D1112616

Group Power

Group Power

Lobbying and Public Policy

Carol S. Greenwald
Brooklyn College of the City University of New York

Praeger Publishers • New York

To David, Paul, and William

Published in the United States of America in 1977
by Praeger Publishers,
200 Park Avenue, New York, N.Y. 10017

Library of Congress Cataloging in Publication Data

Greenwald, Carol Schiro.
Group power.

Bibliography: p. 345
Includes index.
1. Lobbying—United States. 2. Pressure groups—United States. I. Title.
JK1118.G74 322.4'3'0973 74-11921

ISBN: 0-03-038276-9

Printed in the United States of America

12 008 98765

Preface

The thesis of *Group Power* is that interest groups are legitimate, important, and often necessary actors in the development and application of general policies designed to cover multitudes of specific situations and individuals. To support this thesis, the book focuses directly on interest groups at work in the public policy process. A variety of perspectives are used to highlight the roles played by political interest groups and the kinds of relationships that can develop between outside interests and public policy makers.

Part I begins with an analysis of politically relevant attributes of groups ranging from the stimuli for organization and the characteristics of such organization to the representatives of such organizations. After presenting an overview of lobbying and lobbyists as skilled practitioners of subtly tuned techniques, Part II moves on to examine the means groups use to build access to official activities, by the use, for example, of opinion polls, media space, electoral assistance, and campaign donations to candidates.

In Part III the participation of groups in the public policy process is considered. Chapters focus on interest group activities at the agenda-building stage and succeeding stages of program development, policy implementation and evaluation, and on relationships with personnel in Congress and at various levels of the executive branch. The concluding part addresses the question of openness in the democratic process. Examples from the military-industrial complex are used to illustrate elite theory, pluralism, and various forms of modified pluralism. The concluding chapter identifies group influence in terms of specific groups and as a cumulative factor that affects the overall policy-making system.

Throughout the book case studies dramatize the role of groups. These cases feature dairymen, ITT, environmentalists, Common Cause, the AFL-CIO, veterans' organizations, the NAACP, the women's movement, and many more. In each case data were drawn from a multitude of sources. However, for the reader's convenience, footnotes have been kept to a minimum by condensing acknowledgments into omnibus footnotes, and not specifically identifying the source of most comments made by public figures. Nevertheless, the contributions of many scholars and friends in producing the detailed research for these cases cannot be underestimated. Thanks are due especially to two students and friends, Amy Ascher and Tom Block, for their research assistance.

As others before me have said, this book could not have been written without the assistance and support of many people. Bill Brigman and Aaron Dolinsky provided continual encouragement and support during the project. Two families, the Nelkins and the Fishmans, opened their homes to give me a room of my own in which to write. Joanne Baer's typing skills and ability to read sense into often confused drafts helped me meet my deadlines with improved copy.

My editor, Denise Rathbun, prodded me into organizing my ideas for a book and then provided the support, encouragement, and intelligent editing necessary to translate those ideas into reality. I cannot thank her enough for her assistance, insistence, and persistence. Special thanks are also due Jacques Fomerand, a colleague who gave willingly of his time in reading the manuscript, offering trenchant criticism, and helping me with research drudgeries. Finally, I take this opportunity to thank my family and housekeeper for their continually renewed support and stoical acceptance of the inconveniences and absences, both physical and mental, created as by-products of the book-writing process.

C.S.G.

Contents

I

Groups: Why, What, and How

Chapter 1

Interests, Groups, and Public Policy

In 1969 American dairymen had a problem. Traditionally dairymen are Democrats. They supported Senator Hubert Humphrey's 1968 presidential election bid to the tune of $150,000. Now it was January 1969; Republican Richard M. Nixon was President. The need for the dairymen to cultivate friends among new executive decision makers was crucial because the federal bureaucracy has an enormous impact on the dairy industry through programs such as milk price supports, milk product subsidies, import controls on dairy products, school lunch milk programs, and cheese purchases.

Since these dairymen were representatives of a giant agribusiness cooperative, not just one-cow farmers, they followed the example set by business associations and hired a Washington lawyer, Milton Semer, to make their top contacts for them. Semer contacted Attorney General John Mitchell who referred him to Herbert Kalmbach, President Nixon's personal lawyer and chief fund raiser.[1] In a series of meetings beginning in April 1969, Semer told Kalmbach that the dairymen "were without friends in the administration and this was the reason they wanted to make a contribution [to Nixon's 1972 reelection campaign]." Semer reported the gist of Kalmbach's reply: "If we want to go forward with the relationship . . . we should deliver $100,000 in cash."

Fortuitously, the dairymen had recently reorganized their cooperative structure and could meet the demand. In 1968 and 1969 multitudes of small cooperatives in the Southwest, Midwest, and Southeast had merged into three large cooperatives for the production and marketing of milk and milk products. The largest of these is Associated Milk Producers Inc. (AMPI) with 40,000 members in twenty-one states. Mid-American Dairies (Mid-Am) has 20,000 members located in the Midwest. Dairymen, Inc. (DI), is the smallest with 10,000 members in the Southeastern United States. The three groups account for 25 percent of all milk produced in the United States, representing over $1 billion in annual sales.

Economically these cooperatives are similar to large trade associations in size and marketing aggressiveness; politically they resemble labor unions. Both augment member lobbying of legislators with clout purchased through political campaign trust funds that provide contributions to friendly candidates. Dairymen's funds are supplied by a checkoff system that takes a maximum of $99 per member per year, thus giving each trust the potential of raising $1 million yearly.

Semer, AMPI's lawyer, told Kalmbach that his clients had three specific goals in addition to their general desire for access to key bureaucrats and White House staff. They wanted President Nixon to address their 1970 annual convention, to see milk price supports raised to 90 percent of parity,* and to have some tangible identification with Nixon, such as ceremonial pictures. In return, the dairymen would contribute $100,000 to $250,000 in campaign funds during the coming year. Kalmbach cleared the message with H. R. Haldeman, Nixon's chief of staff, who passed responsibility on to Jack Gleason, the White House aide charged with "massaging fat cats." The access route having been established, Semer delivered $100,000 in cash in a little valise to Kalmbach on August 2, 1969. Two weeks later AMPI leaders, Harold Nelson and David Parr, met with Harry Dent, Gleason's boss, in the White House.

True to the dairymen's word, $135,000 from their campaign trust funds flowed to Republican candidates via Gleason and Kalmbach. A previously scheduled state visit from the president of Mexico prevented President Nixon from attending the dairymen's annual convention as requested. Instead, Nixon telephoned the dairymen to express his regrets and invite them to visit him at the White House.

*Parity is the name of a formula that sets the price of a specific commodity such as milk at a level high enough to equal the farmer's purchasing power in 1904–14, the peak years of agricultural prices.

Five days later, September 9, 1970, Nelson and Parr had a nine-minute "photo-opportunity" session with the President in the Oval Office. In a confidential briefing memorandum prior to the meeting, Charles Colson (who had replaced Gleason as the dairymen's White House contact) told Nixon of the dairymen's contributions to the 1970 campaign and of their $2 million pledge to the 1972 presidential campaign. This pledge represented 5 percent of the total projected budget of the 1972 Nixon campaign, and came at a time when Nixon was seeking early money because he feared a tough election contest against Senator Edmund Muskie. Nixon did not mention the $2 million directly in conversation, but he did thank Nelson and Parr for their political support, agreed to have them meet top officials, and said he would attend a future AMPI convention. He then gave them presidential key chains as souvenirs of their visit.

By the end of 1970, the dairymen had met the President, conferred with key aides, and won substantial policy victories such as continuation of the school milk program, setting of new dairy product import quotas, and the largest single increase in milk price supports made by any administration at the beginning of a marketing year—all this in contradiction to the stated Nixon administration proposal to move away from policies "which mean massive subsidies to agriculture."

In 1971 the dairymen wanted to preserve the milk price support level won the previous year. Milk price supports were originally included in the Agricultural Act of 1949 as a means of assuring consumers an adequate milk supply by establishing a minimum price for milk used in manufacturing products. The government maintains the price level set for each year by buying milk products when the price falls to the support minimum. The law restricts the support level range by means of the parity formula.

In the first three months of 1971, the dairymen executed the classic lobbying pincer technique of working with administrators to secure continuation of price supports at the 1970 level of 85 percent of parity, while mobilizing congressional action to aid their administrative efforts and/or override an unfavorable decision. Between January and March, AMPI lost its parity case in the Department of Agriculture (USDA), began movement toward enactment of favorable parity legislation in Congress, and then in a miraculous administrative twist, had the Secretary of Agriculture's unfavorable decision of March 12 changed to a beneficial one at presidential behest. Exactly what had happened?

The usual USDA review process, preceding the annual setting of milk price supports by April 1 of the calendar year, began with a full review of economic data. Analysis by various USDA sections and boards indicated that, in terms of the statutory requirement to ensure an adequate milk supply, there was no need to raise the support price above the current level of $4.66 per hundredweight. Although this sounds like a continuation of 1970's parity level, inflation meant that maintenance of the same dollar amount would reduce parity from the 1970 level of 85 percent to a low of 79 percent. Nevertheless, the USDA decision was routinely routed through the Office of Management and Budget and then sent to relevant White House aides. All agreed on the economic decision to maintain the current price, thereby reducing parity.

Colson, mindful of the political implications, recommended simultaneous announcement of pro-dairy cheese import changes to counteract the effect of the parity announcement. Nixon approved the announcement with the Colson modification, on the advice of Secretary of the Treasury George Shultz, White House aides John Ehrlichman and John Whitaker, and Secretary of Agriculture Clifford Hardin. Secretary Hardin issued the press release on March 12, 1971.

Meanwhile on the money front, in February AMPI agreed to buy $100,000 worth of tickets to a Republican fund raiser to be held on March 24. Based on this promise and other indications of the dairymen's financial support, Hardin, Colson, Whitaker, Ehrlichman, and Nixon's confidant Murray Chotiner recommended that President Nixon meet with AMPI leaders. The decision was made in early February to invite them for a March 23 meeting. However, the dairymen did not make the promised purchase of dinner seats until March 22, at which time they bought a "token" table for $10,000. The $90,000 boycott was visible evidence of their attitude toward the March 12 price support decision.

While AMPI conferred with members of the administration, they also worked with the National Milk Producers Federation to create congressional support for the 85 percent parity level. Between January and March, 13,000 letters went from milk producers to USDA,

50,000 letters went from AMPI to congressmen—all asking for legislation setting milk price support levels at between 85 and 90 percent of parity. Responding to these appeals, eighty-seven congressmen wrote requesting 85 percent, while forty-four merely forwarded constituent requests for increases. In February Nelson and Parr met with key congressional leaders who in turn asked administration leaders to raise the support price.

In the ten days following the unfavorable March 12 announcement, twenty-eight bills sponsored by 118 representatives, and two bills with twenty-nine senators as cosponsors were introduced in Congress. All the bills raised parity minimums to 85 percent or higher. Once the bills were introduced, AMPI proceeded to put renewed pressure on the White House.

Within the Executive Office, memos flew creating political rationales for a presidential override of Hardin's economic decision. The action climaxed on March 23 when the President held at least seven meetings concerned only with the milk support issue, including the previously scheduled meeting with eighteen dairy leaders. The general political consensus among Nixon's advisers was that the President must overrule Hardin in order to gain maximum 1972 electoral leverage from this 1971 decision. As AMPI lawyer Marion Harrison phrased it: "For political, if no other reasons, parity must be set again at 85 percent, even if the President has to do it. The President's name, not the Secretary's is on the ballot."

Secretary of the Treasury John Connally related the issue more specifically to votes, saying the dairymen would only give full credit for "friendly motivation" in a nonelection year, and furthermore the dairymen were threatening "just exactly how many electoral votes they're going to cost you if you veto the 85 percent bill—which they think they're going to pass. And I think they're going to pass it. And they say that it'll cost you Missouri, Wisconsin, South Dakota for sure. Veto will probably cost you Ohio, Kentucky, and Iowa." Justifying his decision two years later, Nixon called this appraisal of the consequences of congressional pressure "a gun to our heads."

He forgot the knife in his back. When the dairymen reneged on their promise to buy ten tables at the March 24 fund raiser, it was an unsubtle intimation of a possibly bleak contribution future. To assure himself that a revised price support decision would secure the $2 million, Nixon made his reversal conditional on advance notification to the dairymen and their reaffirmation of the $2 million pledge.

Undersecretary of Agriculture J. Phil Campbell called Harold Nelson and indicated that the price support level might be increased in order to appease the dairymen. Murray Chotiner, now AMPI's lawyer, and Congressman Page Belcher also told Nelson that the price increase was imminent. On the strength of these comments, AMPI and Mid-Am officials flew to Louisville, Kentucky, to verify their division of campaign contribution responsibilities. A 4:00 A.M. meeting in the Louisville airport with Paul Alagia, director of DI, resulted in a $75,000 commitment from DI's campaign trust fund, $25,000 of it to be made available the following day.

On March 24, after the Kick-Off '72 Republican fund raising dinner, Kalmbach met in his hotel room with Chotiner and the AMPI leaders. As Ehrlichman explained it to Kalmbach: Nixon wanted AMPI to reaffirm its "pledge of $2 million in contributions to the 1972 campaign. . . . There was to be an announcement the next day and this was, in fact, linked to this reaffirmation of the $2 million pledge. . . ." Kalmbach reported the reaffirmation of the commitment to Ehrlichman on the morning of March 25. Later that day Secretary of Agriculture Hardin announced Nixon's March 23 decision to raise the support price of milk to $4.93 per hundredweight, or 85 percent of parity. This support level was one penny higher than any requested in congressional legislation; that one cent cost the government $2 to $10 million more in subsidy money.

The dairymen were justly proud of their victory. As one cooperative leader said, "Mid-Am and AMPI, with some help from DI, got this reversal from the Nixon administration on the price support level. And I can assure you that the TAPE and ADEPT programs, as well as SPACE* played a major part in this administrative decision. This just proves that a minority, regardless of its number, if it is well-organized, dedicated, and adequately financed, can prevail."

The dairymen were to pay $90,000 per month from March 1971 until election day in order to fulfill their $2 million commitment. However, the Republicans could not create dummy campaign com-

*These are acronyms for the separate political campaign funds created by each cooperative.

mittees fast enough to receive the money so the dairymen had paid only $232,500 when a spate of newspaper articles in August, tying their money to the price support decision, caused them to cease all direct contributions. By November, 1972 they had contributed $632,-500 directly and indirectly to the President's campaign. Since the milk price support increase meant $300 million more for the dairymen in the 1971 milk year, they received a 500 percent return on their campaign contribution investment.

THE PUBLIC POLICY-MAKING PROCESS

This case is one especially dramatic example of group action and government reaction—dramatic in terms of costs and timing: it is not often that a President receives a $2 million campaign pledge, a $100,-000 down payment, and then rewards the donors with a price support increase worth from $300 to $500 million. Yet the dairymen's case is also a normal example of opportunities in the public policy-making process for groups with sufficient resources, skill, and inclination to play the game.

AMPI's adventures indicate some of the possible intersections between outside interests and the policy-making process. For example:

1. Routinization and slowness of policy determination made it possible for AMPI to predict the decision-making sequence and find access points.

2. The number of participants in any one decision increases the probability of finding friends in the right places (the milk price support decision involved more than two dozen key participants).

3. The variety of institutions interested in their aspect of an issue gives separate groups openings for their positions. Milk price supports involved congressional committees. Congressmen from agricultural states, USDA, White House staff, the President, and various other independent agencies, bureaus, and so on.

4. Partisan considerations, affecting seemingly technical decisions, made it possible for 1972 campaign contribution promises to affect agricultural decisions made in 1970 and 1971.

5. Manifestations of group policy-oriented activity is immensely varied. At one time or another the dairymen used influential Washing-

ton lawyers, campaign contributions, economic information, vote power,relationships among inside decision-making friends, and letter-writing campaigns.

Generally speaking, the American policy-making process is always the fluid, incremental, open-ended, disorderly, often incoherent maze that the dairymen traversed to such advantage. But it is also a series of coordinated activities related by the need to achieve certain specific purposes. In this sense the policy process is a sequence: problems beget options for solutions which beget policies which beget consequences which beget new problems in a revolving cycle. As problems arise that must be solved, ad hoc coalitions of interested people created temporary alliances to generate decisions. The people involved in this process are "playing politics."

"Playing politics" can mean several things. In terms of issues, politics is a "science of alternatives" in which there are "no permanent friends, no permanent enemies, only permanent interests." Thus the dairymen consistently wanted economic advantages; so when Humphrey lost his bid for the Presidency, they made friends with Nixon's men. From the viewpoint of the participants, politics is the art of exercising infuence in order to achieve their specific ends. The route to power and influence varies for each group and each goal. Indeed, assessment of whether a "political play" has succeeded, that is, whether there is a relationship between group action and policy outcome, is often difficult even for the participants. Very rarely is the connection as clear-cut as that between the 1971 price support decision and money for Nixon's 1972 electoral campaign.

Generally politics is a group game; individuals are important, but usually as members of a team rather than alone. The President made the milk parity level decision alone, but he acted to reverse a teammate, Secretary of Agriculture Hardin, on the basis of differently evaluated information, in order to preempt Congress from winning a victory with electoral consequences. In this context the one-tenth of a percentage point advantage in Nixon's parity level, over those suggested in proposed legislation, takes on connotations of a "win for our side."

As in any game, there are rules—rules of politics. The basic constitutional rule that affects the location of power bases on the playing field calls for checks and balances between and within institutions.

The rule of federalism requires dispersion of decision-making power among three branches of government at each of three levels of government. Multiply these three branches—the executive, legislative, and judicial—by fifty states and 153 cities with populations of over 100,000, then add the three federal branches, for a grand total of 612 major institutional bases from which policy politics is played.

In effect the policy-playing field can be compared to a three-dimensional tick-tack-toe board on which a player in the middle square has the option of building horizontally, vertically, or diagonally along any one or all three dimensions. Policy players can choose to act simultaneously or sequentially within one level, or along all levels. Thus, the dairymen acted horizontally on the national level in going from USDA to Congress to the President. A group with strong state ties, the National Milk Producers Federation, used a vertical play from local members to their congressmen and then horizontally from key congressmen to their White House contacts.

The dispersion of power among branches and levels of government produces duplication, competition, negotiation, and bargaining. Superimposed on this constitutionally designed chaos is the internal competition and duplication within each branch. For example, Congress is a study in mirror images: two separate but equal houses, each with two sets of leaders with different power bases (party leaders who set program guidelines and committee chairmen who write legislation) and two decision-making processes (authorization of new ideas, appropriation of money).

The executive branch consists of the President and his White House staff, plus eight major regulatory agencies, eleven cabinet departments, over one hundred executive departments, and hundreds of independent bureaus and agencies. Although the President is constitutionally responsible for all executive decisions, in reality the bureaucracy goes through its daily routines uninfluenced by presidential desires. The federal judicial system of Supreme Court, courts of appeals, and district-level trial courts is replicated at state and local level. Decisions wend their way upward from lower to higher courts. Internal fragmentation within branches complicates power plays and increases the time dimensions within which policy is made. For example, the congressional bills to set a milk price support minimum at 85 percent of parity were introduced in 1971 but did not become law until 1972 despite all the heat generated by the dairy lobbies in March of 1971. Even within a department, fragmentation produces delay as illustrated by the USDA milk support process which begins seven months before the legal deadline because each decision must be reviewed many times in many places.

Policy content provides a framework for coordination of activities among all the bases and team members interested in a specific decision. The process of developing a policy within and among all these power centers forges alliances among the people themselves, sometimes called "subgovernments." These are working relationships joined together by common policy interests rather than separated by the formal rules of the game. Within these issue arenas, nongovernmental actors become team members. Governmental personnel then work with outsiders to increase their own institutional power base: agency personnel interests merge with clientele expectations in a useful symbiotic relationship. Private groups also forge their own links among the institutional bases that lead to a policy goal.

Groups thus supplement and reinforce governmental policy relationships. By playing politics in this manner, groups create power reserves for decision makers who represent their interests within the policy process, and simultaneously establish contacts across institutional lines. These pragmatic, policy-oriented bridges cross the gaps created by constitutional separation. For example, the dairymen wove links among Congressmen Mills and Albert, USDA Secretary Hardin, White House liaison Clark MacGregor, and presidential aides Colson and Whitaker. All six men were separated by different institutional perspectives and loyalties, but all six were drawn together by a need to make the decision on milk price supports

PUBLIC POLICY: PRODUCT

The product of the governmental policy-making process—public policy—differs from any private decision. First, its consequences are different since the policy decision represents both a specific solution to a problem and a grant of power. Public policies as outputs of government (that entity which claims the legitimate use of force in society) represent authoritative allocations of resources and values.

Therefore, control over a governmental policy decision involves political power.

Second, the scope of public issues complicates the content of the problem. Problems reach government because of the complexity of the subject, the numbers of people affected, or personal situations which lead individuals to seek governmental assistance. For instance a rational transportation policy seems a reasonable request. A private individual, in deciding how to get to work, would develop all alternatives to his problem (that is, taxi, private car, subway, walk), calculate the consequences (time, cost, availability), and pick the most desirable solution. Yet in public policy the variables and contingencies are open-ended and forever changing, leading to a geometric expansion of possible solutions. For example, in transportation:

> The need for new highways depends in part on the need for trucking. The need for trucking depends in part upon how much freight railroads and cargo planes carry. The need for more shorthaul air service depends on the federal commitment to better passenger trains. The need for more downtown parking space depends on whether public transportation can ever coax Americans from their automobiles in any substantial numbers.[2]

Third, public solutions are affected by interaction between the complexity of the subject matter and competing viewpoints and institutional jurisdictions within the system. Consequently public policy is generally a product of compromise, negotiation, and bargaining in which no one wins everything. The intellectually perfect answer and the politically acceptable one tend to be incompatible. The reality of the political decision-making structure makes intelligent issue experts settle for a negotiated answer to the most immediate problem. To observers this often seems a sellout to the most obnoxious or richest participant; yet it can also be seen in bureaucratic terms, that is, to lessen the scope of a decision reduces the number of decision-making points, the complexity of the issue, and its ramifications.

All of these convolutions result in time lags. It takes eight years to build an airport; it took forty years to complete the national interstate highway system. By the time the original plans are completed, the consequences of the initial decision have begun to create new problems. Therefore, the final difference between public and private decisions is the inability to eliminate a problem with any one application of a public policy.

In sum, fragmentation, duplication, complexity, and intentional open-endedness make the process of policy making a series of sequential moves toward limited objectives over long periods of time. Solutions are always partial answers to one aspect of a problem; countless other parts are left hanging. These bitesized decisions only generate new problems which again produce answers based on the smallest common denominator, and so on ad infinitum.

There are always choices to be made concerning the rate and direction of change, so the process is never static, never neutral, and rarely closed to aggressive outsiders seeking access. We will examine the variety of group contributions within this policy-making process by focusing on the who, what, where, when, and how of group activity. But first, we need to define the term group, and then refine that concept in order to isolate the category—political interest group—with which this book is concerned.

INTEREST GROUP DEFINITIONS

An *interest* is "the conscious desire to have public policy, or the authoritative allocation of values, move in a particular, general, or specific direction."[3] A *group* is a collection of individuals bound together by shared attitudes and interactions, real or potential, based on the needs created by the shared attitudes. Groups are "structures of power *which* concentrate human wit, energy, and muscle . . . for the achievement of ends common to the members. . . . Groups exist to fulfill the desires of those who comprise them, to achieve their choices, attain their goals. . . ."[4]

Using these definitions, "interest" plus "group" need not equal "interest group." Interests may exist among random individuals without any of the goal-oriented, shared interaction required to meet the definition of group. Or a group may not encompass all people with an interest in a particular subject. Many women who are interested in equal rights for women are not affiliated with NOW, WITCH, WOMEN, or any other active women's rights group. Therefore, we need to combine the notions of "interest" and "group" into a composite definition of "interest group."

An interest group is a combination of individuals who seek to pursue shared interests through a set of agreed upon activities. This is a very broad definition, limited only by the requirements of individual interaction and goal-oriented activity. The definition says nothing about the basis of the shared attitudes, the nature of group goals, or the relationship between the group and government.

Consequently, to separate interest groups as defined here from random combinations of individuals does require some knowledge of the context in which the action is taking place. For example, four people in a car could be chance passengers occupying the same traveling space or four revolutionaries plotting to overthrow the government. Four hundred people interested in the preservation of the lynx could be a random sample of animal lovers or an organization pursuing a common aim. Four thousand people surrounding the Washington Monument could be an audience of rock fans individually attracted by Gladys Knight and the Pips, or they could be a rally organized by specific interest groups to dramatize their policy objectives.

Alexis de Tocqueville, commenting on Jacksonian America, identified an enduring American characteristic—the tendency to form associations. "The Americans of all ages, all conditions, and all dispositions constantly form associations. They have not only commercial and manufacturing companies . . . but associations of a thousand other kinds, religious, moral, serious, futile, restricted, enormous, or diminutive. . . . Wherever at the head of some new undertaking you see the government of France or a man of rank in England, in the United States you will be sure to find an association."

This book focuses on one species of interest group—the *political interest group.* A political interest group is defined as *one whose shared activities include attempts to influence decisions made within the public policy-making system.* We will use the nouns *interest group, pressure group, lobby, voluntary association,* and *group* interchangeably to mean political interest group. To qualify for this classification, a group need not be 100 percent political; indeed we will later exclude political parties from our study, precisely because they are primarily political employment agencies.

Most groups make use of only those parts of the political process whose routines mesh best with their own or those stages of the process required to implement their own goals. Corporations that prefer dealing with government bureaucracies and their equivalent employee hierarchies are an example of the first category of "partial" political interest group. Social welfare groups, religious groups, civic groups are all examples within the second category. They work within the political process to pass legislation facilitating their own objectives or to help implement and evaluate a program once it has become law. Very few interest groups have a 100 percent identification with government except perhaps organizations of governmental officials or governmental entities or associations that develop to protect certain public policies such as the Citizens Advocate Center, an outgrowth of the government's antipoverty legislation. Even these organizations join with private groups from time to time.

In 1974 there were 12,606 national nonprofit organizations in the United States. Table 1 which lists these organizations in terms of their goals shows that 23 percent represent trade and commercial organizations, while 38 percent are concerned with health, education, science, and social welfare.

The Table bears out Tocqueville's observation that "in no country of the world has the principle of association been more successfully used or applied to a greater multitude of objects than in America."

To move from this general listing to a similarly detailed list of political interest groups is impossible. The various laws that require disclosure of active lobbying organizations—the Utilities Holding Company Act of 1935, the Merchant Marine Act of 1936, the Foreign Agents Registration Act of 1938, and the Federal Regulation of Lobbying Act of 1946—are ignored with impunity. Basic domestic lobbying activities should be covered by the 1946 act, but its scope was narrowed in a 1946 Supreme Court decision to include only those who use *another's* money for the *principal* purpose of communicating *directly with a Congressmen* in order to influence the course of legislation.

By creating an unrealistic, simplistic definition of lobbying, the Court felt it was protecting an individual's First Amendment right to petition his representatives. However, at the same time, the decision made the requirements for annual registration of lobbyists and quarterly filing of expenditures irrelevant. Those who choose to register

TABLE 1. National, Nonprofit Organizations by Goal Category, 1974

Category	*Number*	*%*
Trade and commercial organizations	2,916	23.1
Cultural organizations	1,196	9.5
Health and medical organizations	1,089	8.6
Educational organizations	868	6.9
Scientific, technical, and engineering	817	6.5
Public affairs	791	6.3
Social welfare	752	6.0
Religious	728	5.8
Commodity exchanges and agricultural organizations	608	4.9
Hobby and vocational	607	4.8
Fraternal, foreign interest, nationality, ethnic	484	3.8
Athletic and sports	447	3.5
Governmental, public administration, military, legal	406	3.2
Greek-letter societies	332	2.6
Labor unions, associations, and federations	239	1.9
Veteran, hereditary, and patriotic	218	1.7
Chambers of Commerce	108	.9
Total	12,606	100.0

SOURCE: Margaret Fisk, ed., *Encyclopedia of Associations,* 9th ed., vol. 1 (Detroit: Gale Research Co., 1975).

do, those who do not are left alone. It has been estimated that approximately 2,000 lobbyists ply their trade in Washington, spending over $1 billion annually. However, in 1975 only 1,000 organizations were registered, 77 percent of them business corporations and trade associations. Reported expenditure figures for 1973 totaled only $9.5 million.

Fourteen different committee hearings have been held in the last thirty years to correct deficiencies in the lobbying law, but until 1976 no bill passed both houses of Congress. Then the remains of the Watergate reform impulse led to passage of House and Senate bills which, while different in language, were similar in intent. The bills make no value distinctions between "good" and "bad" lobbying goals; all churches, civil associations, and corporations that meet the definition of lobbying are required to fulfill the disclosure provisions of these bills. As modernized by both bills, the definition of lobbying includes indirect lobbying through grassroots channels, as well as contacts with congressional staff and higher echelon executive branch officials. The definition of lobbyist is broadened to include employees who spend at least 20 percent of their time lobbying, or organizations that pay outsiders $1,250 or more in a calendar quarter to lobby for them. The bills also provide for fairly explicit expenditure reporting requirements and strong administrative and enforcement authority to be given to the General Accounting Office.

The willingness to create a neutral and relevant lobbying law that would require business and other interests to register equally has had a spillover effect onto other laws that obscure the actual variety of political interests. Hidden in Internal Revenue Service regulations are two provisions: one that prevents tax exempt public charities that solicit tax deductible contributions from devoting "substantial" efforts to lobbying; and another that permits businesses and unions to deduct the costs of lobbying activities on issues of "direct interest" to them. This means that corporate advertising, trade association dues, and business lunches that further corporate interests are tax deductible, while public charities seeking generalized health, education, or environmental benefits run the risk of losing their tax-exempt status. Proposed legislation would permit those in the latter group to spend 20 percent of their total budget or $1 million annually (whichever is smaller) for lobbying purposes. Once these reform measures are passed, both the public and government personnel will have a more accurate picture of active political interest groups.

This universe of political interest groups includes both voluntary and involuntary associations. In sociological terms, voluntary associations are all nonstate organizations of individuals who join together voluntarily to pursue common interests.[5] Involuntary associations are either those based on ascription according to some characteristic such as age, sex, nationality, or religion; or those mandated as a condition of employment such as union membership, or as a requirement of citizenship such as military draft registration for designated sections of the population.

However, these distinctions are not as clear-cut as they might seem. Some nonstate voluntary associations are related to the state for purposes of incorporation, tax exemption privileges, or licensing of members. Others are related to the state because the individuals who voluntarily band together are state employees or represent parts of the state apparatus such as cities, state legislatures, or federal courts.

In addition, categories of involuntary association spawn voluntary associations that are important political interest groups. For example, persons over sixty-five, an involuntary category, may be voluntary members of the National Association of Retired Persons, the National Council of Senior Citizens, the Gray Panthers, and other politically active groups concerned with age-related problems. Similarly, the American Legion, Veterans of Foreign Wars, Vietnam Veterans Against the War, and Disabled American Veterans all represent a classification that is a consequence of a mandated involuntary association.

Business corporations represent an important segment of the political interest group universe. They are not really voluntary associations, although employees join by occupying the job. They are not really involuntary associations although most are run along hierarchical, bureaucratic lines that allow little room for the development of individual potential envisioned in the sociological definition of voluntary groups. Yet they are among the most active lobbies, employing individuals to pursue their goals through access and influence in the public policy-making system.

In summary, the variety of political interest groups ranges beyond the definition of purely voluntary associations to include trade associations, unions, and business corporations. The common denominator separating political lobbies from other forms of organized activity is their expressed intention to achieve policy goals by influencing governmental decision makers.

INTEREST GROUPS IN THE POLITICAL SYSTEM

In the formal system of representation in the United States, voters elect individuals to Congress and the Presidency from geographical districts. Within each district there is a range of separate interests—recreational, cultural, economic, ethnic, religious, and social. The handful of people elected to represent you from your slice of territory cannot possibly represent all of your interests. Political parties, the vehicles used to elect most representatives similarly fail to accurately represent all interests since parties must aggregate proposals into winning issue platforms.

It is generally agreed that interest groups in the American system fill this issue gap by carrying their own interests directly into the policy-making process. In the 1976 congressional debate on new lobbying regulations, Senator Lee Metcalf said issue information from groups "is essential in considering legislation. . . . We would have to multiply our staffs fourfold or fivefold if it were not for the information that the lobbyists give us, supply us, and the reliable information . . . upon which we can act."[6] Political interest groups translate social and economic power into political power through the process of articulating specific demands. "Lobby groups and lobbyists define opinion for government with a sense of reality and specificity which political parties, the mass media, opinion polls, and staff assistants seldom, if ever, can achieve."[7]

These demands in turn reflect both status quo needs of established groups and bargaining positions of new interests. However, the ways of the system are more supportive of status quo interests so that groups may promote change, but slowly. In the balance of change and stability, groups tend to be agents of the latter. This is reinforced by their technical function of supplying specialized information to create a range of policy alternatives. A multitude of specialized groups offering advice to a multitude of competing power centers has the potential for facilitating compromise or promoting chaos. The likelihood of compromise is increased within the friendly environment of decision-making subgovernments, especially when groups then cooperate in the implementation of those policies.

Groups articulating new attitudes or championing new causes often have difficulty in penetrating the close working relationships among the insiders. If minority positions—such as unionization of farm workers, desegregation of schools, equal work opportunities for women and minorities—do penetrate the system, groups have acted as a safety valve. Potential unrest is translated into expanded citizen support for government. If demands for change fail—such as negative income tax, free abortions on demand, free health care—those interests denied access to the policy process feel unrepresented. However, the ability of "outs" to get "in" has been increased by the development of public affairs lobbyists who challenge corporate economic interests in the name of clean air, free speech, and everyday taxpayers. These groups also fulfill the informational function of political interest groups by carrying their data directly into the policy process.

The distinction between this group representation of interests affecting large segments of the public and public interests represented though the electoral system can be clarified by contrasting the roles of political parties and lobbies. Lobbies are defined as "all groups or associations which seek to influence public policy in their own chosen direction while declining to accept responsibility for ruling the country."[8] A political party is an organization of groups and individuals that seeks to staff governmental institutions through the process of winning political elections. Parties as organized shared interactions fall within our definition of interest group, but they will be excluded from the universe under examination because their primarily political functions make them a conduit for group influence rather than a competitor within the interest group policy-making role.

Interest groups tend to attract a specialized homogeneous membership concerned with the advancement of specific policy positions. Groups organize minorities in an attempt to implement specific policy in both political and nonpolitical arenas. Parties, on the other hand, are government-oriented organizations, created under state law, led by political officials. Policy for parties is a means, not an end; their end is to win control of the government through the election process because all their rewards such as patronage, influence, and status stem from such a victory. Party membership is broad, inclusive, heterogeneous, nonissue-oriented. In order to garner the majority of votes necessary to win elections, parties play a broker role in politics. They combine assorted interests into broad ad hoc coalitions.

Thus party and group roles are complementary. Both make claims on society on behalf of the shared attitudes and interests of their members. But parties focus primarily on personnel and staffing of government, while groups act mainly as information conduits for the formulation and advocacy of policy ideas.

The communication-broker role of interest groups is important not only at the general policy development level, but also on the personal level. The limited nature of any one group's interests makes it accessible to people who need to relate to society as a whole but are overwhelmed by its scope. Working within a group, whether for senior citizen benefits or tax shelters, an individual can reduce the complexity of government to the level of his own concern. This learning experience provides a basis for citizen identification with the larger political world, for increased confidence in one's own ability to cope, and for heightened identification with and support for governmental processes in general. In this context group participation is an antidote to feelings of helplessness, anomie, and unfamiliarity that exist in most modern societies. In terms of representative government, at the personal level, the broker participation role of political interest groups becomes a means of distributing power among ordinary citizens through their indirect participation in public policy decisions.

There is little disagreement on the functional utility of groups for the American political system, but there is widespread disagreement on the societal impact of such participation. In general the policy benefits ascribed to group participation reflect certain value premises of the observer. Critics of political lobbies feel that, "No public policy could ever be the mere sum of the demands of organized special interests . . . for there are vital common interests that cannot be organized by pressure groups."[9] Beginning with this value point, organized issue-oriented action "is itself a mobilization of bias in preparation for action . . . a method of short-circuiting the majority."[10]

The opposite position, presented by James Madison in *Federalist* No. 10, begins with the premise that men naturally pursue selfishly motivated interests. The role of government is to control this clash through compromise so that public good can emerge from the competition among private interests. Illinois Senator Charles Percy restated this thesis in the 1976 Senate debate, saying that, "Every single time, virtually without exception, that we have a major issue before Congress . . . you have opposing lobbyists. . . . It is possible for us to go to each of these groups—the most articulate, the best groups on both sides and have them prepare the best research that they can." Add to this the value judgment that this participation is not only good, but essential and one has the normative position of group theorists such as V. O. Key who declared that, "At bottom, group interests are the animating forces in the political process. . . ."[11]

Skeptics who assume the middle position in this debate argue that the clash of *all* relevant issues could produce well-rounded policy in the public interest, but in fact *all* interests are either not represented or not represented equally. Speaking in the same congressional debate, Senator Edward Kennedy said lobbying disclosure laws are necessary because "Day after day, lobbyists spend vast amounts of influence money. . . . The interests they represent are rich and powerful. Their operations can easily thwart the people's will and corrupt the public purpose." Others see a similarly dysfunctional interposition of groups between government administration and John Q. Public. Citing the symbiotic relationship between bureaucracies and their clientele groups as a barrier to participation by the general public, these critics view the group brokerage role as the promotion of selfish interest rather than the communication of varied interests.[12]

These judgments are important because they color interpretations of group activities and assessments of group influence. We will consider these views later in an evaluation of the role of groups throughout the policy process.

SUMMARY

Politics is defined as the process of allocating resources and values, a process that is usually diffuse, and slow. Multitudes of power centers compete in the formulation of policy. Groups rather than individuals serve as vehicles for promoting specific ideas within the process, operating between and among the various centers and creating subgovernments tied together by policy interests.

Interest groups are combinations of individuals who seek shared interests through a set of agreed upon activities. Political interest groups use the public policy process to obtain some or all of their goals.

Political parties and interest groups share the task of linking citizens and government. Political parties, however, use policy as a means to aggregate sufficient voters to place their candidates in power, while interest groups are primarily interested in the subject matter of policy rather than policy makers per se. Thus groups have the capacity to provide alternative systems of representation for citizens' views and to connect individual interests with public policies. We shall next consider those characteristics and resources of groups that are important in terms of their public policy participation.

NOTES

1. Information for the dairymen's case study was taken from the Senate Select Committee on Presidential Campaign Activities, *The Senate Watergate Report,* vol. 2 (New York: Dell, 1974), chap. 6; and U.S., Congress, House, Committee on the Judiciary, *Statement of Information,* bk. 6, pts. 1 and 2. 93 Cong, 2d Sess.
2. *Christian Science Monitor,* August 18, 1971.
3. Joseph LaPalombara, *Interest Groups in Italian Politics* (Princeton, N.J.: Princeton University Press, 1964), p. 16.
4. Earl Latham, "The Group Basis of Politics: Notes for a Theory," *American Political Science Review,* 46 (June 1952): 382, 397. The definition also owes a debt to David Truman, *The Governmental Process* (New York: Knopf, 1951), chaps. 1–3.
5. See David Sills, "Voluntary Associations," *International Encyclopedia of the Social Sciences,* vol. 7, ed. David Sills (New York: Free Press, 1968), pp. 362–63.
6. This and other quotations from the 1976 Senate floor debate on lobbying law revision are taken from U.S., Congress, Senate, *Congressional Record,* 1976, 94 Cong. 2d Sess. pp. S 9269–76.
7. Lester Milbrath, *The Washington Lobbyists* (Chicago: Rand McNally, 1963), p. 356.
8. S. E. Finer, "Interest Groups and the Political Process in Great Britain," in *Interest Groups on Four Continents,* ed. Henry Ehrmann (Pittsburgh: University of Pittsburgh Press, 1958), p. 117.
9. George Galloway, quoted in L. Harmon Zeigler and G. Wayne Peak, *Interest Groups in American Society,* 2d ed. (Englewood Cliffs, N.J.: Prentice-Hall, 1972), p. 21.
10. E. E. Schattschneider, *The Semi-Sovereign People* (New York: Holt, Rinehart & Winston, 1961), p. 30.

11. V. O. Key, *Parties, Politics and Pressure Groups,* 5th ed. (New York: Thomas Y. Crowell, 1964), p. 17.
12. See, for example, Henry Kariel, *The Decline of American Pluralism* (Stanford, Ca.: Stanford University Press, 1961); Theodore Lowi, *The End of Liberalism* (New York: Norton, 1969); Grant McConnell, *Private Power and American Democracy* (New York: Knopf, 1966).

Chapter 2

Group Anatomy: Membership, Leadership, Goals

We know that interest groups develop from the shared attitudes of individuals who band together to further their common aims. But, why are persons who hold some interests more motivated than others to form these shared interaction patterns? Why are there 113 apparel trade associations, 114 national labor unions under the AFL-CIO banner alone, and only thirty-one women's rights organizations? Why does an issue such as water resources spawn hundreds of ad hoc organizations, while consumer problems give rise to but a few interest groups?

Answers to such questions lie in the reasons why groups are formed and why individuals join any specific group. This chapter examines the major theories on the sources of interest groups, what we know about people who join groups, and the relationship between characteristics of group members and patterns of group organization and leadership. The final section of the chapter considers group attributes as potential lobbying resources.

GROUP FORMATION

The most common sociological theory of group formation begins with the premise that man is a social animal who develops patterns of thought and activity through group affiliations beginning with the family and expanding through religious, educational, social, and political ties.[1] As society becomes more complex, changes in the social order create situations that are not met by these traditional groups. Thus, immigrants to America founded ethnic societies and fraternal orders to re-create their familiar social patterns. Nineteenth-century sweatshops, fourteen-hour days, and inadequate wages bred "muckraking" groups to generate social reform and unions to improve working conditions.

Establishment of the American National Red Cross dramatizes the link between an existing situation and group formation. Clara Barton, a Civil War nurse appalled by battlefield health facilities, waged a fiery personal battle for forty years against American apathy and elite disdain for charity. In 1881 she founded her organization to provide civilian hospital assistance to soldiers in the field. The Red Cross was granted a congressional charter in 1900 as the culmination of a series of maneuvers to gain status for the organization. Today it is a quasi-official agency with the President of the United States as honorary chairman, the attorney general as honorary counselor, and the secretary of the treasury as honorary treasurer, a fifty member board of governors, a national career staff of 3,600, 10,000 chapter employees, 2 million volunteers, and over 36 million people who each contribute at least $1 annually.

Groups also develop as organized segments of social movements which form when a sector of the population, be it farmers, blacks, women, or army-age men, feels itself victimized by circumstances affecting its social status, pocketbook, or both. Usually such frustrations develop in response to economic boom/bust cycles or ideological discontent, when the difference between anticipated change and reality is too slow or too small. These frustrations are fused into a sense of common identity by a creative leader who uses simplistic slogans and solutions to propagandize the issue.

For example, the movement to end the war in Vietnam was united only by a slogan, "END THE WAR!" Strange bedfellows united to march on Washington, disrupt universities, and burn draft cards in order to dramatize the futility of the war, but disagreement concerning solutions cracked the coalition. Some wanted a battlefield victory, some a negotiated win, others pure and simple withdrawal, still others to send only money not men, or various combinations of the above. This led to a paradox: 70 percent of the American public supported the movement's end the war aim while, simultaneously, Presidents

Johnson and Nixon increased the United States commitment to our Asian allies. Thus, the public opinion impact of the slogan was not translated into a public policy impact because the factions within the movement were unable to agree on the means to implement their slogan.

Groups may linger on as institutional echoes of a movement that has run its course. As socially progressive or once radical ideas are absorbed into the mainstream of American political thought, the organizational remnant left behind becomes a "bourgeois" institution. For example, the League of Women Voters is the modern outgrowth of the National American Women's Suffrage Association, the institutionalized part of the movement that resulted in adoption of the Nineteenth Amendment. The National Grange still exists as a "farm fraternity" one hundred years after the Granger movement of economically discontented farmers swept the Midwest.

Industrialization, urbanization, and modern technology have provided other breeding grounds for new groups. As these forces change the conditions of our lives, they create new interrelationships between individuals, between people and society, between workers and their jobs, an interdependence that generates friction which often leads to new problems. Interests form to represent the differentiated sets of values and issues. Expansion of labor unions from individualized crafts such as printers and builders to assembly-line, mass-production industries and, most recently to public employment and the professions illustrates this relationship. Thus societal evolution provides a never-ending source of interest development.

The enormous growth in American industry after the Civil War led to creation of the corporation as a vehicle to organize this economic power. Many interests organized to represent separate segments of the business community, but in 1912 President Woodrow Wilson, feeling that one organization should exist to speak as the general voice of American business, convened an informal meeting of top business leaders, and the Chamber of Commerce of the United States was born.

Groups entering the political arena reflect the increasingly important role that government plays in economic regulation. Arthur Bentley said seventy years ago that public policy is the result of group activities; yet today the reverse is often true—the impact, real or potential, of public policy can create political interest groups. "In short, we can usefully stand Bentley on his head to supplement Bentley right side up; if interaction among politically active groups produces policy, policy in turn creates politically active groups."[2]

As the scope of governmental activity has expanded to cover everything from atomic submarines to the number of bugs permitted in peanut butter, more and more interests are forming groups as vehicles for political activity. The rapid multiplication of new interest groups, or offshoots of old groups, as a response to the development of new issues is most obvious in the economic sector where a new issue such as nuclear reactors or a crisis such as the oil/energy crisis can cause all varieties of opinions (interests) to organize into interest group action vehicles. For example in the oil crisis year of 1974, over fifty petroleum interests registered as Washington lobbyists.

Yet a question arises as to the timing of organized responses. Why do some situations automatically call forth group activity, while in other cases there is delay or perhaps no organized activity at all? Truman and several other group theorists have suggested variations of an equilibrium theory to explain this puzzle. Equilibrium theory assumes that current actors in the political policy system develop a stable set of working relationships among the private political groups and with their governmental associates. When innovations disrupt this equilibrium, new groups form to restore the status quo ante or forge a new equilibrium.

The theory implies that a group will emerge to act as bargaining agent for any newly politicized interests. It does not consider "tilts" in the system caused by time lags between development of an interest in society and its acceptance within the public policy system or the possibility that some interests such as migrants, ideological minorities, and uncoordinated majorities such as consumers may never be able to meet the entrance requirements of the political policy leagues.

Bureaucratic manifestations of the waxing and waning of environmentalist policy during the decade from 1965 to 1975 provide a perfect illustration of equilibrium theory in action. In 1969 there were twenty-four national environmental conservation organizations; by 1969 there were at least thirteen more. In that year Congress recognized the influence of this new lobby by passing the National Environmental Protection Act (NEPA).

NEPA requires environmental impact statements to precede any federal action affecting the environment and authorizes citizen suits to assure implementation of this provision. The enormous consequences of the Act can be seen by noting that laying of the Trans-Alaskan pipeline was stalled for seven years by litigation to enforce NEPA guidelines. NEPA also created a three-man Council on Environmental Quality within the Executive Office of the President. Its members are appointed by the President with the consent of the Senate. Their task is to analyze current trends in the national environment, to formulate and recommend policies to improve environmental quality, and to help the President prepare the annual environmental quality report to Congress.

Not to be outdone by congressional solicitation of this new political policy bloc, President Nixon established the Environmental Protection Agency (EPA) as an independent agency under Reorganization Plan No. 3 of 1970. The new agency combined air and waste management programs and water pollution programs in an effort to coordinate program planning, enforcement, and research in the areas of governmental action to protect the environment.

In 1973 the international gasoline crisis descended, and the bureaucratic reflection of 1970 power was revised to reflect group power in 1973. Executive Order 11748 created a Federal Energy Office to organize priorities in times of energy shortages and to ensure that the total supply of available energy continues to meet present and future energy demands. A year later the office was renamed the Federal Energy Administration (FEA) as part of a congressional reorganization in the Federal Energy Act of 1974. That this agency is fossil fuel's answer to EPA is indicated in "logs" kept by officials of FEA during its first six months which show that 94 percent of their contacts with lobbyists during this period were with oil, gas, and coal industry representatives.

Thus, within a decade the environmentalists moved from minor political actors on the policy fringe to accepted, centrally located, institutionalized participants and then were moved off center stage by energy interests. Government created a situation favorable to group development by recognizing environmental energy demands; new groups evolved in response to new policy possibilities. Some came to change the existing equilibrium, others to maintain it.

But groups also enter the public policy sphere in response to conditions within private decision-making arenas. Groups that are losing battles in the private sphere move to the larger arena of public policy making in order to attract more adherents by "enlarging the scope of conflict." Rules of the game such as one-party states, secret decision making, and private decisions limit challenges to the status quo. By going public, the size of the audience that may become involved is increased, and, thereby, the chances of reversing privately made decisions. "Every change in the scope of conflict has a bias. . . . By definition, bystanders are not neutral. Thus in political conflict, every change in scope changes the equation."[3]

For example, after the Civil War farmers were being bilked by middlemen and jobbers who took a large percentage of agricultural profits as the condition for transporting food to market. The economic inequalities sparked the Granger movement which blamed the railroads, monopolies, and bankers, but especially the railroads, for the farmers' economic distress. As a result, the government passed legislation to control rates and established the Interstate Commerce Commission to regulate railroads.

Business was again regulated when the Federal Trade Commission was created in 1915 in order to restore the ideal of economic competition by reining in the power of "Robber Barons," such as Rockefeller, Whitney, Vanderbilt, and J. P. Morgan, through enforcement of antitrust legislation. President Theodore Roosevelt used his "bully-pulpit" to lead the "trust-busting" action of government on behalf of those who had lost their private fight. However, in both instances cited the time lag between the discovery of the "private evil" and its public correction spanned at least a decade. Consequently we can conclude that the corporations and utilities have had a better place at the gaming table than the challengers.

Equilibrium theory does not predict winners or losers in the battle for policy-making influence, but merely offers an explanation for the development of groups. Some critics dislike the policy consequences that result from time lags between unearthing of a problem and organized action for a solution. Others argue that the theory does not adequately explain periods when change does not beget groups. For these critics the motivations for joining groups can provide an explanation for gaps in the range of politicized interests.

GROUP MEMBERSHIP

Who joins groups and why? Before quantifying the picture of who joins, it is important to consider the question, "Why join any organization?" since the "why" can explain motivations for joining. Why are some people active in civic, school, and church organizations while others who seem to have the same amount of free time prefer to stay at home? Why does someone join the KKK instead of the Elks? Why do some teachers join unions and specialized professional associations while others just teach? The key question is what's in it for the individual.

Since answers to "what" and "why" will explain the motivations for joining or avoiding different kinds of organizations, these answers can lead us to the "who." Basically, the reasons for belonging to an interest group are either *psychological* (it helps one's outlook) or *material* (it helps one's pocketbook). In real life, the two motivations are often mixed, but here, for analytical purposes, we will separate them.

Psychological Benefits

There are two basic psychological functions of individuals that can be affected by joining a group: an "orienting function" that mediates between the individual and the larger society (in our particular concern, the state) and a "personal identification" function that helps the individual to express personal feelings.

THE ORIENTING FUNCTION. Studies have shown that membership in any kind of organization enlarges a person's capacity to act as a citizen by increasing communication links between people and educating individuals about subjects outside their immediate families.[4] In homogeneous organizations, members are more likely to discuss controversial topics such as politics because they feel secure among friends. Even this limited exercise of talking politics can increase interest in public affairs which, in turn, makes the individual feel more confident of his ability to act constructively through his vote or perhaps through leadership within the organization. In this way the group acts as a step toward the outside world; that is, it serves a "mediating function" of linking the individual and society.

Common Cause is an example of an organization that was specifically created to produce this sense of orientation and interest in society and then to use the enthusiasm generated as leverage to move the governmental system to reform itself. In the fall of 1970, Common Cause sought charter members through newspaper advertisements and a barrage of direct mail aimed at dissatisfied members of the middle class who were interested in America but turned off by "politics as usual," typified at the time by the Vietnam War policy. John Gardner, the founder, offered a message: "Everybody is organized but the people. . . . [We will create] a third force in American life which will uphold the public interest against . . . the special interests that dominate our national life today."[5] The result of this appeal, explicitly couched in terms of a new relationship between citizens and government, was 45,000 members within three months; today Common Cause has over 250,000 members.

In the *Village Voice*, of August 30, 1976, an advertisement headlined "Has National Politics left you in the corridor of lost causes?" Sought members for an organization called All Together. "If you are a woman, single parent, gay, divorced, widowed, never married, lesbian, bisexual, swinger, cohabitator, member of a corporate family, or JUST PLAIN TIRED OF AN UNRESPONSIVE SYSTEM . . . YOU NEED ALL TOGETHER." Member benefits included a journal, a legal assistance program, insurance plans, book discounts, and a membership questionnaire—presented as "an opportunity to be heard." All Together is different from Common Cause, but it too seeks members by referring to their psychological relationships with the political system at large and by suggesting that *this* organization can affect *that* relationship.

THE PERSONAL IDENTIFICATION FUNCTION. Some individuals use groups as an outlet for self-expression which then tends to increase their own sense of personal identity. For them the group provides the security and defense against the ambiguity of the outside world which was once provided by the extended family. Other individuals join groups as a means of creating within the group a sense of personal status which they feel is lacking in their everyday world. The "outsider" composition of personal identification groups is suggested by studies of the Ku Klux Klan (KKK) and the recent rise of interest groups within ethnic categoric groups.

Ethnic categoric groups such as Blacks, Indians, Chinese, or Jews tend to share common characteristics not only because of member interactions and a shared heritage and traditions, but also as a result of outside discriminatory pressures. When interest groups develop within these categoric groups, the organized group tends to strengthen those shared characteristics and increase the cohesiveness of the group members through glorification of their own common heritage.

The psychological feelings of social, economic, and political impotence that lead minorities to form groups are revealed in the dichotomy between group goals and techniques. Groups such as the Black Panthers, the Jewish Defense League, or Chavez's La Causa rose during the 1960s as organized responses to a political call for community power. While it is true that the average members of these groups lacked traditional lobbying resources such as education, money, and a sense of efficacy, their leaders had these resources. Nevertheless, the leaders responded to the psychological bonds of their organizations rather than to demands from the political system. Their political goal was some control over the conditions that affected their own lives, but they refused to play the insider's game in order to win. Their slogan, "Power to the People" revealed a personal identification desire to express the group's "own sense of impotence and desire for self-determination through militant, direct actions that don't necessarily become channeled into more customary forms of political action."[6]

The Ku Klux Klan (KKK) provides similar status for its members, mostly people occupying marginal jobs midway between manual labor and low white collar such as gas station attendants, carpenters, store clerks, and truckers. Generally they lack the skills and education to improve their conditions, but since they have absorbed the American success ethos the contrast makes them anxious. By offering a member the opportunity of superconformity to "symbols of 100% Americanism and his membership in the superordinately defined white race . . .,"[7] the KKK provides an accommodation between the member's ambitious internalized values and the insecure reality of his life. For example, a current Klan poem states: "Black is beautiful/Tan is grand/But white is the color/Of the big boss man." The robe, insignia, and obvious status hierarchy of the organizational apparatus provide a sense of personal security that is reinforced by identification of scapegoats such as "niggers," Jews, and Wall Street bankers, who are blamed for the KKK'ers inability to adapt to society. This mythology gives the member a sense of personal identification with a cause.

In summary, the two psychological functions—orienting and personal identification—as motivations for joining groups tend to divide along class lines. People with education and money are more likely to join Common Cause or Urban Coalition or NAACP-type "orienting" groups that encourage their generalized inclination to participate in nonpersonal activities. People in lower economic and status positions, with less education and income, more commonly join groups that give them a sense of personal identification and security.

> Mainstream organizational membership does serve to reduce powerlessness and to integrate high-status individuals into the political and social systems. Those who begin from a relatively advantageous position may have joined because of their initially higher sense of personal efficacy, which is then increased through group membership. In the meantime, the low-status or status-anxious individual will probably remain outside this mainstream of organizational activity as an isolated individual, as a joiner of "anti" or "fringe" groups, or as an occasional participant in mass protest activities.[8]

Material Benefits

The economic benefit theory of group membership provides an explanation based on external circumstances rather than internal motivations. Essentially there are two versions of the material benefits theory: Mancur Olson stresses the relationship between individual motivation and group benefits, while Robert Salisbury focuses on the relationship between anticipated benefits and group formation.[9]

Olson begins from the assumption that political interest groups generally work for "collective benefits," that is, those which all people in the relevant category can share, such as lower taxes, clean water, higher minimum wage, or agricultural price subsidies. For example, the collective bargaining agent for the instructional staff at the City University of New York is such an entity—its bargaining gains apply to all staff regardless of whether they belong to the union or not. Consequently, many staff members enjoy union benefits but do not join the organization itself.

This is a natural phenomenon since any individual "would prefer that the others pay the entire cost, and ordinarily the person would get any benefit provided whether he had borne part of the cost or not."[10] Consequently rational individuals who seek maximum benefits for minimum personal costs will not join a large, common benefit organization unless membership is a precondition of employment or in some other way nonvoluntary.

Then, why do individuals join groups? For two reasons, Olson maintains. First, the group provides desirable "selective benefits," that is, benefits available only to members, such as the Farm Bureau's educational programs and low-cost insurance, the American Medical Association's or the National Society of Legislative Lobbyists discount gift buying, travel, and insurance benefits.

Second, individuals join groups when the value of the benefit or the need to be seen as a participant is important. Consequently the size of the group itself becomes a relevant factor. In a small group one member may contribute more than his share because he needs the benefits for himself; in a medium-sized group participation or nonparticipation of an individual may be noticeable, thus pushing the individual to contribute to a collective good. In a large organization the addition of one more person rarely matters, so in cost-benefit terms the rational individual will abstain from participating. Among the largest interests, such as business, trade, or petroleum, "The standard for determining whether a group will have the capacity to act, without coercion or outside inducements . . . depends on whether the individual actions of any one or more members in a group are noticeable to any other individuals in the group."[11]

This notion relates back to the earlier question concerning the composition of the organized political interest group universe. According to Olson, individuals take the time to organize collectively in groups only if the group itself is small enough to make their participation necessary or if inducements such as private services and discount prices make membership dues seem worthwhile. His arguments apply most directly to economically oriented associations. However, in the context of charitable work or middle-class organizations working for health, education, and welfare benefits intended for others, his concept of self-interested rationality is checkmated by psychological motivations. Olson's theory does not explain membership in groups such as Common Cause which exists primarily to lobby, which cannot control the benefits that flow from its successes, and which cannot coerce its membership to remain. Salisbury supplements these gaps in Olson's argument by presenting a broader theory that sees all groups as "benefit exchanges" in which an "entrepreneur," the initiator of the enterprise, invests his capital of time, money, and effort to assemble a package of benefits that can be purchased for the price of group membership.

The entrepreneur's potential "market" is the entire range of people he chooses to attract. "If, and so long as, enough customers buy, i.e., join to make a viable organization, the group is in business. If the benefits fail or are inadequate to warrant the cost of membership, or the leaders get inadequate returns, the group collapses."[12] A group may offer fraternal benefits as do the Grange or the Elks ("Best People on Earth"); or the material benefits of trade associations; or ideological satisfactions such as those offered by the KKK, Common Cause, or the Vietnam Moratorium Committee.

The major difference between Olson and Salisbury is the emphasis placed on the group leader/entrepreneur as functionally different from group members. Salisbury argues that the organizer himself must receive special rewards in order to make his leadership role worthwhile. These range from salaries as chief executive to personal benefits as major spokesman for the group. From this vantage point, the lobbying, which seems almost irrelevant in Olson's terms, becomes a part of the leader's profit. In this context lobbying may represent personal choices and values of group entrepreneurs rather-than enactment of member's wishes.

Thus, theories of individual attraction to organizational membership as means to fulfill personal needs or overcome personal feelings of inadequacy, and theories of membership as rational decisions based on cost/benefit analysis add to our understanding of group origins. Human needs are important factors in determining timing, that is, when interests organize and when organized interests turn to the political arena for benefits.

Characteristics of Group Members

The psychological and material motives for joining groups suggest numerous categories of individuals potentially available to join organizations. The next questions are: Which persons actually do join groups? What stimulus motivates them to act on the basis of their interests and predispositions?

The United States has often been called a "nation of joiners," and current data indicate that such involvement is increasing. Table 2 lists organizational memberships by group category. As the table shows 75 percent of the population belong to some organization, although the largest category consists of the 42 percent who listed church affiliations. More importantly, 19 percent belong to two groups, 30 percent to three or more—figures that are up 17 percent from those reported in 1957. However, this does not automatically translate into politically active people or organizations, since only one-third of all organizations could probably be considered political interest groups.

Joiners of voluntary associations are more likely to be male than females, parents than nonparents, married than single, urban or rural nonfarm than farmers, Jews or Protestants than Catholics, frequent voters than nonvoters, and home-owners than renters.[13] Nevertheless, the most frequent correlation between individuals and the likelihood of group membership is socioeconomic standing. As income, occupation, community status, and education rise, so does the possibility of group membership. This is understandable in the sense that education broadens a person's interests so that he or she seeks outside interactions; community status makes community concerns more personally relevant so that an individual will have the rational self-interest motivation to join; those in higher status careers tend to benefit more from group contacts and information; higher income increases the possibility that a person has more time available for nonprofit activities as well as sufficient skills to participate.

TABLE 2. U.S. Organizational Memberships by Group Category, 1974

Group Category	*Percent Belonging*
Church	41.8
Sports	17.5
School service	17.5
Fraternal	13.7
Professional	13.0
Youth	10.3
Literary, art, study	9.2
Hobby	9.6
Veterans	8.9
Service	8.9
Political	4.4
Farm	4.2
Nationality	3.5
Total membership	74.5
Total in two groups	18.9
Total in three or more groups	29.9
Total multiple membership	*48.8*

SOURCE: Robert Salisbury, "Overlapping Memberships, Organizational Interactions, and Interest Group Theory" (Unpublished American Political Science Association paper, Chicago, Ill. 1976), p. 4.

Even a wealthy, white, male Protestant usually must be asked to join an organization or in some way made aware of its existence and its relevance to him. Generally people join social/fraternal groups and community based civic organizations such as the Rotary, PTA, or the League of Women Voters because they are asked by friends or because community norms require participation in certain groups. So most suburban mothers join the PTA the year their firstborn enters kindergarten and cease to pay dues when their youngest leaves school.

Trade associations and professional associations solicit members by sending introductory letters to lists of new people in the field. Often new groups or entrepreneurs who specialize in creating letterhead organizations for their own private gain buy mailing lists geared toward specific ideological or economic groups. For example, in February, 1972, Dependable Mailing Lists, Inc., was offering: "325,000 conservative-minded individuals, List #114, @$25.00 per M; 158,-000 liberal-minded individuals, List #104, @$25.00 M."[14] These lists are usually based on magazine subscription or charge account lists. Some groups ask current members to find a new member or send in names of those who might be interested. These are then added to the lists which become more valuable as they increase in size.

The organizer or group then mails a letter soliciting a membership fee, often sweetening the appeal with a merchandising gimmick, such as the gun control decals sent with the offer to join the National Gun Control Center or the decorative seals that accompany many charity appeals, or with rhetoric designed to make the issue seem of vital importance. For example, the end of the war in Vietnam created a series of new organizations dedicated to universal amnesty for draft resisters. One such organization, Safe Return, sent a solicitation letter in spring 1975 to an antiwar list. The letter included a raft of liberal endorsers, ranging from *Village Voice* cartoonist Jules Feiffer to Congresswoman Bella Abzug to establish the reputability of the organization, and an emotional message recounting the personal trauma of the returned Vietnam veteran who signed the letter. "I wouldn't want you to have to endure the horrors of Vietnam and the years of fugitive life which followed. . . . For the sake of those living underground in exile, in prison, or on the 'street' with a bad discharge, won't you please join us?"

A more unusual form of membership recruitment is illustrated by the National Federation of Independent Business (NFIB) which employs a sales force of 150 people who are paid on a commission basis for each recruitment or renewal they sell. (NFIB members must own and operate independent businesses that are not the dominant employer in the area). The sales person learns a seven-point emotional appeal that begins with a questionnaire seeking views on current national issues, progresses through an overview of the federation, and climaxes with a patriotic call for action on behalf of independent businessmen. "If we each vote on the laws of our land (through the Federation's poll) in a concerted action every month, we can put our country back on a firm foundation."[15] Labor unions employ a similar technique to organize new occupations or bring in new nonunionized firms.

Membership Size versus Cohesion

The size of the membership thus recruited is important politically from two aspects: the size in relation to the total possible member population, and member cohesion, which is defined as the amount of internal membership agreement on the organization's goals. Size in relation to the total possible pool of group members is important when politicians are considering whether the group really qualifies as a mouthpiece for its specific segment of the population. For example, the AFL-CIO claim to speak for labor is seriously weakened by the fact that less than one-fourth of the total working force is unionized, and major unions such as the Teamsters, United Mine Workers, and United Auto Workers are not affiliated with the AFL-CIO.

The American Medical Association used to enjoy the membership of approximately 70 percent of all practicing doctors, but the percentage has now declined to 50 percent. The American Bar Association claims 67 percent of all lawyers as members. By contrast less than 20 percent of all university and college teachers belong to the American Association of University Professors. Twenty-eight million veterans are eligible to join the American Legion or Veterans of Foreign Wars, yet the former has only 2.7 million members, the latter 1.8 million.

While increasing membership may facilitate a group's chances to maintain credibility as spokesman for its issue, membership growth can have internal organizational ramifications that weaken the group's capacity to actually produce member response. For one thing, group expansion encourages the tendency for members to affiliate as "paper members," to be merely dues payers rather than activists. Generally only a fraction of any group's membership are activists, but as the group increases in size the proportion of participants to paper becomes counterproductive. When the vast numbers on the membership roll cannot be counted on to act on behalf of group goals, groups use their money to create substitutes such as political campaign trust funds that provide clout in the name of the inactive members. AMPI's dairy trust fund millions represented a brilliant checkoff scheme, not millions of politically active dairymen.

Secondly, the idea that all members of a group think alike is a useful myth, but untrue. Any two plumbers will probably disagree on various issues despite their common union card. So it is axiomatic that with increased group size comes increased membership heterogeneity. This has two important consequences for the political life of the group. The diversity of members' interests tends to expand the agenda of desirable goals. This in turn may not only dilute the group's political resources, but may also create internal tensions within the group and even within individual members that affect their level of involvement.

People have many interests, "overlapping memberships"[16] in groups, that may lead to explicit conflict between family and job, politics and church, or implicit conflicts over values, goals, and demands for an individual's time. Such conflicts determine the activity level that is feasible for a member. Competing time demands may preclude membership in small action-oriented groups. Therefore, many mothers say they will postpone civic organization work until their children are in school or grown. On the other hand, some organizations may not provide sufficient activities to satisfy their members' expectations. Common Cause responded to member complaints of this kind by creating state boards of directors to pursue "clean up government" campaigns at the state level.

Members faced with time or issue conflicts have several options. They may lose interest in the organization either temporarily or permanently; they may drop out; they may modify their own level of participation; or they may form a new organization. For example, the National Association of Professional Educators was formed in 1975 in California and the Midwest by conservative teachers opposed to the militant stands of the two larger teacher interest groups, the National Education Association and the American Federation of Teachers.

Conflicting interests can also inhibit group consideration of new issues. For example, teachers associations often take no position on parochial school aid because it could split their membership along a religious/ethical axis that is not relevant to their more dominant occupational concerns. Many women's organizations take no stand on abortion for similar reasons. Even economic organizations are not immune to the fractionatizing tendencies of overlapping membership. "It is difficult to get multipurpose business associations to take stands on controversial issues. The broader and more heterogeneous the organization, the greater the probability that some subgroups will dissent on a given issue."[17]

The direct relationship between overlapping memberships and cohesion (the internal togetherness of members) indicates the organizational importance of cohesion as "a constantly operating influence that limits the activities of a group and its leaders . . . "[18] both in terms of goal-related activities and membership participation patterns. The scope and amount of a group's political activities occur within the boundaries set by the internal areas of agreement that form the substance of group cohesion.

GROUP ORGANIZATION AND LEADERSHIP

For most people the term *organization* conjures up visions of desks, telephones, letterheads, and staff. Yet this is merely one stage in the development of group activities, a stage many important interest groups such as Students for a Democratic Society (SDS) or Women Strike for Peace never reached. Therefore, the definition we will use is more flexible. "An organization comes into existence when explicit procedures are established to coordinate the activities of a group in the interest of achieving specific objectives.'[19]

Naturally the National Rifle Association, headquartered in a new nine-story marble and glass building in Washington, D. C., with its 1 million members and staff of 292 is readily identifiable as an organized political interest group. But the International Society of Professional Bums consisting of fifty-one dues-paying members and an answering device on a telephone is also a political interest group duly registered in November 1975 for the purpose of lobbying Congress to do absolutely nothing.

These examples span the range of organizational apparatus, but in both cases a routinized pattern of interaction has been established for the furtherance of group goals. By contrast, the definition does not include what have been termed "potential groups"—those "interests that are not at a particular point in time the basis of interactions among individuals, but that may become such."[20] Such phenomena, often called public interest or public opinion, are important as influences within the policy-making environment, but they are not included within our focus because they lack established procedures as a framework for activity.

When organization is considered in terms of developmental stages, it can provide clues to the internal workings of a group that, in turn, affect the group's political activity patterns. A formal organizational apparatus is often a manifestation of a high degree of group interaction or a reflection of an agreed upon value structure. For example, membership organizations such as unions often allot half their staff to recruitment, while trade associations with a fixed corporate membership base may assign staff primarily to internal communication needs. An office with its lease, typewriters, files, and telephones also suggests permanence and a degree of stability. Sometimes, this effect is deliberately created by a new organization to inspire confidence; more often it is a concrete manifestation of organizational longevity.

Organization charts also indicate the flow of power within a group both in terms of relationships between professional staff and volunteer boards of directors, and among the various subunits or chapters of an interest group. Many volunteer organizations including charities, social welfare organizations, civic groups, and recreational groups, are staff run even though in all other respects they fit the definition of "voluntary association." Often the division of decisions into policy and implementation categories provides a means for staff control over volunteers' participation.

Organization routines and patterns of interaction assume varying degrees of participation and a natural division of labor. Often a volunteer board of directors will conduct most of the policy-making activity, while a small staff of rotating volunteers will do the writing, mimeographing, and mailing necessary to carry out the policy decisions. Or a large paid staff may direct daily activities, leaving the board free to set policy directions, and volunteers to do specific tasks such as running blood banks or disaster relief centers for the Red Cross. In most trade associations there are no volunteer workers except the board which meets infrequently, and a paid staff performs the association's business. In this way either the selected staff or elected directors have, in the words of Robert Michels, "dominion . . . over the electors. . . . Who says organization, says oligarchy."[21]

The struggle in the NAACP over the retirement date of Roy Wilkins, executive director for the last twenty years, illustrates the situation of board-staff conflict. At the NAACP's July 1976 convention, Mr. Wilkins made an unprecedented appeal to the delegates to permit him to retire after the July 1977 convention to be held in his hometown, rather than in January 1977 as requested by the board. The sixty-four-member board felt challenged to assert publicly that it was the elected, appointed leadership of the organization, and that Mr. Wilkins, despite his national reputation, was but an employee of the board, hired on a year-to-year contract. The dispute ended with board decisions to accede to Mr. Wilkins's request, to appoint an administrator to take over most of the actual leadership duties during the interim period, and an expressed intention to never permit any one staff member to become so powerful in the future.

Organization also sets the decision-making sequence which in turn affects the way a group responds to current policy demands. Most national organizations with state and local subdivisions must choose functional chores for the localities and retain the decision role for themselves at the national level. For example, most trade associations are geographically federated, but policy is made by the national board. NOW, the National Organization for Women, despite its 800 affiliates, also makes policy at the national level. By contrast, in the AFL-CIO federation decision-making power is split between the locals and the national board. Thus in the 1972 elections, despite AFL-CIO chairman George Meany's declared policy of neutrality, approximately a dozen unions supported Nixon, while about three dozen supported McGovern.

In tactical terms, loose-knit federations find it harder to gather key people as quickly as the policy-making process may demand. At the same time, when power is diffused within an organization, it is often easier to obtain immediate local pressure when such a tactic is required. When centralized decision-making organizations make snap decisions, they often find field implementation an impossibility. In heterogeneous organizations where a central board is used as a tool for integrating various internal factions, central decisions often reflect the lowest common denominator of agreement—a level that may be too low to be useful for lobbying. In 1972 the Business Roundtable, an organization composed of 160 chief executives of the largest American companies, was formed because it was felt that decision-making by the Chamber of Commerce and the National Association of Manufacturers was too slow and too tepid to be useful for lobbying purposes.

Some federated organizations use member polls and delegate conventions to create yearly agendas and select new officers. The facade of participation seems democratic, but in many trade associations and unions the real policy arguments occur during the drafting of planks for convention consideration. For example, the 1975 AFL-CIO convention gathered during a severe economic crisis, but for the 1,000 delegates and alternates it was a dull, noncontroversial meeting. Without disagreement, eighty resolutions were adopted on topics ranging from support for tax deductible lunches to opposition to the political situation in India.

By contrast the American Medical Association, which is also a federation, has lively conventions at which delegates from affiliated locals make policy decisions that the national board must follow. Thus delegates forced the national organization to accept a national health insurance plan, medicredit, and to work with the Department of Health, Education, and Welfare to implement professional standard review organizations—both of which were previously opposed by the national AMA. At the 1975 house of delegates meeting, delegates also rejected a board suggestion to raise dues, substituting instead a one-year additional assessment to cover the association's financial deficit.

Many organizations secure member participation through issue referenda to discover member preferences. For example, Common Cause offers its members a yearly choice of fifteen current issues; the leadership then acts on those in the top third. The National Federation of Independent Businessmen polls its members monthly by congressional districts, then tallies the results, and mails them to congressmen on a district-by-district basis. National totals are computed and mailed to all members of Congress and relevant executive branch officials. However, since only one-quarter of the membership usually participates in the poll, the federation sends out percentages of the actual vote rather than raw numbers or percentages of the membership as a whole.

On the other hand, the League of Women Voters assures maximum member participation in its selection of issues by conducting a year-long process that begins when local suggestions are forwarded to the national level. The most prominent issues are combined to form a two-year program that is accepted by representatives of local leagues at its biennial national convention. While often inconvenient in terms of securing immediate league response to new issues, the process is essential to maintain the grass roots participatory integrity of the league's internal decision-making processes.

Both conventions and referenda serve "primarily to emphasize unity, to give sanction to previously determined decisions, and, by the appearance of wide rank-and-file participation in policy forming, to strengthen the group internally and make it more effective externally."[22] Such devices may create the illusion of or conditions for cohesion which leaders must then develop and enhance. "The attitudes present in the membership define the tasks of the leaders and the internal political life of the group is made up of a continuous effort to maintain leaders and followers in some measure of harmonious relationship."

Leadership is the term applied to the relationship between the active minority who actually make group decisions and the group rank and file. The exact content of the leader's job varies to meet group demands since it is rooted in this reciprocal relationship between leaders and members. In most organizations, a few tend to rule the many for a variety of reasons.

Leaders inevitably arise in any human group. This created a dilemma for Students for a Democratic Society in the 1960s. Dedicated to a wholly democratic, participatory organization, SDS found itself with de facto leaders who arose out of an unconscious, spontaneous delegation of roles. This clash between reality and philosophy led the leaders to denounce their own position. One, Tom Hayden, said: "Leaders mean organization, organization means hierarchy, and hierarchy is undemocratic. . . . The fine line between leader and organizer must remain clear: an organizer does not impose his ideas on the community."[23]

The processes of leadership development and leadership selection vary with the organization, the people available, and the issues. In terms of the exchange benefit theory of group development, a John Gardner (Common Cause) or a Maggie Kuhn (Gray Panthers) or a Robert Welch (John Birch Society) develop a program which they package so as to attract members who want to buy in, that is, join. A variation of this situation is the outside organizer, such as Saul Alinsky, who makes a career of organizing groups and teaching them political action techniques. Both types of individual create groups, but the former stay with their creation for the mutual benefit of both, while organizers receive rewards from the process itself rather than from developing a particular group program.

Some group leaders emerge from within the group as typified by the labor leaders of the 1960s—George Meany, I. W. Abel, Jerry Wurf, and others. Often leaders move from a single group base to become movement leaders. Crisis situations, such as the Birmingham integration march which catapulted Martin Luther King from chairman of the Southern Christian Leadership Conference to head of the civil rights movement, create leaders by providing a backdrop against which personal qualities of dynamism, self-confidence, and executive ability stand out.

Many middle-class organizations and trade associations have routinized internal leadership selection so that it is customary for last year's first vice-president to become this year's president. Where selection follows an automatic process, it is often in recognition of the fact that only certain types of people will opt for leadership positions which tend to entail a large amount of time and responsibility. Usually civic organizations are led by middle-aged members who have spent years acquiring the expertise and then find the time once family responsibilities decrease. Similarly, the leaders of the AMA and other professional associations tend to be financially secure specialists who have both the time and economic independence to devote to such leadership.

The crucial job for a leader, regardless of his manner of selection, is to maximize the sources of internal group cohesion and act as group spokesman vis-à-vis the outside world. Generally the ratio of internal activity to external salesmanship is affected by the size and heterogeneity of the group. Large, heterogeneous organizations, that is, national unions, veterans organizations, civic organizations, and large trade associations, require considerable leadership efforts to create internal consensus. The leaders must work to keep members aligned through the use of house organs such as monthly newsletters, information backgrounders, action information alerts, and so on. Members of small, homogeneous organizations, such as individual corporations or union locals, are more likely to have an agreed upon set of values that helps the leaders over the consensus hurdle and allows them to concentrate on policy contacts with outside decision makers.[24]

Leaders can satisfy members' desires by acting in terms of their own beliefs which they feel to be representative of the membership or by trying to do what they think the membership wants done.[25] The first option is often impossible to achieve in established organizations since the organizer-leader, as he acquires the skills of leadership, tends to become less typical of the rank and file.

Once in office, the position itself, with the status attached to it, adds to leadership power. This often creates its own communications gap between leaders and followers. Some leaders who seem too far ahead of the rank and file may be called down by members who feel the leader is only using the organization as a means of personal advancement. Others may feel the leader has sold out to the opposition.

This is most visible in labor unions when leaders symbolically leave their trade uniforms behind and wear the jacket and tie uniform of management. After years of working their way up the union hierarchy, these men are no longer firemen or miners or steelworkers, they are union management men; they have a new, totally different career. Union leaders are now paid executive salaries: in 1973, ninety-three union leaders earned over $35,000 a year, three earned over $100,000. Edward Sadlowski, insurgent candidate for president of the United Steelworkers of America in 1977, expressed this sentiment when he said: "The issue of the steelworkers is clearly defined. It is an issue between the haves and the have-nots. . . . Those guys [the leaders] think everything is kosher by virtue of the position they hold. I don't feel they could tell a worker from a boss, and that's tragic."

Leaders who do not satisfy member desires can change or be deposed. John Gardner, the moderate, scholarly patrician who founded Common Cause has become more aggressive in recent years in order to meet the expectations of his hyperactive constituency of middle-class mavericks who want to make changes now. He plays to their antiestablishment attitude with phrases such as: "If you want to clear the stream, get the hog out of the spring." "As the Lord tempers the wind to the shorn lamb, the politician lightens retribution to the fat cat."

Leaders who want to retain ties with their members can do so through control of the organization's internal propaganda machine, spelling out organizational philosophy, setting meeting agendas, and producing written materials. The newsletters, bulletins, and magazines that arrive weekly or monthly are powerful propaganda tools, since they put current, factual information before the members in the context of group goals and strategies. By phrasing information in the context of a member's interests, the group may be able to "orient" the member toward outside events in ways that will also add to the group's strength.

Leaders also maintain their power through development of special skills such as the use of jargon, manipulation of the policy process, and structuring of finances to further their own aims. Jargon is peculiar to most organizations, for example, the League of Women Voters speaks of "items," read "goals," or "consensus," read "group position." Membership rituals of many fraternal organizations serve a similar purpose. Learning the jargon requires an initiation period for the new member during which time the person learns to accept the organization as it currently functions. Then having spent the time to become an "insider," the member wants to maintain his/her investment in the status quo situation.

DEMOCRACY AND INTERNAL GROUP DECISION MAKING

The discussion of leader-led relationships is important in the context of the previous discussion of group functions for individuals and for society as a whole. Groups are seen as providing a means of expressing minority opinions for policy information and as public education tools. They are also viewed as a mediator between both individuals and society and broad interests and society. In each case the group helps to stabilize political relationships by increasing the public's participation in official policy making, thereby increasing public satisfaction and identification with the government. At the narrowest level the leader-member relationship sets the boundaries within which the group serves these functions and creates cohesion, a necessary precondition of effective group action. Consequently group sociologists are divided over the forms of group participation and its democratic meaning.

Generally, the argument over member participation in group decision making is discussed in terms of group structure. One faction argues that in order to assure democratic participation, that is, involvement of all members in decision making, a group should have all the apparatus of a democratic state, such as rival parties nominating candidates for office, divided power between the legislative and executive parts of the administration, and judicial safeguards such as the Bill of Rights guarantees to protect minority views within the group. This emphasis on structural competition implies a positive view of the notion that groups serve a mediating function between individuals and society. The logic is that without guarantees of active member participation, the rank and file cannot acquire the citizen skills and awareness that the "orienting function" of groups requires. " . . . The effective voluntary association is one in which not only membership is voluntary, but the type of activity is also voluntary in that the members choose their goals and the means for obtaining them. Few things would wreck an association faster than to impose a goal or means of action on the members. In other words, pluralism of ends and means is a necessary component of voluntarism in democracy."[26]

A second argument states that structural competition guarantees are unnecessary since private governments and public government are basically different and groups have a homogeneity of opinion unmatched by the public at large. With this homogeneous ideological or issue basis of membership, it is sufficient for the organization to nominate officers at a convention representing the entire membership and then to let the officers act in the members' interests. "Since the organization is the total of its membership and since its goals are the common goals of its members, limitation of its power is not only undemocratic but also irrational."[27] However, since we have seen that total homogeneity of opinion is humanly impossible, this ideal of majority democracy may be carried too far.

The middle ground sees both arguments as unrealistic. The "democratic apparatus" argument is flawed by the evidence on different levels of member participation, different skills among members, the difficulty of securing truly competitive slates of candidates or truly competitive opinions within the narrow confines of any one group's resources, and the primarily administrative role of most group organizational structure. The opposing argument for majority democracy is flawed by evidence that many groups do not tolerate internal minority factions. I. W. Abel, United Steelworkers president, told union dissidents: "We don't want you. We can't afford you. And we are not about to surrender this union to you." The delegates at their annual convention cheered him. Thus dissidents are forced to be silent or leave the group, but usually there is no alternative group for them to join. Unions, for example, have vigorously opposed "dual unionism" because it will weaken the bargaining power of existing unions.

The compromise offered by the third camp is to judge internal group practices by the standard of responsiveness to members' wishes. Representativeness can be attained if members are offered meaningful choices on referenda and at conventions and if they have means of communicating with their leaders in the interim periods. Since leadership effectiveness and performance depend on knowledge of members' desires, a responsive organization will fulfill the needs of the larger social and political system and will also be successful in the narrower terms of its own goals. This emphasis on goals can, however, be misleading since articulate minorities may set organization policy. In addition it takes no note of the role of paper members. All three analyses presuppose the importance of member acquiescence in group processes; what they disagree about is the way to identify "meaningful" involvement or the amount of participation it requires.

GROUP GOALS

The goals of interest groups can be classified in several ways—number, complexity, feasibility, subject matter content, source of the interest, consequences for society as a whole—but in terms of public policy making, goal content is probably the most significant classification. A goal may reflect objective characteristics of the group such as its economic situation, for example, labor unions; or it may arise from shared subjective values such as the American Civil Liberties Union, a civic organization dedicated to the preservation of First Amendment rights. An amusing linguistic distinction is made along these lines by an Englishman, Samuel Finer, who divided groups into "proper interest" groups, those pursuing their own welfare, and "promotional" groups which espouse causes such as peace, health, safety, or morals. Or slicing the pie slightly differently, an American sociologist, Arnold Rose, has divided groups into two individual oriented categories: "expressive" groups which satisfy the personal interests of members, for example, hobby, athletic, professional associations; and "instrumental" groups which aim to solve problems in society at large.

Clark and Wilson have created a three-category classification of goals[28] which is useful in terms of our previous discussion of individual reasons for joining groups and group incentives to lobby. "Material" goals are those having monetary value; "solidary" goals are related to personal rewards or benefits to the individual such as making friends, discussing ideas, having fun, gaining a sense of status; "purposive" goals are altruistic or suprapersonal goals relating to society at large—war, peace, civic reform, civil liberties.

"Solidary" benefit groups are formed by individuals seeking psychological refuge and are, therefore, least likely to venture into the political policy-making arena. But this is not true of every ideological group by any means. The John Birch Society, the Americans for Democratic Action, the Ripon Society, the Americans for Constitutional Action, and hundreds of other groups are politically active in the hope that they can lead the United States policy process toward their own ideological position.

Groups with "purposive" goals, either as their main concern or as additions to a material agenda, as typified by Common Cause, the League of Women Voters, the Sierra Club, and the NAACP, also act within the political process. Nevertheless, the public policy process most readily accommodates groups with material demands, those whose wishes for specific allocations of tangible resources such as grants, subsidies, tariffs, import duties, and so forth, can easily be spelled out in laws and administrative rulings.

Different lobbying patterns are created by the interaction of group size, leadership capabilities, goals, and requirements for cohesion. Larger groups tend to have a more heterogeneous membership which is often reflected in a shopping list of goals. This means that a group will either disperse its energies and work a little on every goal or will arrange the goals in order of priority, only pursuing actively those at the top of the list. In addition, as the numbers of goals increase, the chances for internal conflict between the ramifications of goal A and goal E increase, making the group's lobbying positions more moderate. This is evident in the AFL-CIO where the original goal of job stability has come into conflict with more recent civil rights goals, now being implemented through job quotas. To mitigate the internal strain, the AFL-CIO tends to pursue civil rights and social goals through separate coalitions which provide an organizational distance from the union itself.

If you accept Olson's rational view of group membership, then as size increases, groups will also have to devote more of their money to selective benefits for their own members in order to keep a sufficient membership base. To recapture defecting members, the AMA said in 1975 that "there is nothing a union can do for a doctor that his professional organization cannot do if it is willing." Thus it is now considering new services such as backup malpractice insurance and courses in negotiating techniques for the many doctors employed by health institutions.

Groups pursuing their own economic goals "generally have a more disciplined membership, more affluent treasuries, tighter bureaucratic organization, and a more permanent and indeed also more active clientele" then groups with civic, noneconomic goals.[29] Groups with purposive goals are easy to organize, but they rarely endure. Once the emotional issue—peace, amnesty, gay lib, legal marijuana—has been expressed, it is often difficult to develop a shared program that will serve to bind the group together past its moment of protest. For each category of group, the goals generate a level of organized interaction that in turn limits the forms of group action and the probable life expectancy of the group.

It has been suggested that the tangible or intangible, specific or general content of group goals affects both the role of leaders and their lobbying style.[30] Groups with specific, tangible, usually economic interests cast their leaders as spokesmen for the group. They begin immediately to issue position papers and speak at hearings to communicate their demands, while backstopping their governmental solicitations with a publicity campaign aimed at the general public. By contrast, leaders of groups with intangible, general interests spend the early months of policy making in writing interpretive articles to educate their own membership as a precondition for effective action. They emphasize later contacts with congressmen, stressing the general value preferences of their point of view.

What do groups do when events or success make a goal obsolete? This happens: those fighting to repeal the prohibition amendment succeeded, those seeking to end the Vietnam War won, the China lobby lost the battle to deny recognition to Red China, and the March of Dimes conquered polio. When such an organizational blow strikes, the group either dies, as did the antiprohibition lobby and most antiwar groups, or it continues to exist despite current events either because it still sees the threat as menacing even if others do not (the China lobby) or it develops new issues (the March of Dimes now fights birth defects). Generally since leaders have a vested interest in continuing their positions, they adapt the organizational apparatus to fit the new situation.

V. O. Key summarized the member, leader, goal relationship: "The policies and programs of groups . . . are shaped by the interactions within the group, the experiences of its members, the environmental circumstances affecting the group, and other factors. Interest group activity is not . . . a simple reflex action. Rather, group objectives take shape from . . . all the internal processes leading to group action."[31] Once the mix produces group goals, group attributes are reshuffled for use as group lobbying resources.

GROUP ATTRIBUTES AS POLITICAL RESOURCES

All political interest groups seek access to public decision makers as a precondition to any other policy role. The number of entry points they can be assured of and the nature of the reception they receive are directly related to the way in which group membership qualities, leadership abilities, and goals are perceived by other decision makers. Such attributes must be turned into group resources. Resources include any assets that can be used by groups to influence others to assist them or their cause. These include physical resources such as money, size, and media-attracting capabilities; organizational characteristics including cohesion, geographical structure, and leadership skills; intangibles such as the prestige derived from the membership base or the status of the organization itself, the ideological content of the group's program, and the political environment, especially the nature of the opposition.

These resources can be combined in assorted patterns, sometimes helping a group, sometimes hindering it. The total mix at any one time, any one place, on any specific issue represents the amount of legitimacy that public officials will grant to the group as a representative of those whom it says it represents. This legitimacy, a reflection of all the aspects of groups discussed in this chapter, is the most important asset a political interest group can acquire because it means the group will be accepted as a participant in public policy making for that specific time, place, and issue. Legitimacy must be won or renewed each time a group plays political games. Those who win it easily are dubbed "insiders" or "establishment"; those who rarely succeed are the "outsiders." For all groups the components that create this action base are similar, but the interaction of the three kinds of variables—societal position, internal characteristics, and governmental institutions—makes their chances for political success different.

SUMMARY

This chapter has traced the origins of groups back to societal evolution and individual needs—both material and psychological. The question of who joins was related to the question, why join, providing more evidence for the specific needs that groups fill. Group leadership and the nature of internal decision-making processes were linked with earlier discussions of the systemic functions of groups and will reappear later as group lobbying resources. Similarly, group size, group goals, and group leadership were discussed in relation to the purposes of groups and as a basis for understanding later group actions in the political process.

The next chapter will discuss the conversion of these interest group characteristics into lobbying assets.

NOTES

1. See David Truman, *The Governmental Process* (New York: Knopf, 1951); Arthur Bentley, *The Process of Government* (Bloomington, Ind.: Principia Press, 1949); V. O. Key, *Politics, Parties and Pressure Groups,* 5th ed. (New York: Thomas Y. Crowell, 1964); E. E. Schattschneider, *The Semi-Sovereign People* (Hinsdale, Ill.: Dryden Press, 1975).
2. Harry Eckstein, *Pressure Group Politics: The Case of the British Medical Association* (London: Allen & Unwin, 1960), p. 26.
3. Both quotations are from Schattschneider, *The Semi-Sovereign People*, pp. 4–5.
4. For a summary of the studies on group participation, see David Sills, "Voluntary Associations," *International Encyclopedia of the Social Sciences,* vol. 11, ed. David Sills (New York: Macmillan, 1968), pp. 364–66.
5. Paul Lutzker, "The Politics of Public Interest Groups: Common Cause in Action" (Unpublished dissertation, Johns Hopkins University, 1973), p. 63.
6. Robert Binstock and Katherine Ely, *The Politics of the Powerless* (Cambridge: Linthrop Publishing, 1971), p. 214.
7. James Vander Zanden, "The Klan Revival," in *American Political Interest Groups: Readings in Theory and Research,* ed. Betty Zisk (Belmont, Ca.: Wadsworth, 1969), p. 353.
8. Ibid., p. 299.
9. Mancur Olson, Jr., *The Logic of Collective Action* (Cambridge, Mass.: Harvard University Press, 1965); Robert Salisbury, "An Exchange Theory of Interest Groups," in *Interest Group Politics in America,* ed. Robert Salisbury (New York: Harper & Row, 1970), p. 32–67.
10. Olson, *Logic of Collective Action*, p. 21.
11. Ibid., p. 45.
12. Salisbury, "An Exchange Theory of Interest Groups," pp. 42–43.
13. See Sills, "Voluntary Associations," p. 365; Rose, *The Power Structure: Political Process in American Society* (New York: Oxford University Press, 1967), pp. 224–25.
14. Harvey Katz, *Give!* (New York: Doubleday, 1974), pp. 59–60.
15. John Bunzel, "The National Federation of Independent Business," in *Interest Group Politics in America*, p. 109.
16. Truman, *The Governmental Process,* p. 159.
17. Raymond Bauer, Ithiel de Sola Pool, and Lewis Dexter, *American Business and Public Policy: The Politics of Foreign Trade* (New York: Atherton Press, 1963), p. 339.

18. Truman, *The Governmental Process*, p. 159.
19. Peter Blau, "Organizations," *International Encyclopedia of the Social Sciences,* vol. 11, pp. 297–98.
20. Truman, *The Governmental Process*, p. 34.
21. Robert Michels, "The Iron Law of Oligarchy," in *American Political Interest Groups*, p. 93.
22. Truman, *The Governmental Process,* p. 196, p. 156.
23. From Paul Jacobs and Saul Landau, "Students for a Democratic Society," in *Interest Group Politics in America,* p. 93.
24. See Bernard Cohen, "Political Communication on the Japanese Peace Settlement," *Public Opinion Quarterly* 20 (1956): 27–30.
25. See Norman Luttbeg and Harmon Zeigler, "Attitude Consensus and Conflict in an Interest Group: An Assessment of Cohesion," *American Political Science Review* 40 (1960).
26. Rose, *The Power Structure*, p. 251.
27. Grant McConnell, "Public and Private Government," in *Private Government,* eds. Sanford Lakoff and Daniel Rich (Glenview, Ill.: Scott, Foresman, 1973), p. 32.
28. Quoted in Salisbury, "An Exchange Theory of Interest Groups," pp. 47–48.
29. Eckstein, *Pressure Group Politics*, p. 35.
30. See Cohen, "Political Communication on the Japanese Peace Settlement," pp. 30–32.
31. Key, *Politics, Parties and Pressure Groups*, p. 126.

Chapter 3

Lobbying and Lobbyists

Thus far we have discussed interest groups—shared interactions toward an agreed upon goal—and those characteristics of groups—size, membership, cohesion, goals, status—that can be translated into political assets. In this chapter we will consider lobbyists and lobbying, the agents and activity through which group demands are transmitted to participants in the public policy process. After all, labor is but short hand for over 125 separate unions, business is shorter hand for hundreds of occupations and several hundred thousand individual companies. "Labor," "business," "blacks" do not walk the halls of government; their representatives do. So, just as labor means a diversity of unions, labor lobby means people—lobbyists—who communicate labor's demands to the appropriate decision makers.

Lobbyists are important in their role as representatives of interests within the American constituency and as individuals whose perceptions and experience guide both group strategies and their own pattern of activities. In this chapter we will survey the lobbying scene; in later chapters we will consider lobbying at various stages of the public policy-making process.

LOBBYING

Lobbying has both an honorable and a dishonorable part. Its honorable roots can be traced to the First Amendment right to petition one's representatives, a relationship that assumes freedom invites differences among people which government will harmonize in the best interest of all. The right to petition provides the form of functional representation discussed earlier in which blocs of people with similar problems combine their strength to influence public policy. In *Federalist* No. 10, James Madison said: "The regulation of these various and interfering interests forms the principal task of modern legislation and involves the spirit of . . . faction [groups] in the necessary and ordinary operations of government."[1]

The less honorable view associates lobbying with dairymen buying 85 percent of parity, the Lockheed $2 million bailout, and other instances where minorities sabotage the principle of majority rule. The term "lobby," in referring to groups, has been carried over from the term for entranceway or hallway where representatives of group interests stationed themselves to request favors from legislators. Nineteenth-century lobbying was "an individualized and grossly acquisitive business."[2] As economic developments outran the creation of legal regulatory codes, each new corporation, loan, or franchise was negotiated separately. Illustrious men such as Daniel Webster proudly proclaimed the businesses for which they "worked."

In 1852 congressmen set up a price scale (money or land) for their votes; for example, when Bay State Mills of Lawrence, Massachusetts, wanted modification of wool tariffs, they sent an agent equipped with facts: he lost. Then they sent Thurlow Tweed, "wizard lobbyist," armed with $70,000: he won.[3] The entrepreneurial attitude underlying these deals was expressed by Collis Huntington of the Southern Pacific Railroad to one of his lobbyists: "If you have to pay money to have the right thing done, it is only fair and just to do it."[4] In the nineteenth century this was not hypocrisy, it was the free enterprise way.

Today expansion of governmental activity and concentrations of private economic power have wrecked the easy philosophic assumption that interest + interest + interest = public interest. "Stable unrepresentation," technological media possibilities, diffused needs, and concentrated interests work to upset the original equation. The problem was succinctly put in the Buchanan committee's 1957 congressional report: "And so to the extent that some groups are better endowed than others, there is a disparity in the pressure which these groups can exert on the policy-making process. . . . It is said, for example, that the individual consumer and the billion dollar corporation have equal rights before the law, but are they equal before the lawmakers?"

The two stereotypes of lobbying lead to two extreme interpretations of the role of groups in public policy making. One sees government as divorced from all groups, responding only to vote power and protected from group influence by the intricacy and duplication of the policy-making process. The opposing view sees groups as all-powerful with public decision makers as mere pawns implementing privately arrived at decisions. Reality lies in-between. Groups today function as

> associations of like-minded men who confront government collectively rather than competitively. These groups are politically active through the medium of skilled group bureaucracies, as well as lobbyists . . . before administrative agencies as well as legislative committees, by political action at the grass roots as well as personal persuasion under the capitol dome. They are active in a political process where involvement explains more than external pressure. . . . [5]

If we define lobbying as "one aspect of the efforts of men, characteristically organized into groups, to influence the making of public policy, wherever it is made . . . "[6] it allows us to present a wide-open definition that includes grass roots or indirect group activities such as public relations campaigns, protest marches, intergroup alliances, and group initiated letter or telegram campaigns as forms of lobbying. Theorists might dispute this definition as so broad as to be meaningless, but in terms of practical group power it is indeed relevant because it enables us to extend our analysis of group participation to include the creation of public issues instead of picking up group activity in the middle of the process when issue action reaches the formal agenda of Congress or agencies. For example, to exclude the AMA's socialist smear campaign against medicare or the cigarette lobby's fight to keep tobacco legal or the oil companies advertisements explaining their assessment of environmentalists' demands is to tell only half the story.

Lobbying can also be explained in terms of the function of persons who lobby.[7] Lobbying may thus be defined as *any form of communication, made on another's behalf, and intended to influence a govern-*

mental decision. This definition is much broader than the legal federal definition under which Washington lobbyists register, which limits lobbying to persons who collect money for the primary purpose of influencing legislation by direct communication with congressmen. The two definitions are similar in that both focus on the governmental process, include intent to influence, and involve communication. However, the functional definition is realistic, the legal one is not.

Using the functional definition, lobbying can occur within any governmental institution. And can focus on any decision maker—clerk, staff member, official. It is also not confined to direct communications since these constitute but a small fraction of the time and techniques available to modern lobbyists—for example, testifying, researching, staff consultations, campaign activities. The notion of payment is also less limiting in the functional definition. The legal definition stipulates that money must be collected for the principal purpose of lobbying. Using this loophole, International Telephone and Telegraph Company and William Whyte, U.S. Steel's vice-president (read lobbyist), as well as many others do not register since they do not feel that 51 percent (principal) of their own time or organizational resources are allocated to lobbying (that is, direct communication with legislators).

Nevertheless, the functional definition still separates lobbyists from citizens petitioning their representatives by specifying presentation of another's viewpoint, even if the intermediary is unpaid. Thus if the chairman of General Motors walks the floors of Congress as he and other leaders who are members of the Business Roundtable are encouraged to do, he would be considered a lobbyist. The distinction gets fuzzy when the chairman of General Motors confines his visits to his own congressmen and senators. Is he then a lobbyist or simply an atypical citizen calling on his elected representatives? Title and pay aside, the functional definition stresses the communicator-broker role of the lobbyist as an agent for the translation of social and economic power into public policies. Lobbyists carry demands to government, negotiate results, and transmit decisions back to their group, thus creating an important link between organized interests and public decisions.

Lobbying itself is a form of communication, on a par with input from the media, research sources, political parties, colleagues' advice, and opinion leaders in the community. Viewed in the context of a communications system, lobbying can be seen as a means to affect the behavior of individuals by supplying information. The decision-maker's behavior is conceptualized as the result of his previous perceptions and attitudes plus the contents of the "message stimulus."[8]

There are several forms of communication available to lobbyists, with the most effective being the ability to affect the official's job security or public image. For example, a civil rights-labor coalition tarnished Judge Harrold Carswell's public image and his chances for a Supreme Court appointment by pointing out his judicial ineptness, evidenced in numerous reversals of his decisions by higher courts, and his segregationist bias as suggested in his statements and actions. The strength of potential electoral influence is revealed in the gun control paradox: over two-thirds of all Americans favor gun control legislation, but it never passes Congress because the National Rifle Association its electoral power. "Elected officials sense that the anticontrol voters mobilized by the gun lobby are apt to engage in a kind of bullet voting, and decide their voting preferences on the basis of the gun question alone."[9]

Next in effectiveness is the ability to affect an official's information structure by challenging his own information, supplying new information, obstructing competing information, or reformulating policy alternatives. For example, Keith Stroup, the lobbyist for NORML (National Organization for the Reform of Marijuana Law) focuses his arguments in the context of "not pro-grass, but anti-jail."[10] Common Cause reformulated the policy-making context to favor public financing of elections by creating a public perception of the Watergate excesses—that is, in terms of the undue influence of private money on campaigns and hence on elected officials.

A third form of communication supplies personal rewards to decision-makers, such as ideological satisfaction or monetary gains. While it may be politically expedient for Senator Jackson to be pro-Israel since it helps Boeing Aircraft, the largest employer in his state, it may also be ideologically satisfying since he holds a strong anti-Communist, pronational defense position. The material reward is symbolized by an anecdote that Robert Winter-Berger, retired lobbyist-public relations man, tells, in which Speaker of the House John McCormack ended a tour of his office by pointing to the beautiful blank paneling above his door and saying: "And there is the motto of this place: Nothing for Nothing."[11]

It is the lobbyist's job to select the form of communication most likely to be favorably and accurately received by the intended receiver. This means the lobbyist must chose the target and content of the message with care and skill. Distortion can often occur in a variety of ways: perhaps the message was transmitted through a staff member who altered it in translation, perhaps the official was predisposed to block out the message, perhaps "channels" to the decision maker were blocked by others interested in affecting the same decision, or perhaps other stimuli (for example, problems, people) distracted the person from the lobbyist's message. The subjectiveness of the entire process puts a premium on both the lobbyist's skill in judging the situation and the quality of the information transmitted.

LOBBYISTS

Lobbyists are salesmen for their groups, but they sell information and ideas instead of toothpaste. The bribe-offering, cigar-smoking entrepreneur of the past has been replaced by a smooth-talking, sophisticated business man who works the nooks and crannies of power. "[T]he main part of a lobbyist's job in practice is to circumvent the legislation that already exists, to cut through red tape, to get priorities and preferences for clients who have no legal right to them."[12] Dita Beard, ITT's lobbyist, said that "she represented ITT in the process of trading votes, favors, and people. Her job was to head off situations adverse to ITT in Congress and the administration before they turned into legislation or appointments. A favor for Dita went into the record books for repayment, on demand, from the bank called ITT."[13]

The average private interest lobbyist is a fairly well-educated, fairly well-paid, middle-class, middle-aged male who lives in Washington, D.C. Contrary to popular mythology, only one-third of the Washington lobbying corps are ex-congressmen. Most are full-time career employees of their association or business, who fit lobbying, in terms of direct contact with officials, into a busy schedule. For example:

> An executive of a trade association has to concern himself, not only with national politics, but also with organization, finances, membership, meetings, bulletins, and magazines, correspondence, inquiries, staffing, and the like. He must follow legislative and administrative developments . . . collect economic statistics, business news, and scientific and legislative reports. . . .[15]

Since the majority of trade associations work primarily with the executive branch, and since the scope of federal regulation has been steadily widening, the number of associations headquartered in Washington has been increasing yearly, from 19 percent in 1970 to 26 percent in 1975, with the result that it is now the fourth largest industry in Washington. In 1974 there were "430 registered lobbyists within walking distance of the White House."[16] William Utz, of the National Shrimp Congress, explained that: "The reaction time to new rules and regulations is faster if the headquarters is based in Washington. If you have an ear here, you can translate things as they happen. . . ." Washington headquarters also facilitate more interorganization communication and less regional bias. Indeed, the phenomenon has spawned a group of its own: the National Association of Professional Bureaucrats, whose motto is, "When in Doubt, Mumble."

Counterparts to private lobbyists work for the government. Despite a 1913 law prohibiting government expenditures for federal government lobbying, all executive departments and the White House executive office have congressional liaison staffs that communicate (read "lobby") with Congress on matters of importance to them. Congressmen, also assume the role of lobbyist, as in the dairymen's case when Congressman Wilbur Mills (the chairman of the Ways & Means Committee) called Secretary of the Treasury George Shultz to seek higher milk price supports.

The most powerful and colorful of all such lobbyists is always the President himself. President Kennedy was the first President to institutionalize the function by creating an office of congressional liaison. Yet, although this office coordinated executive branch lobbying and maintained continuous contacts with legislative personnel, Kennedy still had over 2,500 separate contacts with congressmen in 1961 alone.[17] President Johnson continued to emphasize the personal touch. He would invite congressmen for dinner in groups of fifty. After cocktails, the ladies would go with Lady Bird for a White House tour and the men would join the President for a two-hour briefing. Around 8 o'clock P.M. dinner would be served, and the guests would leave by 11.[16]

President Ford lobbied when he called fellow-Republican Senator Charles Percy to try and swing his committee vote behind the President's Cambodian aid bill in 1974. His request was couched nicely, "I'm hoping that if, after you've looked at it, you can see your way to help out in the full committee [vote]. It would be extremely appreciated. . . . Chuck, I can't ask for anything more. . . ."[17] But behind the smiles lay the constitutional powers of the President to administer laws, appoint personnel, veto bills, and withhold information covered by the executive privilege of privacy.

The rules of American politics encourage government actors representing one level of government or institution to pursue shared interests through a set of agreed upon activities centering on other governmental levels or institutions. Since this is our definition of interest group, for our purposes these groups or government spokesmen for groups are lobbyists. However, governmental personnel acting in such capacities must be analytically separated from governmental personnel acting as the source of official decisions. Decision makers also act in their official capacities, as when Secretary of Agriculture Hardin made his price support decision and President Nixon countermanded it.

The official as government decision maker differs from the official as spokesman for specific interests because in the first capacity his decisions regarding rules and allocation of resources are reinforced by government's exclusive control of the legitimate use of force within society. This final legitimate authority enables an official to "exercise against all groups and individuals certain powers which they may not exercise against him. The concept of officiality . . . is the sum of the technical differences which are rooted in the social understanding as to who does what to whom. . . . "[19]

In combining the duties of governmental liaison and group administrator, each lobbyist develops a style that can be defined in terms of the ratio of time spent in the office to the ratio of time spent "out on the hustings." In Washington over 70 percent of the lobbyists interviewed in Milbrath's 1963 study were *administrators,* spending over one-half of their time at the office. These men may be lawyer-lobbyists such as Tommy "the Cork" Corcoran who have no need to appear; they merely telephone. For example, when a tool and dye company was in trouble with the Pentagon and its retained law firm, Covington and Burling, got nowhere through regular channels, the law firm routed the case to Cocroran. He listened to the problem for an hour, made one telephone call to the Pentagon, announced the problem was settled, and billed the client $10,000.[20]

Other less glamorous, administrator-style lobbyists are association directors who fit calls into their bureaucratic schedule. John Post, executive director of the Business Roundtable, sees his job as one of "legislative intelligence—reading, following legislative developments, and contacting staff members on occasion. . . . " These administrators are informants who convey information from clients to committees and vice versa. For example, the six or seven chamber of commerce lobbyists testify at hearings, gather information, and keep abreast of legislative developments. Du Pont's seven government affairs employees work primarily at "collecting, evaluating, and disseminating information to company officials. . . . "[21]

An alternative role is that of *contact man,* in which the lobbyist walks the halls, becomes friendly with key staff, and sees his job in terms of *whom* not *what* he knows. Such lobbyists often represent constituent organizations, such as labor or environmentalists, or specialize in supplying political information to legislators. This would be the style of a Winter-Berger, who declared that, "a lobbyist who has two or three good connections in high places in Washington can represent an unlimited number of clients, achieving more for them in five minutes than they could achieve in five months. In Washington, it is the quality, not the quantity of one's connections that counts. . . ."[22]

A final lobbying style is the *lawyer-lobbyist.* Traditionally these have been characterized as the stars of the lobbying profession. Washington lawyers are a special breed who represent whole industries by creating law rather than litigating it.

> The Washington lawyer rarely litigates cases, he tries to appoint judges. He does not write to his congressman, he seeks to deliver a majority on

> the committee. . . . He is in a very real sense the interface between public and private interest. . . . His private practice steps on the brass rail of public policy every time he has an expense account luncheon.[23]

A new form of Washington lawyer, the Nader breed, challenges the traditional lawyer loyalty to only the client, arguing that in the situation of the lawyer-lobbyist there is an additional responsibility to the public good. Thus Nader, "seeks distributive justice for the greatest number of people, practices before all branches of government . . . and remains undeterred and undetoured by parochial client interests or control."[24]

Regardless of style, lobbyists belong to a "political skill group." They are technicians and tacticians who play their group's resources to maximum advantage. The access required for group input in the policy process basically boils down to personal relationships between officials and lobbyists in which the group spokesman (lobbyist) commands sufficient respect for himself and/or his group to obtain a hearing; the official, in turn, supplies useful up-to-date, inside information. This relationship becomes the basis for contacts with other decision makers. Since a group's resources and position in society also affect its chances of access, lobbying alone is not equivalent to the total influence potential of a group, but lobbyists are an integral part of the group's leadership resources. Lobbying cannot turn sows' ears into silk purses, but it can display either one to the best advantage.

TECHNIQUES

Lobbyists must deal with three levels of program: long-range purposes (policy); overall plans to implement the purposes (strategy); and specific actions to carry out the strategy (tactics). Generally group goals (policy) are an inflexible resource with which the lobbyist must work since they reflect group needs* rather than political realities. However, strategy—the determining of goal priorities and methods of achieving them—is often influenced by the lobbyist's assessment of

*See Chapter 2.

the receptivity of the political environment. Tactics are solely the province of the lobbyist.

The techniques of communication may be categorized in several ways. Lobbying information can be directed by *target:* 1) upward to selected key officials; 2) spread out among all rank-and-file decision makers; 3) downward to activate constituent pressure; or 4) laterally to develop alliances with other groups.

Communications can be categorized by *content:* 1) straight facts related to broad public issues or technical specialized points: 2) subjective arguments that use accurate facts arranged to support the group's position; 3) political information regarding constituents' or colleagues' attitudes on an issue; or 4) indirect evidence to suggest the group's poll power.

Techniques can be divided according to the *method of communication:*[25] 1) direct contact with decision makers; 2) indirect contact via constituents, mass media, and so on; or 3) social and personal devices designed to secure and maintain access to the decision makers.

Direct Techniques

Direct techniques include presenting arguments and/or facts directly to decision makers, participating in bill drafting, or testifying at hearings. Lobbyists consider these the most effective, simplest, and cheapest of all techniques, but due to competing pressures on national decision makers, such access is rarely available. In direct relationships lobbyists try to become auxiliaries to decision makers, providing information to activate, reinforce, strengthen, and remind the official of his commitment to the issue. An ITT lobbyist explained that:

> When you work with these politicians, remember you have to prepare the whole goddamned smear. Write the letters, the "off the cuff" comments, the press releases, everything. Believe me, they use most of our stuff; some don't even proofread what we write. . . . The responsibility we accept is to keep them out of trouble.[26]

Since congressional action occurs primarily in committees, most lobbyists stress their relationships with committee members and staff.

The vice-president of Pennzoil has said "We try to develop friends on all the committees charged with responsibility in areas that would affect this company. When a bill we're concerned about comes up, we want to have a chance to explain our position."

An American Legion lobbyist emphasized the usefulness of bill drafting, and suggested that committee chairmen be asked to introduce bills. The number of members contacted later concerning the legislation depends on their calculation of its chances. "If we are in doubt about it, we try to cover as many members of the committee as we can. If we felt reasonably certain that it was going to go through without too much trouble, we wouldn't try to cover too many. If it was very controversial legislation, I would try to cover every member of that committee and many others besides."

Generally lobbyists make friends (contacts) first with their philosophical allies or members from their districts; for example, Ford Motor Company has plants in 66 congressional districts in 24 states. This translates into 114 "home" legislators. Goodyear has plants in 52 congressional districts in 26 states: 104 legislators. Issue groups tend to work with ideological allies—the environmentalists with Senator Muskie, antihunger groups with Senator McGovern, antiabortionists with Senator Buckley. Often these men chair subcommittees dealing with the same subject, thus adding institutional power to their attitudinal preferences. Robert Winter-Berger paid a mutual acquaintance $1,000 for an introduction to Jerry Ford since he wanted to work with ideologically compatible Republican congressmen.[27]

In general lobbyists agree on certain essential rules to follow when meeting with officials: be pleasant and inoffensive, be well-prepared and informed, be personally convinced of your arguments, use the soft sell, convince the official of the issue's importance to him in his constituency or in terms of the public interest, and leave a written summary behind. Rules gathered from a set of twenty-eight women lobbyists are slightly more personal: do not carry a briefcase to a meeting since the official may think it contains a tape recorder; do not lie, double-cross, or make mistakes; do not lobby at a party until coffee is being served; eat where lawmakers eat; smile till your face aches.

Both lists stress pleasantness and competence, reflecting the reality that lobbyists have little with which to threaten legislators. "Pressure is a tactic only opponents engage in."[28] It becomes a subjective phenomenon: the difference between pressure and persuasion lies in the mind of the receiver.

HEARINGS. Hearings are considered a mixed blessing by most lobbyists. Most congressional hearings are stacked by the committee which issues invitations and seeks to schedule the speakers in order to maximize the desired point of view. Sometimes committees may schedule hearings as a favor to vociferous groups who want a show of action. The advantages of hearings are that they publicize issues, provide free publicity for groups, build a public record to support an issue in its developmental years, and permit the lobbyists to perform for the "home folks." Disadvantages include the poor attendance and closed minds evident at most hearings, and the relegation of information produced to back shelves and "read later" piles.

Nevertheless, a glance at the roster of most hearings indicates the current range of interested groups and the current slant of politically relevant opinion, as indicated by order of appearance. For example, John Gardner, Common Cause's chairman, was so disliked by former Congressman Wayne Hays that his testimony on public financing of elections was scheduled for the last day of hearings before Hays' committee despite the key role played by Common Cause in the development of the legislation.

Indirect Techniques

All indirect techniques seek to create policy changes by using group members, interested unaffiliated citizens, and/or the media as springboards for the group's message. Groups use writing campaigns, advertising campaigns, rallies, protest marches, walkathons, telethons, and telegrams. The purpose is twofold: first, to impress public officials with existing political grass roots support for the group and its program; second, to generate a favorable atmosphere in terms of the public at large which will facilitate the group's chances for turning proposals into public issues. It took environmentalists a decade to convince lovers that sunsets were signs of pollution rather than romance.

The techniques can be arranged along a continuum ranging from the cheapest, most direct forms of constituent-official contact at one end to the most expensive and indirect methods at the other.

CONTINUUM OF INDIRECT TECHNIQUES

Least Expensive		*Most Expensive*
group alliance	walkathons	advertising
contact of	marches	direct mail
member and officials	rallies	campaigns

Generally noneconomic interests, working within the system, use member-official contacts to secure policy changes; economic interests, or well-financed nascent interests, use advertising to produce citizen interest and response; and poor groups or those with unaccepted and/or intensely felt positions use crowd scenes to gather support through the presence of numbers.

CONSTITUENT ACTION. Constituent action means letters/telegrams/telephone calls from citizens to elected or appointed officials. There are two techniques:[29] "the rifle" approach singles out specific targets or constituents to make the contacts, while "the shotgun" approach sprays everybody in sight. The "rifle" approach zeros in on key officials, using either important constituents or friends of the official to present the group's case. For example, in 1972 when ITT was having antitrust problems, its president, Harold Geneen, met with three cabinet members, three White House aides, five senators, five representatives, and the chairman of the Federal Reserve Board—that's the rifle approach—a key man talking to government's key men. When lawyer Tom Corcoran visits congressmen, he is paid to provide entree, not information. As one representative described a recent visit: "He knew nothing about the issue and was paid to deliver access. . . . He came in . . . told a few jokes, set the tone, and left."

The "rifle" technique forms the basis for Business Roundtable lobbying. Each year the Roundtable concentrates on a few bills of key importance to business; for example, in 1974 they opposed the federal land use bill and the consumer protection agency. Their members, all corporate presidents, then sit down with key officials. The influence of these men makes it easier for them to "get the business view planted, and the reasons behind it. Make government sit up and listen . . . roll a little thunder here . . . a heavy weight business outfit . . . ready to use its left. . . ."[30]

The "shotgun" technique is used by organizations with congressional district strength either in economic or electoral terms. Traditionally, trade associations, unions, and civic organizations have mobilized writing campaigns to representatives.* Most of these groups communicate monthly with members through bulletins, research backgrounders, and action calls, so it is relatively easy to insert a request for membership action. The request sometimes reflects an internal organizational need to involve members as much as it reflects the external political situation. Constituent letters expressing personal interpretations of an issue, even if the arguments are group-supplied, can have an impact since representatives will view them within the context of their obligation to their electorate. While the system sounds simple, the technique can easily boomerang unless timing and member response are both on target. If the mail consists of canned statements of fill-in-the-blank postcards, if it arrives after the time of decision-making flexibility has passed, or if it irritates the recipient, it will prove counterproductive.

The classic example of group power derived from grass roots participation was the Anti-Saloon League in its fight for prohibition. It was said that the group's director, Wayne Wheeler, "controlled six Congresses, dictated to two Presidents . . . and was recognized by friend and foe alike as the most masterful and powerful single individual in the United States."[31] To kill proposed gun control legislation in 1965, the NRA triggered 12,000 letters from members to Congress within one month. Traditionally citizen groups, professional groups such as the AMA, and labor unions have schooled their members in the art of constituent pressure. The Women's Lobby, Inc., uses a variant of the constituent-legislator technique that stresses personal home district contact. It has a network of correspondents in every state who publicize "wrong" votes within the district. These members also visit their representatives during congressional recesses. The rationale is that to combat deep-seated attitudes, a personal presence is needed. Carol Burris, the group's Washington lobbyist, explains: "They know

*Western Union has instituted a service whereby "public opinion" telegrams may be sent to any public officials at a cost of $2.00 for fifteen words. Large groups can send mailgrams consisting of 100 words or less at a negotiated quantity discount rate for multiples of the same message.

how to deal with a piece of mail or a telegram, but dealing with a living person in your office is a different thing. You just can't file her away. It's hard to be rude . . . it's easier to accept the fact that she believes desperately in what she's fighting for."

As corporations are being permitted to behave more like people, they respond by adopting the concerned constituent technique. In 1973 the National Association of Manufacturers said, "The basic thrust of our new 'grass roots input' program is to capitalize on the basic strength of NAM—to vastly increase the extent to which our membership . . . become energized in legislative efforts." The Chamber of Commerce has computerized its membership lists by congressional districts. When member action is required, the computer selects those people to be notified and sends them written instructions. Local committees have also been set up to work in the districts to counter creation of a consumer protection agency, to oppose breaking up of the oil companies, and to support some of President Ford's anti-inflationary vetoes. Now that the Chamber and the NAM have merged into the Association of Commerce and Industry, the organization plans to concentrate on grass roots lobbying.

Working along the same lines, ITT has systematized its grass roots approach by assigning every politician to a senior ITT manager for cultivation. Each manager makes routine reports to the Washington office on the "activities, disposition, and temper of his charge." With manufacturing operations in forty states, ITT has "a goddam grass roots movement, first class."[32]

Some groups seek to mobilize constituent-legislator contact by providing group ratings of legislative records rather than by sending specific policy alerts to their membership. A legislator usually will claim ratings are inaccurate in that they substitute partial activity for the whole, or because groups choose votes that represent motives other than a legislator's animosity toward the group's program. This was especially true in the days before the "teller vote" was recorded, when roll-call votes often reflected the final vote on a total bill package rather than the more crucial content votes that occur as amendments, motions to recommit to committee, and so on. Despite legislators' hostility, groups see voting records as an indirect way to call public attention to their vote power resource, as well as a method of educating members on their issues. Several dozen groups play the ratings game including half a dozen labor unions, the American Conservative Union, the Chamber of Commerce of the United States, the Consumer Federation of America, Environmental Action, the National Council of Senior Citizens, and the National Education Association.

ALLIANCES. The creation of interest group alliances can magnify the impact of grass roots lobbying by multiplying numbers of involved members, while simultaneously creating interval organizational breathing space by shifting contentious or broad issues from a group's home headquarters to a different institutional location. The pooling of resources also permits distribution of the work load to take advantage of each group's special talents, the combining of monetary resources, and the multiplication of possible working contacts.

Examples of alliances can be found in relation to any major public issue:

- The Leadership Conference on Civil Rights, 139 civil rights, civic, social welfare, religious groups and labor unions, was responsible for passage of the major civil rights legislation of the 1960s.
- The Labor-University Alliance in the early 1970s lobbied to set a date for ending American participation in the Vietnam War and supported candidates committed to active programs for social change.
- The Council on National Priorities and Resources was created to lobby for more domestic and humane programs in the federal budget. This group draws upon the diverse resources of the United Auto Workers, the National Farmers Union, the National Education Association, the National Conference of Catholic Charities, and Common Cause, among others.

The narrow issue focus of most coalitions maximizes group effectiveness. "A well-financed outfit working on a single bill or issue can really do a job, compared with one . . . interested in hundreds of bills."[33] Alliances are able to project a public image of active unity despite the fact that the coordinators are really "a handful of men mobilizing a large number of passive supporters in whose name they acted under a variety of hats."[34]

This in turn generates a new group resource: the ability to affect the flow of information on a subject. Since policy content reflects available information, those who control content thereby acquire indirect influence over policy. Thus alliances achieve major impact by

> building a series of fronts through which [groups can] speak. Since such fronts come to be regarded by the general public and Congress alike as the representatives of important interests, those who controlled what these groups said, controlled thereby the accepted image of what the issues were and how the major interests felt about them.[35]

CLIMATE CONTROL TECHNIQUES. Lake Erie almost died before the public became sufficiently aroused to force public action; coal mine cave-ins took thousands of lives before mine safety legislation was enacted; until the asssassination of President John F. Kennedy, it was not a crime to kill a President; smog smothered Los Angeles for decades before automobile manufacturers were forced to pollute less. In all of these instances, conditions persisted until group activity seized on the problem and turned it into a public issue. To play down or dramatize issues, to present their interpretation of the situation, to win friends and influence people, political interest groups use techniques ranging from sophisticated, expensive, multimedia advertising campaigns to mass membership sit-ins, protests, boycotts, demonstrations, and marches. Regardless of the means used, the desired result is first to educate the public to accept the group's viewpoint and then to activate sections of the public to force governmental decision makers to deal with the problem.

ADVERTISEMENTS. Most major companies use institutional advertising to subliminally reinforce the textbook axiom that business is good for America and their business is particularly good. For example, the Association of American Railroads stresses institutional advertising to build good will for the railroads. They spend over $1 million annually "promoting the railroads generally as an important part of our economy. . . . [We] might go four or five years without advertisements dealing with specific legislation."

In the oil crises days of 1973 the American Petroleum Institute and the American Gas Association, two of the industry's major trade associations, spent $12 million on three energy campaigns. Mobil Oil Corporation has run a nationwide series of "educational" advertisements, such as those appearing on the "op-ed" (opinions) page of the *New York Times,* replete with basic facts supporting Mobil's interpretation of current policy issues. Congressman George Brown, Jr., was so angered by one advertisement's misrepresentations and half-truths that he sent a public rebuttal in which he countered company facts with his own.[36]

The March of Dimes uses similar institutional advertisements to retain its position as one of the big four among American charities. One ad shows a soft, loving picture of mother and babe with the comment: "Give a child the gift of Life/Support the MARCH OF DIMES." It is difficult to refuse motherhood, but perhaps the kind-hearted reader should know that the March of Dimes deals with birth defects, not birth itself, and that only 6 percent of the millions raised is spent on research.

Public relations campaigns also sell issues. For example:

- CARE began a 1975 campaign against hunger with an advertising gimmick. Every individual is asked to give up one meal a week and to send the money thus saved to CARE. The ad, showing an empty plate, says: "Starvation Stalks Millions. Who Cares? I Care."
- The J. Walter Thompson advertising agency is donating its time to create a new campaign promoted by the Committee for Hand Gun Control that seeks to circumvent the National Rifle Association by focusing on bullets, which it wants included among the objects controlled by the Federal Hazardous Substances Act. Their slogan: "You need a bullet like you need a hole in the head."
- NORML, the "pot" lobby, uses public service ads to make their issue visible. Lobbyist Stroup wants "to communicate moral outrage, the pain of what it's like to be locked up."
- The AMA spent between $7 and $12 million in 1962 alone to combat medicare by stigmatizing the concept as socialist.

To wage successful public relations campaigns requires a combination of group resources: money, leadership skills, community status, a reputation for informational expertise, membership commitment, and overall legitimacy. Consequently, such campaigns are insider techniques in the sense that they are used primarily by established groups pursuing some version of an acceptable goal. For groups with less leverage within the system, less money and more manpower, less acceptable goals and more intense commitment, the available public education techniques are the techniques of protest—marches, rallies, demonstrations, walkathons, or less productively, riots.

PROTESTS. Protest is "a form of collective expression, disruptive in nature, designed to provide its users both with access to decision makers and with bargaining leverage in negotiations with them. . . . protest is a device which cuts through some of the subtle biases in the contest to influence public decisions."[37] Normally protest is linked in the public mind with powerlessness, but it need not be so. Since its essence is a combination of threat and moral appeal, it may be used to dramatize indignation. An example of this use of protest was the "Jobs Now" Rally of May 1975, which attracted 40,000 unionists to protest unemployment and generate action on a package of public works bills designed to create jobs. "If the government can subsidize the copper companies and Lockheed, why can't it subsidize us?"[38] In May 1976, 20,000 people rallied before the United Nations in support of freedom for Soviet Jews. Neither labor nor the Jewish community is politically impotent or friendless, but because these issues are intensely important to members of both groups, they march to reinforce the internal cohesion of the group and to advertise the depth of their commitment.

However, protest activity is more generally developed by relatively powerless groups (those with a modicum of resources sufficient to initiate action, but insufficient to act alone) as a way to acquire bargaining leverage within the going political system by appealing to outsiders in the media, government, and more established groups to carry their cause forward. Protest as a strategy becomes "a mode of political action oriented toward objection to one or more policies or conditions, characterized by showmanship or display of an unconventional nature and undertaken to obtain rewards from political or economic systems while working within the systems."[39]

Examples from the last decade span the issue gamut from civil rights to student rights to urban conditions to hippie utopias. The early 1960s were characterized by marches, sit-ins, and boycotts to dramatize the need for civil rights legislation. In 1963 boycotts and demonstrations occurred in 800 communities, climaxed by the August 28 March on Washington. Martin Luther King led 200,000 people to the Washington Monument where he delivered his famous

"I Have a Dream" speech. The late 1960s saw a wave of violence as marches turned into riots: 34 dead, 856 injured, 3,000 arrested, and $200 million in damages.

In 1966 Cesar Chavez, leader of the migrant farm workers in the lush California valleys, struck against the grape growers. Robert Kennedy and the media took up "la causa," and table grapes became a symbol of protest against working conditions for all minorities. Results of the national grape boycott showed that sales were off by 12 percent in 1968. In 1975 the United Farm Workers, now unionized, marched 110 miles to focus attention on their boycott of Gallo wines.

Between 1967 and 1971, the anti-Vietnam War movement engaged in a wide range of mass involvement techniques: the 1967 nationwide local demonstrations, October 1967 March on the Pentagon, January 1968 counter-inaugural, 1969 nationwide day of moratorium in honor of war dead, and the seventeen days of spring protests in 1971 beginning with Vietnam veterans reenactment of the war as they saw it, followed by a middle-class, middle-aged demonstration by 200,000, followed by the "people's Lobby" that sat in at key decision-making centers, and climaxed by the Mayday Tribe who tied up Washington traffic and offices in order to implement their motto—"If the Government won't stop the War, the People will stop the Government."

The common thread linking the constantly revising anti-war protest groups, spanning the years and coordinating the demonstrations, each different in tone and membership, was the need to dramatize to the American public that the Vietnam War was responsible for deaths abroad and current misery at home. The policy of war became an issue of domestic priority with which Congress began to deal. These groups had to use protest tactics because they were powerless, not in middle-class resources perhaps, but in legitimacy, since they were advocating the un-American position of opposition to an ongoing war.

The role of organizations and leaders and the relationship between protesters and their communities differs in ethnic and ideological protests.[40] For blacks, and other racial minorities, protest is accepted as a normal form of political participation for people routinely cut off from effective access. By contrast, white protesters tend to be high on the socioeconomic scale because they are engaging in an act of nonconformity by community standards; thus their intensity of commitment and middle-class resources insulate them from hostile community reactions. Yet in any protest the use of the technique signals that the group is weak in traditional lobbying resources. Lacking legitimacy or organizational resources, groups use galvanizing devices to secure governmental access or speed up the pace of governmental activity.

SERVICES

The true currency of lobbying is information, but since the world of decision makers is a small one where everyone knows or knows of everyone else, information is often communicated socially. Lobbying is a business, government is a business: on both sides participants seek to gain money or programs. Lobbyists, especially those representing financially successful private interests, have expense accounts. In addition, seasoned lobbyists, have a wide range of contacts.

Decision makers, even officials, are only human. So a lobbying assist for an environmental cause from movie star Robert Redford may win "Brownie points" from a celebrity buff in Congress. Or free entertainment, free cars, free drinks, free sex will appeal to some decision makers as enjoyable benefits. In this sense social lobbying can be more effective than money as the added sweetener that causes a decision maker to change his mind. If officials accept monetary bribes, it is a conflict of interest; if they accept sex, it is shockingly indiscreet. Members of the press pounce because official indiscretions, banned by law and outlawed by public standards of morality, make headlines.

From the lobbyist's viewpoint, social relationships in Washington are no different from those found on Wall Street, in the banking community, or in any other small decision-making world. Social relationships may grease certain access routes, but it would be an oversimplification of a complex process to attribute any one vote or public decision to one dinner party, one night with a *Playboy* centerfold, or one $1,000 "loan." Washington lobbyists almost unanimously rate bribes, broads, and booze as near zero in influence effectiveness.[41] They describe these tactics as leftover myths perpetuated today in order to snare headlines, explain defeat on issues, or improve the electoral position of challengers for public office. Practitioners categorize friendship, money, and meals as devices for maintaining access, gathering information, and trading tips, rather than securing actual votes. Friendship means that the lobbyist often acts as informal broker—trading information and voting preferences among colleagues within the official congressional or bureaucratic system. The frequency of use of any one of the social avenues of access by any one lobbyist depends upon his reputation, his organization's goals and resources, and the location of decision makers important to him.

Consider money. "Money is exchanged: money for favors, money for deals, money for government jobs."[42] Elected representatives need money to run costly election campaigns. As Dita Beard said, "These guys are businessmen pure and simple. They are in the business of getting reelected; and if you are ever in doubt as to how to deal with the bastards, keep that in mind. It is a very rare son-of-a-bitch . . . who is so entrenched that his reelection is not the first consideration in any goddamned thing he does."[43]

Yet Dita's second office was in a social setting—a private club near Congress frequented by Republicans. "Dita's special drinking table was at the far end of the cocktail lounge . . . near the piano and next to the bar. From this vantage point Dita watched the comings and goings from the dining room, main bar and conference rooms." Taking nature into account, Dita said, "I try not to catch them on the way to the men's room, otherwise they're fair game."

Until 1975 congressmen could receive unlimited honoraria for speaking engagements, a monetary incentive totalling $940,000 to senators alone in 1974. Since 1976 congressmen may receive up to $25,000 net for outside engagements. The top ten organizations granting honoraria to senators in 1975 included the American Mining Congress ($9,000), the United Jewish Appeal ($8,500), American Podiatry Association ($6,000), American Bankers Association ($5,-250), and the National Town Meeting ($4,000). Congressmen also have financial holdings in corporations that may be an indirect monetary influence on the way they vote.[44]

But there are other forms of monetary exchanges; for example, Nathan Voloshen,* a lobbyist who worked out of Speaker McCormack's office, was asked by Parvin-Dohrmann Company to lift a Securities and Exchange Commission suspension on the trading of

*See Chapter 6.

their stock. McCormack arranged a meeting with SEC Chairman Hamer Budge, followed by a second meeting later in the day, and within the week the suspension was lifted. The grateful firm paid Voloshen $50,000. He paid McCormack $15,000 and McCormack's administrative assistant, Martin Sweig, $10,000.*

Favors also can be given in kind; for example, General Motors leases Cadillacs to the Pentagon brass for a mere $100 a year, while the same deal for the average citizen costs several thousand dollars a year. Until 1970 Ford Motor Company leased insured Lincoln Continental sedans to key committee chairmen and ranking minority members for $750 a year, compared to $4,000 a year for a private individual. Other companies offer corporate airplane service to commuting representatives, discount prices on the necessities of life, and so forth, all designed to purchase receptivity—step one on the road to influence.

Dorothy Ellsworth, lobbyist for the Brotherhood of Railway, Airline and Steamship Clerks, regularly purchases thirteen season tickets to Redskin football games, which she gives away to representatives who ask for them. Hospitality at official conferences, such as governors' conferences, is paid for by industry: at the 1975 New Orleans Conference a sumptuous dinner paid for by the Mid-Continent Oil and Gas Association displayed a sign saying, "The seafood you are eating tonight is delicious proof that the oil and seafood industries can thrive and survive in the same waters."

Social gatherings are another form of contact used constantly by those seeking new friends and allies. Groups sponsor approximately 1,500 cocktail parties a year, and are invited to the same number of campaign collection parties by elected officials. The numbers make partying a chore; but parties are deductible as a business expense for the simple reason that business is often conducted informally over coffee or cocktails. Perle Mesta, "the hostess with the mostest" in the 1950s, said she "never gave a party without a purpose." A 1976 Government Accounting Office report disclosed that between 1969 and 1974 Northrop Industries paid Madame Chennault, a well-

*Both Voloshen and Sweig were caught and convicted: Voloshen was fined $10,000 and given a one-year suspended prison sentence; Sweig was fined $2,000 and given a two-and-one-half year jail sentence.

known member of the Washington social establishment, $160,000 to give parties at which 200 guests at a time were wined, dined, and "sold" the F-5 jet fighters made by Northrop. Then in a bit of bookkeeping sleight of hand, Northrop billed the Pentagon for the expense, listing Madame Chennault as a consultant.

Smaller social gatherings take place at elite institutions such as Burning Tree golf course, where President Ford plays, or at little-known, insider clubs such as the 116 Club. To reach the club, one goes through an alley, enters a gate, climbs up a flight of stairs, and then walks past six houses. Membership is limited to 200 legislative relations specialists, key government decision makers, and a few nonresidents. Dues are $500 initiation and $20 per month. Its advantages are privacy, proximity, and good food.

The sex scandals of 1976 that rocked stalwarts such as Congressman Wayne Hays from office suggest that sophistication is increasing rather than the practice decreasing. Elizabeth Ray, the "Washington Fringe Benefit", whose tales led to Hays's resignation, said she worked for both lobbyists and later congressmen "strictly to date public officials in exchange for political favors."[45] Perhaps, the notion of access as business is summed up in the statement by Common Cause lobbyist Dick Clark. "The job description of a lobbyist is not nine-to-five. . . . There is no such thing as a social contact."

SUMMARY

This chapter has defined lobbying as those forms of communication between outside groups and government decision makers designed to influence the content of their decisions. Lobbyists, politically skilled experts who represent groups, analyze policy-making layouts, pick targets, and select techniques to reach the most receptive officials at the most opportune times. Lobbying is an individualized process; the content of the verb "to lobby" is as diffuse as its practitioners are numerous.

The techniques of lobbying can be ranged on a continuum from direct inside face-to-face contacts with decision makers to public hearings where decision makers are shared to indirect communication through members of the group to advertising campaigns that sell a point of view to protest actions that demonstrate the need to be heard. The techniques of gaining personal access to decision makers range from money to personal support/services/gifts to election campaign assistance to demonstration of a crisis requiring immediate official attention. All these methods of operation, and various combinations thereof, will be examined in the following chapters.

NOTES

1. James Madison, *The Federalist Papers,* No. 10 (New York: Modern Library, 1937), p. 56.
2. Edgar Lane, *Lobbying and the Law* (Berkeley: University of California Press, 1969), p. 5.
3. Karl Schriftgiesser, *The Lobbyists* (Boston: Little, Brown, 1951), pp. 8–9.
4. Lane, *Lobbying and the Law,* p. 23.
5. Ibid., p. 46.
6. Ibid., p. 11.
7. This definition is derived from Lester Milbrath's in *The Washington Lobbyists* (Chicago: Rand McNally, 1963), pp. 7–8. The legal definition is found in *United States v. Harriss* 347 U.S. 612 (1954), where the Court redefined lobbying.
8. Raymond Bauer, Ithiel de Sola Pool, and Lewis Dexter, *American Business and Public Policy: The Politics of Foreign Trade* (New York: Atherton Press, 1963), pp. 466–67. See also Milbrath, *The Washington Lobbyists,* chap. 9.
9. Michael Harrington, "The Politics of Gun Control" in *Annual Editions 1975/76* (Guilford Conn.: Dushkin Publishing Group, 1975), p. 211.
10. Patrick Anderson, "The Pot Lobby," *New York Times Magazine,* January 21, 1973, p. 8.
11. Robert Winter-Berger, *The Washington Pay-off: A Lobbyist's Own Story of Corruption in Government* (Secaucus, N. J.: Lyle Stuart, 1972), p. 13.
12. Ibid., pp. 16–17.
13. Thomas Burns, *Tales of ITT: An Insider's Story* (Boston: Houghton Mifflin, 1974), p. 107–8.
14. Bauer, Pool, and Dexter, *American Business and Public Policy,* pp. 348–49.
15. Map in *National Lampoon* (1974): 4809.
16. Laurence O'Brien, *No Final Victories* (New York: Ballantine Books, 1975), p. 113.

17. Alan Otten, "By Courting Congress Assiduously, Johnson Furthers His Program," in *The Modern Presidency,* ed. Nelson Polsby (New York: Random House, 1973), p. 191.
18. John Hersey, *The President* (New York: Knopf, 1975), p. 74.
19. Latham, "The Group Basis of Politics," *American Political Science Review* 46 (June 1952): 390.
20. Joseph Goulden, *The Superlawyers* (New York: Weybright and Talley, 1971), pp. 148–49.
21. *National Journal* (1975): 513.
22. Winter-Berger, *The Washington Pay-off,* p. 15.
23. Joseph Califano, "Ethics and The Washington Lawyer," reprinted in U.S., Congress, Senate, *Congressional Record,* 93 Cong., 1st Sess., September 25, 1973, p. E6043.
24. Joseph Page, "The Law Professor Behind Ash, Soup, Dump and Crash," in *Styles of Political Action in America,* ed. Robert Wolff (New York: Random House, 1972), pp. 1301–2.
25. These techniques are adapted from Milbrath's classifications in *The Washington Lobbyists,* chaps. 11, 12, and 13.
26. Burns, *Tales of ITT,* p. 34.
27. Winter-Berger, *The Washington Pay-off,* pp. 34–37.
28. Harmon Zeigler, "Interest Groups in the States." in *Politics in the American States,* eds. Herbert Jacob and Jacob Vines (Boston: Little, Brown, 1967), p. 138.
29. V. O. Key, *Parties, Politics and Pressure Groups,* 5th ed. (New York: Thomas Y. Crowell, 1964), pp. 134–35.
30. *Congressional Quarterly Weekly Review,* November 23, 1974, p. 3180.
31. Congressional Quarterly, *The Washington Lobby,* 2d ed. (Washington, D. C.: Congressional Quarterly, Inc., 1974), p. 2.
32. Burns, *Tales of ITT,* p. 31.
33. D. Matthews, *U.S. Senators and Their World* (New York: Vintage Books, 1961), p. 188.
34. Bauer, Pool, and Dexter, *American Business and Public Policy,* p. 378.
35. Ibid., p. 372.
36. See U.S., Congress, Senate, *Congressional Record,* 93 Cong., 1st Sess., July 30, 1973, p. E5206.
37. Peter Eisenger, "Racial Differences in Protest," *American Political Science Review* 68 (1974): 593, 605.
38. *Business Week,* May 12, 1975, p. 81.
39. Michael Lipsky, "Protest as a Political Resource," *American Political Science Review* (1968): 1195.
40. Eisenger, "Racial Differences in Protest," p. 601.

41. Milbrath, *The Washington Lobbyists,* chap. 13.
42. Winter-Berger, *The Washington Pay-off,* pp. 39–40.
43. Burns, *Tales of ITT,* p. 35. The following Beard quotation is found at *ibid.,* pp. 109–110.
44. *Congressional Quarterly Weekly Report,* July 31, 1976, pp. 2050–54.
45. Elizabeth Ray, *The Washington Fringe Benefit* (New York: Dell, 1976), pp. 17, 21.

II

Building Access to the Policy Process

Chapter 4

Group Access and Climate Control

In the previous part we looked at interest groups—their membership, organizational structure, and goals—and lobbyists—political interest group agents—in the public policy-making process. Now let us turn to the general environment that surrounds the political decision making process, an environment of opinion created from the feelings, beliefs, values, and symbols currently accepted as real and true by the American public and acknowledged as such by official decision makers. The content of opinions within an overall opinion climate changes constantly but gradually, unless dramatic events such as the Gulf of Tonkin incident during the Vietnam War or the "Saturday night massacre" (when Special Watergate Prosecutor Archibald Cox was fired by President Nixon) catalyze an immediate reaction. This general decision-making climate is distilled from an amalgam of specific public opinions as the aroma of cooking reflects the stew's ingredients.

Political interest groups seek to use or create an issue-opinion relationship to supplement or support the narrower lobbying tools of direct or grass roots government-directed communications. Groups use the broad brush, community-directed techniques of propaganda, publicity, and public relations to produce a favorable public opinion environment for their ideas. Abraham Lincoln underscored the importance of public opinion in the policy process when he said: "He who molds public sentiment goes deeper than he who enacts statutes or pronounces decisions. He makes statutes or decisions possible or impossible to execute." Modern communication techniques have turned Lincoln's intuitive notion into a science: advertising and public relations personnel now merchandise election campaigns and policy proposals.

GROUPS AND PUBLICS

To begin to play the game of politics, interest groups need access to decision makers. "Access, therefore, becomes the facilitating intermediate objective of political interest groups. . . . Perhaps the most basic factor affecting access is the position of the group or its spokesman in the social structure."[1] Consequently groups are always trying to improve their public image. Some name prestigious people to their boards of directors, such as the President of the United States as honorary chairman of the Red Cross. Others use communications techniques to convince the general public that the group's activities and membership reflect middle-class all-American values and goals; for example, Western Electric advertises: "There are still some things Americans know how to do best. . . . We make things that bring people closer." Similarly International Paper Company: "Why International Paper is helping to develop a 1 million acre forest on land it doesn't own. . . . We want to be sure there'll still be enough wood products around when your kids grow up."

Economic power does not automatically translate into an equal amount of political influence so business seeks to create a climate of public support to protect itself—if necessary—from political repercussions. Despite the fact that representatives of these big businesses could gain access to the policy-making arena through their companies' economic clout, they still feel the need to advertise their homey, helpful side in order to make American consumers like them. For example, "good guy" advertising by the oil companies kept the public unaware of their size and monopolistic practices until the price of gasoline and oil company profits escalated simultaneously in 1973.

At the other end of the spectrum, Ralph Nader also uses the impact of propaganda to build his reputation with the public at large and thereby increase his political clout. Combining the language of a muckraker with the logic of a lawyer, Nader delivers his message to the press in colorful, moral, newsmaking language. Both his programs and popularity are products of specifically targeted campaigns. The result: a June 1975 Harris poll showed that 76 percent of the public felt Nader was "keeping industry on its toes." Business and good government/citizen/environmental groups seek to use the media—television, radio, newspapers, magazines—to enhance their status, but it is easier for business to use media effectively. First of all, business interests are generally concerned about narrow issues directly affecting a specific constituency that can be targeted in public relations campaigns. Public interest issues, by definition, affect all the people and, as such, are often harder to pinpoint and identify with any one person's specific interest. Consequently these issues are harder to advertise and sloganize.

Second, the tax laws favor business' use of communications techniques.* While advertisements might be a natural way to make individuals identify with the impact of pollution on their lives, the costs of such advertising are prohibitive unless they are tax-deductible. Tax-deductibility takes two forms. Organizations that are classified as tax-exempt institutions may receive tax-deductible contributions, but they may not use this money to buy media time or space for lobbying purposes since lobbying by charitable groups is prohibited in the tax code. However, the tax code does permit businesses advertising *in their own self-interest* to deduct such expenditures as business expenses—yet even their advertisements *in the public interest* are not tax-deductible.

This inequity reflects the current legal definition of lobbying. The lobbying impact of indirect, or grass roots, or public relations communications was written into the 1946 Federal Regulation of Lobbying Act. Congress recognized the importance of this technique by defining lobbying as any attempt "to influence, *directly or indirectly,* the passage or defeat of any legislation by the Congress of the U.S."[2] However, the Supreme Court eliminated indirect activities because "The language of the Act is so broad that one who writes a letter or makes a speech or publishes an article or distributes literature . . . has no fair notice when he is close to the prohibited line."[3] Therefore an attempt

*A favorable rule bias does not necessarily mean that that group wins. Environmentalists still have strong public poll support despite their reduced advertising budgets. It does mean more quantity in business advertising.

to realistically define a category of government-influencing techniques was removed to avoid possible violations of the First and Fifth Amendments.

Despite inequities and unrealities in the law, groups continue to compete in the public forum in order to persuade the silent majority. Sometimes large membership or public interest groups measure responses in terms of letters or coupons mailed to decision makers. In other cases the generalities recorded on public opinion polls indicate a group's effectiveness. As in a self-fulfilling prophecy, these group-initiated activities assume and at the same time create the truth of the political axiom that public opinion sets the boundaries within which acceptable public policy is made.

Public Opinion

Opinions are expressions of attitudes. Most people have opinions, whether or not they are based on supporting facts. For example, a 1972 survey of public attitudes concerning foreign assistance to poor countries showed that despite widespread lack of knowledge and misperceptions concerning current policies, over two-thirds of the public supported such programs. However, such opinion, the stuff of weekly opinion polls, rarely translates directly into policy because it is but one general input into a highly complex process.

Indeed, most politicians rarely look to polls for guidance on citizen concerns. They see the public as an overlay of specific groups—butchers, bakers, candlestick makers—rather than an undifferentiated mass. When a situation becomes large enough or complex enough to require settlement by outside parties, a particular interest is born that seeks such action. "That which intervenes between the perceived problem and the government outcome is a public, a group of affected parties. . . ."[4] Thus the public opinion the politician sees is really a composite of many publics' opinions.

> A policymaker generally assesses any group's views according to the group's importance to him, as well as according to his assessment of the particular issue's actual importance to the group. Those whose political support is essential but uncertain carry greater weight than those whose support can be taken for granted, and those whose support is unattainable are often disregarded.[5]

From the perspective of the political interest group, the complexity of public opinion as a phenomenon facilitates its manipulation so that a part of the public may seem to be *all* public opinion. Groups affect the content of public opinions, blurring the line between educational and propagandistic messages.

The content of an opinion and its value as a political resource are always specifically related to a topic, time, and place. As a political resource for group participation in policy making, a particular opinion is defined in terms of the size and political interest level of the public involved, the willingness and/or ability of that public to act upon its opinions, and the intensity, stability, rationality, and factual content of the opinion itself. For example, public opinion on medicare is really shorthand for many opinions—the opinions of doctors, hospital administrators, patients, old people, poor people, taxpayers. Each of these opinions can be analyzed in terms of its size, intensity, and so forth. Many of these separate opinion publics may contradict each other, or they may complement each other by arriving at similar conclusions along different informational paths.

Attraction to a topic—the necessary precondition for formation of *any* public opinion—is created by lobbyists for government and private groups. Governmental agencies, congressional committees, and outside interest groups feed the media a steady diet of information. Editorials, commentaries, and news reports are often credited with stimulating congressional mail without thought to the sources that provided the initial news data. Thus, in a reciprocal relationship, public policy actors both create and accept the national consensus called public opinion.

Political interest groups seek to make their "public" appear to be the largest, most intense, and most rational component of public opinion. The type of audience that a group seeks to motivate varies with the size of the group, its members' characteristics, its internal stability, and its goals. For example, smaller interest groups are likely to use public relations techniques in order to enlarge their potential pool of allies within the general public since their own member nucleus is so small. Being small, they also tend to be more homogeneous which in turn creates a high enough level of internal cohesion to permit group leaders to look outside to the general public. As an example, Ralph Nader's organizations seek citizen allies since they lack a traditional go-to-meetings membership. Businesses also compensate for their small base of loyalists by seeking public identification of their economic interest with broader aspects of the public welfare. Thus, arguments for protection of U.S. shoe manufacturers from foreign competition are couched in terms of American jobs and balance of payments.

Heterogeneous groups such as large trade associations spend most of their time on internal informational programs in order to achieve quasi-unanimity as a precondition for any action. For example, in 1973 the American Petroleum Institute's 300 members could agree on industry-wide positions only for building the Alaskan oil pipeline and against a windfall profits tax so, despite the plethora of energy/oil issues in 1973–74, these were the only concerted campaigns the API could undertake. Large, homogeneous organizations such as unions and farm organizations, or small, prestigious groups such as professional societies also lobby their members first, not to create cohesion, but to use existing agreement to generate member letters to officials. For the large group, member action advertises the group's voting base and member political involvement. In professional organizations, members can promote their group's view by "merchandising" their community status to influence the opinion of laymen with whom they come in contact.

There are several approaches to seeking outside allies among the public at large. Some groups may try to activate all possible publics or specific strata within the public in terms of their individual relationship to the group itself. A diagram of the possibilities would show the group in the center of the circle surrounded by concentric circles representing degrees of involvement: closest would be active group participants, then passive members, fellow travelers (nonmembers who identify with the group's goals), potential sympathizers, neutral citizens, and at the outermost circle, the definitely unreachable, hostile individual. Thus, public interest lobbies consciously address their messages to concerned middle-class citizens or students joining public debate for the first time. John Gardner, chairman of Common Cause, called effective communication "the most powerful single weapon of the public interest lobby. . . . The problem and solution must become the subject of public discussion. . . . The issues must be dramatized. If the public is apathetic, it must be aroused. If there is already public indignation, it must be channeled."[6]

Or groups may approach individuals in terms of their issue orientation. Again moving from those nearest the group, the communications would attract the public interested in the group's own issues, the attentive public interested in various public issues, the general public sporadically interested in issues, and finally the rarely interested, inattentive, indifferent, alienated publics. Mobil Oil's advertisements every Thursday on the "op-ed" page of the *New York Times* illustrate this issue technique. The ads were placed there because "we felt we had to address ourselves primarily to opinion leaders as the group best able to grasp complex issues."[7]

Public Relations and Private Goals

Groups often create public relations campaigns in order to make their programs appear synonymous with the public interest. For example, Keep America Beautiful* (KAB) the group that promotes antilitter campaigns is supported by the beverage and packaging industries which are fighting against returnable bottles and reuseable packages. Thus, their slogan, "People Start Pollution. People Can Stop It" (reminiscent of the NRA's "Guns Don't Kill; People Do") might be read as truth or as an industry redefinition of the problem.

Another example is the Advertising Council, a nonprofit business-media consortium of industrial giants formed during World War II to provide free propaganda services in support of the United States war effort. The council still exists, now spending $4 billion a year in free advertising for an assortment of campaigns. Their most famous is Smokey the Bear, a recently controversial one was WIN (Whip Inflation Now). Critics have pointed out that while it may seem that the campaigns are of a public service nature, they also serve private corporate purposes by ignoring, for example, industrial causes of pollution, litter, and highway deaths in favor of human culprits (slobs, drunken drivers, and so on). Indeed, thirty congressmen wrote a letter protesting the council's involvement in the WIN campaign which they termed partisan and controversial.[8]

*The discrepancy between slogan and sloganeers became so large during the 1975–76 debate over reuseable bottles that the Environmental Protection Agency withdrew from the organization.

In both KAB and the Advertising Council business has acted as a "silent partner," using the technique of "front organizations" or nicely named alliances to increase the legitimacy of their efforts or to deflect the content of public debate in order to help themselves. By contrast, the private electric power companies have been blunt about their successful twenty-five-year public relations campaign to turn public opinion away from support of public power companies. Testimony during the McClellan Committee Hearings on lobbying activities in 1957 included the following statement on the electric companies' advertising program (ECAP):

> By the end of 1952 the *[Saturday Evening] Post* had carried 128 ECAP advertisements. . . . They are reprinted here to show how one industry, advertising its cause consistently and persistently, has been able to help shift the great weight of public opinion. . . . ECAP advertising is designed to win public support for the business-managed electric light and power companies.

In March 1974 the American Electric Power Company placed an advertisement which said that a national policy of generating less energy would undermine the national economy and, therefore, the Clean Air Act should be modified to expedite coal-fired electricity generation. Russell Peterson, chairman of the Council on Environmental Quality, responded in a letter to the company calling the content of the ad "nonsense" and the ad itself, irresponsible. Chairman of the company Donald Cook then wrote to President Nixon requesting an investigation of Peterson's letter. The President took no action except to return Cook's letter. Both advertising programs, even though over twenty years apart, assume, as suggested by Peterson's immediate reaction, that such advertisements will help private companies to secure legislation through manipulation of the climate of opinion.

Merger of the National Association of Manufacturers and the U.S. Chamber of Commerce is designed in part to provide the organizational resources for a massive public relations campaign which will turn the post-Watergate, antigovernment mood into a probusiness asset. The new group plans to promote business problem solving as an antidote to big government programs. In 1975 the NAM produced a multimedia entertainment package to explain the free enterprise system and the problems of government intervention in simple terms. The packaged production rents for $3,500 with live talent, $500 without. Thus the major business trade associations have come to the realization that political clout can begin by developing those elements in the policy-making environment that support a probusiness climate of opinion.

Of course, groups also use public relations campaigns to pursue specific objectives as opposed to creating a climate of opinion. Thus, NORML, the marijuana lobby, uses radio spots to promote decriminalization of marijuana by focusing on the inequities of the law and the consequences of long prison terms meted out for possession of one marijuana cigarette. Another example is ASH, the anticigarette group, which seeks to restrict smoking in public places using slogans such as "Smoking should be confined to consenting adults in private" and "Caution: Your smoking may be hazardous to my health." For businesses that agree to set aside nonsmoking sections, ASH provides signs advertising: "We have fresh air for nonsmokers."

Groups also use grass roots campaigns to protect established positions. "Throughout most of its history, the NAM has, in its propaganda and through other means executed a series of retreats to prepared positions. The AMA since the early 1930s has performed a similar maneuver."[9] The AMA battle is a classic example of defensive public maneuvering. The idea of national health insurance was first broached in 1935; thirty years later in 1965 a narrower version of health care for the aged became law. While the AMA could not kill the idea permanently, opposition by this prestigious group, assumed to have special professional knowledge, obviously slowed down passage of a bill.

The AMA public relations campaign concentrated on maintaining a negative public image of medicare among the articulate, attentive, middle-class segments of the population. While support for a national health program ranged from 53 to 65 percent among the least attentive and nonattentive segments of the public during 1960–64, support among the attentive public dropped 10 percentage points, from 47 to 37 percent.[10] Simultaneously the AMA's public relations campaign used substantive arguments related to the possibility of increased bureaucratic interference in medical practice to arouse their own membership.

Then, relying on the prestige of a doctor in an average community, they used personal contact and local advertising campaigns that emphasized symbolic issues. These public arguments called federal medical care the first step toward socialism, the beginning of the welfare state, and the end of quality medical care in America. The same issues were raised in three national campaigns during 1964 and 1965. In October 1964 radio announcements, television spot dramatizations, and a series of advertisements in 8,000 newspapers argued against the bill. In early 1965 a similar campaign, which cost $829,484 according to public records, urged acceptance of the AMA substitute bill, "eldercare." In June 1965, in a last-ditch but doomed media effort, advertisements in 100 major papers plus a national hour-long television program urged rejection of the House-passed bill then being debated in the Senate.

Many public-directed campaigns seek to produce citizen responses such as letters which reinforce the image of the group as a functional link between citizen interests and public policy makers. In this sense groups fill a vacuum created by the general lack of citizen interest in governmental activities. Politicians may feel safer when they know the general boundaries of acceptable action, but they rarely seek out general public opinions on specific legislative proposals. This gives a group the opportunity to do three things simultaneously: mold an environment amenable to its values and goals, supply information during the policy debate, and satisfy the politician's need to have current soundings of popular sentiment.

> The articulate leadership group acts as a multidirectional conveyor belt, carrying information and opinion upward to policy makers and downward or across to colleagues, constituents, or citizens in an effort to create a "public opinion" for which it might again be a sounding board upward. Particular organizers or types of organizations specialize at different times in particular aspects of the conveyor relationship; but collectively the articulate public both leads and follows, formulates and persuades. It *is* "public opinion," it *represents* "public opinion," and it *creates* "public opinion."[11]

A study of group communications, attitudes, and actions relating to trade legislation in the decade 1953–62 dispelled the myth of a small clique of business tycoons dictating congressional decisions. Instead businesses and trade associations organized alliances that appeared to be composed of multitudes of united individuals, but were instead "a handful of men mobilizing a large number of passive supporters in whose name they acted under a variety of hats."[12] The emphasis was on grass roots activity designed to energize local businessmen and interested citizens. Research, letter writing, local meetings, press conferences, news releases and bulletins, created a climate of public opinion in which these groups could influence selection of key issues and then contribute their information to the public debate. By changing the general decision-making environment through these alliances, the groups became "nodes in the communication process," able to channel public discussion and, thereby, become an indirect but important factor in the formation of that policy.

> . . . Although the pressure groups' propaganda activities did not persuade anyone by the direct impact of what was said, by engaging in apparently futile activities those organizations arrogated to themselves the roles of authoritative spokesmen for particular sides or interests. By thus seizing a portion of the field of battle, they became effective organizers of the communication process.[13]

In 1976 Harold Willens, a California businessman interested in combatting the economic power of the oil companies by divestiture, founded Citizens for Energy Action. The group wants to use business expertise to counter oil company informational resources. Willens' goal is "to become the legitimate counter opinion on energy matters, so that when the administration makes a statement about energy policy, the press will seek us out. . . ." His group wants to become a "communication node." Likening the oil company claim to a monopoly on information to similar claims by witch doctors in primitive societies, Willens reduces his purpose to the basic democratic denominator: "What we're trying to cultivate is citizen common sense, which is the best weapon to balance the bureaucratic urge for more power. It only takes common sense."[14]

THE LANGUAGE OF GRASS ROOTS CAMPAIGNS

As manipulation techniques replace outright face-to-face demands, greater emphasis is placed on the "strategy of proper public presentation of demands, of selling the group and its objectives to the public, of mobilizing a long-run mass support."[15] The language of persuasion is categorized as educational or propagandistic. Educational language usually deals with the dissemination and discussion of accepted ideas, attitudes, and subjects. Propaganda is defined by David Truman as "any attempt, by the manipulation of words and word substitutes, to control the attitudes and consequently the behavior of a number of individuals concerning a controversial matter."[16] Education connotes neutral communication. Propaganda involves the *intention* to influence attitudes by words rather than force. Often the line between propaganda and education lies in the eye of the beholder. For example, is patriotism an educational exercise explaining accepted values or propaganda designed to rally support for the establishment?

Essentially the propaganda process is a psychological one. The propagandist must ensure that the intended message reaches the individual and stimulates or produces the desired attitudes. This is not a simple task. People tend to select information that fits their predispositions because the assimilation of new information is uncomfortable. To scale perceptual barriers, public relations experts use prestige symbols or the idea of majority support to construct a bandwagon psychology. Or they couch new information in terms of important symbols such as rules of the game or slogans such as "Free Enterprise," "The American Way," and "Progress is our most important product." For example, Texaco used pretty cheerleaders, marching bands, and firewords in a commercial that spelled out the all-American need: "Trust Texaco."

Language itself plays a key role by setting the context of an activity so that it becomes desirable or undesirable, honorable or dishonorable. In the following sentence four actors are all selling goods or services, yet the terminology makes the first actor seem more legitimate and moral than the last. "If General Motors sells cars, it's called advertising; if the National Institute of Health sells psychiatry, it's called education; if a streetwalker sells sex, it's called soliciting; if a street urchin sells heroin, it's called pushing dope."[17]

Most groups tend to paint the opposition as bad, their own aims as good. Slogans or eye-catching pictures, often unrelated to the basic message, are used to solicit attention. For example, a lovely five-year-old proclaims that a telephone call "is the next best thing to being there"—yet she is probably too young to even dial. Or the March of Dimes, which researches cures for birth defects, solicits public sympathy with a Madonnalike portrait of a loving mother and her perfectly formed baby.

A message may contain facts, rumors, opinion, or various combinations thereof. Generally "educational" messages for the attentive public are mostly verbiage with key parts of the message in large letters, qualifying comments in telephone-book-sized type. Slogans to attract numbers of people are usually printed in bold type and surrounded by space or pictures. For example, a recent Amtrak (railroad) advertisement to woo airline business used a cartoon format to contrast Amtrak's pleasant trip with the harried checkpoints of airline travel. A bus company advertisement, seeking to end Amtrak's federal subsidy, framed its message "Amtrak. It's a vicious circle. Every time it comes around it costs us another $1 billion . . ." in an oval of railroad track.

Messages are also repeated many times with only subtle alterations in form. The variety of media outlets permits an interest to vary its pitch but maintain slogan continuity by shifting the surrounding copy format to suit the particular media form. Media include radio, television, books, newspapers (dailies and weeklies), specialized magazines, general reader magazines, and assorted educational/intragroup materials. Selection of the proper outlet can make the difference between public relations success and failure. For example, the anti-Tydings gun group sought contributions in *Gun Magazine* advertisements—a likely target audience for contributors. By contrast, public interest groups or broad issue coalitions usually take full-page advertisements in the five major national newspapers in order to reach a maximum number of attentive public members with one effort.

An Allied Chemical Company advertising campaign praising profits as necessary ingredients in economic growth was designed for certain specific audiences: opinion leaders, Allied employees and stockholders, Wall Street, cities where Allied plants are located, legislators, labor unions, and college presidents. To reach these targets, the advertisements were placed in eighteen college newspapers, six regional trade in-house publications, five magazines (*Newsweek, Forbes, Chemical Week, Business Week, The Smithsonian*), and five newspapers (the "op-ed" page of the *New York Times,* the "Sunday Outlook" section of the *Washington Post,* the *Wall Street Journal,* the *Houston Post,* and the *Houston Chronicle*). Thus this $350,000 campaign was precisely targeted to reach the maximum number of readers in those groups. The Business Roundtable spent $1.2 million to promote the concept of free enterprise in a series of editorial advertisements in the *Reader's Digest* designed to educate Middle America.[18]

The media act as a catalytic agent, spotlighting issues, interest groups, and activities, thereby creating public demands. Media coverage of the civil rights protest activities, for example, generated pressure for civil rights legislation in the 1960s. Vietnam has been called the first "living room war," the first war to be seen in living color on the evening news for seven years. The media also focused attention on group activities opposed to the war and helped legitimize opposition to current military activity.

> The public often needs considerable stimulation before it becomes sufficiently aware of issues to provoke some action. The media often interact simultaneously with each segment in the policy process, setting the agenda for the interaction of leaders with groups and the mass electorate. . . . The media then are a catalyst for action, stimulating and encouraging and even rationalizing the opinion-policy process.[19]

Interest groups need the media to create widespread discussion and involve the public. The media, as businesses that thrive on controversy, need the battle of competing interests to make public events salable. In these terms the Supersonic Transport issue became a 1971 media feature when environmentalists formed the Coalition of Citizens against the SST and produced thousands of fact sheets, new research data, and local action. The media picked up the issue, turning arguments into battles. As the broader public became involved and angry at being taken for granted, the issue became one of environmental and national priorities rather than employment and security. The new context killed the SST.[20]

The Media, Grass Roots, and the Nixon Impeachment Interest Groups

The use of the media to generate constituent activity and the symbolic content of such appeals is well illustrated by the role of interest groups in the Nixon impeachment debate. Both sides couched their appeals in terms of fair play, constitutional principles, and the similarities between the impeachment process and a trial. The first and largest group against impeachment was the National Committee for Fairness to the Presidency organized by Rabbi Baruch Korff when the *New York Times* rejected his letter to the editor. With a bank loan and money saved for a vacation, Rabbi Korff launched a series of ten advertisements placed in 200 newspapers. The advertisements, beginning in August 1973, emphasized the anti-Nixon bias of the news media and the Senate Watergate Committee hearings.* The text reiterated Korff's belief in the President and urged citizens to "speak out in defense of the principles which have built and sustained our society."

Money and members poured in: 10,000 members within a month; 160,000 by February 1974; 223 local groups by May 1974. Eventually $600,000 was raised and spent primarily for advertisements, but also for local campaigns and lawsuits to remove the Watergate hearings from television. The Committee for Fairness also collected 1.5 million signatures on a petition supporting the President. Rabbi Korff characterized his membership as "ordinary people, just blades of grass" who felt that the press and political left were unfair to President Nixon. Indeed, after the President's resignation, the group adopted new but sequential goals: policing the media for "liberal" bias and raising money to pay Nixon's legal fees.

A second national anti-impeachment group, Americans for the Presidency, was organized by Donald Kendall, president of Pepsi-Cola. The group ran an advertisement in 100 newspapers in February

*Rabbi Korff's interpretation of the tape transcripts as proof that "the President is human" suggests the perceptual bias that propaganda tries to overcome; for the public at large, disclosure of the contents of the tapes sent Nixon's poll popularity down to 26 percent.

1974 listing the names of prominent Americans who supported Nixon. The text of the advertisement couched the issue in separation of powers terms, but a spokesman for the public relations firm that produced the ad said its main aim was identification of those famous supporters.

On the proimpeachment side, several organizations developed educational—that is, primarily informative—campaigns. The AFL-CIO and the American Civil Liberties Union (ACLU) distributed impeachment handbooks containing information on the process and possible charges. The Americans for Democratic Action (ADA) distributed 500,000 copies of an eight-page pamphlet on the "theme that impeachment is a trial process that allows the President to have his day in court." Common Cause, maintaining its procedural focus, lobbied for open, fair, and thorough procedures in the Judiciary Committee inquiry and for strict rules in the event of a Senate trial.

In contrast, the ACLU also launched one of several full-scale propagandistic grass roots letter-writing campaigns. Two full-page advertisements in the *New York Times* asking for volunteers and funds said: "There is only one thing that can Stop Impeachment now. Your Silence." The League of Friends of Thomas Jefferson asked citizens to clip its advertisements and mail them to congressmen or Judiciary Committee members. The ads began: "Wake Up America!"

The Committee for the Resignation of the President asked citizens to send money and grant permission to use their names in future advertisements, "If you believe that President Nixon has violated the trust placed in him by the American people and that he should resign. . . ." The National Committee on the Presidency asked for $25 from voters in sixty vulnerable election districts in order to make impeachment an election issue in those districts and to elect proimpeachment representatives. Their direct mail appeal began: "We are a group of ordinary citizens like yourself, who want to preserve your Constitution."

To handle impeachment as a policy decision both sides decided that direct lobbying of Congress would be discourteous and counterproductive. Instead groups used the written word to generate constituency activity aimed, first, at forcing action despite congressional hesitancy and, second, at creating public understanding of the impeachment process so that the anti-Nixon sentiment could be translated later into support for the constitutional process and, if necessary, development of the issue in the 1974 congressional elections.

The rhetoric on both sides recalled the propaganda efforts of the Founding Fathers. Note the committee names: Committee for Fairness to the Presidency, National Committee on the Presidency, League of Friends of Thomas Jefferson, Americans for the Presidency. All of these play on the constitutional issue—conjuring up the institutional mythology of the Presidency rather than the personal image of a mere man. The advertisements were wordy, designed to be read, and phrased in terms of the American sense of fair play.

The impact of the campaigns can be measured in two ways. In terms of mail, the House Judiciary Committee received 429,367 letters favoring impeachment and 143,676 against by May 1974.[21] Individual congressmen reported similar deluges of mail. The polls also reflected increased public information: in the Gallup poll of June 22–25, 1973, 69 percent opposed impeachment, 19 percent favored it, although only 49 percent approved of Nixon's performance in office. By April 12–15, 1974, one-third opposed impeachment, while 52 percent favored it. Since the "no opinion" column only gained three percentage points during that period, the majority of the shift was movement from a negative to a positive view of the impeachment process.[22]

A CASE IN POINT: GROUP PUBLIC RELATIONS AND THE MIDEAST CRISIS

Public relations is not a substitute for political action. It can support other insider skills such as negotiation and litigation, or it can rationalize the need for less "proper" actions such as bribery or violence. In either situation, public relations seeks to set the stage; the group must follow through with action. The basic material for these grass roots campaigns is the drama of daily political life. Consider the Mideast crisis of 1973–74 when, during one time period, the public had to make sense of an Arab-Israeli war, the Arab oil embargo, lines at gasoline pumps, home heating oil shortages, gigantic oil company profits, arranging and rearranging of governmental mechinery to deal with the crisis, environmental alarms over increased pollution and ecological damage, and complex arguments for greater reliance on oil, gas, uranium, coal, or solar energy.

In this kind of situation, where the public is inundated with conflicting issues and solutions are ambiguous, political interest groups have an opportunity to explain the situation from their individual perspectives. So, during the Middle East crisis the Arab lobby, the Jewish lobby, the oil lobby, and the environmentalists all pushed their own explanations of the problem, its cause, and the solution.

The issues involve three kinds of basic United States interests in the Mideast: an emotional and military commitment to the state of Israel, an economic interest in Arab oil, and a strategic interest in avoiding any cold war conflicts in the area. Each lobby arranged these priorities in ways advantageous to its own bargaining positions. However, their perspectives need not necessarily lead to policy clashes for two reasons. First, adhering to the style of propaganda, lobbies tend to couch substantive disputes in procedural terms that emphasize the rules of fair play, public interest rhetoric, and so forth. For example both Arabs and Jews seek Mideast peace in the context of American national interests, which means help for a democratic nation to the Jews, an evenhanded policy (fair play) to the Arabs. Second, propagandizing groups may truly be seeking apples and oranges—and so have no substantive issue conflict at all. Thus ethnic and environmental lobbies discuss the Middle East problem in separate but parallel contexts.

Assorted simplifications can be cast on the public waters to be picked up by separate publics receptive to a group's perspective. A brief look at activities of some of these groups during this period illustrates the possibilities of communications designed to influence decision makers by bouncing attitudes from the environment into the policy-making arenas.

Ethnic Lobbies

Jews represent 2.8 percent of the American population, 4 percent of the national vote. Senator James Buckley characterized Jews as "extremely effective in doing what the Constitution encourages; that is, peaceful assembly and the right to petition. I only wish others were as good at it as the Jews are." Politicians define Jews as liberal, traditionally Democratic, activist, well-educated, and quick to send constituent opinion to congressmen when necessary.

For example, in April 1973 Senator Henry Jackson introduced an amendment to the Soviet most-favored-nation trade bill making passage of the bill contingent upon a liberalization of Soviet emigration policies for Jews. The amendment represented not merely a concession to the lobbying skill of the 300 or more national Jewish organizations. It reflected American indignation at being outsmarted in the Soviet wheat deal, resentment at Nixon's usurpation of power over trade negotiations, the feeling that Russia should not get something for nothing, and the desire to reaffirm through export the American ideal of freedom of movement.

The Jewish groups backed Jackson's amendment with media advertising plus direct lobbying and constituent letter-writing campaigns. Jewish leaders met with White House aide Len Garment and held a meeting with key congressmen to sensitize them to the issues involved. Jewish contributors visited their representatives; constituents inundated their senators with two to three dozen letters per day. Jewish lobbying organizations added seventy-eight cosponsors to Jackson's bill, and then convinced Congressman Wilbur Mills to sponsor the House bill, with its 238 cosponsors. With this show of support, the measure passed Congress while the White House, despite fears for the amendment's effect on East-West détente, did little to publicly oppose it. This kind of congressional response reflects not only Jewish voting strength, but also their ability to mobilize group members on specific issues.

In terms of Israel per se the major Jewish lobbying organization is the American Israel Public Affairs Committee (AIPAC) which emerged twenty-one years ago from the American Zionist Council. It is now an umbrella lobbying organization, acting as agent for other interested groups that cannot lobby directly because of their tax-exempt status. AIPAC's executive committee is composed of the presidents of all the major Jewish organizations; their budget of $400,000 is raised through members' dues.

Although AIPAC has an effective congressional lobbying team and can summon grass roots pressure when necessary, Executive Director Morris Amitay says, "Our point of strength is not that we are so highly organized, but that so many people are committed to Israel." Amitay couches his pro-Israel appeals in terms of American interests because public sentiment rests on more than the Zionist desire for a homeland. It reflects American attitudes and values: "A sense of something owed the Jewish people after the Nazi holocaust, shared religious roots and democratic ideals, admiration for the pioneer spirit of the Israeli nation builders ... empathy for the underdog ... geopolitical cold war realities of the 1950s. . . ."[23] The $3.7 billion in credits and loans for military equipment and the $1.2 billion in economic aid given to Israel since the 1950s is evidence of this generalized American support for Israel.

Amitay says AIPAC "would be relatively ineffectual if the other 97 percent of the U.S. population did not share a widespread sympathy for Israel." Until recently the Arabs accepted this American attitude as inevitable; however, in the last two years the policy environment has been modified by the need for oil, the Arab performance in the 1973 war, a diminished cold war atmosphere, and the beginnings of sophisticated Arab public relations campaigns in America.

There are two major Arab lobbies: the Arab Information Center, sponsored by foreign states through the Arab League, and the National Association of Arab-Americans, formed in 1972 by Arab-Americans to present the Arab point of view to Congress and the American public. Four thousand members contribute $25 to $100 in annual dues to support its efforts. The Arab League gives the Information Center approximately $500,000 per year, which it uses to staff centers in five major cities and to provide public relations films and speakers.

The Arab lobby, just like the Jewish lobby, couches its appeals in terms of American interests and American values. Thus, they seek "evenhandedness in the Middle East": supporting Israel, but not giving it "carte blanche." Richard Shadyac, former president of the Arab-American organization says: "Our clout has to be on the basis of seeking justice and objectivity in the Middle East. We are giving Congress a viable alternative."

Just as Israel provides sightseeing trips for government officials, so too does this new Arab organization. Just as AIPAC produces a weekly newsletter, the *Near East Report,* which is sent to all relevant officials, so too the Arab Information Center has begun publication of a biweekly newsletter, *The Palestine Digest.* The Arabs are trying to emulate their competition so that some day their success may be attributed, as is Jewish success, to "a combination of United States national interest, widespread public support, community activism, and an effective Washington operation."[24]

The Oil Lobby

The oil lobby has traditionally secured access to key decision makers by the campaign donation route. Advertising campaigns either touted specific industry products or identified the oil industry with American symbols such as progressive enterprise, private ownership, individual businessmen. Their advertisements are written in the language of the self-conscious to answer anxieties in such a way as to reassure individuals while solidifying the private, hidden power of corporate oil.[25]

The American Petroleum Institute (API), an outgrowth of a World War I government-sponsored committee, is the trade association for the major oil companies. It has between 260 and 350 corporate members, and 7,000 individual members, who collectively represent 85 percent of the industry's total business volume. Dues to this nonprofit, tax-exempt organization are a business-related tax deduction: eight companies pay $1 million or more in dues. In 1973 API was reorganized to provide a more informational, aggressive, public relations, and direct lobbying adjunct to complement efforts of the individual companies.

At the time of the October 1973 Arab-Israeli war, the big four companies, Exxon, Texaco, Mobil, and Standard Oil of California, which together with Saudi Arabia form the Arabian American Oil Company (Aramco), sent a memo to President Nixon two days before he ordered the massive emergency arms lift to Israel. The message concerned a secret meeting that American company officials held with King Faisal of Saudi Arabia in which he warned that aid to Israel would mean cutbacks in crude oil production. At the same time the American companies were urging the Saudis to increase their prices. This helps American companies in two ways: first, by increasing their gross profits; second, by reducing the oil companies American taxes since they can charge off the royalties paid to the Arabs against their American tax liability.

After the war and the increase in oil prices, the public blamed the oil companies. The companies began a series of massive advertising campaigns, again tax deductible, to convince the public that other factors caused both the oil crisis and the embarrassingly high profits of the oil companies in the fiscal quarter following the gasoline price hike. The media blitz was designed to counter the news columns by transforming "a policy crisis into an 'oil crisis.' "[26]

In 1973 and 1974 API spent approximately $1 to $2 million on advertising, expanded its direct lobbying division from three to eleven lobbyists; instituted a policy analysis division to provide input during the congressional bill-drafting process, held news conferences to counter media misinformation, and provided news releases, speakers, and assistance to local media outlets and regional associations. In addition, at a cost of $30 to $70 million, the major companies themselves are currently training executives in news techniques, are promoting their subsidies of public television programs, and are perfecting their advertising rebuttals to current government proposals. The oil executives say, "This business of communication has become as important as finding more oil." One public relations firm hired to teach the new communicators states, "Our greatest market seems to be among companies where Ralph Nader has just been."[27]

Mobil Oil's advertising program provides an example of the current approach. Mobil's chairman of the board explained his company's program as an effort to use paid advertising to counter public misinformation. Advertisements were placed in fifteen to twenty newspapers in 1973, later in one hundred papers. The basic pitch was that America was becoming unnecessarily reliant on outside producers of oil because the government was not permitting industry to develop adequate domestic resources. Discussing the *New York Times* "op-ed" advertisement series, he said: "We try to surprise readers . . . with our selection of subject matter, our headlines, and our brisk and often irreverent text. We try to be urbane, but not pompous. . . . In sum, we think the exercise has been useful, . . . and sufficiently productive to continue."[28] For example, four headlines on the profit issue read:

Now about those record profits or ours. . . .
We just spent three months' profits in one morning.
Just two cents.
Are oil profits big? Right. Big enough? Wrong.

The content of this "idea advertising" antagonized many specialists who caught Mobil in half-truths, misleading explanations, and self-serving solutions. Representative George Brown, Jr., answered one Mobil "open letter" to congressmen with a detailed refutation of every point. He said that if Mobil were seriously interested in solving the energy crisis, "they would take the millions of dollars they are now spending on misinforming the American public and spend it on research and development."[29]

In an interesting twist CBS and ABC television stations refused to accept viewpoint advertisements. A letter from the CBS legal department, dated February 27, 1973, read: "It is the general policy of CBS to sell time only for the promotion of goods and services, not for the presentation of points of view on controversial issues of public importance." Nevertheless, using other television stations and newspapers, the oil industry is still pursuing its basic postwar technique of using advertising to make people feel a partnership with the oil companies, by merchandising an "endless and sugar-coated repetition of a 'few plausible facts.' "[30]

Environmental Lobby

A political joke in 1974 was that the best way to keep warm would be to burn the environmental protection laws. To pessimists this seemed indicative of the times. The period 1973–74 saw the way cleared for building of the Alaskan oil pipeline, delay on meeting the requirements of the Clean Air Act, and executive department decisions and presidential messages emphasizing energy at the expense of environment. However, optimists saw the energy crunch as a blessing in disguise since it had created a front page crisis that made people aware of finite resources twenty years earlier than environmentalists had anticipated. Environmental Protection Agency Administrator Russell Train said: "Our energy and our environmental ills both stem from essentially the same source: the patterns of growth and development that waste our energy resources just as surely and shamefully as they lay waste to our natural environment."

The strength of the environmental lobby is diluted for two reasons. First, while specific segments seek specific policies there is no overall agreement on one set of environmental priorities to serve as a base for reeducating Americans to a new life style. Second, most of the organizations active in the environmentalist movement are educational, nonprofit, tax-exempt groups that cannot lobby. Two important exceptions are the Sierra Club and Friends of the Earth. The Sierra Club has grown from 7,000 in 1952 to 160,000 in 1974. The club uses paperback books and "sensational newspaper and magazine advertisements simultaneously to build membership, raise money, influence legislation. . . ."[31] Indeed its activities have been so successful the Internal Revenue Service took away the club's tax-exempt status in 1966 after it ran a series of advertisements to prevent a dam project that would have flooded the Grand Canyon.

The president of the Sierra Club during the 1950s and early 1960s, David Brower, was ousted for such flamboyance. He founded Friends of the Earth to serve as an umbrella lobbying vehicle for groups restricted by the tax laws. His staff of four works to provide support for the public relations and citizen activity campaigns of other groups. During the 1973–74 oil crisis, the environmental lobby accepted short-term delays as a substitute for elimination of the entire set of laws gained during the late 1960s and early 1970s. Senator Clark summarized the environmentalists' 1973 position by saying: "We need to develop a balanced approach to energy policy. Environmental laws should not be made the scapegoat for energy shortages. We are not faced with a simple choice between cold homes and dirty air."

These groups also advertise. In March 1973 a full-page Sierra Club advertisement in the *New York Times* asked William Ruckelshaus, EPA administrator, to "Hang Tough." The advertisement then cited facts and statistics indicating clean air was more economical than dirty air and urged citizens to write letters in support of the strong Clean Air Act. The ad said: "Your letter will be like a vote that can help change our world forever. Your letter will be your commitment to clean the air for once and for all . . . or at the very least, mail the coupon on this page to Mr. Ruckelshaus now as your encouragement that he hang tough, very tough, on the Clean Air Act."

Each of these lobbies—Jews, Arabs, oil producers, and environmentalists—plays the public relations game in order to shape a decision-making environment that will enhance its own chances for access to decision makers. Each lobby is limited by internal differences of opinion that affect both the content and coordination of its public relations efforts. However all four use the media to expand their ideas beyond their own membership and potential membership to those members of the attentive public who will pass their message on to the public at large.

These four campaigns in the Middle East propaganda war illustrate the flexibility of climate control techniques. Each interest highlighted a different facet of the problem: Jews emphasized democracy; Arabs, oil; oil companies, economic repercussions; environmentalists, resource allocation. Sometimes the four competitors were in direct conflict, proving V. O. Key's point that "where competing interests are organized, propaganda is essential."[32] But sometimes the arguments slid by each other, enabling an official who makes policy in small incremental bites to side with each group on separate issues and still maintain a consistent position for himself. Consequently it is impossible to attribute any specific policy decision to the opinion climate of the moment. As in news briefings where the official gives important news "off the record," the public opinion activities of groups are on "deep background."

SUMMARY

In this chapter we have considered the various educational and propagandistic techniques that groups use as indirect access routes for improving their own status in society or promoting their goals. By supplying information—be it symbols, slogans, or facts—that alters the decision-making milieu, groups can become important indirect influences on the policy process. Groups act as conduits between the public and politicians, supplying information on the activities of politicians to their own members and interested bystanders who in turn carry the information to others in ever-widening circles. The final result, as measured by public opinion polls and mail, is a general support level among the citizenry that politicians refer to when implementing specific policies.

Media-education, as well as campaign services and campaign cash contributions, are all indirect methods used by political interest groups to enter the public policy game. In the next two chapters we will examine groups at work in the electoral process where they use their skills to turn group positions into party platforms and election issues, and where they use their money and services to help candidates committed to their goals.

NOTES

1. David Truman, *The Governmental Process* (New York: Knopf, 1951), pp. 264–65.
2. Federal Regulation of Lobbying Act of 1946 (pl. 79–60), sec. 307 (author's emphasis).
3. *United States* v. *Harriss* 347 U.S. 612 (1954). Justice Douglas dissent.
4. Charles O. Jones, *An Introduction to the Study of Public Policy* (Belmont, Ca.: Wadsworth, 1970), p. 19.
5. This quotation and the information that precedes are from John Sewell and Charles Paslillo, "Public Opinion and Government Policy," reprinted in U.S., Congress, *Congressional Record,* 93 Cong., 2nd Sess., July 1, 1974, pp. H6091, H6089–94.
6. John Gardner, "Letter to the Membership," *Report from Washington* (September, 1970), p. 8.
7. U.S., Congress, Senate, *Congressional Record* (daily edition), 93 Cong., 2nd Sess., June 17, 1974, p. E3948.
8. U.S., Congress, Senate, *Congressional Record* (daily edition), 93 Cong., 2nd Sess., December 4, 1974, p. E6955.
9. Truman, *The Governmental Process,* p. 251.
10. James Strouse, *The Mass Media, Public Opinion and Public Policy Analysis: Linkage Explorations* (Columbus, Ohio: Charles E. Merrill, 1975), pp. 14–15.
11. Bernard Cohen, "Political Communication on the Japanese Peace Settlement," *Public Opinion Quarterly* 20 (1956): p. 28.
12. Raymond Bauer, Ithiel de Sola Pool, and Lewis Dexter, *American Business and Public Policy* (New York: Atherton Press, 1963), p. 365.
13. Ibid., p. 359.

14. "Crusade," *The New Yorker,* June 14, 1976, p. 29.
15. Samuel Eldersveld, "American Interest Groups," in *Interest Groups on Four Continents,* ed. Henry Ehrmann (Pittsburgh: University of Pittsburgh Press, 1958), p. 1934.
16. Truman, *The Governmental Process,* p. 223.
17. Paul Eschholz, Alfred Rosa, and Virginia Clark, eds., *Language Awareness* (New York: St. Martin's Press, 1974), p. 40.
18. *New York Times,* December 12, 1975.
19. Strouse, *Mass Media, Public Opinion and Public Policy Analysis,* p. 270.
20. *Christian Science Monitor,* September 29, 1971.
21. *Christian Science Monitor,* June 11, 1974.
22. Strouse, *Mass Media, Public Opinion and Public Policy Analysis,* pp. 155–56.
23. *Time,* March 10, 1975, p. 24.
24. Information in this section is from *Congressional Quarterly Weekly Report,* August 30, 1975, p. 1871.
25. See Robert Engler, *The Politics of Oil* (Chicago: University of Chicago Press, 1961), chaps. 13, 14, 15.
26. U.S., Congress, Senate, *Congressional Record,* 93 Cong., 2nd Sess., November 18, 1974, p. S19473.
27. Ibid., p. S19474.
28. Ibid., June 17, 1974, p. E3948.
29. Ibid., July 30, 1973, p. E5206.
30. Engler, *The Politics of Oil,* p. 475.
31. Odom Fanning, *Man and His Environment: Citizen Action* (New York: Harper & Row, 1975), pp. 110–12.
32. V. O. Key, *Politics, Parties and Pressure Groups,* 5th ed. (New York: Thomas Y. Crowell, 1964), p. 130.

Chapter 5

Building Access through Electoral Activities

ITT (International Telephone and Telegraph Company) is the model of a modern major conglomerate, expanding in the 1960s by acquisitions and mergers.[1] Between 1961 and 1968 ITT acquired fifty-two American and fifty-five foreign corporations; in 1969 the board approved the acquisition of thirty-three more companies. To halt the process, Richard McLaren, assistant attorney-general of the Antitrust Division of the Department of Justice, initiated cases against three of the proposed 1969 mergers because ITT's

> history in the last decade makes it the most acquisitive corporation in the nation's history. Indeed, ITT is the archetypal example of the diversified corporation which has grown almost entirely by acquisitions. It has swallowed some 101 companies in widely varying fields in the last ten years.

McLauren was hired for his reputation as a trust buster. ITT seemed to provide a perfect opportunity for him to take a conglomerate antitrust case to the Supreme Court. Yet on July 31, 1971, several days after the Justice Department had indeed filed an appeal to the Supreme Court, McLauren announced an out-of-court settlement of the case that gave ITT all it had requested two years earlier. ITT gave up six subsidiaries, which earned less than $40 million, and kept Hartford Fire Insurance Company, which earned $105 million.

The official reason for McLauren's about-face was the company's plea of economic hardship as documented in a study commissioned by White House aide Pete Flanigan and given to McLauren. A more persuasive reason lay in Nixon's aversion to any antitrust litigation. The tapes of an April 1971 meeting with John Ehrlichman reveal Nixon saying: "I don't know whether ITT is bad, good, or indifferent. But there is [sic] not going to be any more antitrust actions as long as I am in this chair. . . . [Trust busting] was all right fifty years ago. . . . . It's not a good thing for the country today." Acting on this attitude, Nixon immediately dialed Deputy Attorney General Richard Kleindienst and told him: "I do not want McLaren to run around prosecuting people, raising hell about conglomerates, stirring things up at this point. Now you keep him the hell out of that. Is that clear? . . . My order is to drop the goddamn thing."

A third version, offered by Jack Anderson, based on a purloined memorandum from Dita Beard, ITT lobbyist, to her boss, Bill Merriam, suggested that the solution had little to do with ITT's internal economic situation and less to do with presidential philosophy. Her version linked the decision with ITT's offer to provide $400,000 through its Sheraton Hotels Subsidiary in order to enable Nixon to hold the 1972 Republican National Convention in San Diego. The general sentiment in San Diego and within the Republican National Committee was rather negative, but Nixon wanted the convention held on "his turf," within commuting distance of his Western White House, in a place where he felt safe.

The $400,000 offer was made by Hal Geneen, ITT president, to Congressman Bob Wilson at dinner on May 12, 1971, as Wilson complained about the possibilities of attracting the convention and the need for "up-front" money from the business community. To Wilson and Geneen, it was a business deal—promotion and business for Geneen's hotels in San Diego. To others, in the context of the antitrust litigation maneuverings, it seemed a bribe. In the Beard memorandum she made that sort of link explicit:

> Other than . . . [Attorney General] John Mitchell, [California Lt. Governor] Ed Reinecke, Bob Haldeman, and Nixon . . . *no one* has known from whom the $400,000 commitment had come. . . . Our noble com-

> mitment has gone a long way toward our negotiations on the mergers eventually coming out as Hal wants them. Certainly the President told Mitchell to see that things are worked out fairly. . . . Mitchell is definitely helping us but cannot let it be known.

Seven days before the ITT case was dropped, the Republican National Committee decided to hold the convention in San Diego. When the ITT pledge became public knowledge, the Republican National Committee moved the convention to Miami.

Ethics aside, the incident illustrates one of the many kinds of electoral process relationships that develop between political interest groups and political party activities. Group activities related to the national presidential nominating conventions range from competition to host the convention (cities lobby the parties), to testimony and lobbying before the platform committees, to direct participation as duly elected political party/interest group delegates. Groups also work at securing nominations for friendly politicians and then developing issues for "their" candidates, providing person power to do the work, and finally getting out the vote on election day. Political interest groups that can claim voting blocs—Jews, blacks, women, Catholics—play on this relationship in order to secure candidate promises and access to electoral decisions. This chapter will focus on these party-group relationships in terms of the group need to create two politically necessary bases—personal access to elected officials and public acceptance of the group's ideas.

RELATIONSHIPS WITH THE MAJOR POLITICAL PARTIES

Interest groups and political parties can perform reciprocal services because, while both act as conduits between citizens and their government, the former emphasize policy content while the latter are concerned with filling public offices. Political interest groups serve politicians as a convenient tool for identifying and reaching key blocs within the voting public. And in a reciprocal sense, the political habit of gearing campaigns to voting blocs creates a role for the political interest group as organized spokespersons for bloc concerns. For the candidate, group support offers the advantage of campaign personnel and services, a dependable source of support within the district, reliable exposure to a specialized audience, and, perhaps, a bloc of votes in November. Candidates speaking to a group address its dominant concerns; thereby groups inject their issues into the campaign. Thus the group's dual capacity to speak both for and to its constituency implements the democratic notion of citizen participation through the expression of voter issue preferences in the electoral process and at the polls.

From the group's vantage point, coordination with party activities has several advantages. First, it is another way to ensure access to officials who are either receptive to the group's ideas or indebted to the group itself for electoral assistance. Second, groups with the advantage of membership strength can use the electoral process as a way to illustrate this group resource. While it is true that no group can deliver its members' votes as a neatly wrapped package, it is also true that in the folklore of politics, tales abound of close contests won with the support of key organized minorities. To be safe, politicians prefer to work with groups rather than test the cliché.

Third, participation in party politics offers groups a chance to shape campaign issues in various ways. They may seek to influence the national party platforms in order to have specific policy liens on the winners or just to shape the general contours of political debate. Groups also inject their policy positions and candidate choices and value judgments into individual campaigns when they rate candidates' past performances, provide workers and literature for those they support, and generally advertise the campaign, from the group's perspective, in their newsletters.

Most major political interest groups maintain a facade of nonpartisanship, supported by their issue-oriented interest in the selection of officials, while simultaneously aligning themselves with one or the other major party. For example, despite the well-publicized neutrality of George Meany in 1972, the public generally associates the AFL-CIO with the Democratic Party. Conversely, big business is considered Republican. However, all business is not Republican; all labor is not Democratic. Variations occur along ideological, geographical, policy, and socioeconomic lines. Both party and group seek to motivate voters to vote on the basis of information that they provide.

Consequently it is of mutual interest to parties and allied groups to cooperate for maximum electoral efficiency.

The dispersion of party power throughout the levels of government in the federal system, coupled with the fact that political party power flows upward from the grass roots, permits groups to be geographically partisan. That is, a group may support different political parties and their candidates in different states and localities and/or across the three levels of government. The multiple access points of this three-dimensional system create numerous options for groups. A group may assist candidates with important policy-making positions such as President, governor, or legislative committee chairman; it may help only marginal candidates in order to maximize its access should the candidate win; it may work to create an ideological bias within a legislature by supporting only "liberal" or "conservative" candidates. Once a group has determined its strategy, it implements that strategy by participating at various stages in the selection and election processes.

NATIONAL PARTY PRESIDENTIAL NOMINATING CONVENTIONS

Convention Sites

Conventions mean big business as indicated by ITT's 1972 offer of $400,000 to establish its Sheraton subsidiary's new San Diego hotel. To win the convention prize, cities act as special interest groups and appoint lobbyist-public relations citizen committees to present their case. As with any public decision, the process begins early: for example, city presentations were made to party selection committees in 1974 for site decisions in 1975 for conventions in 1976.

The Democratic National Committee's (DNC) twenty-member site selection committee was inundated with statistics, offers of assistance and gifts as two cities—Los Angeles and New York—lobbied for this 1976 tourist bonanza. The Los Angeles booster group gave each committee member a Hollywood director's chair, personalized with the member's name, and promoted the glories of Los Angeles and its 210,000 square feet of convention hall space in a film produced by

Universal Studios. The size of the convention center, despite its lack of grandstand space for an audience, was the city's main asset. However Los Angeles was faulted by committee members for "its physical sprawl, its remoteness for the majority of convention delegates, and for the unpredictability of government leaders" (a euphemism for Governor Brown's lack of enthusiasm and indecisiveness).

New York City gave committee members authentic athletic jerseys worn by Joe Namath, Catfish Hunter, Walt Frazier, and Tom Seaver and bushels of apples signifying the New York City nickname, "The Big Apple." Madison Square Garden, while not a convention center, offered grandstands for 15,000 spectators and nearby accommodations for delegates. New York City was faulted by the committee for "relatively high prices, its congestion, the uncertainty of municipal finances, and the danger of civil strife." In the final hours when it appeared that New York City might win if these fears were alleviated, the New York City booster team produced the leaders of key unions who pledged to provide city services during the convention period, and the city agreed to spend $1 million for modification of Madison Square Garden. The committee's decision was 11 to 9 in favor of New York City, then 14 to 6, and finally unanimous. It reflected DNC Chairman Robert Strauss's desire for "a good stage on which to display the story, the principles, the character, and the drama of the Democratic Party. . . ."

The seven-member Republican site selection committee had to choose among Kansas City, Cleveland, and Miami. Kansas City won after agreeing to spend $500,000 and demonstrating the availability of 13,000 hotel rooms within reasonable distance of the convention center. But, as in the case of the Democrats, image played a deciding role. President Ford preferred the image of the friendly Midwest, heartland of America, rather than the Miami site where Nixon was nominated twice.

For both cities the 1976 convention decisions had local and national consequences. New York City originally estimated that the 3,000 DNC delegates would spend $200 million for assorted services. By convention week this estimate had dropped a zero, and was down to only $20 million. More important than tourist revenues was the chance to host 3,000 politically active Americans and to upgrade New York City's image during its period of fiscal catastrophe. Kansas City had similar considerations in mind. As Mayor Charles Wheeler, Jr., said, it would erase the "cowtown" image of the city and put it into "the big leagues" in terms of competing for other national nonpolitical conventions.

National Party Platforms

Platforms provide a formal mechanism for incorporating outside interests into a governmental position paper. Platforms are both internal accommodation documents designed to placate various factions within the party in order to achieve unity during the presidential campaign and a series of promises to the public. The nominated candidate pledges to support his party's platform and to implement its goals. Consequently platforms provide a forum for groups with new issues seeking to create public understanding of their long-term goals, as well as an opportunity for established groups to push for implementation promises.

Every four years, platform committees hold a series of meetings where people testify on issues they want included in that year's platform. Sophisticated organizations produce elaborate booklets for consideration, such as the AFL-CIO's sixty-two-page itemization of seventy topics. Common Cause used literature, supplemented by members' letters to platform committee members, urging incorporation of the group's structural reform proposals. In 1976 the Democratic Platform Committee accepted all of Common Cause's planks; the Republicans accepted four of its proposals.

Final platforms of each party differ in content and emphasis, reflecting the ideological bases of each party and the accumulation of interests each considers essential. For example, the 1976 Democratic platform contained strong urban aid platforms (a reflection of the series of publicized meetings that the Democratic Conference of Mayors held with presidential candidate nominees), sought repeal of Section 14(b) of the Taft-Hartley Act allowing states to require nonunion shops, supported common site picketing (organized labor's two major bread-and-butter goals), opposed a constitutional amendment to ban abortions and endorsed the Equal Rights Amendment (women). The 1976 Republican platform supported opposite provisions and, indeed, almost dropped a forty-year-old plank endorsing the ERA. The plank was only saved at the last minute by the intensive lobbying of ERA supporters and the personal decision of Phyllis Schlafly, leader of the anti-ERA forces, to withdraw her minority report and concentrate on electing Ronald Reagan the Republican presidential candidate.

Actually the role played by women provides an instructive example of how platform fights are symbolic of group acceptance (for itself or its ideas) within the political process. Gloria Steinem commented on the shift of the women's lobby between 1972 and 1976 from outsiders to insiders, pointing out that the abortion issue controversy in the Republican platform debate had no parallel in New York City. Democrat women had fought that losing battle at the 1972 Democratic convention. Now these women were insiders who had their plank accepted quietly despite Carter's reservations. In 1976 the women's groups in the Democratic Party moved from the symbolic level of platform language to the nuts-and-bolts level of national party rules, arguing for a 50-50 division of delegates in 1980. Dilution of the women's suggested language became the media's "women's issue," which hid a more important agreement to make the women's division of the party serve its feminist constituency, as the minority division serves its clientele. The trade-off signified a new level of participation by womens' groups: "women were sophisticated enough to be using the threat of a floor fight to bargain on entirely different issues."[2]

Convention Delegates

The identification of interest group participation within national party convention delegations is usually based on a subjective classification of the delegate body by outside observers. Various aspects of a multiassociational human being are isolated by different observers so that one affiliation of that person leads to the identification of a group's role which later is used to deduce the group's influence in the convention process. For example, a twenty-nine-year-old, Jewish, black, male, Detroit automobile assembly line worker could be categorized by his age, religion, color, sex, geographical location, or occupation. Only the last affiliation would place him as a member of a special interest group as defined in Chapter 1 (the other categories fall within our definition of categoric groups) yet if the delegate is identified by any of the first five attributes in the public mind he becomes a member of that "group," even though in analytical terms such a political interest group may not exist. Thus, in explanations of group electoral participation, group roles often rise and fall in relation to the human attributes identified as relevant by the commentators of the moment.

This definitional problem can be illustrated by examining the process of creating a convention delegate body that is considered representative of party membership. Any definition boils down to the subjective perceptions of current leaders and candidates. In their search for representativeness, different factions can divide the same party in opposite ways. As an example, in 1972 the Democratic delegate selection rules characterized previous conventions as overrepresentative of white, middle-aged, middle-class males and specified more representation for women, minorities, and youth. However, the middle-aged, middle-class white males identified themselves as liberals, conservatives, ethnics, union representatives, party leaders, and so on. Labor unionists accounted for approximately 10 percent of the delegates in 1968 and 1972, but in 1972 they were defined as part of the white male bloc rather than separated by the ethnic and occupational identifications of the past. Thus labor as a convention subgroup was analyzed in 1968, ignored in 1972.

When the new rules worked and the 1972 convention delegates included 23 percent youth, 15 percent blacks, and 38 percent women, the subdivisions among the white, middle-aged males who had been "categorized" out of the convention resented their lack of representation. As George Meany said of the New York delegation: "What kind of a delegation is this? They've got six open fags and only three AFL-CIO people on that delegation! Representative?"

For groups unable to participate inside convention halls, there is always the street. The Hippies and Yippies of the 1960s have been replaced by "Right to Life" antiabortion rallies and "Gay Alliance" marches on behalf of homosexual's rights. But regardless of the group's goal, its purpose is to use the television exposure provided by convention street scenes to advertise its message. If these protesters prove "successful," they will move inside next time around since it is the historical role of a party to absorb, neutralize, and use such outsiders. However to a protester of the 1960s, being a 1976 delegate was a journey from "no to nowhere. . . . Now there was nothing we could do but watch Jimmy Carter co-opt our leaders, steal our songs and even our language for his speech."[3] The complaint stands as affirmation of the symbiotic relationship between parties and political interest groups in an election year.

GROUP SERVICES TO PRESIDENTIAL CANDIDATES AND CAMPAIGNS

Groups are attracted to candidates for several reasons. First, they might win, eliminating the access problem for those who were their "first" friends. Second, candidates are excellent vehicles for promoting specific issues or general ideological orientations. Ellen McCormick, the Long Island housewife, who was the eleventh presidential primary candidate to qualify for matching federal funds, entered the race in order to popularize the "Right to Life," antiabortion viewpoint. Stalemated in Congress on a proposed constitutional amendment, checkmated by Supreme Court decisions upholding the right to abortion, the "Right to Life" movement decided to use the public financing component of the 1974 campaign finance laws as a way to fund prime-time prolife television commercials. As Georgia's "Right to Life" chairman, Jay Bowman, explained it: "She's not a serious candidate. But she can get equal time [on television] for the prolife message—and she can get the federal government to pay for it."

The next-best thing to running a message-only candidate is to advise a regular political one. For example, Carter's advisers included three of Ralph Nader's raiders; Joe Browder, leader of the Environmental Policy Center; UAW president Leonard Woodcock; Jack Conway from Common Cause and the American Federation of State, County, and Municipal Employees; and Mary Zon from AFL-CIO's Committee on Political Education (COPE). The list reflects the public interest and labor positions in the Democratic national platform.

A third position, one step removed from the candidate himself, but still concentrating on the issue aspect of campaigns, is to try to influence the issue content of a campaign. Common Cause did this in "Campaign '76" through an elaborate citizen network whose members asked candidates the same governmental reform and budget-oriented questions wherever they went. They also compiled issue profiles of all presidential candidates that were mailed to the primary American media outlets as resource material. Common Cause questions forced candidates to respond to budget and conflict of interest issues; its monitoring of candidate statements earned the group a position as a "communication node" that translates into lobbying effectiveness.

The League of Women Voters approached the same goal in 1976 by sponsoring five televised regional town meetings at which candidates for the presidential nomination responded to audience questions backed up by queries from issue experts. During the presidential election campaign, the League sponsored four ninety-minute nationally televised debates—three between President Ford and Jimmy Carter, one between the vice-presidential candidates. To sponsor the programs, the League had to get a ruling from the Federal Elections Commission that its $150,000 cost would not constitute a private contribution, which is illegal under the 1974 campaign law. The FEC ruled that because of the League's record of nonpartisan political activity it could organize the debates.

A final, rather indirect way to inject issues into campaigns is to rate incumbents either on issues selected to reflect the member's overall philosophy or on issues related to a specific topic. Nineteen organizations rated candidates in 1972; by 1976 over fifty organizations played the ratings game.[4] Comparing lists of issues is like comparing apples and oranges, however, since each organization has its own definition of "key votes" and the number used to create a list varies widely.

The selection process reflects a group's internal organizational structure and goal requirements more clearly than it reflects congressional action per se. For example, the Americans for Democratic Action (ADA) selects a broad range of votes that are then narrowed down by two dozen congressional aides who select approximately two dozen reflecting their issue concerns, that are then approved by the ADA executive committee. Voting records are computed, and congressmen are given plus or minus ratings indicating their deviance from the ADA's definition of "liberal." The Americans for Constitutional Action (ACA), their conservative counterpart, has created an elaborate system from which is derived a "consistency index" indicating the percentage of times congressmen vote "for safeguarding the God-given rights of the individual and promoting sound economic growth by strengthening constitutional government, against 'group morality,' a socialized economy, and centralization of government power."[5]

COPE selects approximately twenty social program and labor issues of interest to all workers, not just unionists. The Chamber of Commerce lists ten selected votes of importance to the business community, but does not endorse candidates or make campaign contributions. The National Council of Senior Citizens adopted the ratings technique in 1974 with a list of nine issues ranging from vocational rehabilitation to farm programs. They did not include the vote on the rise in social security benefits for senior citizens because they said there were no key votes recorded on this issue. Their newsletter explained that: "The real battles which culminated in a two-step, 11 percent 'cost of living increase' . . . were held behind closed doors and over telephone wires between leading members of the House and Senate, the council, organized labor, and the White House."[6]

The effect of endorsements and ratings is elusive. Often those endorsed/rated do not seek the favor, indeed, they find it a disadvantage since it gives challengers a handle for attack. Senator Eagleton has repeatedly asked the ADA to eliminate his rating because "my high rating is about as politically useful in Missouri as a pro-Arab position in New York." Others criticize ratings as partisan, misleading, unscientific, and incomplete. Nevertheless, groups continue to use them as an educational/public relations tool that publicizes the role of the group vis-á-vis congressional action, and links group positions with candidate identities in the hopes of influencing voting behavior.

Environmentalists have coupled ratings with massive publicity campaigns in a small number of targeted districts with notable success. Generally since such groups see themselves as splinters rather than voting blocs, they prefer to focus on marginal contests where their limited strength may tilt the outcome. In 1970 Environmental Action coined the term "Dirty Dozen" and applied it to the twelve congressmen whom they wished to defeat on the basis of their environmental voting record. Between 1970 and 1974, thirty-one individuals received this designation: nineteen have been defeated, five resigned.

A second environmental group, the League of Conservation Voters, works with other environmental groups to assist in key campaigns, provides computer breakdowns of incumbent voting records, and gives campaign contributions to selected candidates. In 1970 the League gave $45,000 to twenty-two candidates, sixteen of whom won. In 1972 they endorsed fifty-seven candidates, and forty-three won; in 1974, thirteen of the seventeen to whom they contributed money won. Chairperson Marion Edey said, "The races we won were mostly where opponents were willing to campaign on environmental issues. We lost where opponents fogged up their own or our candidates' environmental records or managed to divert the argument off the subject."

Ms. Edey's comments go to the heart of the problem concerning group influence on members' voting behavior. Generally so many other factors influence members on the way to the polls that it is difficult to show a causal relationship between voting behavior and particular group efforts. The possibility of ascertaining the real influence of an issue in an election is made even more awkward by the tendency of each group involved to attribute a candidate's victory (or defeat, if that was desired) to the influence of its issue.

For example, in 1970 Senator Joseph Tydings (Democrat, Maryland) was defeated for reelection. Tydings attributed his defeat to "the National Gun Lobby, a powerful and selfish special interest group . . . [which] has apparently decided that I imperil their profits and marked me No. 1 on their national purge list."[7] The National Rifle Association (NRA), as a tax-exempt organization, was unable to acknowledge any personal role in Tyding's defeat, but it did heap credit on CAT (Citizens Against Tydings) which opposed his election because it considered gun control a civil liberties issue that should remain unregulated by government.

The organization spent between $50- and $60,000, raised from advertisements in *Gun Week,* for publicity: 150,000 bumper stickers, 175,000 brochures, 30 full-page advertisements, and numerous radio spots. Tydings invited attack on his gun control stance because he made the issue an important part of his campaign, as indicated by his discussion of gun control in two of six sixty-second television commercials and his emphasis on the topic in campaign speeches. Yet the executive director of his campaign, in an election postmortem discussion of his narrow defeat [by 25,000 votes], said, "Well, the left-handed Lithuanian vote didn't go for him."[8] This is a shorthand, offhand way of saying that the vote margin was so narrow and the possible reasons so numerous it would be impossible to isolate the deciding factor.

However, for the NRA it was easy to claim success. Using Tydings' words, they headlined a postelection article in *The American Rifleman:* "Antigun Leaders Toppled." In their explanation Senators Tydings and Thomas Dodd (Democrat, Connecticut) were defeated because of their progun control stance, while Senators William Proxmire, Hugh Scott, and Hubert Humphrey won reelection after they reversed earlier stands in favor of the 1968 Gun Control Act. The promotional tendencies of the interest group, by simplifying the complexities of the real world, make it impossible to reconstruct the actual role played by issue groups in a campaign. Tyding's excuse becomes accepted as truth, and the myth of group electoral power is reinforced.

For those groups interested in candidates' campaigns rather than candidates' issue positions, there are a variety of "soft services," also known as "in-kind" services, such as printing, mailing, providing campaign workers, and so forth, that groups can make available to candidates of their choice. For example, the American Medical Political Action Committee (AMPAC) hires field representatives to activate members politically. AMPAC shows films that instruct doctors in the ways of politics, conducts workshops, provides political speakers, and creates letter-writing campaigns. In the "how to talk politics to patients" training film, a doctor says: "Patients trust our judgments when they ask us to take care of their health. I think they'll buy our opinions on congressional candidates."[9]

Businesses often provide soft services for candidates in lieu of hard cash; these range from use of the company plane for campaigning to stamps, stationery, and reproduction services for mailings. Since the average cost of one candidate mailing to a congressional district is $12,000, that is a nice soft service. Companies often donate advertising expertise by letting a candidate use their public relations company or lend other company employees to candidates while continuing to pay their salaries.

Testimony from the Senate Watergate hearings showed that in 1972 the dairy cooperatives lent an employee to Wilbur Mills' presidential campaign effort and continued to cover her pay and the cost of her Washington apartment. In 1970 AMPI paid $12,000 for advertising company bills in Hubert Humphrey's senatorial campaign. In 1968 they spent $90,711 to print a collection of Lyndon Johnson's messages to Congress entitled "No Retreat from Tomorrow."

In 1974 the National Committee for an Effective Congress (NCEC), which formerly supported liberal candidates with cash donations, created a program of "campaign support services." NCEC hired political consultants in polling, media use, fund raising, and so on, and "rented" them at wholesale prices to over fifty candidates. The cost to NCEC was $125,000; the results were thirty-five victories for their candidates.

The most well-known form of indirect contributions are the advertisements in national party convention programs that are purchased by large companies and unions at outrageous prices. In 1972 the minimum price for a black-and-white full-page advertisement was $10,000 to a top of $25,000 for the back cover ad. Proceeds are used to defray convention costs, and sales are made in a bipartisan manner by salesmen for both parties. This results in duplication of most advertisements including Coca-Cola's back page ad in each convention program. Since 1968 such corporate contributions have been legal and tax-deductible, increasing their desirability as a form of corporate political participation.

GROUPS AND VOTERS

The electoral college system, which maximizes the importance of populous states, also maximizes the influence of bloc voting—labor or black or Jewish—that is concentrated in major cities. It has been estimated that unions may provide a net gain of 2.8 million votes for Democrats in presidential elections, approximately one-eleventh of the total popular vote necessary to win during the 1950s.[10] Notions of a causal relationship between ethnic, religious, occupational, or age characteristics and voting behavior are promoted by the media, which discuss electoral activities and consequences in such terms. Thus, the 1972 Nixon vote was characterized as support from 54 percent Catholics, 39 percent Jews, 58 percent urban dwellers, 59 percent blue-collar workers, 48 percent of the youth vote. Organized segments of such blocs seek to capitalize on this form of political shorthand by claiming that their activities make such identifications possible. Therefore groups, particularly mass membership organizations, seek to mobilize their membership through voter registration drives or issue-oriented materials. However since members usually belong to more than one group with political interests, and since political values of individuals precede their group membership, most groups can only reinforce rather than change voting inclinations.

Nevertheless, political interest groups that represent segments of the categoric group considered a voting bloc emphasize their ties to maximize their own group impact. By way of example, in 1976 forty-five civil rights, black, labor, and business organizations formed the National Coalition on Black Voter Participation, to implement "Operation Big Vote," a major drive to register at least one million more blacks before the November 1976 election. The goals of the organization explicitly relate this goal to the broader purpose of enhancing black policy-making influence, increasing the number of black elected officials, and providing a base for a permanent black lobby. Blacks were pleased with their successes at the 1976 Democratic National Convention and in subsequent meetings with Jimmy Carter. They attributed this success to their preelection timing of demands. Basil Paterson, black national committeeman from New York, said: "We've got the pivotal votes. Now the task is to set our demands and frame them in realistic terms. The commitments must be gotten before our consideration is delivered." Again the myth is implemented.

Using similar electoral mathematics, the Catholic Church hierarchy, represented by the National Conference of Catholic Bishops, linked the 1976 Democratic Party need for at least 60 percent of the Catholic bloc vote to the Church's need for commitments on antiabortion policies. Church sponsorship in each congressional district of political "prolife" committees designed to publicize the issue, combined with President Ford's attempt to "Republicanize" working-class urban Catholics, made abortion a campaign issue despite the similarity of the candidates' views. Thus, the Church, an organized segment of the Catholic community, made its issue a lightning rod despite the fact that polls show no religious polarization on the abortion question.

Similarly in 1972 both presidential candidates sought to ensure the Jewish vote by emphasizing their pro-Israel positions to the point where eight major Jewish organizations publicly deplored the crass wooing of a bloc vote by overemphasis on this one issue. However, the intensity of the drive for the vote of 3 percent of the American population reflects the predominance of Jews in three industrial states —New York, Illinois, and California. In New York, Jews account for 14 percent of the electorate; 85 percent of them vote. Despite the fact that Nixon's Jewish vote probably reflected domestic anxieties symbolized in the "law and order" slogan, the self-fulfilling prophecy linking Israel/interest/vote continues to persist. Consequently despite all the scholarly findings that groups cannot corral members' votes, the Monday morning quarterbacks perpetuate the contrary myth by explaining election results in terms of political interest categories.

A CASE IN POINT: LABOR AND "SOFT" PARTY POLITICS

Organized labor's activities within the party system illustrate how one special interest group can parlay the range of options discussed in this chapter into enormous political clout.

Labor as a political force is an abstraction that quickly dissolves into several parts when examined closely. One part is the AFL-CIO apparatus commanded by President George Meany and Alexander Barkan, director of the Committee on Political Education (COPE). COPE is really an independent political machine that can be cranked up for any candidate to spew forth money and organizational supports such as voter registration drives; computer information banks with voter, candidate, and election law information; and assorted publications designed to inform and motivate union voters. Another part of labor consists of the large independent unions such as the United Automobile Workers (UAW), the Teamsters, the United Mine Workers (UMW), and the International Longshoreman's and Warehouseman's Union. A third part consists of those unions among the 114 affiliated with the AFL-CIO that do not follow the national command, preferring to spend their money independently rather than through COPE. Finally there is the union member as an individual who may or may not be influenced by pressures from his national, state, and local unions. Often these four segments work at cross-purposes to each other—supporting opposing candidates, offering electoral power which is not really there.

Within the Democratic Party, labor often endorses candidates during the primary stage, thereby bringing along with them the support of other liberal issue groups such as the ADA, ACLU, NAACP, and NCEC.[11] For example, in 1960 John Kennedy's candidacy was advanced by union advocates such as the UAW, United Steel Workers, and Textile Workers Union of America, who endorsed him despite his less than enthusiastic civil rights record, and persuaded the black groups to join with them. Conversely, labor opposed Lyndon Johnson because key unions felt he was too committed to southern legislators and Texas oil interests to use the Presidency to help labor. The British newspaper, the *Economist,* said: "It is doubtful whether the unions could swallow the gnat of Senator Johnson's nomination, even if this refusal subsequently obliged them to digest the camel of Mr. Nixon's Presidency." His unacceptability to labor made it difficult for Johnson to gather other liberal support, and hence impossible to win over northeastern delegates, since the party pros in those areas "would not risk the alienation of organized labor."[12]

In 1968 the labor contingent at the Democratic convention accounted for approximately 10 percent of the delegates, members of the party infrastructure that handed the nomination to Hubert Humphrey. Those in attendance later received "Order of the Buffalo" lapel pins as symbols of Eugene McCarthy's remark that he lost to Humphrey because "these old labor people, they just dig in and put their heads down. Like buffaloes. You couldn't budge them."

With Nixon elected in 1968, Meany began to push for congressmen to counter Nixon's antilabor program while at the same time moving the Democrats toward a centrist position in 1972. Thus, the action went on at two levels: an issue level and a personnel selection level. On the issue level Nixon sought to woo labor with his busing and war positions, but his wage and price controls led Barkan to state that "labor's primary political goal in 1972 [is] the defeat of Richard Nixon's bid for reelection." Labor also moved to create a task force for the protectionist Burke-Hartke trade bill, which labor wanted to make a 1972 campaign issue in order to dramatize the need to protect

American jobs. COPE's local apparatus was used to run teach-ins, hold mass meetings, generate advertising campaigns, and solicit candidate commitments to back the bill.

At the same time labor was working within the Democratic Party to find a suitable presidential candidate. Barkan boasted that, "We aren't going to let these Harvard-Berkeley Camelots take over our party." Yet, even with thirteen labor leaders on the Democratic National Committee, the McGovern reformers eliminated labor as a representational category—as a basis for delegate selection quotas.

In February 1972 the *New York Times* quoted a labor leader as indicating three options: "We could go all out for Muskie right now and probably guarantee him the nomination. We could go for Hubert, and give him a fair shot. . . . Or we can just elect our delegates and watch." Choosing the third option, 300 labor delegates were at the convention, but no longer in the inner circle of power. As one labor leader complained: "No one paid any attention to me. . . . I felt as I were at a Republican convention." United Steel Workers' President I. W. Abel, in his nominating speech for Humphrey, summarized traditional labor's attitude: "We're tired of the politicians who denounce big labor and 'labor bosses' on Monday and then come to us on Tuesday with their hands outstretched."

Nixon continued to try and mollify labor by removing the traditional antilabor rhetoric from the Republican platform and by releasing imprisoned Jimmy Hoffa, ex-president of the Teamsters Union. Nevertheless, stung by the indifference of the McGovernites to the importance of labor within the Democratic Party and unable to swallow the Nixon economic program, the AFL-CIO Executive Council decided, in July 1972, to remain neutral in a presidential race for the first time since their merger in 1955. Individual unions would be free to go their own ways; COPE would concentrate on congressional and selected gubernatorial races. The Teamsters, Iron Workers Union, Seafarers International Union, and others supported Nixon. Thirty-three of the affiliated AFL-CIO unions supported McGovern, as did the UAW.

After the 1972 election, Joseph Beirne, President of the Communication Workers Union, reflecting the more liberal union posture, said, "We should have a greater say in what the Democratic Party does by participating in its restructuring, serving on the Charter Commission, and making our voice heard on all policy decisions." In 1973 eleven of twenty-five DNC seats were held by labor leaders, and Robert Strauss, new national chairman, was elected with labor approval. However by December 1974, when the Democrats met in Kansas City to adopt a new charter, the division between the Meany/Barkan traditionalist position and the more aggressively liberal position of the UAW, the Communications Workers of America, and the American Federation of State, County, and Municipal Employees had widened. The former renounced Strauss and the continuation of implicit delegate quotas for women and minorities.

The split was formalized as a position of noninvolvement in political party affairs taken at the February 1975 meeting of the AFL-CIO Executive Council. Meany said:

> We came to a unanimous conclusion that the AFL-CIO has no desire to influence the internal structure of either the Republican or Democratic parties and we have no desire to allow the Republicans or Democrats to interfere with our internal affairs.
>
> We have a political party and it is known as COPE, and we are going to continue to improve it, strengthen it, maintain it, in order to try to elect labor's friends to the House and to the Senate and to the state legislatures, irrespective of political parties.[13]

The thirty-five-member Executive Council voted to remain officially aloof from both presidential preference and delegate selection primaries in 1976.

Instead individual unions were encouraged to act on their own. Nine liberal unions,* the core of McGovern's union support, immediately organized the Labor Coalition Clearinghouse. Their goal was "to ensure a strong labor voice at the Democratic convention irrespective of the primary results." Whereas in previous years, labor members had run as COPE supported delegates committed to the labor-backed candidate, they were now urged to jump on any ticket. So in New York State ninety-five union members appeared scattered

*The nine unions are the United Auto Workers, National Education Association, International Association of Machinists, United Mine Workers, Communication Workers of America, American Federation of State, County, and Municipal Workers, International Union of Electrical Workers, Graphic Arts Union, and Oil Workers.

over Jackson, Udall, Harris, and Carter slates. The coalition acted in 18 states, with the result that 418 of the 550 union member Democratic delegates were elected from coalition unions. "Organized labor spent over a half million dollars electing these delegates, financing their travel and convention expenses and, in some cases, even providing them pay for missed days of work." Labor influence within the Convention, in its coalition form, seemed reestablished when Carter met with clearinghouse leaders for half an hour to touch base before selecting a vice-presidential running mate.

However, union support is important not merely for its delegates or money. In addition to its political contribution fund, COPE also has three other funds that encourage voter registration efforts; produce educational materials such as handbills, leaflets, posters; and support the administrative activities of the central COPE office. Barkan says that when a candidate is given a choice between $5,000 in cash to spend as he pleases or $25,000 to "work the union membership for a candidate, most candidates take the former. I never fail to be amazed at the shortsightedness of many candidates. I don't have a high regard for the pragmatic intelligence of most candidates."[14]

COPE's "soft services" are phenomenal. For example, in 1960 COPE handled an all-out registration drive in fourteen key states providing manpower, money for offices, parade floats, posters, advertisements—even baby-sitters. COPE published and distributed 10 million leaflets listing the voting records of incumbent congressmen on ten key issues, and five million leaflets showing Kennedy voting "right" 91.6 percent of the time, Nixon voting "wrong" 76.6 percent of the time. Union power on behalf of former Senator Estes Kefauver of Tennessee provided 60,000 telephone calls, mailed 300,000 copies of his campaign literature, distributed 160,000 leaflets, and created a file on 65,000 union members in the state.[15]

In 1968 the AFL-CIO registered 4.6 million voters, printed and distributed 55 million pamphlets from Washington and 60 million from local unions, used 8,055 telephones in telephone banks in 638 localities manned by 24,611 union member volunteers, provided 72,225 house-to-house canvassers, and 94,457 Election Day volunteers to car pool, baby sit, and poll watch.[16]

For the 1972 elections COPE determined to register 75 percent of its 13 million members and did. In addition, COPE fed information into its computer data bank on the voting residences and participation records of all AFL-CIO members in the thirty-eight states with 50,000 or more unionists. COPE's research division also produced information on all incumbents and many challengers, as well as materials for 'educational' issue campaigns in congressional elections. On Election Day over 100,000 volunteers worked as doorbell ringers, vote solicitors, and drivers in order to get out the vote.[17]

In 1974, 110,000 volunteers donated time through COPE to run register-and-vote campaigns, handle telephone banks, do polling and canvassing, check registration lists, distribute materials, and get out the vote. Money from regular union dues finances these services since they are directed at members by members. As of 1976, the COPE computer bank has 14 million union members listed by address, political district, and registration states. COPE's 1976 services will cost the AFL-CIO $550,000 for computer time and $2.8 million for staff, leaflets, and postage. However, in 1976 COPE is more valuable than ever to candidates. Because these soft services are limited to internal union communications, their "in-kind" value is not considered a contribution to any candidate. Thus, the language of the campaign finance law gives labor's soft services a cutting edge.

SUMMARY

This chapter has explored the nonmonetary forms of group electoral participation ranging from group representation among delegates nominating party candidates to group informational activities such as publication of voting records, candidate ratings, issue-oriented campaign literature, and advertisements. Organizations with political interests also perform quasi-partisan activities such as registering voters, distributing literature, and getting out the vote on Election Day.

These services and campaign donations indirectly promote group interests through the selection of government decision makers who support similar policy positions or feel sufficiently obligated to the group to grant it a hearing when requested. In terms of favoring one party over another, group efforts probably cancel out each other, but in terms of furthering specific policy positions, membership groups such as labor and environmentalists have a "poll power" advantage that matches the "money power" advantage of business.

In the next chapter we will see how groups use money to create electoral obligators as a means of securing later policy-making access.

NOTES

1. Information for this case study was drawn from Anthony Sampson, *The Sovereign State of ITT* (New York: Fawcett, 1973), chaps. 8–10; Nixon Transcript of his Conversation, April 19, 1971; *Congressional Quarterly Weekly Report,* March 11, 1972, pp. 519–24.
2. Gloria Steinem, "Kissing with Your Eyes Open: Women and the Democrats," *Ms,* July 26, 1976, pp. 6–8.
3. Marlene Nadle, "A Radical Resigns from the Democratic Party," *Village Voice,* August 2, 1976, p. 41.
4. See *Congressional Quarterly Weekly Report,* May 22, 1976, pp. 1285–1307.
5. Congressional Quarterly, *The Washington Lobby,* 2d ed. (Washington, D.C.: Congressional Quarterly, Inc., 1974), p. 64.
6. Ibid., p. 65.
7. See *The American Rifleman* (August 1970): 52, also (December 1970): 22; and John Bibby and Roger Davidson *On Capitol Hill,* 2d ed. (Hinsdale, Ill.: Dryden Press, 1972), pp. 25–51.
8. Ibid., p. 50.
9. See Judith Robinson, "American Medical Political Action Committee," in *Political Brokers: People, Organizations, Money, Power,* ed. Judith Smith (New York: Liveright, 1972), p. 76.
10. Harry Scoble, *Ideology and Electoral Action* (San Francisco: Chandler Publishing, 1967), pp. 159–62.
11. Nicholas Masters, "Organized Labor Bureaucracy as a Base of Support for the Democratic Party," in *Pressure Groups in American Politics,* ed. H. R. Mahood (New York: Scribner's 1967), pp. 157–60.
12. Ibid., p. 158.
13. *New York Times,* February 19, 1975.
14. Jonathan Cottin and Charles Culhane, "Committee on Political Education," in *Political Brokers,* p. 108.
15. Masters, "Organized Labor Bureaucracy," pp. 156–57.
16. Herbert Alexander, *Money in Politics* (Washington, D.C.: Public Affairs Press, 1972), pp. 174–5.
17. *Christian Science Monitor,* March 9, 1973.

Chapter 6

Money for Access

Within a four-year cycle, Americans vote to fill over 500,000 public offices from dogcatcher to President of the United States. The total cost for 1972's national extravaganza was $400 million; the presidential candidates spent $94 million: forty-nine million by Richard Nixon, forty-five million by George McGovern— at a cost of $1 per voter. In this chapter we will consider the rules of this money game and how changes in the rules since 1971 have rearranged the starting positions of the players—the interest groups, the "fat cats," the politicians, and the political parties.

> Money itself is neutral. It gains political meaning only from the way it is used and the purposes sought through its use. . . . The operations of campaign financing are affected by shifts in the interests that assert claims through them . . . what sort of people want a part in financing political activities affects the ease of raising money, the procedures for doing so, and the rewards expected.[1]

For example, twenty-nine noncareer ambassadors contributed $1.8 million to Nixon's reelection campaign. Between 1972 and 1974 President Nixon appointed thirteen new noncareer ambassadors, eight of whom donated a minimum of $25,000 for a grand total of $706,000. The three ambassadors to the Benelux countries contributed $568,-000, which amounts to $22.05 per square mile for those small nations.

Despite disclaimers of any quid pro quo when asked at the Senate Watergate hearings why these people gave such large contributions, a typical reply was, "I cannot imagine that he would have given those kinds of monies without that belief [that he would be considered for an ambassadorship]." What's in it for them is the prestige, excitement, glamour of an ambassadorial post.

Another example concerns legal "persons"—corporations—not people. Corporations per se have been banned from making direct campaign contributions since a 1907 law was passed in the wake of insurance company scandals in 1900 and 1904. Yet in 1972 nineteen corporations and two dairy cooperatives were caught contributing $1.5 million in corporate funds to Nixon's reelection campaign. The total fines paid by the companies and individuals involved amounted to $149,000, or less than 4 percent of their total campaign contributions. In terms of personal penalties, the twenty-one individuals involved fared equally well: only two were discharged from their jobs; the rest are still drawing six-figure salaries and living the comfortable, corporate good life.[2] The question of what's in it for them relates less to those meaningless punishments and more to contributions as a means of translating economic power into political power. The incident illustrates several important aspects of relationships between economic institutions and political men.

To the politician, $100,000 contributions are crucial in terms of planning overall campaign strategy and allocating later fund-raising resources. To those corporations, all among *Fortune*'s 500, the need to raise instant cash may have been awkward in terms of their normal cash-flow procedures, but the amounts involved are "peanuts"—small enough to be hidden under expense accounts or insurance premiums. This discrepancy between the significance of the amount of money in economic and political terms has enabled corporate "persons" to use campaign contributions as a way to ensure their access to political persons, beyond that which might be available to them in terms of their employee voting power base or their economic strength in particular constituencies. Thus the raising of campaign money becomes entangled with the representational issue of whether money from special interests *should* short-circuit representation through the ballot box.

CAMPAIGN COSTS

There is "no neat correlation . . . between campaign expenditures and campaign results. . . . Yet it is clear that under some conditions the use of funds can be decisive. And under others, no amount of money spent by the loser could alter the outcome."[3] This is especially true in general elections where a basic amount of money is essential to secure competition, visibility, and voter education, but overall campaign resources also include party organization, the candidate's own personal resources (charisma, incumbency, past record), the issues, his alliances with groups and media in his district, and the level of development of his own campaign organization. Money helps because it has the advantages of "transferability" between geographic areas and "convertibility" into information, time, intelligence, visibility, even charisma—by buying others to substitute for candidate deficiencies in any of these areas.[4]

Nevertheless, money is most important in the nominating process where a basic amount of "up-front" money is needed in order to prove candidate viability, hire staff, and pay for early expenditures. Even to depend on direct mail for over one-half of all campaign money, as George McGovern did, requires money for the first letters. The importance of getting over this "choke point" is symbolized in souvenirs such as McGovern's sterling silver FMBM pin given to those responding to his first mailing. FMBM means "For McGovern Before Miami" (for McGovern before he was nominated by the party at the Democratic convention in Miami). AMPI's milk money was important to President Nixon precisely because it represented "one of the three largest and earliest pledges to his campaign at a time when he trailed in a presidential poll."[5] That $2 million pledge accounted for one-twentieth of his entire projected campaign budget of $40 million.

Pressure for the contributor's dollar has been heightened by the rapid escalation in campaign costs. Will Rogers observed: "It takes a lot of money to even get beat with." It has been said that Abraham Lincoln raised $200, spent 75¢ on a keg of cider, and gave back the rest. Today that $200 would buy only three seconds of prime time on television. The figures for total spending in presidential election years tell the tale—50 percent increases every four years—1964: $200 million; 1968: $300 million; 1972: $400 million.

One reason for the increase is the growth in the size, mobility, and ballot independence of the American voter. Pollster Lou Harris said that 1972 showed a "new, highly independent change group [as] the moving force in American politics." The calendar length of campaigns has also increased. A candidate running the primary route could appear in thirty-three primaries or state conventions beginning in New Hampshire during the first week of February in an election year. For example, Senator Walter Mondale declared his noncandidacy in 1974, two full years before the 1976 elections. Senator Henry Jackson began his fund-raising plans for election '76 in 1974 with a series of three-hour planning luncheons for key contributors and fund raisers, followed by local fund raisers in major cities, and culminating in a 1975 direct mail solicitation campaign. By mid-1975, Jackson had a pre-1976 war chest of $2.1 million.

Campaign techniques per se are also increasingly expensive. "In 1968 the Nixon-Agnew campaign was the 79th largest television advertiser . . . ranking between Schlitz Brewing Company and Monsanto. The Humphrey-Muskie campaign ranked 109th between Sperry-Rand and Standard Oil of N.J."[6] In 1972 sixty seconds of prime time on CBS cost between $40,000 and $55,000, which was the lowest commercial rate for such periods. In the same year both presidential candidates spent $1 million on polls to explore voter sentiment, $1 million on jet travel, $10.5 million for radio and television advertising, and $12 million for direct mail fund-raising solicitations. Contested elections, long primary fights, millionaire candidates, computer analyses of the electorate—all increase election costs, all intensify the need to generate money.

Candidates unanimously agree that soliciting funds is the most odious of all campaign duties. It is distasteful, time-consuming, demeaning, and tedious. Joseph Cole, national finance chairman of the Democratic National Committee told a House Elections Subcommittee hearing in 1973:

> I have seen the tribulations of trying to meet the expenses of a campaign.
>
> . . .
>
> I have sat next to the presidential candidate, who was tired, who was weary, and concerned with the issues and not able to handle them, not

> able to prepare, not able to think about them because he has to go downstairs at 7 in the morning to shake hands with a guy from whom he may get a large contribution.
> It goes on all day long and all night long, and I was asked at the Senate hearings how much time do you think a presidential candidate spends on fund raising? And I said at least 70 percent of his time, and I think all of his waking hours. It is really demeaning, demeaning to go through.

Much of the money for national elections is gathered through the auspices of the party's national finance committees; for congressional races, from congressional campaign committees. Both parties use direct mail solicitations and versions of "time payments"—for the Republicans it is "sustaining members" who give a fixed amount each year, for Democrats it is pledges paid over time. The Republicans also have a quota system whereby state parties pay money to the national committee. In return the national committee provides expertise and services such as polling, media assistance, and so forth.

The Democrats have been using fund-raising telethons in recent years. In 1974 the performance resulted in pledges of $7.1 million, receipts of $6.3 million. Both committees and candidates also raise money at campaign dinners ($5,000 per table), luncheons, breakfasts, and other social events. The congressional finance committees traditionally hold spring fund-raising dinners. In fact the above $100 threshold for reporting donations under the 1971 campaign law was designed to just exclude the basic dinner ticket price.

Contributors are divided into two categories: a small category of big givers, and a large category of little givers. Eighty percent of the money comes from the first category; 70 percent of all contributors belong in the second category. This relationship is indicated by the Republican budget created to guide fund raising in 1972. Targeted to raise $40 million, the chart suggested seven contributors of $1 million or more, 100 contributing $100,000 to $500,000, 125 contributing $50,000 to $99,000, 150 contributing $25,000 to $49,000, 100 contributing $10,000 to $24,000, 100 contributing $5,000 to $10,000, and 500 contributing $1,000 to $5,000. Thus, over half the money was to come from 107 individuals, while 4 percent was targeted to come from small contributors of $100 or less.[7] In 1972, 187 people each contributed over $50,000; 45 people gave the Democrats $7.5 million, 142 gave the Republicans $17.7 million.

WHY GIVE?

People give for a variety of reasons. The stereotyped notion of the politician's viewpoint was expressed by old-time Pennsylvania boss, Senator Boies Penrose: "I believe in a division of labor. . . . You send us to Congress; we pass laws . . . under which you make money, . . . and out of your profits you further contribute to our campaign funds to send us back again to pass more laws to enable you to make more money." A more modern politician, Jesse Unruh of California had a similar explanation: "The buddy system works. The rich and powerful know the rich and powerful. Political contributions are the singletree between the mule's ears; the singletree is there to get the mule's attention."

Large businesses often see campaign financing as a buffer to protect themselves against government action. "It is not so much that we want something done *for* us, as that we want to avoid having something done *to* us." Claude Wild, Jr., of Gulf Oil was more precise: "Sixty-one agencies of government have something to do with energy. . . . I did not think that we wanted to be discriminated against." William Powell of Mid-American Dairymen explained their $2 million pledge in more positive terms: "I have become increasingly aware that the soft and sincere voice of the dairy farmer is no match for the jingle of hard currencies put in the campaign funds of the politicians. . . . Whether we like it or not, this is the way the system works." The National Education Association (NEA) dabbled in contributions in 1972 for the first time and noticed some attitudinal changes. As their director, Stanley McFarland, put it: "It doesn't mean that we own them, of course, but the door is sure opened a little wider for us to get in and present our problems."

But economic access is not the only reason to contribute. A California lawyer-fund raiser gives eight candidate-related reasons for individuals to contribute:

> First . . . because they know the candidate personally. Second, because they like him or believe in him. A third group simply likes to feel involved. Another group is the problem solvers: they think they can solve the world's problems through the candidate. Then there is ego money: people who want to be seen around the candidate. There's

> loyalty money. It comes from people who know the guy's going to lose but they're going to stick by him. There's sure-thing money: people who want to be with a winner in anything. And there's just-in-case money, which comes from people who back one candidate but give money to the other, too, just in case he should win.[8]

Many of these contributors are "fat cats" (that is, wealthy individuals) who are already politically active, but want to assure themselves of personal access. Another California fundraiser, Eugene Wyman, explained that: "There's a tremendous ego trip involved with power. Generally the man who gives money doesn't ask for any business favors for himself, but he may want the candidate over for dinner or have him attend a wedding or bar mitzvah. All the donor wants to know is that if he wants to talk to somebody in power, he's got the access."

Presents to contributors touch this same vein. In 1972, $5,000 would bring the donor an RN pin with a diamond chip, $12,000 brought a pen and pencil set with an embossed seal and signature, $25,000 led to dinner at the White House, and $100,000 meant you were eligible for an invitation to take a federal appointment. George McGovern gave all contributors membership in his Million-Member Club complete with card and button, but for $10,000 one could join the Woonsocket Club and wear an 18-carat gold lapel pin.

Many contributors both large and small, from culled mailing lists or the $100,000 Club give to the party and candidate who agrees with their political philosophy. Stewart Mott, heir to a General Motors trust fund and philanthropist for liberal causes, spent close to $400,000 in 1968. In 1972 he said: "I am prepared to spend something on the order of $300,000 if things fall into place. I'm willing to open my checkbook widely and creatively." A similarly motivated contributor, movie theater heiress June Degnan, said, "I would have supported King Kong if he'd run against Lyndon Johnson." She gave Eugene McCarthy $60,000 and helped him raise $2 million more.

This motivation has led some commentators to define "ideological" contributors as

> one of the means by which the class power position of the corporate rich is maintained.... The greatest impact of election financing is on the

> attitudes of would-be candidates, who understand how necessary it is to get early money to start up their campaigns. . . . The big givers do not back those who might threaten the system. Campaign financing reinforces the system. . . .[9]

For example, in 1968 Stewart Mott wanted candidate Hubert Humphrey to change his Vietnam position in order to "qualify" for money. Humphrey refused. In 1968 both candidates were asked to support oil depletion allowance quotas as a precondition for financial assistance. Nixon pledged and received; Humphrey did neither.

A final reason why people give is that donors are dunned for money. This was exemplified in the approaches of the 1972 Nixon fundraisers. The Nixon Reelection Committee devised two corporate solicitation programs. The first emphasized the individual employee contribution approach, which neatly circumvented the corporate gift prohibition, yet enabled a pooling of company contributions so that "the combined contributions from you and your associates will maximize recognition of your group's support of the President."[10] The program generated $2,791,134 during the summer of 1972.

The second program covered the same terrain, except that industries rather than individual corporations were the targets. Industry leaders were selected to coordinate contributions, thus playing on interindustry competition for the presidential ear. The 1972 report on this program indicates that $7 million was raised. The nine most productive industries were pharmaceuticals, petroleum products, investment banking, trucking, textiles, carpets, automobile manufacturers, home builders, and insurance. Amounts ranged from a high of $885,000 to the insurance companies' contributions of $319,000. However, this list is misleading as indicated in a later study by Congressman Les Aspin. By his count, 178 oil companies and/or their officials contributed $5 million, or 10 percent of Nixon's total contributions.

Defense contractors would not play the 1972 industry pool game because none wanted another leader to get extra fund-raising credit. Defense contractors gave $2,555,740 to Republicans and $319,983 to Democrats. Forty-eight percent of this money was acquired in "secret" gifts prior to the April 7 deadline. However, regardless of the year, and despite the fact that the bureaucracy is predominantly

Democratic, the military-industrial complex usually donates primarily to Republicans. Perhaps their big business ideological ethic prevails over any notions of campaign access advantages, or perhaps the symbiotic relationship between the Pentagon and its contractors frees them from the obligation of giving money in order to secure access.

In pleading guilty to violation of the anticorporate contribution statute, American Airlines Chairman of the Board George Slater said:

> . . . Most contributions from the business community are not volunteered to seek a competitive advantage, but are made in response to pressure for fear of the competitive disadvantage that might result if they are not made.

Gulf lobbyist Claude Wild, Jr., said:

> I considered it considerable pressure when two Cabinet officers and an agent of one of the committees that was handling the election asked me on various occasions . . . for funds—that is just a little bit different than somebody collecting for the Boy Scouts.

RULES OF THE GAME

The revelations of Watergate abuses in the system of financing elections were made possible by revisions in the rules of the game. Until 1971 the process of contributing was regulated by sections of the Hatch Act and the Federal Corrupt Practices Act. These laws limited individual political contributions to a maximum of $5,000 per candidate per year and set strict limits on campaign expenditures for House, Senate, and presidential races. Corporations, unions, and government contractors were forbidden from making contributions. The Clerks of the House and Senate were designated as supervisory personnel, responsible for collecting reports on all contributions and expenditures of $100 or more by political committees (that is, those operating in two or more states on behalf of federal candidates in the general election). The law was such a sieve that writer Richard Harris said it "assures that the financial practices of practically everyone who attains national office will be corrupt."[11]

To circumvent contribution limitations, and escape gift taxes, individuals divided their money into contributions of $3,000 or less, sent to individually incorporated, virtuously named dummy political committees. For example, Nixon's main fund-raising committee had to keep track of 450 dummy committees set up to collect $3,000 contributions. One of the reasons AMPI never fulfilled its $2 million pledge was that the Republicans could not create separate committees fast enough. Each committee needed a charter, a chairman, a treasurer, and a bank account. To assure anonymity, the committees were organized in the District of Columbia, given innocuous names such as "Americans United for Honesty in Government," and employees of the banks involved rather than the members of reelection committee were used as officers.[12]

The law led to the $99.99 federal general election contribution special. State elections and all primaries were also excluded from the law so that money could be given in quantity during the primaries, and the surplus carried over. Political committees were incorporated in the District of Columbia or in only one state in order to evade reporting requirements. Candidates neglected to file expenditures exceeding the unrealistic 1925 limitations by using the loophole that money handled by treasurers without the candidate's "knowledge and consent" need not be reported. Using these guidelines, four senators officially reported no expenditures for their 1964 election campaigns. Parties circumvented the rule by creating multitudes of committees, each of which spent up to the legal limit. These evasions were practiced openly by everyone since the attorney general had never prosecuted a violator.

Then in 1971 the rules were changed. Common Cause sued both national party committees and the New York State Conservative Party for violating expenditure and contribution limitations. The Court gave the group standing to sue—the right to present its case as representatives of all Common Cause members interested "in maintaining the effectiveness of their votes." The impetus for reform that had been gathering since the 1968 election began to move in earnest. The Federal Election Campaign Act of 1971 closed many of the old loopholes such as the definition of political committee, set media expenditure limits for campaigns, eliminated the challenged contribution and expenditure limitations, and provided for an expanded and reinforced disclosure system of contributions or expenditures in excess of $100. However, practical politics—collection of maximum amounts of anonymous money—delayed the President's signature on the bill until February 7, 1972, which meant that the law went into effect on April 7, 1972, after five primaries and numerous fund-raising dinners had taken place. Stringent monitoring of disclosure processes by Common Cause, and strict procedures established by the supervisory officers who now included members of the General Accounting Office, led to the most accurate record of expenses to date. It also revealed the inadequacy of disclosure as a way to prevent abuses of the contribution process.

In 1974 the Federal Election Campaign Act Amendments created a new ball game for 1976: strict limits on individual and group or corporate contributions, stringent expenditure limitations, an independent enforcement agency to supervise the law, and a system of mixed public and private financing of presidential elections.

The day the new law took effect, Senator James Buckley, former Senator Eugene McCarthy, and nine other individuals, third parties, and interest groups that participate in elections challenged the constitutionality of all major provisions of the 1974 Amendments. It took a year for the case to proceed through the courts. During that time probable candidates for 1976 and the newly created Federal Election Commission (FEC) proceeded to implement the law as it stood. On January 30, 1976, one week before the New Hampshire primary, the first presidential primary of the 1976 season, the Supreme Court upheld most of the new law: contribution limits, public financing of presidential elections, the principle of an independent enforcement commission, and mandatory comprehensive disclosure requirements.

Citing the need to spend money to implement the free speech concept, the Justices eliminated expenditure limitations for candidates (unless they chose to accept public subsidies in which case they also had to accept the private money-raising limitations attached as conditions), and permitted individual citizens to spend unlimited amounts for candidates and issues as long as they were completely independent of any candidate's campaign. The Court also required the joint presidential-congressional nomination method for FEC commissioners in the 1974 Amendments be rewritten to conform to the traditional presidential nomination/Senate approval method that preserved the constitutional notion of separated powers. Benignly, the court gave Congress a thirty-day grace period to enact this simple change; passage of the 1976 Amendments took 111 days.

A look at the impact of rules changes on union and corporate campaign contributions illustrates the important political consequences of changes in language.[13]

The 1925 Corrupt Practices Act

Under this law, corporations and unions could create separate, segregated political action committees (PACs) to solicit and make contributions. However if they held government contracts, they could not establish PACs. Unions took advantage of this provision to establish COPE and its counterparts. Corporations were less ambitious; those that did create PACs funded them by inviting/urging/coercing employes to donate money to company good government funds from which campaign donations were made to company friends. For example, Electronic Data Systems Corporation, a computer firm, funneled $100,000 into the presidential campaign of Wilbur Mills through seventeen dummy committees with names such as "Fiscal Sanity Committee." At Chemical Bank/New York Trust Company, vice-presidents and above were invited to give to the company Fund for Good Government. Monsanto Corporation used a payroll deduction plan from 1968–1975, wherein amounts were extracted monthly from executive paychecks and put in special accounts in a local bank. Union Oil Company of California and TRW, a large defense contractor, had similar payroll deduction plans for employees. At Union Carbide a letter went from executives to their division managers urging "voluntary" contributions.

These funds gave up to $100,000 in thousand-dollar lots or less to friends. A Union Carbide official explained the general rationale for the fund and listed their criteria for giving assistance:

> As citizens we feel we have an obligation to support candidates [in states and districts] where we have production facilities. . . . If they are going to win, if they have been helpful in the past, reasonable on issues, we will find people in the corporation who will help these guys.[14]

Corporations unwilling to go to the trouble of setting up PACs had two other ways of securing campaign funds. The first one required employees to give "independently," as separate individuals. In 1972 American Shipbuilding Company created fictitious bonuses for eight employees who gave the money, less taxes and deductions, to the Committee to Reelect the President. The transaction was papered over with backdated memoranda, creation of a new real bonus plan, and entry of some expenditures under "research."

ITT had a similar plan. In 1960, one of the executives, Mr. Naylor, was designated to give, but refused to perform. The initial memorandum to him stated that: "Hal has given me a selected list of top executives to contribute to the election campaign. You are down for $1,200. This can be financed for you by the company if necessary. . . . You will be expected to recover the amount by covering it up in your traveling expense account." When Mr. Naylor refused, Geneen replied, "Well everybody does it. It's paying off big in Washington."

Using the second method, corporations funneled money through company lawyers or public relations firms, which covered up the transactions with fictitious expenses such as the dairymen's lawyers did in the case of AMPI contributions. Or money was hidden under false entries. Thus:

- 3M Company hid a $634,000 fund from 1963 to 1973 by keeping it on the books as insurance premiums and payments to foreign legal counsel.
- Northrop Corporation, a defense contractor, laundered over $1.2 million between 1961 and 1973 by passing it through a Paris-based consulting firm.
- Gulf Oil Company laundered its money through its Bahamas subsidiaries.
- Ashland Oil Company, Phillips Petroleum, and Goodyear Tire and Rubber Company all used the Swiss bank route.
- American Airlines charged its slush fund of $275,000, used between 1964 and 1973, to entertainment costs.
- Braniff International Airways balanced off $1 million by selling 3,626 airline tickets that were never registered on the company's books.

The 1971 Federal Election Campaign Act (FECA)

Although this legislation kept the provision of the 1925 law that permitted noncontractors to establish PACs, it eliminated the contractor clause completely. Immediately contractors entered the void and established PACs. Common Cause challenged TRW, a major defense contractor with a long-standing PAC, and won; TRW dissolved its PAC. But labor became worried, since a majority of the major unions as well as a majority of the top 500 corporations have government contracts.

The 1974 FECA Amendments

Changes included permission for all corporations and unions to establish PACs. The law limited contributions from a PAC to $5,000 per candidate per election but did not specify whether it applied to one PAC per entity or whether regional or state or conglomerate subdivisions could establish "sub-PACs." Individuals could contribute only $1,000 per candidate per election for a maximum of $25,000 per year, so business quickly decided to put PACs into the "fat cat" void. As UAW counsel Stephen Schlossberg said: "You can't buy a candidate for $1,000 or $5,000. You can't even rent one for that. But if you could proliferate [PACs] for $40,000 or $50,000, maybe you could rent one for awhile."

On November 18, 1975, the FEC ruled in response to a Sun Oil Company request for clarification that businesses could solicit voluntary contributions from both employees and stockholders to be distributed by management to candidates of their choice. Given the green light, and educated at Chamber of Commerce seminars on the mechanics of creating legal PACs, business entered the field of special interest campaign contribution committees. Eighty-nine such committees existed in 1974; by October 1976, there were about 500.

Labor and political interest groups also wasted no time in adding PACs: between January and October 1976 labor PACs increased from 160 to 225. Where formerly several broadly based funds would serve as umbrella money brokers for everyone, now each interest wanted its own PAC. Overall 246 new PACs were created in 1975 for a total of 745 in existence. By September 1976, 1041 PACs were in operation.

The 1976 Amendments

The 1976 Amendments dashed such hopes. A PAC and all its subsidiaries were held to the $5,000 per candidate/per election maximum. The manner of fund-raising solicitations was also spelled out: corporations can solicit contributions from stockholders and their families and from managerial, professional, supervisory, and administrative personnel without limitations; unions can do the same for their members and families. Twice a year both kinds of PACs may make written solicitations of all employees in a corporation, so long as anonymity of the donors is maintained. All corporations, unions, and other interest groups must disclose any expenditures for internal political communications to members if the amount spent exceeds $2,000 during an election period.

Ironically the laws that were passed to erase the impact of special interest money in electoral politics have become instead a boon to a new breed of electoral interest group—the corporations. Instead of eliminating such influence, the changes have encouraged expenditure of ever-increasing amounts of special interest money. A look at some figures is illustrative. In 1972, 153 individuals gave $20 million to President Nixon's reelection campaign; in 1974, 24 individuals gave over $25,000 to assorted congressional candidates; in 1976, no one gave more than $1,000 to any candidate in presidential primaries, and the presidential election was financed solely with public funds from the presidential tax-check-off fund. In 1972 labor made donations of $8.5 million ($4 million in congressional races); in 1974 labor PACs gave away $6.3 million; in 1975, gearing up for 1976, $6.6 million was on hand by December 31st; and by October 1, 1976, labor PACs had spent $5.8 million in congressional races. Business PACs contributed $4.5 million in 1974, and had $8.8 million on hand at the end of 1975. By October 1, 1976 business, professional, and agricultural PACs had spent $7.5 million in congressional campaigns, almost $2 million more than their labor counterparts. Overall, direct contributions to congressional candidates in 1976 totalled between $22–23 million, twice the $12.5 million lavished on congressional races in 1974. It is estimated that corporate and business PACs alone will give triple the amount of money in 1978 that they gave in 1974. Clearly the new law has made the PAC access technique both legal and lucrative.

ALLOCATING FUNDS

Although PACs give money in the name of assorted interests—business, civic groups, ideological organizations, professional associations, and issue groups—certain uniformities exist within categories. First, most of the noncorporate economic funds are supplied by dues from members of the affiliated, nonprofit, tax-exempt organization or from voluntary contributions, such as union member $2 tickets that are sent to COPE, the AFL-CIO's political fund. Ideological funds draw from established mailing lists because most have only a small membership base. Problems occur when too many groups/unions/associations solicit the same people for contributions. One fund raiser labeled the problem "the incestuousness of their mailing lists."[15]

Second, recipients are generally selected either by the fund's board of directors, for example, Business Industry PAC (BIPAC) the National Committee for an Effective Congress (NCEC), or by local and state committees that forward suggestions to the national level, American Medical PAC (AMPAC), COPE. The method used seems to develop out of the parental organization's structure. Federated groups such as the AMA or AFL-CIO place more emphasis on grass roots participation, secure more funds through local fund raising, and combine the monetary emphasis with political participation activities designed to involve their members in the electoral process.

The level of the electoral races in which groups involve themselves also seems to follow this principle; thus AMPAC and COPE (national PACs in federated organizations), give to both state and federal candidates, while BIPAC, NCEC, and other unitary national groups focus on Congress alone.

> Political money flows according to strategy designed to have the most effect with the fewest dollars. As the Senate is relatively liberal and visible and has power in foreign affairs, Senate contests are of interest to groups such as the National Committee for an Effective Congress or the Council for a Livable World. On the other hand, since the House tends to be conservative and often can exercise an effective brake on liberal legislation, conservative groups such as BIPAC and AMPAC send "veto dollars" to legislators who are in key positions to block or revise bills.[16]

Criteria for selection of candidates involves considerations such as the issue orientation of the candidate, chances for success, potential as an ally if elected, and political party affiliation. The exact weighing of these factors provides the major differences among the groups. Specific labor unions tend to concentrate on congressmen sitting on committees that enact legislation of interest to that union. Trade associations also give to key committee members, primarily incumbents, although they often hedge their bets by giving to both sides. Ideological groups target funds for key districts where a challenger with their viewpoint might oust an incumbent of the other persuasion. Corporations fall someplace between ideological groups and single industry unions or associations; they never give to both sides in the same race, and frequently give money to "home state" representatives rather than relevant committee members. [17]

Third, although the total amount of money given through campaign committees has steadily increased from $5.7 million in 1964 to $12.5 million in 1974, individual PACs tend to give approximately the same size gifts to recipients regardless of the year or the total amount the committee has to spend: several thousand dollars in Senate races, $500 to $2,500 in House races. A few groups also single out a handful of key races for extra-large contributions; for example, in 1974 AMPI gave $32,000 to Congressman David Bowen's campaign (he is a freshman member of the dairy subcommittee). Labor gave the most primary election money ($168,700) in 1974 to millionaire Howard Metzenbaum to defeat John Glenn in Ohio; Glenn still won. Between May and August, the unions apologized for guessing wrong by donating $75,400 to Glenn.

The big three among the special economic interest campaign committees are COPE, BIPAC, and AMPAC.

COPE (Committee on Political Education), representing the AFL-CIO, was organized in 1943 as the first political action arm of a political interest group. It still commands more manpower, money, and electoral clout than any of its imitators. Its goal, according to Director Alexander Barkan, "is to win elections not arguments. I look on myself as a political pragmatist. I want to win. I'm not interested in winning arguments and losing elections."[18] COPE usually distributes $1 million among all congressional candidates: approximately

$10,000 to senatorial candidates, $2,500 to candidates for the House. In 1976, COPE endorsed 28 Senate and 362 House candidates; 68 percent of their Senate candidates won, 71 percent of those for the House.

BIPAC (Business-Industry Political Action Committee) was formed in 1963 to counteract COPE. Affiliated with the National Association of Manufacturers, its contributions go to representatives, usually Republicans, in close races, "where our money may tip the scales."[19] Candidates must also believe in "protection of 'the principle of individual freedom' and [pledge] to 'represent the competitive, free enterprise viewpoint.'"[20] In 1976 BIPAC spent approximately $300,-000 in 18 Senate and 105 House races, with special concentration on 8 Senate and 20 House seats. Although their overall level of success was 56 percent in the Senate and 43 percent in the House, they only won 25 percent of their important Senate contests, and 20 percent of the important House seats.

AMPAC (American Medical Political Action Committee) was created in 1961 as an offshoot of the AMA to educate doctors to be politically active and to provide assistance to candidates for political office. AMPAC was designed to buy the "right to a dialogue,"[21] so although most of their money goes to representatives who support the AMA viewpoint, some goes to strategically located opponents in order to secure access. Money is usually given to incumbents in competitive races. Between 1972 and 1974, AMPAC gave $1.5 million to 300 congressional candidates; in 1974 its contributions of $1.5 million made it the largest special interest contributor. In 1976 AMPAC again spent over $1 million in congressional races.

Among ideological/issue committees, liberal groups are better financed, larger, and more numerous than their conservative counterparts. Some of them developed from an issue base such as the antiwar movement, conservation, or equality for women. The biggest and oldest group is NCEC (National Committee for an Effective Congress), organized in 1948 to elect liberal legislators. It raises money from an 80,000-person mailing list. In 1976, NCEC endorsed 100 House candidates and 13 Senate candidates. They won in 69 percent of their Senate races, 73 percent of the House seats.

Its conservative counterpart would be ACA, Americans for Constitutional Action, founded in 1959. However, an ideological split within conservative ranks has left ACA destitute, able to contribute "in-kind" services, but no money. Instead, the Conservative Victory Fund, established in 1970, gave approximately $125,000 to twenty-three House candidates and three Senate candidates, all Republicans who are "ideologically pure."[22] ACA supported 10 Senate candidates and 153 House contenders in 1976. Half their candidates won Senate seats; 79 percent of their House candidates won. However, another ideologically conservative group, the Committee for the Survival of a Free Congress, spent $250,000 in 62 House races, and won in only 18 percent of them.

THE QUID PRO QUO

In the 1972 congressional elections, money from political campaign committees accounted for $9.7 million (14 percent) of the $69.7 million reported by the candidates.[23] PACS contributed $8.4 million directly to candidates, $1.3 million indirectly through congressional campaign committees. Business, agricultural, and professional committees accounted for $3.3 million; labor for $3.6 million; and ideological/issue groups for $1.5 million. The economic sectors spent more on winners than losers, perhaps because they favored incumbents—business giving them 60 percent of their funds, labor 53 percent. Approximately one-quarter of labor PAC funds went to no-incumbent races. The miscellaneous ideological/issue category split their funds almost evenly: 36 percent challengers, 33 percent incumbents, 31 percent no-incumbent races. Political party biases of business and labor were also evident: business favored Republicans 2:1; labor favored Democrats 8:1. In 1974 similar practices prevailed although all groups increased the total amounts spent and labor put an emphasis on supporting challengers in order to create a "veto-proof" Congress (bringing the "incumbent-challenger" support ratio down to 2:1). In 1976 the "liberal" organizations (COPE, NCEC, ADA, UAW) and the "conservative" organizations (ACA, BIPAC, CSFC, NCPAC) duplicated contributions for only 12 candidates. Nine of the 12 were incumbents, 8 were Democrats, 11 were winners. Only Rosling, a Republican from Hawaii, with contributions from COPE, BIPAC and NCPAC, lost. This small percentage of duplication, a dozen men among approximately a thousand candidates, suggests the thoughtfulness of PAC contribution patterns, and the tendency of congressmen to have definite records which lead to their cultivation by mutually exclusive combinations of interests.

Common Cause data on the 1972 congressional elections indicate that the average expenditure by incumbent House candidates was $60,000. So what did the special interest group get for its $1,000 or even $5,000 (8 percent) contribution? Even a cynic would have to assume that to buy any self-respecting representative would cost more than $1,000. Muckrakers tote up examples of money given and votes recorded, but is the correlation as simple as that?

In 1974 the Maritime Union political committee divided $333,300 among 141 representatives who voted for the Energy Security Transportation Act which would have required that 20 to 30 percent of oil imports be transported in American ships. Was this money thanks for past services or a prepayment on the future? New Jersey Democrat, Senator Harrison Williams raised $34,600 from a securities industry fund raiser in 1975 at the same time that legislation affecting the industry was before his committee, and two weeks after he amended the bill to their liking. Was the $34,600 a coincidence or a bribe? Is the timing difference between these two examples significant?

Alabama Senator John Sparkman attracted most of his campaign funds in 1972 from out-of-state interests under the jurisdiction of his Banking, Housing, and Urban Affairs Committee because, if he lost, Senator William Proxmire, known for his antibusiness stance, would have become committee chairman. If the funds had all been from groups within Alabama, would this be a less obvious case of self-interest? The UAW wanted to defeat the Fisher amendment to the 1975 energy bill, which would have placed penalty taxes on "gas guzzler" cars after 1977: among the forty-three recipients of $2,000 each in 1974 UAW funds, twenty-two voted against the amendment and nineteen voted for it.

To accept the direct causal relationship interpretation between campaign donations and helpful votes is to ignore many equally relevant forces—ideological compatibility, district economic needs, the sequential piecemeal form of congressional decision making, the need for available factual information, party cues, and so on. In most cases the contribution suggests a close relationship between politician and interest group based on a shared identification of values, economic views, friends—indeed the common ground that led to contributions in the first place.

Looking at it from another angle, interests do not buy big votes—war or peace—but on small issues, of importance to a contributor, and irrelevant to the representative, the representative will probably go along. As Maryland Senator Charles Mathias explained it:

> Where it counts is in the small votes—the ones that don't seem so important. Say there is a bill to make 100,000 acres of public timberland in Wyoming available to the lumber people. . . . I don't care very much because the case doesn't affect Maryland directly. So then a lumber dealer in Baltimore who gave me $1,000 in the last election comes and presents the lumber people's side. I might think, Oh, well it's a trivial thing to me and important to him that I might as well go along.[24]

SUMMARY

This chapter has focused on money—in the form of campaign contributions—as a political resource. We have examined the various reasons why people contribute money—economic, ideological, psychological—and the ways in which candidates raise money—by mail, through interest group contacts, or from the small number of wealthy Americans who contribute to politics. *Money buys access, not influence.* Money provided at key points, such as early in the campaign, enables an individual to create a viable campaign.

However, money alone cannot win campaigns. Money alone cannot assure continued meaningful access to officials unless other factors such as commonality of interests, useful information, and friendship develop to supplement the campaign donation. Whether money *should* buy access is a value question related to one's view of the proper way for meshing assorted needs and interests into the policy process.

Before considering the normative issues, in the next section we will turn to groups actually lobbying in the public policy-making process in order to assess both their options and actions.

NOTES

1. Alexander Heard, *The Costs of Democracy* (Chapel Hill, N.C.: University of North Carolina Press, 1968), pp. 3, 12.
2. *New York Times,* August 24, 1975.
3. Heard, *The Costs of Democracy,* p. 16.
4. David Adamany, *Campaign Finance in America* (North Scituate, Mass: Duxbury Press, 1972), pp. 2–3; see also chap. 3.
5. Senate Select Committee, *The Senate Watergate Report,* vol. 2 (New York: Dell, 1974), p. 302.
6. "Comment: The Federal Election Campaign Act of 1971: Reform of the Process?" *Georgetown Law Journal* 60(1972): 1309.
7. Senate Select Committee, *Senate Watergate Report,* p. 83.
8. *Time,* October 23, 1972, p. 29.
9. David Nichols, *Financing Elections: The Politics of an American Ruling Class* (New York: New View Points, 1974), pp. 7, 49.
10. See Maurice Stans' letter to corporation officers, Senate Select Committee, *Senate Watergate Report,* p. 127.
11. R. Harris, "Annals of Politics—A Fundamental Hoax," *The New Yorker,* August 7, 1971, p. 37.
12. Senate Select Committee, *Senate Watergate Report,* p. 318.
13. Information in this section comes from Common Cause, *In Common* (Spring 1976), pp. 3–14, and from interview data regarding 1976 contributions.
14. W. Pincus, "Silent Spenders in Politics—They Really Give at the Office," *New York,* January 31, 1972, p. 40.
15. Congressional Quarterly, *Dollar Politics,* vol. 2 (Washington, D.C.: Congressional Quarterly, Inc., 1974), p. 54.
16. Herbert Alexander, *Money in Politics* (Washington, D.C.: Public Affairs Press, 1972), p. 177.
17. *National Journal,* April 10, 1976, p. 475.
18. Jonathan Cottin and Charle Culhane, "Committee on Political Education," in *Political Brokers: People, Organizations, Money, Power,* ed. Judith Smith (New York: Liveright, 1972), p. 90. The 1976 data on COPE, BIPAC, AMPAC, NCEC, and ACA come from *Congressional Quarterly Weekly Report,* November 6, 1976, pp. 3136–44.
19. Ibid., p. 128.
20. Ibid., p. 123.
21. Ibid., p. 76.
22. See Congressional Quarterly, *The Washington Lobby,* 2d ed. (Washington, D.C.: Congressional Quarterly, Inc., 1974), pp. 61–72.

23. These statistics are from Common Cause press releases for their 1972 and 1974 election monitoring project or Lester Sobel, ed., *Money and Politics: Contributions, Campaign Abuses and The Law* (New York: Facts on File, Inc., 1974).
24. Harris, "Annals of Politics," p. 48.

III

Public Policy: Process and Product

Chapter 7

Making Private Problems Public

So far we have been considering groups per se and the access techniques they use to develop their positions within the public policy-making process. With this chapter, we will shift our focus to groups at work within the public policy-making process. As sketched in Chapter 1, the policy process resembles a three-dimensional tick-tack-toe board with multiple decision-making centers on three levels of government. Add to this a concept of working relationships based on issue agreements and conflicts rather than on the hierarchial paths of formal organization charts. Then superimpose a decision-making attitude that deals with all of this structural complexity by focusing on small, specific aspects of multifaceted problems so that the number of decision-making points required to coordinate a solution is thereby diminished. The sum is a process in which it is easier for government to consider, one by one, national highway speed limits, oil depletion allowances, atomic energy plant safety, and strip-mining practices than to coordinate all four as aspects of a total national energy production and conservation policy. The public policy-making system well deserves the adjectives most commonly used to describe it: open-ended, pluralistic, government-by-whirlpool, fragmented, incremental, fluid, evolving, constantly changing.

For a political interest group, the organized chaos of this tick-tack-toe system presents unlimited lobbying options. Groups take advantage of the fragmentation to use different techniques at different points in the policy process. However, for purposes of analysis, we will reduce the process to one level—the national government—and then artificially simplify it by considering policy making by stages although in reality all parts of the process and all decision-making centers move simultaneously.

In the following chapters the total policy-making process is divided into separate stages: agenda building, the process of moving a problem from the general social, economic, and cultural scenes to public decision-making centers; as well as four stages of the public policy process —problem identification, program development, policy implementation, and policy evaluation. This chapter continues with a survey of the kinds of public policy choices that lobbying groups face, followed by examination of the initial stage of agenda building. Chapters 8 and 9 will focus on group-institutional relationships, Chapter 10 on policy implementation and evaluation.

THE PUBLIC POLICY PROCESS AND LOBBYING CHOICES

Groups must select the best times and places for lobbying. "Best" means many things: it is related to group goals, resources, timing both in terms of internal cohesiveness needs, and in terms of decision-making stages and environmental conditions such as competition, cooperation, friendliness, hostility from officials and other groups. "Best" translates into group choices that can be separated for analysis into two types, although again in reality they are interrelated. Choice 1 concerns the locus for action: what stages of the process, what institutional forum(s), and what specific subset(s) of policy players. Choice 2 requires a decision as to the type of government response that the group wants: subsidies for itself, regulation for all those in a category of business or type of activity, or manipulative policies that use the implicit threat of strong governmental sanctions to force groups to act against their own selfish interests or realign those interests in terms of a perceived public need.

The term *public policy-making process* refers to a series of goal-oriented activities that occur in, among, and around governmental institutions.[1] A specific policy topic passes through various decision-making centers, each of which has sufficient power to affect an idea in passing, but insufficient authority to mandate acceptance of its viewpoint on others involved in the process. The four stages of policy making are linked in circular fashion since evaluation leads to identification of new problems which initiates the process again. But the fact that the sequence is continuous does not imply that it need be logical or orderly. Personnel, stages of development, and time sequences intertwine much as characters in a television soap opera interrelate. In both cases an actor or issue may take center stage for weeks or months and then fade away. Observers know that the actor or issue still exists, offstage, because of frequent references by the current cast, but it may be months before the actor reappears. Similarly political interest groups appear and reappear in the policy process. The pattern of their behavior may seem to have no overall purpose from an outsider's perspective, but it usually reflects groups' Choice 1 and Choice 2 decisions.

Choice 1

Just selecting an institutional framework provides an array of alternatives. A group may focus on legislative, bureaucratic, judicial, or White House decision-making arenas; for example, the dairymen went first to the White House executive office to get milk price support parity levels. Or groups may lobby two arenas at the national level; thus the dairymen worked simultaneously with President Nixon *and* with midwestern congressmen in their bid to maintain the parity price. Or a group may take advantage of the three levels of government in our federal system to focus on institutional arenas at different levels of government. This can be done in a cooperative way as when New York City, lobbying for money to end its descent toward bankruptcy, sought state legislation as a necessary precondition for federal aid legislation. Or it can be done competitively: no-fault insurance advocates unable to secure national legislation used state legislatures to implement their goal.

Within any institution a group must pinpoint the best decision-making center. Groups interested in writing legislation may work with the relevant congressional subcommittee or bureaucratic subdivision. Those groups entering the process at a later stage may work on staff revisions of legislation, try to block further committee or floor action, or seek modifications when policy reaches the implementation stage. Thus, "right to life" groups, seemingly stymied at all points in the decision-making process, were able to have an amendment inserted into the 1976 Labor-HEW appropriations bill that prohibits the use of public funds (for example, Medicare) to pay for abortions unless the life of the mother is endangered. By tagging a controversial policy issue to a necessary appropriation bill, the group was able to make a policy gain.

In a book written to advise Washington corporate representatives (lobbyists), Lewis Dexter warns against lobbying in Congress except "when the executive department is almost uniformly hostile and when there is some access to the Congress. . . . The important consideration, of course, is what alternative courses of nonlobbying action are open . . . where the chances of success are better."[2] This advice suggests that Choice 1 decisions generate sequential activities, but they may also lead to simultaneous activity on separate institutional fronts as illustrated by the dairymen and ITT.

Choices related to the locus of action also include calculations of the best time to enter the process. When a group initiates an idea, it has the luxury of plotting the entire path through all processes and policy centers. Usually, however, a group learns of an issue in midstream and has to make immediate decisions based on existing limitations. Or a group finds that its policy plan has been checked by counterplans from other groups or other issues that intersect with its own proposal. Keeping such complications in mind, let us run down the sequence of policy-making stages from the group's perspective.

Problem identification is a crucial stage because the way in which personal, individual problems are expanded into general issues requiring public attention will determine their governmental path from problem to policy. Problems move from private troubles to demands for public action when people perceive that the problem is too large to be handled personally or when it is assumed that governmental assistance will produce a better solution. As the "sponsor" group approaches government for support on an agreed need or to settle some disagreement, the choice of governmental representative is crucial. Generally groups sponsoring new ideas seek someone who agrees with their viewpoint to carry their problem into the policy process. A friend, with similar views is crucial because the choice of government spokesperson, and that person's location in the policy-making process, can determine both the official definition of the specific issue to be settled and the kind of government response that might be used.[3]

Program development is the stage at which the outside problem is taken into the public policy process and a solution formulated for consideration by Congress and the President in their capacities as representatives of the people. Thus, it is a two-part process. First, some part of the bureaucracy or a congressional subcommittee *formulates* a plan to meet those aspects of the problem that have been defined as needing immediate attention. Since earlier we characterized the policy-making process as spasmodic, incremental, and cautious, it is logical to assume that most planners (unless faced with a crisis) will nibble at problems, preferring to resolve those sections of the issue that can be integrated into existing structures, existing interest group-bureaucracy arrangements, existing perceptions of similar problems. Many ideas never get farther along in the policy process than this point. They remain ideas that have not been redefined into a proposal with a plan and a price tag.

Once a plan is formulated, it must be accepted by Congress in its capacity as representative of the people. This procedure is called *legitimation.* It may take one year, or many years, or an idea may be kicked around in various proposed forms and never become law. Medicare spent twenty years in the development process; the Equal Rights Amendment was introduced yearly from 1923 till 1972 (nearly fifty years) until it was finally approved by Congress for ratification by the states. The attrition rate is very high: generally only about 3 percent of the thousands of proposals introduced yearly in Congress survive to become public laws.

The legitimation procedure is accomplished by sending the plan through the gauntlet of congressional subcommittees, committees, House and Senate floor votes, and presidential acceptance of the final product. In this process, different sets of officials touch base with groups of importance to them, thereby providing opportunities for previously unrepresented interests to affect the policy. Thus the procedures are designed to "ensure that decisions made are traceable to a numerical majority. That is not to say that a majority of the citizenry is actively involved in making policy, but rather that, at several points along the way to policy, numerical majorities are formed. The result is a system of layers of numerical majorities. . . ."[4]

The cumulative effect of this process presumes that all groups, individuals, and interests considered relevant by the official decision-makers will have had input into the process. Representational problems arise when groups that feel a problem is relevant to their concerns are not similarly perceived by government officials and so are not invited to participate. Or when relevant interests lack the organizational base and resources to participate. Or when relevant ideas are excluded because they or their group have not been accepted into the general policy milieu surrounding a specific policy decision. Or when a specific interest group can checkmate a collection of numerically large groups because it has the power to stop action at a necessary point in the process.

Despite the seeming specificity of legal language, most laws are written to permit a maximum amount of administrative flexibility in interpreting congressional intent. *Policy implementation* thus becomes a series of administrative rulings and court decisions (often incorporated in later legislation), the content of which reflects the structure of the administrative agency, its dominant clientele groups, and its level of subject matter expertise. As in preceding parts of the process, decision makers bend over backward to cultivate obvious support groups and placate vocal antagonists. Quite often new groups, not included in the program development stage, may be successful in influencing the development of policy substance through implementation.

The vast amount of administrative discretion created by "thou shalt" statutory language provides opportunities for bureaucrats to take the cautious path of incrementalism and least resistance, and thus content themselves with "symbolic" administration of the new laws. Laws administered symbolically use guidelines that make minimal changes in the status quo, as contrasted with an aggressive application of congressional intent that might shake up the status quo. Both forms of administrative action—the aggressive and symbolic—often coexist because, while political activity means concrete benefits for a few specific groups, for the masses it produces only symbols.

For example, school desegregation actually affects only that small percentage of the population with children in racially unbalanced schools, but the Supreme Court's decisions are interpreted by all the spectator-masses to fit their own needs of expression. Thus the same act may symbolize bigotry or equality, discrimination or favoritism to different segments of the mass public. When President Nixon told the Department of Health, Education, and Welfare in 1974 to stall administrative implementation of desegregation by deemphasizing busing, he was having an actual effect on perhaps 10 percent of the population, a symbolic effect on the other 90 percent.

In the fourth stage of the policy-making process, *policy evaluation,* those who initiated the process, those who developed the policy, and those who feel its effects judge the activity in terms of its original goals and its current repercussions. The notion of evaluation may be summarized in the saying that generals always fight the last war; that is, they act in the present on the basis of evaluations of the most recent past. So, too, domestic policy is considered in relation to what preceded it as well as in terms of what might have been.

Legislators, administrators, journalists, interest groups, and affected individuals all evaluate a program using criteria such as costs in terms of time, money, manpower; relief from the original situation; political support for the policy; and any new problems it generates. Various institutionalized forms of evaluation exist such as congressional oversight of administrative activities, program budgeting that allocates dollars so as to ensure dollar value for services, and presidential commissions to provide ad hoc judgments of currently volatile situations. Often outside evaluations by the media, muckrakers, researchers, or the affected population spark the official reviews; for example, Ralph Nader has become synonymous with the role of administrative gadfly, exposing rot in programs such as food inspection, mine safety, and nuclear energy plant safety systems.

Since situations change over time, and the lag between the initial perception and this reexamination may be several years, most public problems do not self-destruct in the sense that the first solution eliminates the initial problem and is in turn eliminated also. Consequently reactions at this final stage usually range along a continuum from simple satisfaction with the plan as it is to procedural/technical modifications to resolution of related but new problems to total reformulation of the policy. Thus, policy making proceeds as a continual recycling of demands involving outside groups and official government representatives in the selection of solutions based on "proximite choices and limited information. . . ."[5] Political-interest groups use their lines of access to enter those decision-making centers and those policy stages where they feel their position will be most influential.

Choice 2

Group calculations in Choice 1 (what forums? what actors?) are related to this second choice, policy objectives, because the kind of government policy requested depends to a considerable extent on which decision makers and structures the group believes will respond to the affected interests. A group may ask government to act in one of four ways: first to remain uninvolved in the problem (noninvolvement is itself a form of action). If government action is desired, the narrowest policy involves *subsidies* to the petitioning group; a broader form of policy *regulates* an entire industry or activity; the broadest form uses regulations and subsidies to *manipulate* an entire reward system in order to benefit currently disadvantaged groups.

Subsidies harness the individual's profit motive to governmental goals by providing government payments to induce increases in specific activities. For example, farmers are paid subsidies to encourage them *not* to plant certain crops; oilmen are given tax advantages (read "subsidies") in order to encourage oil exploration. Medicare, Medicaid, food stamps, mass transportation capital grants, and "buy American" trade policies are all subsidies because, in each instance, the government is paying individuals to participate in specific government policies. The total cost for major federal subsidies in FY1970 was $64.4 billion, for FY1975 it was estimated at $95 billion.

Regulation affects categories of interests as interests rather than through individuals' behavior. Regulation sets the conditions under which certain activities may take place. Generally speaking, if the purpose of subsidies is to encourage action, the purpose of regulations is to discourage it. Antitrust, labor mediation rules, transportation rates, minimum standards for food and drug purity, clean water and sulfur-free air are all governed by federal regulations that seek to set a federally mandated minimum standard of acceptable behavior. Regulations are more visible than subsidies since they apply to entire industries, enabling those within the regulated sphere to jockey for advantage, those outside to compare their position with the regulated. The key political issue in regulation relates to the way in which the rules (for example, licensing, taxation, prohibition, adjudication) are drawn, since this will determine the location and style of the politics of implementation.

Both of these types of government intervention are implemented through volumes of detailed government regulations that require affected groups to follow a series of explicit instructions. However, the primary locus for subsidies and regulative decisions is not the same. Subsidies tend to be enacted in specific terms by Congress because they represent an understandable product of the congressional barter system. For representatives subsidies are tangible "goodies" to take home to their constituents. Regulations are usually formulated so that administrators make the decisions that affect the regulated. Thus begins a cycle in which groups with strong ties to administrative centers use their clout to shape the new legislation or modify its implementation.

The broad approach embodied in the initial regulation may be whittled down politically in a series of ad hoc exceptions and exemptions for friends of the regulators. This is politically possible because laws are not implemented as one complete chunk. Each section and subdivision is broken down into parts which, in turn, are applied through a series of specific requirements. For example, when the Federal Elections Commission implements the campaign finance law, it does so by considering the number of PACs per corporation, the definition of public presidential candidate debates as a private contribution or public service, the kinds of information that candidates and groups must file for the public record. From such pieces the total scope of actual regulation will emerge.

From the group perspective, the best policy involves techniques that serve the group's true goals and are developed in decision-making arenas where the group has strength. For example, groups with a strong congressional power base, such as agricultural groups, may seek subsidies since these are primarily allocated through a process of congressional committee trade-offs. Large businesses will opt for regulation since Congress will pass the broad legislation, but the crucial decisions about detailed rules and their enforcement are made by the agencies, where industry is well-represented.

The form of public policy requested may also reflect an interplay between group goals and political realities. Consider gun control: the

NRA prefers no governmental action at all, but, when faced with postassassination insistence that restrictive legislation be passed, it opted for innocuous reporting/registering regulations rather than a law with criminal penalties for owning certain guns. Progun control groups such as Ban the Bullet have developed a goal that permits them to face political reality and circumvent Congress where the NRA has superior clout by seeking a Food and Drug Administration ruling that bullets are covered by the Hazardous Substances Act which the FDA implements. Thus the general aim of gun control has been redefined into a bureaucratically possible goal that would curtail the sale of bullets rather than ban the sale of guns. It is indirect but logical.

The tendency of regulative and subsidy policies to reinforce the conservative, status quo bias of public decisions marks them as political rather than technological solutions to problems. Both subsidies and regulations encourage or inhibit current activity patterns, those activities that politically active groups have a stake in preserving. By contrast, decisions made in economically and technologically rational terms would seek to reorganize behavior patterns by devising new incentives "to spur individual decision makers in their own self-interest, toward socially desirable actions."[7]

Continued reliance on these old-fashioned, politically oriented mechanisms for dealing with modern, technologically complex social and economic problems has impeded government success in terms of the fourth policy technique: manipulation. Manipulative policies are broad, very visible government plans designed to redistribute "life chances" (that is, opportunities for personal development and economic advancement) through government intervention. Welfare, civil rights legislation, social security, tax reforms such as the negative income tax are all manipulative policies that influence the reward structure of private activity in order to shift advantages from "haves" to "have-nots." The breadth of such programs and their impact on large segments of society guarantee both visibility and heated debate over who benefits at the expense of whom. Manipulative (often called redistributive)[8] policies tend to be umbrella policies that use both regulation and subsidies as specific techniques for achieving the overall goal. Often manipulative policies are symbolic ones, incorporating governmental hopes and values, which may or may not be implemented within a politically reasonable time. Civil rights became a constitutional norm with the passage of Amendments in the 1860s, but specific laws were not applied until the 1960s. Sometimes groups take advantage of the fact that in reality the definitive line between subsidy-regulative and manipulative policies is often blurred; thus, the AMA characterized medicare as socialized medicine (manipulative) when in fact it was initially a system of subsidies to encourage private action, that is, public payment for services by private doctors.

New Yorker reporter Elizabeth Drew has suggested that the issue of redistributive government intervention has been settled in the affirmative, but the nature of intervention, that is, the kinds of private problems that require the social and/or economic restructuring implicit in manipulative policies is still being debated. She divides the last forty years of government activity into three stages: (1) the post-depression era when government designed insurance and regulatory systems to prevent future economic catastrophes; (2) the 1960s when government tried to remake our social and cultural system by changing opportunities for various categories of "losers" in society such as the poor, the blacks, the uneducated; and (3) the 1970s when government has been faced with a politics of "resource constraints" that requires people to make changes in personal life styles in order to preserve common goods such as air, water, and space. Such generosity toward others has usually been seen only as a temporary wartime sacrifice. Indeed, the social reorganization programs of the 1960s foundered on these shoals; there was not enough time, money, or official commitment to wear down "human resistance, class resentments, political opposition." Without the supportive efforts of citizens, government manipulation cannot create "new national forms of behavior. . . ."[9]

The choices for groups are, as one can see, neither easy nor frivolous nor unimportant to the life of others. The manner in which groups establish and implement their goals affects the content of the public policy agenda. Therefore, the next questions to be considered are the ways in which a problem becomes part of the public policy agenda and the way in which group choices affect public development of an issue. Using energy-environment issues as examples, let's trace how the method of reaching government determines the perceptual and institutional context in which the issue is discussed, which in turn limits the possible policy alternatives.

BUILDING A PUBLIC AGENDA

Did you ever wonder why the environment did not become an issue until the late 1960s although pollution has been with us since the Industrial Revolution? Or why poverty became an issue in 1964–65? Or why American involvement in Indochina began in the middle 1950s but public agitation and dismay did not explode in the streets until 1967–68? One answer lies in the rhythm of public issues. "Issues have runs like plays. They make an opening splash, excite everyone's interest for a while, are written about and talked about, and then fold."[10] We may never know why a problem becomes a priority: what event catapults it from the general issue pool to classification as priority. It seems clear that problems exist (often in worse shape), long before public recognition of their importance, and that problems persist long after that spotlight has turned onto other things.

Nevertheless, in terms of public policy making, certain kinds of socially rooted domestic conditions lend themselves to an interplay between the media and the public which, in turn, generates an interest-issue cycle. The cycle moves upward to a "heightening public interest and then [downward to] increasing boredom. . . ."[11] At the cycle's beginning, a publically unperceived problem exists. Then dramatic events trigger media attention which focuses public attention. With public awareness comes the naive assumption that technical tinkering can resolve the issue. Laws are passed and institutions created to implement that resolve.

Time passes and the condition persists, bringing the realization that success requires a commitment of money and resources that the public is unwilling to make. Realism dampens public interest and the media move on in search of more dramatic, entertaining news—the source of "new" major problems. The laggard issue is moved off center stage into that policy-making limbo in which the institutions created in its peak period continue toward the goals established at that peak. When new, related issues or unexpected crises bring the problem back to public notice again, it is at a higher level of attention, effort, and concern because it was once a top priority issue.

Groups may use organization and strategy to create or extend events in order to generate media excitement and activate the issue-interest cycle that links public opinion to the public policy-making process. Problems can be escalated into disputes when individuals or interests seize an event or introduce an attitude designed to promote sufficient controversy to create a public policy. Do-gooders, candidates for public office, groups that feel disadvantaged by private arrangements, or groups created by unique events such as tornados, assassinations, strikes, or riots all act as agents to translate events into issues.

> [Public policy] winners tend to be those who have formed groups, identified and clearly articulated their values, located the critical decisional points in the system, effectively used dollars to win public support, manipulated symbols, selected political tactics appropriate to the time and place, and who will spend their time, energy, and financial resources on efforts to influence government. Losers are those who have not done these things, or have not done them well.[12]

Interest groups with access to available, involved officials have a better chance of creating the conditions for official action than groups that lack access because of their insufficient organizational resources or the unacceptability of their demands. Groups with access use the process of creating public issues to not only indicate problems but also to offer their perception of the key issues and their version of the public interest solution that should become public policy. "In fact, by the time an issue arrives at an actual choice point, its fate may already be decided. . . . The crucial question may be whether or not it gets on the governmental agenda, how it is defined by that time, how visible it is [to the public], and what social influences have been activated in the process."[13]

The process of moving an issue from the general socioeconomic environment into the governmental policy process is called *agenda building.* An agenda may be defined as "a general set of political controversies that will be viewed at any point in time as falling within the range of legitimate concerns meriting the attention of the polity."[14] There are two kinds of governmental agenda: the *systemic* agenda that is an informal amalgam of popular priorities, values, and concerns considered suitable for public decision making; the *formal* agenda that consists of those items on legislative calendars, administrative schedules, and judicial dockets that are actually to be considered by governmental decision makers. Usually items reach the systemic agenda as a prelude to formal public action since the systemic agenda is a reflection of current community opinion.

The key notion here, that the development of public issues reflects the involvement patterns of various segments of the public, is similar to the key explanation offered by E. E. Schattschneider for understanding public policy making. To Schattschneider, politics is a struggle over the substance of public policy in which power lies in the definition of alternatives. "He who determines what politics is about runs the country because the definition of the alternatives is the choice of conflicts, and the choice of conflicts allocates power."[15]

The game of politics is played by greater and lesser aggregations of people and groups. The "socialization of conflict" (that is, the ways in which conflict is expanded) plus the intensity, visibility, and direction of specific issues determine both the content of an issue and the players' moves. Policy outcomes depend on the number of bystanders—that is public citizens—who can be involved in the issue. Thus, once again, a crucial factor in the game of politics is numbers: the involvement of publics (attentive and/or mass) to an extent that will support various forms of governmental activity in any given dispute. "Government responds only to those who ask. . . . Who gets what, when, where, and how is the product of more than pure chance."[16]

Environmental Issues and the Public Agenda

The environmental issue cycle that moved from a "pollution" peak in the late 1960s and early 1970s to an "energy" peak in 1972–73 and then stabilized at an "ecology" issue intermediate position in 1974–75 illustrates both the overall process of putting (or getting) problems on formal agendas of government and the rise and fall of priority subproblems within a general issue area.

The historical legacy of public interest in the environment reflects a lack of concern for common goods and an enthusiasm for private gain. For example, during Lincoln's presidency, 75 million acres of public land were given to the railroads; by the end of the nineteenth century, 180 million acres were gone. In 1901 President Roosevelt's initiatives in developing a public park system were thwarted by the popular congressional war cry: "Not one cent for scenery."[17]

Nor is this merely an historical attitude. As recently as 1960, the report of President Eisenhower's Commission on National Goals covered fifteen topics in 372 pages, but included only five paragraphs on air and water pollution. The Brookings Institution (a "liberal" research center) in a 1973 listing of pressing concerns for the new Nixon administration to tackle similarly failed to list ecological issues.[18] How does one reconcile this with President Johnson's 1965 call for environmental beautification as a national priority or with President Nixon's annual environmental messages beginning in 1969 and his first energy message in 1971? What happened to change public attitudes? What caused public leadership initiatives on environmental issues and generated a decade of increasingly stronger environmentally related legislation?

One answer can be drawn from our earlier discussion: it lies in the dynamic of a three-way relationship among current events, political initiatives, and public response. President Johnson's environmental initiatives reflected his personal Texas rancher's preoccupation with environmental conditions. His crusade to end water pollution and Lady Bird Johnson's concern for national beautification both generated media attention as reflected in increased press coverage of environmental issues; for example, *New York Times* coverage of pollution articles doubled between 1964 and 1965.[19] "Trigger events" such as the Santa Barbara oil spill, Los Angeles smog battles, pesticide-related deaths, and polluted beaches provided further grist for the media mills.

In addition, average citizens began to connect the idea of environmental degradation with the increased noise, odors, and smog of industrial urbanized living.[20] The pervasiveness of such problems became obvious as middle-America took to the road to seek fun and recreation. By 1968, 79 percent of all American families owned a car. The beaches and parks, once the purview of the rich, were now flooded with vacationers and their litter. Highways became parking lots jammed with cars producing obvious noise and odor pollution.

An environmentalist public opinion—especially among the educated, the middle-class, the young, and the affluent—began to grow and develop.

> It seems apparent that between 1960 and the early 1970s, the nation made an extraordinarily rapid transition, in terms of social awareness, from environmental indifference to political concern: during this transformation, "ecology" rose from virtual political invisibility to political salience. . . . It is clear that the major takeoff period for major public interest . . . was the era of 1965–70.[21]

By 1968 public opinion polls showed that approximately 50 percent of the public had some interest in environmental quality. By 1970, 90 percent in one survey mentioned the problem of water pollution; 53 percent in another survey rated the reduction of air and water pollution as a major priority issue. A 1970 *Fortune* poll showed over one-half of the executives polled were interested in government regulation and national industry standards.[22]

With spreading affluence came rising standards. The public began to include increasing numbers of offensive smells, fumes, and noises in their general definition of pollution.

> Pollutants are those substances which interfere with the use of air, water, or soil for socially desired purposes. . . . The definition hinges on the concept of human use, and thus, . . . the definition of what constitutes pollution is dependent on the public's decision as to what use it wants to make of its environment. It becomes a public decision, a voicing by the community of its concept of the public interest.[23]

These subjective definitions enlarged the concept of pollution on the systemic agenda of community concerns, thereby permitting government decision makers and interested groups to consider a broader array of public issues under the rubric of environmental problems which might be placed on the formal agenda of government.

The zenith of proenvironment public activity was reached on Earth Day, April 22, 1970. This day was envisioned by its initiator, Senator Gaylord Nelson, as a national teach-in on environmental issues. During the six months of planning for this national day of coordinated public activities, public opinion polls and the content of congressional debates showed that environmental concerns had moved ahead of other national issues. On Earth Day itself, marches, teach-ins, theatrics such as car buying, dirt dumping, and "guerrilla" street theatre skits turned the day into a media happening. In summing up the experience, Senator Nelson said: "You can be sure there will never be another political campaign like the one in 1968 when not one of the three candidates for president considered the environment an issue worthy of a major speech. It is nothing short of remarkable how rapidly this issue has been thrust into the politics, the conversation, and the literature of the country. . . ."[24]

This increase in public enthusiasm and raised consciousness was reflected in legislation and administrative reorganization. In the 1960s environmentalist, sports, and civic associations had joined together to pass initial regulatory legislation such as the 1963 Clean Air Act, the 1965 Water Quality Act, and the 1967 Air Quality Act. Group organization built first at local and state levels.[25] Traditional environmentally concerned organizations such as the Sierra Club, the National Wildlife Federation, and the Izaak Walton League trebled their membership. The League of Women Voters adopted antipollution as a study item in 1956; in 1969 it created an umbrella coalition of thirty-eight organizations to work together to obtain full funding of new waste treatment plant legislation.

Since 1969 an array of groups devoted solely to environmental lobbying have been established: Friends of the Earth (FOE), Environmental Action, Natural Resources Defense Council, the Fisherman's Clean Water Action Taskforce (Nader), and others. In addition governmental lobbies such as the Conference of Mayors seek subsidies for more sewers, waste treatment plants, and air purification systems. Medical societies consider the relationships between pollution and health, scientists lobby for research funds to develop nonfossil sources of energy. Industry pollution committees have proliferated to both lobby and study new and proposed regulations. Currently over 5,000 national organizations lobby, disseminate information, and hold meetings concerned with the environment/ecology/energy issue.

During this period of community activity, policy makers were also beginning to question the traditional economic assumption that water and air were free common goods. The economic pricing system that rewarded industry abuse of water and air as discharge receptacles by not including such aesthetic/social costs in consumer prices was under attack. Nader's research groups, and government itself, in reports by the General Accounting Office, and later, the Council on Environmental Quality, questioned the success of regulatory legislation passed in the early 1960s. Thus, by the late 1960s, the stage was set for pollution to become a major public issue.

From 1969 to 1972, true to the curve of the issue-interest cycle, escalating public demands, backed by consistent public opinion, moved pollution from the systemic to the formal agenda. Strong, new legislation such as the National Environmental Protection Act of 1969, the Clean Air Act Amendments of 1970, and the Water Pollution Act Amendments of 1972 were enacted. Congress acquired major new properties for public recreation and refused to continue funding the environmentally obnoxious SST (supersonic transport). President Nixon killed the Cross-Florida Barge Canal project in order to save the water supply of the Everglades. In addition he incorporated the new interest into a Council on Environmental Protection in the Executive Office of the President, later adding the Environmental Protection Agency (EPA) as an independent agency in Reorganization Plan No. 3 of 1970.

A close look at the environmental policy outputs revealed that action was more cosmetic (symbolic) than real (effective). EPA was politically weak, since like any new agency, a period of relative quiet is needed for the creation and consolidation of supportive clientele relationships with outside interests that serve as a base for fighting bureaucratic wars. However, the older bureaus whose jurisdiction was affected by the new laws began immediate skirmishes and attacks designed to protect their old policy making positions. Consequently, EPA was unable to effect a major change in the breadth or vigor of implementation as suggested by the budget statistics: in 1955 pollution expenditures were 3 percent of the federal budget; by 1972, despite the new group pressures and new legislation with administrative directives, pollution expenditures were still only 5 percent of the total budget.

Anti-pollution laws themselves were primarily regulatory, with incentives (subsidies) for waste treatment plants and other capital improvements added in the 1970s legislation. The ambivalence of government toward action is indicated by the emphasis on regulatory responsibilities delegated to state and local governments with federal supervisory and enforcement powers. Even in 1970s legislation, when the "delegated standards" approach was abolished in favor of the goal of complete pollution abatement, government's technique was still industry regulation, with the difference being that Washington would now set guidelines for progress.

The ambivalence reflected industrial reluctance to spend the amounts necessary to curb the discharge of pollutants or to remodel their current machinery. It has been estimated that, "If carried out as intended, current pollution control laws will require over the next decade, expenditures of up to half a trillion dollars by consumers, business firms, and governments, and substantial changes in industrial practices and the style of consumer living." Governments alone will spend $104 billion for pollution control facilities in the 1972–81 decade.[26]

In agenda-building terms, the environment had "arrived" as an issue on both systemic and formal agendas by the mid-1960s, but pollution peaked as a subissue in 1971–72 and began a downward slide into bureaucratic limbo. Energy was standing in the wings waiting to rise to front and center. Beginning in 1970, the United States began to import almost a quarter of its oil supply, the dominant source of domestic energy. By 1973 the amount was 36 percent, 2.3 billion barrels a year. In 1972 England dramatized the relationship between energy and economy when a national coal strike put 1 million people out of work and within five weeks had brought the country to a standstill. Predicting from this event, *Forbes* magazine in October 1972 stated that "energy is about to replace ecology as the pet of Washington politics." Yet as late as Spring 1973 "it was impossible to convince the head of a major Washington television news bureau that this country would be facing an energy crisis."[27]

Energy as we are now aware, was gaining public issue awareness without media preparation. The triggering event was the October 1973 Arab oil boycott. Arab oil-producing nations, angry at United States military support for Israel, cut off all supplies of foreign oil. Gasoline prices soared; gas stations closed. The boycott resulted in gas lines, truck strikes, speed limit reductions, carless Sundays, home heating shortages, industrial fuel allocations, and panic. Suddenly environment was back as a priority, but now positions of the subissues were reversed, with energy conservation superseding pollution control as a priority. The interrelatedness of the issues is obvious! "If electric utilities burn coal instead of oil, we reduce dependence on imports but we risk befouling the air. If we strip mine low-sulfur western coal . . . we may help keep the air free of sulfur but we may also despoil hundreds of square miles of western land and pollute the tributaries of western rivers."[28]

Thus, as is true of many issues, the "energy issue" is really shorthand for an enormous complex of interrelated issues:

> inflation, recession, and unemployment; transportation; the balance of payments; housing; taxes; cities; economic concentration and antitrust; regional differences within the United States; arm sales abroad; the environment; architecture; America's relations with its European allies and Japan; and relations between the wealthy and the poor nations of the world.[29]

The dispute involves oil interests, automobile manufacturers, unions, consumers, foreign nations, environmentalists, all users of energy, producers of nonfossil forms of energy, and all the many subdivisions within each category. Each participant views any particular solution from the perspective of its own primary problem.

Consequently, in this issue area as in others, coalitions change membership from one aspect of the issue to another as groups remain internally consistent to their own priorities. Since the groups' working relationships within government do not change, involved officials also tend to work from issue to issue rather than holding back to support a rationalized comprehensive energy solution. The 1975 congressional attempt to save energy by taxing cars on the basis of fuel efficiency suggests the problem. This solution placed the UAW, normally a liberally oriented, proconservation union, on the side of its employers, the automobile manufacturers, because the gas guzzler tax would have reduced employment for Detroit workers on large car assembly lines.

Thus the timing of the Arab boycott coincided with growing domestic strife between the energy companies and environmental control advocates. Business fought back, countering the ecologist's litany of planetary doom with their own claims of fuel scarcity and economic depression. Environmentalists saw this as merely a means to counter their success, a suspicion reinforced by public policy making in the 93rd Congress: Clean Air Act standards were lowered; construction of the Alaskan pipeline began, immune to further court challenges such as those that had held up activity during the previous seven years; ocean oil drilling and exploration for shale oil on federal land were renewed; the President established a Federal Energy Administration to ensure a sufficient supply of energy for America; and the Emergency Energy Act was passed which countermanded many of the standards set by EPA.

Just as it appeared that pollution control might be sacrificed as the scapegoat of the energy crisis, another "trigger event" occurred: the major oil companies reported enormous company profits. The ten largest oil companies reaped over $5 billion in profits in the first six months of 1974. This confirmed public suspicions, as reported in an earlier Gallup poll, which showed that more people attributed the energy crisis to the oil companies than to any other factor. As the boycott receded, and public indignation focused on the traditional target of monopolistic big business, energy slid down the issue-interest peak.

Since the end of 1974, the environmental issue has been in that state of official confusion indicative of unresolved problems and insufficient public interest in specific policies. A comparison of the legislation passed during the "pollution decade" with the muddled, contradictory legislative record of the energy crisis period suggests that public opinion indeed plays a role in agenda building by setting priorities for governmental action. One news commentator explained the current confusion by saying: "We probably do not have a government policy because the truth is, at this moment, we have no consensus or what that policy should be."[30]

The lower echelon status of environmental issues is also suggested by the rise of an accommodation subissue: ecology, or conservation of *all* resources—air, water, and fuel. The new issue reflects both public opinion disarray and group strategies. The environmentalist groups, fearing greater erosion of environmental legislation if they fought back at the peak of the energy crisis, acquiesced in moderate delays of political control measures while arguing that such controls are only a marginal cause of the energy crunch. Senator Dick Clark was one of those urging this moderate approach: "Environmental laws should not be made the scapegoat for energy shortages. We are not faced with a simple choice between cold homes and dirty air."[31]

A public opinion shift toward an ecology/energy balance was reflected in a *New York Times* comment that conservation and technology could benefit both sides.

> Amid the rush to a trillion dollar g.n.p., personal and national thrift went the way of the rumble seat. The conservationists changed and became environmentalists concerned with water and air pollution and the effluents of affluence. Last winter's oil embargo may help revive this American tradition of saving, for conservation offers the fastest and surest means of cutting down dependence on imported oil. Conversely . . . an advanced, highly sophisticated technology . . . can be used to ease environmental problems while it seeks solutions to the energy shortage.[32]

The rise of ecology as a compromise policy area also indicates the problems of attempting manipulative policies, that is, government intervention to rearrange the private distribution of rewards in an area of "resource constraints" where no one interest can emerge as a real winner. In addition attitudes have changed since the 1960s. Planners of President Johnson's War on Poverty assumed that there were inexhaustible resources—enough to cure any evil—until they discovered that their resources were inadequate. Energy issues begin from inadequacy, from a concern with shrinking resources, and from the knowledge that the past practice of buying off interests with logrolling subsidies or settling one issue through regulation while other problems remain untouched cannot work when scarcity has decreased room to maneuver and the number of affected interests increases daily.

This environmental agenda shows that in over a decade media attention focused on environmental disasters plus government initiatives developed an environmentalist public opinion oriented toward air and water pollution control, the most visible forms of environmental decay. Public demands were formalized in legislation and bureaucratic apparatus designed to end pollution. As the costs and time required for total abatement became apparent, public commitment decreased. Then just as the pollution issue was fading because of public disinterest, the energy crisis revived it in terms of the new agenda item. Pollution was lumped together with other environmental concerns under the rubric of ecology or conservation. The public policy process is now responding to issues in the new context of energy/ecology tradeoffs.

SUMMARY

This chapter has summarized the workings of the policy-making process and the techniques used to implement government objectives in terms of their potential for interest group involvement. The sporadic, segmented, piecemeal nature of policy-making sequences is ideal for group participation through those members of the government with whom they have developed working relationships. The chapter divided the overall process into four stages: problem identification, program development, policy implementation, and policy evaluation. Policy outputs were classified into three action categories on the basis of the governmental technique employed: subsidy, regulation, and manipulation.

The final section of the chapter examined the first step in the policy sequence: getting a private problem onto the public agenda for consideration. The whole issue of environmental problems, and the subissues of pollution, energy, and ecology, provided an example of the way public leaders, private groups, and the media create public interest in certain issues, as well as the importance of this public concern as a precondition for action.

In the next chapter we will consider how groups work with Congress to create programs and how these programs then become public laws.

NOTES

1. There are many excellent discussions of public policy making. This section has benefited from Peter Woll, *Public Policy* (Cambridge, Mass: Winthrop Publications, 1974); Charles Lindblom, *The Policy-Making Process* (Englewood Cliffs, N.J.: Prentice-Hall, 1968); and Charles O.

Jones, *An Introduction to the Study of Public Policy* (Belmont, Ca.: Wadsworth, 1970).

2. Lewis Dexter, *How Organizations Are Represented in Washington* (Indianapolis: Bobbs-Merrill 1969), p. 62.
3. Jones, *An Introduction to the Study of Public Policy,* p. 39. See also Roger Cobb and Charles Elder, *Participation in American Politics: The Dynamics of Agenda Building* (Baltimore: Johns Hopkins Press, 1972), p. 27.
4. Jones, *An Introduction to the Study of Public Policy,* pp. 72–73.
5. Ibid., p. 146.
6. Randall Ripley, ed., *Public Policies and Their Politics* (New York: Norton, 1966), p. xi.
7. Allen Kneese and Charles Schultz, *Pollution, Prices and Public Policy* (Washington, D.C.: The Brookings Institution, 1975), p. 7. See Chapter 1 for an application of these general comments to the problems of pollution.
8. See Theodore Lowi, "American Business, Public Policy, Case Studies, and Political Theory," *World Politics* 16 (July 1964).
9. Elizabeth Drew, "A Reporter at Large: The Energy Bazaar," *The New Yorker,* July 21, 1975, pp. 35–72.
10. "Talk of the Town," *The New Yorker,* March 24, 1975, p. 31.
11. Anthony Downs, "Up and Down with Ecology—The 'Issue-Attention Cycle,' " *The Public Interest* No. 28 (Summer 1972): 39.
12. John Straayer and Robert Wrinkle, *American Government, Policy and Non-Decisions* (Columbus, Ohio: Merrill, 1972), p. 44.
13. Ibid., p. 30.
14. Ibid., p. 151.
15. E. E. Schattschneider, *The Semi-Sovereign People* (Hinsdale, Ill.: Dryden Press, 1975), p. 68.
16. Straayer and Wrinkle, *American Government, Policy and Non-Decisions,* pp. 3, 44.
17. Walter Rosenbaum, *The Politics of Environmental Concern* (New York: Praeger Publishers, 1973), p. 11.
18. Ibid., chap. 1; Kneese and Schultz, *Pollution, Prices and Public Policy,* pp. 2–3.
19. Cecile Trop and Leslie Roos, Jr., "Public Opinion and the Environment," in *The Politics of Ecosuicide,* ed. Leslie Roos, Jr. (New York: Holt, Rinehart & Winston, 1971), p. 55.
20. For a summary of the social and economic background factors see Downs, "Up and Down with Ecology," pp. 43–46; Rosenbaum *The Politics of Environmental Concern* pp. 12–16; J. Clarence Davies III and Barbara S. Davies, *The Politics of Pollution,* 2d ed. (Indianapolis: Pegasus,

1975), pp. 7–9; Kneese and Schultz, *Pollution, Prices and Public Policy,* chaps. 1, 3.

21. Rosenbaum, *The Politics of Environmental Concern,* pp. 18, 14.
22. Trop and Roos, Jr., "Public Opinion and the Environment," pp. 57, 60.
23. Davies and Davies, *The Politics of Pollution,* p. 3.
24. Odon Fanning, *Man and His Environment: Citizen Action* (New York: Harper & Row, 1975), p. 34.
25. For a discussion of environmental groups, see Davies and Davies, *The Politics of Pollution,* pp. 88–100; Trop and Roos, Jr., "Public Opinion and the Environment," p. 62; and Fanning, *Man and His Environment,* chaps. 6–10.
26. Kneese and Schultz, *Pollution, Prices and Public Policy,* p. 1; *New York Times* November 9, 1974.
27. U.S., Congress, House of Representatives, *Congressional Record,* 93 Cong., 2nd Sess., July 1, 1974, p. H6093.
28. Kneese and Schultz, *Pollution, Prices and Public Policy,* pp. vii.
29. Elizabeth Drew, "*A Reporter at Large,*" p. 35.
30. Frank McGee, "NBC White Paper," 1973.
31. U.S., Congress, Senate, *Congressional Record,* 93 Cong., 1st Sess., September 12, 1973, p. S16407.
32. *New York Times,* October 20, 1974, p. 14.

Chapter 8

Group Interaction with Congress

Groups work toward governmental decisions that further their own goals, but at the same time decision makers seek interest group support for a variety of reasons: to secure technical information; to implement federal directives; to coalesce political support for an official, department, or policy; and/or to ensure electoral support from identifiable blocs of voters. Two-way relationships are formed from mutual need and are reinforced by patterns of friendship and by decision-making routines.

Each group's representatives must find the path of substantive decisions in their area. Yet the enormous diversity and duplication of federal structures complicates the simple functional reasons for group-government interaction. First consider the problem of size. The federal bureaucracy employs approximately 3 million civilians; Congress consists of 535 elected representatives and a staff of over 16,000; the federal court system includes 506 judges and justices. Second is the problem created by dispersion of decision making among the myriad subdivisions of each large entity; for example, there are over 2,000 separate entities within the federal bureaucracy. A bureaucrat may be one of the 5,000 employees in the Executive Office of the President or among the 129,000 employees of the Department of Health Education, and Welfare. The congressional system is divided into 52 committees, 360 subcommittees, and 7 joint committees. The court system consists of 102 courts arranged in two appellate levels and a district court system.

In order to get anything done amidst this structural chaos, most decisions are really made by small numbers of individuals scattered throughout the government who share similar policy concerns. It is at this level that the 5,000 registered and unregistered lobbyists enter to seek policy decisions. The outside lobbyists work with those government actors interested in their policy goals. In time, as like-minded people work together on related issues, patterns of interaction become established. These patterns become *action centers:* functional, issue-based alliances that coordinate personnel and procedures in order to form decisions. Action centers evolve from the moves of policy-oriented players who need to connect with each other in order to score.

Centers may become important "fulcrums of balance"[1] between the ongoing concerns of a government institution and the wishes of the political party currently in power. Bureaucrats below the level of presidential appointee are able to act as policy entrepreneurs since their offices are the main repositories of policy-related information and their careers are protected by civil service safeguards. Bureaucrats seek to preserve their structural autonomy because it reinforces their policy-making autonomy. Interest group support is used to increase the power base of governmental actors (bureaucrats and congressional staff) by providing them with an outside source of political strength and/or necessary information. Each power center strives "to become self-sustaining in control of power in its own sphere. Each seeks to aggregate the power necessary to its purposes. Each resists being overriden."[2] Sometimes these centers are called "whirlpools," suggesting the intensity and closeness of the established relationships. Sometimes they are called "subgovernments," a term that highlights the permanence of institutional patterns created by similar moves to make similar policy points.

These action centers tend to develop at two levels—the presidential level and the mid-bureaucracy level. On the presidential level executive liaison personnel representing the Executive Office of the President and appointed executive branch personnel work with congressional leadership to pass the President's legislative program. Action centers at the mid-bureaucracy level typically link a middle-level executive branch component such as bureau or office executives with staff members of the congressional committees that authorize and appropriate for their programs and with leaders of the nongovernmental interest groups that support these programs.

Over the years decision-making patterns based on the policies involved become institutionalized. Decision-making shortcuts called "routines" develop as a way of simplifying policy options.

> It is often wiser to employ a routine than to make detailed calculations about the ramifications of alternative decisions for the host of economic, social, and political criteria that are potentially relevant. . . . However, routines also help to isolate the actors from certain inputs. It is in this way that the routines bring equilibrium and conservatism to the political system.[3]

For example, incrementalism is a perfect routine since it limits decision makers to options within the range of last year's decisions and this year's narrow shifts in program. Basic social and economic goals are not considered; instead established participants seek modification of current policies.

Thus action centers depend on stable relationships through which the members develop and implement policy. When desired policies require the partisan, personal, priority characteristics of presidential level action centers, groups seek such allliances. When policy requires technical information or the expertise of tenured civil servants, then groups work with mid-level action centers. The presidential action center is more personal and less permanent than mid-level centers since its members reflect temporary electoral victories. The institutional linkages between the Executive Office and department liaison offices have been in place since the early 1960s and stand ready to be used by incoming presidents, just as the agency/congressional committee/clientele group action centers remain linked in spite of personnel changes (although at this lower staff level the tenure span is more nearly fifteen years than four). Groups use their information-providing capabilities and/or their influence over appointments and electoral votes to form working alliances with whichever action centers affect their interests.

In order to analyze group participation in the policy process, we will divide one continuous sequence of overlapping activities into two separate parts. Here we will consider the techniques employed by groups seeking access and input within the congressional policy making system. Chapter 9 focuses on group relationships with executive bureaucracy components and denizens of the presidential executive office. In chapter 10 we will switch from institutional linkages to a process focus and examine group activities designed to affect the development, implementation, and evaluation stages of public policy making. The courts will be considered separately since tradition and function have combined to make judicial policy making/lobbying relationships separate and different.

CONGRESS

Usually when people think *lobbying*, they think *legislature*. This reflects the "constitutional" view, in the sense that the farmers felt that Congress would be the main arena for the resolution of conflict; congressmen would be human envoys representing the most basic, dominant, visible, and important interests in their districts. Congress was planned as an institution of minorities whose raison d'etre in the constitutional scheme of checks and balances was to protect organized minorities from stultification by organized majorities. This attitude was embedded in the very structure of the institution, and has been enhanced by the accumulation of rules, norms, and procedures that define the legislative process.

The major procedure for congressional implementation of its protection mandate is the passing of legislation, including appropriations for federal spending. In addition to lawmaking, Congress involves itself in administrative matters through oversight hearings, which investigate the progress of specific programs or agencies. The Senate's confirmation power provides opportunities for congressional checks on major administrative and federal court appointments; its ratification power permits public discussion of American treaty commitments prior to accepting them (often evaded by using executive agreements which require no senatorial consent).

In servicing their constituencies, Congressmen may represent their publics through their votes and by casework, which consists of errands for constituents wanting help with bureaucratic red tape. Indeed many requests made by lobbyists are really only casework for a group constituency seeking information or expediting government action for specific interests.[4] Thus the roles assigned to Congress require coordination of public needs with representatives of important interests and with other branches of government; action centers provide pathways for implementing these roles.

From the viewpoint of the lobbyists, there are two important aspects of Congress that affect the role. First, since congressmen are elected, all things being equal, groups with broad vote power or with economic clout in districts across the country will have easier access to congressmen. Second, the structure of Congress makes committees the major action centers for policy development, so lobbyists are encouraged to develop special relationships with those committee staff and senior members who need their information and expertise as legislative input. Since committee membership is fairly stable, it is a worthwhile lobbying investment. Duplication of functions, leaders, and committees, which is built into the bicameral congressional structure, enables lobbyists to use their ties with any key action center to kill legislation they cannot correct. The internal dispersal of power and authority also maximizes the lobbyist's ability to parley a useful bit of information or help from a key inside lobbyist into a policy success.

Committees

In terms of both legislative structure and process, the committees remain the major source of personal power and the major forum of legislative activity. "Committees remain the kiln in which the stuff of legislation is baked, the important point of entry to the congressional power elite, a major route to attainment of the respect and deference of colleagues that members eagerly seek. Congressional size, work load, and rules promote, if not compel, their primacy."[5] Committees also disperse power among many competing policy subdivisions. Committee subject matter jurisdiction is not related to 1970 priority issues which means that there are no single major committee centers for currently important topics such as poverty, transportation, or energy; instead, aspects of each subject are scattered among various committees.

For example, the development of a coherent energy policy is complicated by the fact that fourteen House committees and twenty-eight subcommittees, sixteen Senate committees and thirty subcommittees, three joint congressional committees and seven subcommittees all claim jurisdiction over parts of the issue. Bills related to air pollution are processed through the House Committee on Interstate and Foreign Commerce, the National Environmental Protection Act came out of the Committee on Merchant Marine and Fisheries, water bills and billboards go to the Public Works Committee, and wilderness bills are processed through the Interior Committee. Dispersed authority for overlapping policy areas has meant that agencies spend many man-hours in separate hearings on similar subjects; for example, the U.S. Energy Research and Development Administration, in its first 135 days of existence, sent witnesses to testify at the formal hearings of six full committees and twenty-seven subcommittees of thirteen other committees.[6]

During the 93rd Congress, an effort was made to streamline and modernize committee jurisdictions in order to increase the overall congressional role in policy development. Representatives of six interest groups testified at the hearings* and three submitted material for the record.** Each witness offered suggestions for subject matter rationalization and gave examples of committee overlaps that had impeded his or her own lobbying activities. Relating the pluralistic committee decision-making situation to opportunities for interest group access, the representative from the American Bar Association noted that:

> There are over 200 subcommittee chairmen with . . . some share in fiscal-monetary-credit policy matters. . . . The resulting congressional environment invites pressure tactics—of either the carrot or stick variety—by lobbying forces representing all manner of private interest groups, since action may be stopped or modified at any one of many legislative stages.[7]

Attacking the lobbyist-legislator relationship directly, several good government groups recommended committee rotation for congressmen in order to broaden their knowledge, weaken the seniority sys-

*NAACP, AFL-CIO, Nader, Committee for Economic Development, Common Cause, League of Women Voters (LWV).

**Chamber of Commerce, Federation of Homemakers, American Bar Association.

tem, and break up "the unholy trinity: the longstanding and underground alliance of a committee member with a middle level bureaucrat and a special interest lobbyist concerned with the same subject matter. Such alliances are the product of ripened acquaintance and mutuality of interest. . . .[8]

In a letter to Congresswoman Julia Hansen, sponsor of the committee reorganization legislation, Congressman John Dingall argued that both jurisdictional simplification of committee subject matter concerns and rotation of congressmen would be disastrous from the standpoint of member effectiveness and independence. Member rotation among committees would "dissipate expertise. . . gained over scores of years which cannot be equated with the superficial knowledge of private individuals, academics, and the bureaucrats downtown."[9] For the same reason he also would not tinker with existing subject matter assignments since again the new committees would lack the experience/expertise reservoir found among current committee members.

He argued strongly against one-issue committees, calling them "cockpits." For example, an Energy and Environment Committee would "pit conservation organizations against the oil companies and power companies on a day-to-day basis." One-issue committees would also be less likely to have moderate members who would be willing to compromise because of possibly adverse electoral consequences if they opposed key interest group positions. For example, a labor committee could cause "direct political peril.. . . The result will be a committee of extremists totally dependent on either the side of labor or the side of management."

Both statements assume that the current system of overlapping jurisdictions and member expertise on similar subjects gained in different issue contexts permits "broad participation by members without particular axes to grind. . . ." Dingall equates member independence and committee compromise on legislative language to "balanced" committees such as his Merchant Marine and Fisheries Committee which has "a constituency in the Maritime industry, and also in broad areas of conservation and the (sic) environmental concern." Thus notions about the impact of action center behavior patterns were important considerations throughout the committee reorganization debate.

The Legislative Process

The legislative process may be viewed as a slow-moving conveyor belt that carries programs through the various power centers forming the legislative policy-making machine. On an industrial assembly line, thousands of individual pieces of raw material are tumbled into the process, but only hundreds of complicated finished combinations emerge from the other end. So too in the legislature, where thousands of proposals, often duplicates of one another, are combined into major pieces of omnibus legislation that eventually become law. For example, in the 94th Congress, 24,283 bills were introduced into committees, 3,156 bills were reported out for consideration by one or both houses, and 588 public bills were enacted into law. In percentages, 2 percent of the ideas tumbled into the committee hopper in 1975–76 made it through the entire process and emerged as American public law.

The process itself can be divided into three stages:

1. During the *committee consideration* stage, committees winnow out major ideas for examination, hold committee and/or subcommittee hearings to gather information, rework the bills to reflect their ideas, and then write a report recommending the committee product completely or with reservations. All bills that never leave committee are considered "killed."
2. Bills reported out by committees reach the second stage: *floor action* at which time they must secure majority agreement from those congressmen voting on the matter. The rules of each house are sufficiently different to permit lobbyists to play one house against the other in terms of amending committee bills. However, if the legislation is passed in different forms by each house, it must be reconciled in a conference committee. This report must be accepted by both houses before a bill reaches the final stage.
3. The *President* may nullify congressional action by vetoing any legislation, which then cannot become law, unless the veto is overruled by a two-third's vote of the members of each house of Congress.

If a proposal were to go through every possible stage of the legislative process, it could be changed or killed at any of thirteen points.

This gives the advantage to those groups that would maintain the status quo, and to those that have well-developed working relationships at any of the key checkpoints.

The importance of adjusting lobbying coalitions and tactics in order to meet each hurdle is illustrated by the surprise demise of a bill proposed by the American National Cattlemen's Association to create a special board to promote beef consumption. The House voted 263 to 112 to reject the conference committee version of the bill which included a referendum provision weighted in favor of corporate cattle producers. The American Farm Bureau Federation, Consumer Federation of America, trade associations, and farm groups representing the smaller cattlemen joined with urban congressmen to defeat the bill.

The Business Roundtable similarly scored a coup when, working through the "house counsels" of its member organizations (all *Fortune* 500 corporations), the group was able to kill an important antitrust bill by having the House Rules Committee recommit it to the Judiciary Committee rather than send it to the floor for a vote.

Rules and Norms

Committee importance in the legislative process is reinforced by rules and norms that structure Congress's internal relationships. Legislative rules range from the formal, codified precedents and rulings of the Chair to informal, unwritten expectations called norms.[10] Among the most important rules from the perspective of outside groups are those relating to policy development relationships, since these determine the positions of greatest policy-making importance to groups.

The unwritten rules governing individual work patterns stress committee work as the route to internal prestige, and require *specialization* in selected subjects as a precondition for congressional effectiveness. Usually members specialize in something important to their constituency and/or subjects within the jurisdiction of their committee that interest them. Thus Massachusetts Senator Ted Kennedy is an expert on health, Senator Edmund Muskie of Maine on air pollution, Louisiana's Russell Long on taxes. These men chair committees or subcommittees dealing with these issues and are listened to in debate or asked for voting recommendations when their specialty is under consideration.

Between 1964 and 1974, approximately two-thirds of the House and over one-half of the Senate membership was new.[11] These freshmen came determined to reform the old seniority system and committee procedures in order to redistribute policy-making power. By 1975 their efforts had culminated in a system of widely dispersed institutional power bases: committee chairmen were forced to defend their records before the party caucus every two years, thereby undercutting the security of seniority as the only path of committee advancement. Subcommittees were given more staff and greater responsibilities. The distribution of committee assignments was redesigned to permit fairer assignments for freshmen. "Sunshine" legislation opened to the public all committee meetings.

These reforms have increased the dispersal of policy-making power and at the same time have made it possible for individuals to build personal reputations based on issue expertise rather than seniority-based autocracy. The new distribution has also affected the importance of the norms of "apprenticeship," "courtesy," and "reciprocity," all of which assume that it is advantageous to maintain a personally neutral, respectful atmosphere in which business can be conducted. *Apprenticeship* refers to the waning tradition whereby new members observe the action in the beginning, rather than jumping in and making waves. *Courtesy* forbids insults between members and requires referring to each other in debate by state rather than name —a device that preserves bargaining space between competitors. *Reciprocity* is the institutionalization of bargaining and compromise so that ad hoc majorities can be formed and reformed as issues change.

The consequence of congressional structure and norms for the legislative process are (1) to narrow the arena in which many critical decisions are made, (2) to limit the number of key decision makers on any given issue, (3) to give power to committees and subcommittees and (4) to increase the importance of reciprocity and the superior bargaining resources of those in leadership positions as a means of balancing the decentralizing consequences of issue specialization, duplication of committee functions, and dispersal of power.

While this may not be the best system for producing rational policy, it is tailor-made for interest group participation in the policy process.

Specialization enables groups to concentrate on developing relationships with particular committee staff and ranking congressmen since they will have the most impact on legislative substance. Although seniority has been weakened in the 94th Congress by rules changes that allow the Democratic Party caucus to elect chairmen, the prerogatives of seniority and the tendency to choose leaders from among ranking committee members still ensure a continuity of relationships that makes the effort to develop committee ties worthwhile.

Increased committee staff and expanded subcommittee roles may make it harder for some groups to maintain all the necessary committee contacts, and it may make the specialized information services of groups less essential. Open committee meetings will facilitate greater participation by citizens groups and other underfinanced lobbies. Openness helps all outside groups by making accurate information on congressional activities accessible at no cost to those who choose to observe the action.

Reciprocity has several assets from the viewpoint of the group. First, it increases the likelihood that a deal made within one committee will be honored at later stages since committees expect similar treatment from each other. Issue specialization plus reciprocity means that groups need to activate only those individuals directly interested in their issues, and can then hope that their colleagues will follow their voting cues.

Second, the emphasis on committees and the corollary emphasis on subject matter expertise, when coupled with the electoral need to represent constituency interests, leads to coalitions formed around issues rather than along strictly partisan or ideological lines. Thus groups select allies on an issue-by-issue basis; compromise and negotiation proceed within relatively flexible channels. Finally, reciprocity assumes that today's enemies are tomorrow's allies—a bargaining situation enhanced by the norms of courteous interpersonal communication.

LEGISLATORS AND LOBBYISTS

The myth of lobbying power holds that lobbyists are powerful enough to be considered the third branch of the legislature. This notion of powerful lobbyist and spineless legislator is supported by scandals such as the offer of a $5,000 bribe to Senator Clifford Case for his vote on a natural gas bill, or the Nathan Voloshen scandal in which he traded on Speaker John McCormack's prestige in order to get favors for clients; or the case of Senator Daniel Brewster, convicted in 1972 of taking a bribe in a postal vote case. Indeed, Senator Brewster's office was a classic example of an office run by and for special interests. His office was

> one where lobbyists wrote speeches, where a federal job was purchased for cash, where money flowed into [assistant's] and the Senator's pockets and where the Senator's signature was so widely copied by staff members that they even signed it to [the Senator's] final divorce decree.[12]

These stories seem to support Woodrow Wilson's observation that "The government of the United States at present is a foster child of special interests."

Numbers support the myth also. Approximately 2,000 persons register annually as lobbyists, but it has been estimated that the number of corporation vice-presidents, Washington lawyers, public relations men, and independent entrepreneurs who fit our functional definition of lobbying (that is, seeking to influence governmental decisions) totals over 5,000 people or ten lobbyists per congressperson. Eight out of ten of the largest corporations have Washington representatives, although only approximately 300 businesses actually registered lobbyists in 1975.

At the other extreme are analysts who see lobbies as underfinanced, overburdened, internally divided, and relatively powerless vis-à-vis legislators:

> Congress is not a passive body, registering already-existent public views forced on its attention by public pressures. Congress . . . is rather the major institution for creating and initiating political issues.[13]

The average chief executive of a trade association must perform his organizational chores in addition to lobbying. Trade association policies must accommodate the interests of all members, so heterogeneous and/or large associations tend to take very general issue positions representative of the lowest common denominator opinion within the association. Dissatisfaction with this slow-moving, nonspecific approach has led corporations to use trade associations for back-up research while they depend on their own man in Washington to keep abreast of daily happenings of direct interest to their company. Similarly dozens of specialized trade associations, often composed of only a dozen members, have been formed to complement the work of the peak associations (Chamber of Commerce, AMA, American Petroleum Institute). Yet trade associations have some assets that compensate for their lack of policy-making effectiveness. First, the notion of an industry position as compared to a company one has the strength of numbers. Second, corporate leaders prefer to let associations lobby because of "a desire for anonymity by management and their suspicion that active legislative programs are faintly unrespectable.[14]

The middle view places legislators and lobbyists in a transactional bargaining relationship in which the scope of the issue and the scope of the conflict (that is, the number of persons, groups, and interests involved) determines the relative influence of lobbyists in any specific policy situation. In the relationship between congressmen and lobbyists, the advantage lies with the officials since they do the voting. As such they are the only actors capable of translating group goals into public policy. In addition, the legislator is in a position to offer positive assistance to the lobbyist, such as arranging committee hearings for group measures that will never pass, leaking important strategic information, inserting group letters and articles into the *Congressional Record*—and just plain friendship. On the other hand, an annoyed legislator can use the hearing device to investigate lobbyists or just threaten to no longer cooperate.

> The senators have what the lobbyists want—a vote, prestige, access to national publicity, and the legislative "inside dope." Moreover, the lobbyist wants this not just once but many times over a number of years. The senators are in a position to bargain. They need not give these things away.[15]

Friendship between legislators and lobbyists is a two-way street; it may produce the few minutes advance notice needed to best one's opposition, but it may also oblige the lobbyist to play down a position or do a favor for the legislator. For example, Washington lawyer,

Tommy "the Cork" Corcoran, when asked why he was so successful, said, "I get my information a few hours ahead of the rest." Another lobbyist, asked to explain the uses of senatorial friendships, explained: "You can't go far on friendship alone. Oh, maybe once a senator would push a little bill for you because you were his friend. But a senator is like a well—you can only draw on it so many times.[16] On the other hand closeness with legislators can lead to identification with their interests, an identification that legislators may exploit. As another lobbyist said, "Whenever I get a call from a senator who says 'Hello, Johnny-boy, come on up for lunch today,' I know that he's going to do something we won't like."[17]

The main service that lobbyists provide for legislators is the collection, transmission, and dissemination of information: technical information on the ramifications of proposed legislation, as well as political information on the impact of the bill on a company and/or the legislator's district or within Congress itself. Lobbyists can generate grass roots support for legislators' positions, compile background information for speeches and draft legislation, prepare witness schedules for hearings in order to highlight particular viewpoints. Representatives Abner Mikva stated that the real weapon of public interest lobbyists as effective tax lobbyists was their comprehension of the issues. "They haven't got any troops. All they've got is their intellect."[18]

The basic relationship underlying all these varieties of activity is relaying information necessary for action to cooperative congressional insiders in order to generate congressional interest in the group's issue. Consequently the natural point of intimate contact is between the expert committee staff member and the lobbyist. Staff members and lobbyists trade information. Staff members want to know the specific problems of various industries, groups, and so on; the lobbyist wants a feel of general solutions under consideration. Staff relationships are also crucial for lobbyists because, while congressmen suggest the generalities of legislation, the staff draft the technical language that will affect specific interests.

Probably one of the closest informational relationships exists between lobbyists specializing in tax laws and the staff and members of the Ways and Means Committee and the Joint Committee on Internal Revenue Taxation. This subgovernment is based on expertise since, in tax legislation perhaps more than in other areas, "a few carefully chosen words or a properly placed phrase in a new law can save—or cost—a corporation millions of dollars in taxes."[19] The lobbyist experts work with committee staff in supplying testimony, trading technical information, and editing bill drafts and then the committee report that provides a legislative history to guide later court decisions. Robert Brandon, tax specialist with Nader's Tax Reform Research Group, "is such a part of the process in the House that he moves freely in and out of the anteroom just off the committee's hearing room. . . . Moskowitz [Common Cause lobbyist] enjoys similar privileges on the Senate side."[20]

The relationship between lobbying and special interest provisions was illustrated in September 1976 when a Nader specialist's leak to *New York Times* reporter Eileen Shanahan led to two long articles on the special interest provisions in the 1976 omnibus tax reform bill. Pressure from Senators Kennedy and Proxmire forced Senate Finance Committee Chairman Russell Long to hold a hearing to reconsider seventy-three such provisions. The hearings uncovered amendments benefiting only one or two specific companies or individuals:

- Senator Michael Gravel's provision helped two trade associations in the material-recycling business (both had contributed to his campaign).
- Senator Robert Dole put in two amendments granting oil depletion allowances to trusts held by Senator Long's relatives.
- Senator Walter Mondale wanted an amendment to provide tax credits for homeowners who installed clock thermostats, a benefit for Minnesota-based Honeywell, Inc.

As the list suggests, businesses were able to obtain special favors by linking their benefit with broader constituency interests. Lobbyists interested in real estate taxes and foreign income and capital formation benefits came lobbying accompanied by businessmen from the legislators' home district or had legislators' offices flooded with mail from them.

The good government groups found it harder to build a bandwagon for the general notion of tax reform. Thus many of the public interest groups' initial gains in adding tougher revenue-producing provisions were whittled away during the mark-up sessions. Senator Muskie, complaining about the $2 billion floating away through tax loopholes, recalled Senator Long's comment that the definition of loophole depends on whose ox is being gored. Long also told Muskie that "There is always a majority for 'reform' but very seldom a majority—after the special interests have done their work—for any particular reform."

During a 1972 subcommittee mark-up session on the Fair Credit Billing Act, the agenda was supplied by the American Bankers Association, and Senator Bill Brock, son of a bank director, shepherded the anti-consumer agenda items through the committee. "When the tallies were all in, the banks had rammed through, wholly or in part, fifteen of their twenty amendments. One weary senator muttered . . . We began with the Fair Credit Billing Act. We wound up with the Bank Protection Act of 1972."[21] This type of relationship is not atypical; for example, in the 1973–74 fight to create a consumer protection agency, the lobbyist for the Grocery Manufacturers of America wrote part of the Government Operations Committee's minority report opposing the bill.

Lobbyists' information is usually slanted to benefit the group's position, but at the same time lobbyists must never lie. Reliable information is the source of their influence, the precondition for their access to decision-making situations. Thus, in 1974 the coal companies couched their arguments against a tough strip-mining land reclamation bill in terms of the energy crisis; in 1975, with gas available and jobs disappearing, they switched their emphasis to the negative impact that limits on strip mining would have on available jobs in coal mining regions.

Lobbyists fill many kinds of voids in the congressional dispersed power structure precisely because information is such a highly valued commodity. Success reflects the lobbyist's skill, knowledge, and expertise. A good lobbyist will analyze all introduced bills to find out the sponsor, the reasons the bill was introduced, "and he will see if anything can usefully be said, and by whom, to the member or to the people at whose request the bill was introduced."[22] Timing and content of messages are very important in securing a good reception from congressional personnel, since the lobbyist's resources compete with the media and with cues provided by expert colleagues, political party leaders, and the President. Thus, when "inside lobbyists" that is, legislators or staff who will argue for the group) seek to move a group's proposal, the group's role within that policy process is obviously augmented.

Often lobbyists are devoutly interested in an item of little significance to most people, proving again the adage that an intense minority can win over an apathetic majority. Take, for example, the issue of the Veterans Day celebration date. Until 1968 it was celebrated on November 11th. In 1968 Congress passed the Uniform Monday Holiday Act which set the observance for four holidays on the nearest Monday. Under pressure from veteran's organizations, the matter was again brought up for consideration. The vets argued that "The historical significance of a November 11 commemoration far outweighs the convenience of a three-day weekend. . . .[23] Opposing them were the Discover America Travel Organizations, Inc., the Calender Reform Political Action Group, and the National Council for Monday Holidays (an alliance of seventeen travel-related corporations, trade associations, and unions). They argued that the Monday date increased tourism and decreased traffic fatalities since it was no longer a one-day holiday.

In 1975 Congress returned Veterans Day to November 11th after a promise from Congresswoman Pat Schroeder that "We have not declared war on Monday holidays. . . ." The congressional reversal indicates the successful federalism strategy of the veterans who had used the eight previous years to pressure states into restoring the original date, so that by 1975 Congress was nationalizing the independent actions of forty-six states.

The congressional process makes it easiest for lobbyists to influence the language of narrow policy decisions that affect only themselves, and moderately easy to influence broader issues if a coalition of groups can present a united front that legislators will accept as the voice of all relevant interests, but rarely possible to affect the outline of redistributive policies because of their scope and generality. On distributive issues such as tax breaks, subsidies, or new capital expenditure projects, groups and legislators may engage in *logrolling*, a term meaning that each group uses its own access points to gain its goals and then supports other groups on parallel proposals.[24] Commodity groups make such trades, but so do seemingly opposed groups as indicated by the pragmatic alliance between the American Medical Association and the cigarette companies in which the companies contributed $10 million to the AMA for cancer research, and the AMA remained aloof from the debate over a health warning in cigarette advertisements and on packages.

On broad issues such as aid to education, revenue sharing, and so on, groups form *alliances* to decrease their work loads, increase their bargaining resources, and present unified demands to which decision-makers must respond. One of the oldest, most effective, and famous alliances is the Leadership Conference on Civil Rights, an alliance of labor unions, church groups, civil rights organizations, and civic groups which was responsible for coordinating the successful group strategy that helped pass strong civil rights legislation in the 1960s. The Conference grew from thirty organizations in 1949 to sixty-five in 1963 to over 125 by 1971.

During the congressional debates on the 1964, 1965, and 1966 civil rights legislation, the Conference, under the leadership of NAACP lobbyist Clarence Mitchell, organized monitoring corps who sat in in the galleries to make sure their supporters were on the floor for crucial votes. The Conference maintained constituency pressure on legislators by mail and in visits by delegations of hometown folks. Two dozen or more lobbyists from Conference organizations such as ADA, AFL-CIO, NAACP, and others visited their key friends in each house. Each organization contributed its contacts and resources (time, money, members) to create success.

SUMMARY

In this chapter we have seen that Congress provides a meeting ground for groups with widely divergent policy interests and varied abilities and resources for participation in the policy process. Generally the 1970 congressional rules reforms have made Congress more accessible to more groups, but at the same time these reforms have lessened the predictability of success for any one group. This paradox arises because the openness of the new rules tends to break up the one-to-one committee staff/lobbyist relationships of the past which were the anchor of stable lobbying alliances. Now, although the currency of lobbying remains technical and political information, the opportunities for using it effectively have increased as the potential of subcommittees, party caucuses, and individual congressmen to change policy has increased.

The nature of group lobbying—the kinds of intergroup alliances and indirect activities required—is closely keyed to the nature of the policy desired. The narrower and more specific the issue, the more likely a group is to act alone. As issues broaden in terms of costs and/or benefits, groups generally form lobbying coalitions in order to produce an outside consensus that will be translated into policy. The openness and flexibility of group lobbying patterns in the congressional environment contrasts with the rather formal relationships, discussed in the next chapter, between groups and the executive branch.

NOTES

1. J. L. Freeman, *The Political Process* (New York: Random House, 1955), p. 10.
2. Douglass Cater, *Power in Washington* (New York: Random House, 1964), p. 17. Griffiths calls such centers "whirlpools," Cater calls them "subgovernments."
3. Ira Sharkansky, *The Routines of Politics* (New York: Van Nostrand Reinhold, 1970), pp. 5, 9.
4. See Lewis Dexter, *How Organizations Are Represented in Washington* (Indianapolis: Bobbs-Merrill, 1969), pp. 80–101.
5. Charles L. Clapp, *The Congressman* (New York: Anchor Books, 1963), p. 314.
6. U.S., Congress, Senate, *Congressional Record,* 94 Cong., 1st Sess., June 25, 1975, p. S11487.
7. U.S., Congress, Senate, House of Representatives, Select Committee on Committees, *Hearings: Committee Organization in the House,* 93 Cong., 1st Sess., vol. 3, part 2, June–July 1973, p. 342.
8. *Ibid*., p. 242.
9. This series of quotes is from U.S., Congress, *Congressional Record,* 93 Cong., 2nd Sess., July 9, 1974, p. E4856.
10. See Malcolm Jewell and Samuel Patterson, *The Legislative Process in the United States* (New York: Random House, 1966), p. 362–75; and Lewis A. Froman, Jr., *The Congressional Process* (Boston: Little, Brown, 1967).
11. See Congressional Quarterly, *Inside Congress* (Washington, D.C.: Congressional Quarterly, Inc., 1976), chaps. 1, 3, 4.

12. David Vogler, *The Politics of Congress* (Boston: Allyn and Bacon, 1974), p. 215.
13. Raymond Bauer, Ithiel de Sola Pool, and Lewis Dexter, *American Business and Public Policy: The Politics of Foreign Trade* (New York: Atherton Press, 1967), p. 478.
14. Paul Cherington and Ralph Gillen, *The Business Representative in Washington* (Washington, D.C.: The Brookings Institution, 1962), pp. 62–63.
15. Donald Matthews, *U.S. Senators and Their World* (New York: Vintage Books, 1960), p. 188.
16. *Ibid.*, p. 191.
17. *Ibid.*, p. 189.
18. Daniel Balz, "Tax Report: Attorneys Perform Dual Role as Lobbyist, Policy Makers," *National Journal* (1975): p. 1382.
19. *Ibid.*
20. *Ibid.*, p. 1380. Tax lawyer David Richmond said he prefers to seek change through Congress since it is the quickest route; "To litigate may take five years. To run the gamut of administrative procedures may take three years. In Congress, decisions may be reached in a matter of months," p. 1381.
21. Jack Anderson, April 4, 1972.
22. Dexter, *How Organizations Are Represented,* p. 58.
23. See *New York Times,* August 5, 1975.
24. See David Truman, *The Governmental Process* (New York: Knopf, 1951), chaps. 11, 12.

Chapter 9

Group Access to the Executive Branch

Despite the enormity and heterogeneity of the executive branch bureaucracy, from the group perspective it more nearly resembles the pigeonhole separateness of post office boxes than the freewheeling maze of access points found in Congress. Most groups create direct relationships with the specific subdivisions of the bureaucracy that handle their subject matter or supervise the distribution of grants for which their group qualifies. This limits the number of access points for each group, but it still permits vertical play-offs between the political and career levels of the bureaucracy.

From the standpoint of interest group relationships with the executive branch, that giant enterprise may be divided into four segments: the presidential office, the department and agency levels influenced by presidential appointees, middle-level bureaucratic subgovernments, and the regulatory agencies. Each part is characterized by a different pattern of relationships that reflects the amount of time the principals expect to have to do their jobs, the subject matter, the degree of independence from electoral and partisan politics, and the work norms that affect behavior patterns of the executive branch actors.

THE PRESIDENCY

Although textbooks depict the President as leader of *all* the people, lines of access for special interests *among* the people exist within the

Executive Office of the Presidency. Traditionally Presidents have distrusted the permanent bureaucracy, an attitude that leads to duplication of department policy-making roles within the Executive Office. Now "interest group brokerage" has been added to earlier duties of policy coordination and administration, partially to accommodate group demands for a policy-making role at this level and partially with an eye toward the next election.

> During the late 1960s and early 1970s a large number of special assistantships or semi-institutionalized offices were set up explicitly to serve as brokerages or clearinghouses to provide greater access to presidential attention for professional, demographic, or specialized organizations. The interests thus provided for comprise a veritable index of middle- and upper-middle-class American society. . . . Once their foothold is established, interest groups are certainly more able to transmit to the President their urgent priorities and play upon the potential political backlash that could arise should their representation be discontinued.[1]

For example, in the modern presidential bureaucracy there are offices for economics, energy, environment, consumers, and drug-abuse prevention; special assistants for military affairs, civil rights, labor relations, cultural affairs, education, the aged, health and nutrition, physical fitness, and volunteerism; ad hoc portfolios for regulatory agencies, Wall Street, governors, mayors, intellectuals, women, blacks, latinos, ethnics, "the Jewish community," and youth.

President Ford went one step further in 1976 and created an Office of Public Liaison, with a twenty-three person staff headed by public relations man William Baroody, Jr. His job was to devise settings for dialogue between the administration and outside groups: holding regional town meetings or conferences featuring the President, inviting eighty people to the White House for Tuesday discussions of various issues, providing formal briefings when requested by important groups, and scheduling biweekly Wednesday meetings in the cabinet room for eighteen to thirty important interest group leaders.

The importance of these symbolic advisers to outside interests is suggested by the strenuous efforts of the scientific community to restore its White House niche. President Eisenhower first brought scientific advisers into the Executive Office; President Kennedy formalized the relationship with the creation of an Office of Science and Technology to offer advice on technological decisions in terms of their benefits for national security and the general welfare. Then under Presidents Johnson and Nixon, such advice was requested less often, so in 1973, as part of Reorganization Plan 1, President Nixon eliminated the office and transferred its functions to the National Science Foundation. Within months, prestigious scientists and research centers were complaining that without an oversight office in the White House to weigh competing viewpoints, there was no coherent national science policy and, consequently, a decline in research productivity.

In the National Science and Technology Policy, Organization, and Priorities Act of 1976, the Office of Science and Technology Policy was reinstated as part of the Executive Office. It and three other new committees will study future priorities in scientific and technological research. The President's adviser will also provide specific advice in all fields related to science, assist the Office of Management and Budget (OMB) in making decisions on federally supported research, and prepare an annual Science and Technology Report for the President and Congress. As with the environmentalists' agitation in the late '60s, scientific community pressure produced two symbols of access —an office within the Executive Office and a message counterpart to the State of the Union message.

Advisers in the White House and members of prestigious Executive Office components such as the director of OMB also act as spokesmen for interests seeking to use presidential influence in support of their policy positions. Thus, in the case of an independent consumer agency during the Nixon years, Associate Budget Director Frank Cartucci, OMB Director Roy Ash, White House Special Assistant Peter Flanigan, and others voiced business' position against the bill.

Flanigan represented business interests in the Nixon White House. As one steel executive said, "He's the guy who people in our industry turn to. And we wouldn't turn to him unless he came through."[2] Or as a Commerce Department official put it: "Peter Flanigan is to the Department of Commerce what Henry Kissinger is to the Department of State." Indeed the range of Flanigan's assignments indicates the importance in terms of policy outputs that such ties had for outside groups.

> [He] supervised the White House's relations with the Federal regulatory agencies . . . looked after the President's consumer affairs program . . . persuaded steel companies to roll back prices after they had announced an increase . . . brought security executives into a meeting with the President for a pep talk when the stock market was depressed, drew up a plan to revitalize the nation's merchant marine, persuaded the CAB to permit an air fare increase that it initially opposed, got the Italian shoe industry to adopt import restrictions to limit competition with American shoe makers, and tried to negotiate a textile import limitation with the Japanese.

The President himself becomes involved with interest groups in several ways. First, in his symbolic role as Chief of State, he often has "photo opportunity" sessions with representatives of national interest groups. For example, during the week of March 10, 1975, John Hersey recorded that President Ford had meetings, lasting four to fourteen minutes, with Miss America, Miss Cotton, the Easter Seal poster child, and the high school winners of the Veterans of Foreign Wars Voice of Democracy contest.[3] Such visits provide groups with proof of their national importance; they provide the President with pictorial verification of his role as leader of the people.

Presidents also meet for longer, more substantive sessions with issue-oriented groups on matters related to their programs or electoral interests. For example, in that same week, President Ford discussed food with a Soviet trade delegation on a U.S. tour sponsored by Pepsi-Cola, met with the editors of *Fortune* Magazine, spoke to editors of the National Newspaper Association who were at the White House for a reception, and talked with retiring Secretary of Labor Peter Brennan and building trades union leaders. Along the same lines, the President makes speeches at the annual conventions of important groups such as President Nixon did with the dairy farmers or President Ford did at the annual convention of the Air Force Association, the Radio and Television Correspondents Association, the Veterans of Foreign Wars, and others.

In yet another variation on the same theme, President Ford invited 100 coal industry executives to a day-long parley with top administration members to discuss the role of coal in energy Project Independence. While government executives praised the coal industry, industry executives took this opportunity to request relaxation of

Clean Air Act standards, the veto of a conservationist-oriented strip-mining bill, increases in the depletion allowance for coal, and a permanent investment tax credit. The day ended with a private dinner, hosted by President Ford, at the State Department.[4]

The President often seeks support from domestic interest groups, especially when foreign policy ventures are affected by congressional policy activities. For example, President Nixon invited fourteen Jewish leaders to the White House for an hour-long meeting during which the President tried to assure the Jews that the Jackson amendment linking Soviet emigration policies to a bill granting them most-favored-nation status was unnecessary. Nixon cited messages relayed to him via the Soviet Embassy in an effort to lessen Jewish support for the Jackson amendment which, at that time, had enough cosponsors to pass. While Nixon was seeking to dissipate the effects of Jewish strength in Congress, President Ford in September 1975 called in thirty-three leaders of American Jewish organizations for the opposite reason. He asked them to use their congressional leverage to secure a massive affirmative vote in favor of stationing American technicians in the Sinai as part of an Egyptian-Israeli agreement.

During the 1974 Arab-Israeli war, the Aramco oil companies (Exxon, Mobil, Texaco, and Standard Oil of California) sent a memorandum to President Nixon urging him not to send aid to Israel. The message was sent as a result of the companies' meeting with King Faisal of Saudi Arabia, who threatened to take away Aramco's oil concession if it did not get its message through to Americans. The memorandum said:

> There is a high probability that a single action taken by one producer government against the U.S. would have a snowballing effect that would produce a major petroleum supply crisis. . . . We are convinced of the seriousness of the intentions . . . any actions of the U.S. government at this time in terms of increased military aid to Israel will have a critical and adverse effect on our relations with the moderate Arab producing countries.[5]

The memorandum was delivered by messenger on October 12, but the President did not see it until October 14 after he had ordered a massive arms lift to Israel.

This kind of presidential-interest group policy-oriented relationship is directly related to outside circumstances. Thus, in August 1970 President Nixon said we should "strive for an environment that not only sustains life but enriches life, harmonizing the works of man and nature for the greater good of all."[6] By December 1973, with the election behind him and the Arab oil boycott in process, the same man told his aides that "I'm going to have to propose some things that will drive the environmentalists up the wall. . . . How are we going to get the coal out of the ground without driving them out of their trees?" Such presidential desires to revere trees or drive environmentalists out of them are directly related to current public opinion soundings and the strength of specific groups in the policy-making process. The enormous range of presidential activity permits the President to solicit aid from groups when he needs them, and palm them off when the pressure lessens.

President Nixon's use of White House initiatives to further his 1972 reelection plans presents a most striking, indeed, illegal example of White House manipulation of government policies in order to gain interest group support. Under the "Responsiveness Program," Fred Malek worked with the Domestic Policy Council and ad hoc interest group oriented committees to cultivate previously Democratic voting blocs such as blacks, Hispanics, the elderly, labor, and so on by offering government grant programs, appointments, and program initiatives. For example, the White House Spanish Speaking Constituent Group Task Force was to use the resources of the executive branch to "stroke this community. . . ."[7] The White House group was also instrumental in channeling federal funds to Spanish groups and independent businessmen. Similarly, to woo the black vote, group leaders such as James Farmer exchanged election support promises for federal funding.[8]

In any interest group encounters at the presidential level, the personal initiative usually lies with the President. His symbolic and administrative strengths give him the overwhelming advantage. However, the need for group support when the President seeks reelection or needs backing for a controversial policy is tacitly acknowledged by the incorporation of spokesmen for group interests in explicitly labeled positions within the White House staff.

THE BUREAUCRACY

Government bureaucracy refers to administrative institutions that implement programs, establish new emphases for government action, represent the government's symbolic concern for certain groups such as blacks, business or labor, and meet the geographical and technological needs of the country as it develops. In the process of expanding from the nine agencies that served George Washington to the 2,000 agencies, boards, commissions, departments, and corporations of today, a crazy patchwork mixture of form and function has emerged. But it would be wrong to assume that no intent lies beneath the balkanized, feudalized structure called the federal bureaucracy.

> Organizational arrangements are not neutral. We do not organize in a vacuum. . . . Organizational arrangements tend to give some interests, some perspectives, more effective access to those with decision-making authority. . . . As Richard Neustadt has pointed out: "In political government, the means can matter quite as much as the ends; they often matter more."[9]

New programs are placed in bureaucratic locations for political as much as programmatic reasons; often subdivisions of a single department can be pursuing diametrically opposed objectives. For example,

> The Department of Agriculture was purporting to regulate pesticides while promoting their use. Water pollution abatement was in the Department of the Interior, whose constituency included many sorts of water polluters. Airplane noise was under the Federal Aviation Agency whose main job was nurture of the noisemakers.[10]

The size of some cabinet departments makes it impossible not to create such conflicts: HEW is really a vast holding company with 400 programs, 129,000 employees, and a budget of $118 billion a year. Within its jurisdiction are eight agencies, twenty bureaus, and forty program clearinghouse centers. Conflict among programs and priorities is inevitable.

An alternative to incorporating new programs into existing frameworks is to reward a large or vociferous constituency with a separate institution. Clientele groups and dependencies prefer agencies to represent only their interests since such separation reinforces their mutual dependency. In this way the entire bureaucracy as well as separate departments become microcosms of conflicts of interest in the outside world.

> The Commerce Department protects the interests of private industry generally, the Bureau of Mines defends the coal and oil industry, the FPC promotes natural gas and electric power, and the EPA and CEQ represent the environmentalists.[11]

When departments such as Commerce and Agriculture were created, the economic population involved was enthusiastic because the action symbolized their political importance. On the other hand, when agencies such as the National Labor Relations Board (NLRB) or the Council on Environmental Quality (CEQ) were created, the constituent population perceived the new institutions as a threat to their own current internal power relationships. For example, when EPA was established, it took 6,000 employees from fifteen different agencies. Created as an election ploy to appease the environmentalists, it represented a threat to economic interests—many of whom successfully resisted relocation from their old departments. Consequently today EPA shares airplane noise level monitoring decisions with the Federal Aviation Agency, environmental radiation level decisions with the Nuclear Regulatory Commission, and pesticide regulations with USDA.[12]

History and constituent pressures can also create situations in which two institutions perform overlapping functions, but due to institutional loyalties and their own clientele interests, neither one talks to its bureaucratic counterpart. For instance, there is little communication between the Department of Commerce and the Federal Trade Commission, or between the Department of Labor and the NLRB.

Once established, a "clientele" agency becomes a status symbol not to be tampered with lightly. Thus when President Johnson proposed a merger of Commerce and Labor, back to the original model of 1903, the Chamber of Commerce called it "contrary to the best interests of the country."[13] It would have represented a loss of face for both interests. The same feelings surfaced in 1972 when the building industry opposed renaming HUD as the Department of Community Development because the word *Housing* would no longer be in the department title.

The relationship of outside interests and bureaucratic components is never more clearly revealed than when a President suggests an executive branch reorganization. When President Nixon proposed a regrouping of executive branch entities into goal-oriented, functionally related departments, he antagonized interests "anxious to preserve their pipelines for putting influence in or getting money out."[14] As former HEW Secretary John Gardner told a congressional committee: "It took them [special interests] years to dig their particular tunnel into the public vault, and they don't want the vault moved."

The idea of super-departments appeals to those who see it in policy terms as a means of coordinating related programs and at the same time decreasing the influence of any one special interest. Reorganization opponents look at the issue from the recipient's viewpoint and "worry that the benefits of having their 'own' program will be diluted if it is submerged in other activities of a new departmental conglomerate." Their argument is buttressed by those who feel that broad program mandates encourage governmental vagueness in implementation. The goals of community development, economic affairs, and similar catchall agencies are "too abstract to serve the concrete needs of effective government programs."[15]

Nixon's plan to create a Department of Community Development by adding community/urban development programs found throughout government to the basic HUD structure illustrates the issue. Nixon wanted to move approximately a dozen programs into HUD:

From the Department of Transportation (DOT): the Federal Highway Administration and Urban Mass Transit Administration,

From the United States Department of Agriculture (USDA): Farmers Home Agriculture and the Rural Electrification Administration,

From the Department of Commerce: the Economic Development Administration and five regional commissions,

From the Office of Economic Opportunity (OEO): community action programs and also the independent Appalachian Regional Commission.

The merger was opposed by the highway lobby, farmers, veterans, actors, preachers, homebuilders, and the League of Women Voters. The farm lobbies feared that they would be submerged in an urban-oriented department, as did NACO, the National Association of Counties. The veterans feared that the next round of suggestions would transfer the veterans mortgage program from the Veterans Administration (VA) to this new department. The highway lobby feared a raid on their trust fund. The League of Women Voters, Common Cause, National Council of Churches, and Actors Equity Association all argued that moving community action programs to this high-level department would bury them under layers of bureaucracy. Only the Conference of Mayors favored the plan since it would provide them with one-stop shopping for all their government assistance.

Program possessiveness adds emotional overtones to normal interest group needs to develop informational and personnel ties with key bureaucratic action centers. The result is a "mosaic of symbiotic professional and consulting ties . . . between public officials and special interest and policy elites."[16] Such linkages once created give inside groups a defensive advantage over their competition and provide a measure of political independence based on group support for the bureaucratic unit.

Presidential Level of Bureaucracy

The presidential level of bureaucracy refers to the approximately 2,500 appointive officials who are selected directly by the President or indirectly by his appointees. They sit atop the executive departments, agencies, commissions, boards, and government corporations, caught between the need to carry forth the President's program and the need to advance the interests and strengths of their bureaucratic base. Outside interest group input at this level occurs mainly during the appointment process or through membership on advisory commissions.

Group influence over appointments is strongest for those positions such as Secretary of Labor, Commerce, Agriculture or Transportation, where the department develops policy for specific economic interests. Similarly, officials in charge of subsidy and grant programs or single interest regulatory programs may be vetoed by their clientele groups. The veto role is considered essential because, as Senator Hubert Humphrey explained, groups look to these officials to represent them "in the councils of government [and] to provide them with leadership and assistance. They especially look upon the Secretary . . . as their champion and chief defender and promoter of their legitimate interests."[17]

Group opinion is usually requested informally before a name is submitted to the Senate for its "advice and consent," thus negating the chances for groups not consulted initially to reverse the process at the congressional hearing level. Most confirmation hearings are pro forma affairs where opposing groups can testify but rarely win. Consider the hearings of each of the following winners:

- Claude Brinegar, formerly a Union Oil of California executive, and a known antimass transit advocate was opposed by the Highway Action Coalition when he was nominated as Secretary of Transportation.
- Walter Hickel and Stanley Hathaway both received flack from environmentalist groups when they were nominated as Secretary of the Interior since they were western governors with proindustry, anticonservationist records.
- Earl Butz was vociferously opposed as Secretary of Agriculture by the Farm Bureau, the National Farmers Union, and the National Farm Organization (NFO) because he was seen as a spokesman for agribusiness, who felt that the demise of the small farmer was inevitable since farming was a business today instead of a way of life. As Oren Stanley, president of the NFO said:

> Businessmen wouldn't accept appointment of a national labor leader as Secretary of Commerce; laboring men and women wouldn't accept appointment of the president of General Motors as Secretary of Labor; and farmers shouldn't be called on to accept appointment of Earl Butz as Secretary of Agriculture.[18]

When Nixon appointed Peter Brennan as Secretary of Labor in 1972, he rewarded the blue-collar, conservative supporters of his reelection by choosing a former construction trades union leader, one of the "hard hats." He also exacerbated the liberal-conservative split within the AFL-CIO, as well as the split between labor and its civil rights allies since Brennan was known for his anti-integrationist stance. Furthermore this same choice enabled Nixon to rebuff AFL-CIO leader George Meany by violating protocol and selecting a lower echelon labor chieftain. As one labor leader summarized his official reaction: "I'm like a man watching his mother-in-law drive his new Cadillac over a cliff. My feelings are mixed."[19]

By 1973 any honeymoon between Meany and Brennan was over. Brennan promised Meany to support strong minimum wage legislation, and then went before Congress to testify for a very weak bill. Meany said Brennan "ducked" the real issues, ignored labor's historical record, "betrayed" labor, used "threadbare arguments," and spouted "utter nonsense." "In his very first appearance on legislation before a congressional committee, this lifelong union man presented the discredited line of the U.S. Chamber of Commerce."[20]

In 1974 the VA administrator, Donald Johnson, former national commander of the American Legion, was drummed out of his job by the two other components of his subgovernment: the leaders of the veterans committees in Congress and the various interest groups. Since subgovernments are held together by policy commitments, when Administrator Johnson began to follow the White House line in terms of appointments, budget cuts, and program directions instead of heeding the wishes of his subgovernment coordinates, they forced Nixon to fire him. The front issue was a lack of sufficient health and education benefits for Vietnam veterans. The real issue was stated by Senator Vance Hartke who requested "a change of policy that would make the head of the VA an advocate of the veteran rather than an adversary." As these examples suggest, appointments have both symbolic value as evidence of an interest group's strength in the inner circles of decision making and policy complications.

Groups also combine appointments and policy interest through the mechanism of *advisory committees.* There are six types of public advisory commissions: those of a general advisory nature, scientific and technical ones, industry or special clientele committees, specific task advisory committees, research and study committees, and public conferences. From the interest group viewpoint, the most important are the industry advisory committees "composed predominately of members or representatives of a single industry or group of selected industries or of any subdivision of a single industry made on a geographic, service, or product basis."[21]

The committees provide a means for officials to seek collective input and/or public support from those who will be affected by forthcoming decisions. For those who are asked to join such committees, it is a source of personal prestige, a means to seek friends among important officials, and an important source of inside information related to present actions and future directions. For example, when the White House was courting the dairy lobby's campaign contributions, White House assistant Jack Gleason asked their attorney, "Are there any people in the Associated Dairymen's Group whom we ought to give priority consideration for some of the Department of Agriculture advisory boards or commissions? We can play this pageantry pretty far. . . ."[22]

Those who like the advisory committee concept see it as an affirmation of representative government that "reenforces the idea of citizen participation in today's government. It suggests the need for an appreciation of the citizen and the client by the official."[23] To critics of the system, these committees represent a way to institutionalize the reality of unequal access to decision makers.

In 1973 there were 1,250 advisory committees within the executive branch: 241 created by statute, the rest formed by government officials who feel such input "to be in the public interest in connection with the performance of duties imposed on that department or agency by law."[24] The total cost for committees in 1973 was $31,110,810; the average cost per committee was $18,970.[25] Of the 22,256 positions on federal advisory committees and commissions, 19,000 are public citizens appointed by the President or by one of the heads of the forty-five departments and agencies that operate these committees. Not only do these committees tend to overrepresent insider organizations and big corporations, they are also unrepresentative of women and black categoric groups: only 11 percent of the positions in 1975 were held by women, 4 percent by blacks; 50 percent of the committees were all white, 36 percent were all male.

Most of these committees deal with specific policy areas. For example, in 1970 Secretary of Commerce Maurice Stans asked President

Nixon to create a voice for industry to counter the newly created Council on Environmental Quality. So President Nixon established the National Industrial Pollution Control Council (NIPCC) in April 1970 to facilitate regular communication with him, the Council on Environmental Quality, and outside interests. The council consists of sixty-three industry members on a central committee and 136 other industry leaders on thirty specific issue subcommittees. NIPCC dilutes policy decisions that will cause economic problems to its companies by issuing statistical analyses that support their own claims or prohibiting government acquisition of unfavorable data by classifying it as confidential trade data. NIPCC's committees, as requested by Stans, contain no representatives from consumer, academic, environmental, or public interest groups. In reality NIPCC acts as "a massive, government-established public relations arm of the world's worst polluters."[26] Yet these men have the ear of the cabinet and Executive Office, while relevant but excluded agencies such as EPA are denied such ready internal access.

Committee composition usually reflects the uses for which such advice is sought. NIPCC serves as a defensive barrier that protects industrial polluters. By contrast, the Advisory Committee on Smoking and Health, established in 1962 by the surgeon general, was composed differently because its function was different. The surgeon general wanted a prestige group to assess all available knowledge on this issue and make recommendations that could be used to build public support for smoking controls.

Impetus for the committee came from four national health charities*, whose members requested such a committee from President-elect Kennedy in 1961 and from the surgeon general in a January 1962 meeting. Nevertheless bureaucratic wheels moved slowly until a Senate resolution calling for the committee and a pointed question at President Kennedy's May 1972 press conference produced an immediate response. Asked by a reporter what he was doing about the smoking and health issue, the President asked the surgeon general what *he* was doing. The result was announcement of this committee.

*American Heart Association, American Cancer Society, American Public Health Association, National TB Association.

Since the executives wanted a report that would generate public support for health-related action, they permitted the tobacco industry, health associations, professional associations, and federal agencies to review a list of 150 proposed members so that none could later weaken the impact of the findings by claiming a stacked committee. One blackball from an interest or any previous public statements on smoking and health issues disqualified a nominee. The final committee of ten well-known doctors was announced in May. They worked fourteen months to review 11,000 documents, interview hundreds of people, and finally produce a 387-page report, *Smoking and Health,* which concluded that the evidence showed cigarette smoking sufficiently hazardous to one's health to warrant appropriate remedial action.

While such committees have important control over federal implementation of specific government policies, the Advisory Council on Federal Reports, a private council funded by business, affects the data-gathering intiatives of all federal agencies. The council was created by the Budget Bureau to implement the Federal Reports Act of 1952 which sought to regulate the burden of government paperwork requirements by having Budget Bureau coordination of any information collected by agencies from ten or more persons. This coordination function has become a regulatory function. The council in connection with OMB reviews all proposed questionnaires prior to their approval.

The council feels that it has no decision-making authority since OMB makes the final decision, that it only provides OMB with "a completely frank expression of the business point of view."[27] Yet at the same time it acknowledges that it plays a "chokepoint" function analogous to the Rules Committee's agenda-setting function in the House of Representatives. In justifying this role, Charles Stewart, council chairman, said:

> It is in the public interest. If every form which is proposed by every government department or agency is launched throughout the U.S. without some overall review procedure, without some checkmate, industry would be overwhelmed. . . . There must be a review procedure at the federal level. . . . This is necessary from a number of standpoints. It is necessary to control burden. It is necessary to avoid overlapping. It is

> necessary to avoid "fishing expeditions" which are totally unfair to that portion of society to which they are addressed. . . . It is necessary to ensure that whatever questionnaires are released will produce results that are as meaningful as possible.[28]

Sounds reasonable, but Edward Berlin, former assistant general counsel of the Federal Power Commission (FPC), said that in his experience they were not just advisory committees.

> These committees do not advise the Budget Bureau; rather they determine what the Budget Bureau will accept or reject as far as FPC and other agencies are concerned. . . . I certainly felt that I would be shirking my responsibilities to the FPC were I not able to negotiate with the industry representatives and come up with something they would agree to let us have. That was the nature of the ball game.[29]

In a world where information is a power base, the ability to prevent government from acquiring necessary data or alteration of the method of inquiry can modify or prevent any subsequent government initiatives. From this viewpoint both kinds of industry involvement in advisory committees provide inside advantages for the participants, close off the flow of information (in violation of the very justification for their existence), and reserve important policy access points for leaders of established interests.

Mid-Level Bureaucratic Relationships

At the middle bureaucratic action center level, bureaucrats and representatives of special interests benefit from a symbiotic support relationship based on similar perceptions of key issues, mutual needs, and long-term technical information ties. In overall policy terms groups can affect the creation, development, implementation of public policies by

> helping to recruit and approve executive branch advisers; suggesting the framework within which policy changes are made; proposing and framing special legislation; building coalitions of support for, or opposition to, policy changes; and influencing the research and evaluation that take place in particular policy areas.[30]

From the lobbyist's point of view, such relationships provide an optimum way to have continual policy inputs. On the bureaucrat's side there are also advantages since his organizational independence from both congressional and presidential directives is often directly related to his degree of dependence on the interest group clientele that benefits from his decisions. Clientele groups can also increase "their" bureau's clout with Congress, run interference with OMB for its policy interests, rally public opinion behind agency programs, and affect the chances for successful implementation of programs.

The classic case of an independent subgovernment action center is the Army Corps of Engineers which improves and builds flood control projects.[31] It is an awesome combination of technical knowledge and political strength shared by the Army Corps of Engineers, congressmen on the public works committees, and the National Rivers and Harbors Congress, an interest group that includes legislators, corps members, and local interests such as local and state governments, building contractors, unions, water transportation companies, and so forth.

On an organizational chart the Corps of Engineers is responsible to the secretary of the army. Its civil division, which builds domestic rivers and harbors improvements, is composed of 35,000 civilians led by 250 military officers. However the corps is a prime source of domestic pork barrel projects for individual congressmen, favored for constituency benefit purposes since each project is visible and fully paid for with federal funds. Consequently in the last 150 years the corps has spent $18 billion to build and maintain 19,000 miles of commercial waterways selected and approved without Department of Defense (DOD) interference.

Each project is selected after going through an eighteen-step decision-making process that includes participation by the Rivers and Harbors Congress, the Corps of Engineers, and the congressional committees. The sequence excludes such seemingly logical participants as the Department of Defense, subdivisions of the Department of the Interior, the President himself, and the many presidential commissions on water resources that have been created over the years. The corps calls itself "the engineer consultants to, and contractors for, the Congress of the U.S." and uses this special relationship to circumvent presidential attempts to cut its budget or change its plans.

Only recently has the environmental movement begun to erode some of the corps's independence. For example, President Nixon halted work on the cross-Florida barge canal in the interests of preserving the water supply of the Everglades. Environmental interest groups are using the environmental impact statement requirement in NEPA to challenge the corps' method of estimating project costs and benefits. Over fifty lawsuits have been filed including a 1974 suit brought by a group of western railroads, the Sierra Club, and the Izaak Walton League specifically to prevent a corps' plan to replace and expand locks on the Mississippi River, but more generally to challenge the traditional decision-making processes and independence of the rivers and harbors action center.

In every policy area program development and bureaucratic interest group relationships shift constantly as both sides seek "to keep a favorable balance of political support over political opposition. . . ."[32] Since these relationships are dependent upon policy content, the same group may be an ally on one issue, an adversary on another. For instance, the AMA fought with HEW Secretary Robert Finch to oppose his choice of John Knowles as undersecretary of health, yet a year later worked with HEW to overturn Nixon's veto of a hospital construction appropriations bill.

The policy emphasis of clientele relationships tends to limit the effectiveness of interest groups to their own area of expertise. Therefore, many corporations have Washington offices, staffed with personnel who act daily as salesmen, international resources, and ambassador-brokers.[33] These offices represent a pragmatic acknowledgment of the intimate regulatory ties linking business and government. Over 100 agencies regulate some aspect of private economic activities from energy production to paperwork procedures: General Electric deals with eleven agencies that have a *direct* regulatory impact on its conduct.

The men representing such corporations engage in selling their company's performance in order to win contracts and grants, but they also participate in policy-making functions by furnishing technical information either to their employers or government counterparts, expediting government action, and making sure that their company's viewpoint is known to appropriate members of the executive branch. Multipurpose groups and trade associations, lacking an informational specialization, tend to be less closely tied into these middle-level bureaucratic relationships, unless it is in the interest of an industry to provide a united front in order to increase its bargaining clout or where businesses wish to express anonymous opinions through their associations.

Independent Regulatory Commission Relationships

Independent regulatory commissions (IRC) differ from other parts of the executive bureaucracy because they are created as adjuncts of Congress, located within the executive branch, but free from its "influence, direction, or oversight. . . . [The commissions are] responsible to Congress and subject to the oversight of Congress."[34] For example, over thirty bureaus, agencies, and departments participate in development of transportation policies, but only the Interstate Commerce Commission (ICC) and the Civil Aeronautics Board (CAB) are independent regulatory commissions. It was assumed that IRCs would be able to function as centers for politically independent economic experts because they would not be part of the bureaucratic authority hierarchy; their commissioners would serve fixed terms instead of at presidential pleasure; and their supervisory activities would be limited to a single area of economic activity. But, in practice, this independence has not developed for several reasons. First, Congress, once it has discharged its public obligation by creating an agency to solve the problem at hand, tends to lose interest. But the regulators cannot ignore Congress: commissions need continuing appropriations, new legislation or revisions of old, appointments and reappointments that require Senate confirmation.

Second, the President has developed an indirect influence over agency personnel since the 1950s when a Truman reorganization plan gave him the right to name commission chairmen, and these chairmen in turn were permitted to appoint their top staff members. This power, coupled with a high commissioner turnover rate, means that one President may appoint a majority of commissioners, thereby stacking the commissions with ideological friends. For example, in President Nixon's first term he filled twenty-eight of the thirty-eight positions on the CAB, FCC, FPC, ICC, and SEC, including all six chairmen.[35]

Presidents also indirectly control the scope of agency activities through OMB approval of all agency staff appropriations.

Third, the lack of congressional interest in commissions once they are created, plus the lack of executive interest in policies it cannot supervise, leaves a policy-interest vacuum that is filled by the regulated groups whose livelihood and goal success are intimately affected by these commissions. "The men and women who regulate industry in the public interest deal occasionally with the White House, frequently with select members of Congress, and constantly with executives of regulated industries."[36] Consequently the indirect policies of patronage has replaced the issue-based politics of other executive bureaucracy-interest group relationships.

> At one time or another everyone has played the game [of patronage and privilege]. . . . The regulators have played because they owe their jobs to political appointments. White House aides and members of Congress have played because regulated companies are important constituents. The regulated play because they cannot afford not to.[37]

The game begins when Presidents clear potential nominees with key interests in order to be forewarned of opposition during the confirmation process or perhaps to repay an industry campaign contribution or as a courtesy extended to business interests that the President needs to develop a climate of public confidence in the economy. Congressional politics also influence appointments in terms of initial sponsorship of nominees or through the confirmation process; for example, among FCC appointees: Robert Bartley was a nephew of Speaker Sam Rayburn, Nicholas Johnson a protégé of Senator Harold Hughes, and Kenneth Cox a close friend of Senator Warren Magnuson.[38] The politics of reappointment blends the two outside pressures. Commissioners interested in reappointment remember the case of FPC Commissioner Leland Olds, rejected for reappointment because he felt the FPC had the power to regulate natural gas! The moral was clear: tread on the friendly side of interests and congressmen who can affect your future.

Despite the unwritten rule to appoint commission chairmen from outside the regulated industry, more and more commissioners and their deputies have industry ties. The rationale is a need for expertise as well as sensitivity to political problems. A study of nine regulatory commissions showed that between 1960 and 1975, 30 percent of the appointees came from the regulated industry; from 1970 to 1975, the figure increased to 50 percent.[39] Personnel-industry ties are further reinforced by the practice of circular employment, whereby regulatory employees learn the byways of government and then leave for lucrative jobs with the industry they once regulated. For example, four of the six FCC commissioners who left between 1970 and 1975 now work for or are legal counsel to communications companies. Between 1960 and 1975, 37 percent of the eighty-five persons who left nine regulatory commissions went to work in the industries they had regulated.

Regulated interests continue the links established during the nomination process by meeting formally at hearings, informally in nonpublic meetings where pending cases are discussed, and socially for golf, cocktails, or dinner. Typically in 1974 TWA lobbyist Thomas K. Taylor played golf three times with CAB Chairman Robert Timm, joined him for part of his European vacation, lunched with all five board members every two or three months, and lunched with CAB staff members every two weeks. Industry representatives greet new commission appointees and offer help in initiating them into the subject matter complexities. The new commissioner soon receives invitations to industry sponsored parties, weekend hunting trips, and annual conventions where he is keynote speaker. Favorable articles appear in industry trade journals, bank loans are arranged, stock tips circulate, and the offer of future employment comes up in informal conversation. To the lobbyist, all this is business. "The lobbyist's hospitality and contributions are part of the mortar of the politics of regulation. Indeed, regulated industry has no real power over the regulators except for the power to offer jobs."[40]

Inevitably human relationships turn regulation in the public interest into protection of private interests. Typically the regulatory commission cycle begins with citizen complaints escalating to a crisis of discontent that is placated by congressional establishment of a watchdog agency to protect the public's interest. Initially there is enthusiasm, public approbation, and political rewards. But as industry experts are hired, problems multiply faster than commission staff resources can handle them, and public attention moves elsewhere; the regulated groups step into the attention vacuum thereby beginning the co-optation process. Homogeneous clientele and the lack of coordination among agencies, commissions, and departments facilitate development of these symbiotic relationships.

The result is acquiescence by osmosis. The regulator sees only those whom he regulates, begins to identify with their interests as they become his friends, and eventually accepts the notion that the public interest is the same as the interested public he sees. These psychological and institutional relationships create what David Truman called the "inflexibility of the established web."[41] Working along the same wavelength, accepting the same values, schooled in the same decision-making routines, groups with minimum effort can use regulators to gain policy benefits that would take a much greater investment of time, money, and publicity to guide through Congress.

In policy terms, the results are status quo, industry-oriented actions. As former FTC Commissioner Frederick Engman said:

> Most regulated industries have become federal protectorates, living in a world of cost-plus, safely protected from the ugly specter of competition, efficiency, and innovation. . . . Our airlines, our truckers, our railroads, our electronic media, and countless others are on the dole. We get irate about welfare fraud. But our complex systems of hidden regulatory subsidies make welfare fraud look like petty larceny.[42]

SUMMARY

In this chapter we have examined action center structural relationships between interest groups and executive branch subdivisions. Action centers developed as a pragmatic way to coordinate policy-related activities among people interested in similar policy areas. While some action centers have acquired a considerable amount of policy-making independence either from age or by the alignment of strong political interests, all action centers consist of psychologically and intellectually attuned policy makers whose common interests set the parameters of issue development in their particular area.

These centers arose to meet the need for action in government; they continue because they are politically useful. The multitude of separate decision-making authorities, the duplication of subject matter responsibilities, and the fragmentation of policy permit industries and politicians to create ad hoc coalitions of politically, emotionally, and geographically related allies. The role of outside interests in relation to both congressional or executive allies is related to the group's ability to influence appointments, election, and future job security, as well as its command of issue-related information that the government needs. Groups use these resources to secure sympathetic access to decision makers. As Chapter 10 indicates, this access is essential if interests want to influence the content of government policy.

NOTES

1. Thomas Cronin, *The State of the Presidency* (Boston: Little, Brown, 1975), pp. 123–24.
2. *New York Times,* March 20, 1972. All three quotations are from this article.
3. John Hersey, *The President* (New York: Knopf, 1975).
4. *National Journal,* March 29, 1975, p. 479.
5. Jack Anderson, July 19, 1974.
6. Both quotations are from J. Clarence Davies III and Barbara S. Davies, *The Politics of Pollution,* 2d ed. (Indianapolis: Pegasus, 1975), p. 102.
7. Senate Select Committee, *The Senate Watergate Report* (New York: Dell, 1974), p. 337.
8. Ibid., pp. 376–77.
9. H. Seidman, *Politics, Position and Power* (New York: Oxford University Press, 1970), p. 14.
10. *New York Times,* December 13, 1973.
11. Davies and Davies, *The Politics of Pollution,* p. 101.
12. *New York Times,* December 2, 1975.
13. *Business Week,* January 14, 1967, p. 140.
14. The next three quotations are from Large, "Overhauling Government Is Not Easy," *Wall Street Journal,* in U.S. Congress, *Congressional Record,* 92 Cong., 2d Sess., June 21, 1972. p. 59818. See also U.S. Congress Senate, Commission on Government Operations, *Hearings: Establish a Department of Energy and Natural Resources,* 93 Cong. 1st Sess., July, August, September, 1973.
15. U.S., Congress, Senate, *Congressional Record,* 92 Cong., 2d Sess., June 21, 1972, p. S989.
16. Cronin, *The State of the Presidency,* p. 99.

17. Hubert H. Humphrey, U.S., Congress, Senate, *Congressional Record,* 92 Cong., 1st Sess., April 23, 1971, p. S19453.
18. Ibid.
19. *New York Times,* December 1, 1972.
20. Victor Riesel column, April 17, 1973.
21. Executive Order 11007, President John F. Kennedy, February 26, 1962.
22. U.S., Congress, House of Representatives, Judiciary Committee, *Statement of Information,* Book VI (1974), p. 118.
23. David Brown, "Testimony" at *Hearings: Advisory Committees,* U.S. Congress, Senate, Commission on Government Operations, 91 Cong. 2nd Sess., October 1970, pp. 33–34.
24. Executive Order 11007.
25. U.S., Congress, *Congressional Record,* 93 Cong. 2nd Sess. June 20, 1974, pp. S1145–46.
26. Lee Metcalf, "Vested Oracles," *Washington Monthly* (July 1971): 46.
27. Brown, *Hearings: Advisory Committees,* pp. 40–41.
28. Ibid., p. 43.
29. Ibid., pp. 75–76.
30. Cronin, *The State of the Presidency,* p. 99.
31. This information is derived from Arthur Maass, "Congress and Water Resources," in *The Politics of the Federal Bureaucracy,* ed. Alan Altshuter (New York: Dodd, Mead, 1968), pp. 283–96; Leslie Roos and Arthur Maass, "The Lobby That Can't Be Licked," *Harpers,* pp. 71–80; and U.S. Congress, Senate, *Congressional Record,* 94 Cong., 1st Sess., August 20, 1975, pp. 8768–84.
32. Seidman, *Politics, Position and Power,* p. 32.
33. See Paul W. Cherington and Ralph L. Gillen, *The Business Representative in Washington* (Washington, D.C.; The Brookings Institution, 1962), and Lewis Anthony Dexter, *How Organizations are Represented in Washington* (Indianapolis: Bobbs-Merrill, 1969).
34. U.S., Congress, Senate, Hubert H. Humphrey, *Congressional Record,* 93 Cong., 1st Sess., November 29, 1973, p. S21405. The seven major ones are Interstate Commerce Commission (ICC), Federal Trade Commission (FTC), Federal Power Commission (FPC), Federal Communications Commission (FCC), Securities and Exchange Commission (SEC), Civil Aeronautics Board (CAB), and Atomic Energy Commission (AEC).
35. *New York Times,* May 5, 1973.
36. Louis Kohlmeier, Jr., *The Regulators: Watchdog Agencies and the Public Interest* (New York: Harper & Row, 1969), p. 69.
37. Ibid., p. 35.
38. *Business Week,* February 28, 1970, p. 64.

39. The statistics are all from the *New York Times,* November 7, 1975, and August 19, 1975.
40. Kohlmeier, *The Regulators,* p. 77. See also *Business Week,* February 28, 1970, p. 64.
41. See David Truman, *The Governmental Process* (New York: Knopf, 1951), pp. 467–69.
42. Speech by Commissioner Frederick Engman, Federal Trade Commission, October, 1974.

Chapter 10

Process: The Policy-Making Activities of Groups

Patterns of group behavior in the policy process depend on key differences in group strategies and needs: differences related to the stage(s) at which policy influence is desired; to the distributive, regulatory, or manipulative purpose of the policy; and to the lobbying resources of the outside groups themselves. In reality all stages of policy making are occurring simultaneously which makes it possible for groups to work on policy at several stages, or carry several policies along at one stage. Keeping the confusion in mind, for the sake of analysis, we will simplify reality and consider the stages as a linear sequence, beginning with development, then implementation and finally evaluation.

In chapters 8 and 9 we examined structurally determined access points that link outside interests and congressional/executive branch decision centers. In this chapter we will analyze the action that takes place within this institutional framework. How do groups work with or against governmental decision-making centers in order to secure their policy objectives?

Two levels of action centers coexist during the policy process: the subgovernment level of congressional committee/bureaucratic middle management and the ad hoc, partisan level of presidential politics. The former emphasizes program-oriented implementation activities; the latter seeks to pass current presidential programs. Interest groups may participate in both institutional arrangements and often play one against the other in order to gain time, money, or policy changes.

Economic interests, especially large-scale industrial interests, prefer to work unseen within the bureaucratic structure either as subgovernment members or members of institutionalized presidential advisory mechanisms. Generally speaking, groups that want federal money in one form or another tend to play congressional and administrative ends of a subgovernment against each other: first, to achieve the largest possible funding grant and then to ensure maximum flexibility in using it. Public interest groups, noneconomic interests, and groups with broad social policy goals try to work with presidential level action centers in order to increase their political clout, maximize conditions for substantive policy change, and/or seek policy plays to circumvent entrenched subgovernment alliances.

POLICY DEVELOPMENT

Once a problem has been identified and defined as an issue for the public agenda, it must be developed into a program, which, if successfully negotiated through congressional and executive branch approval procedures, becomes a legitimized public policy. Programs are ideas that have been defined in terms of dollar value. Ideas by themselves are "free goods, a program is an economic good."[1] Most good ideas never become programs. Those that do have demonstrated that they meet an identified need, will produce visible results within a limited time period (in order to qualify for more money), and will appeal to as large a clientele group as possible (in order to maximize administrative and congressional support bases).

Outside groups, especially the highly organized and wealthy, supply information through established administrative channels, such as task forces, advisory committees, or expert panels. Groups with mass memberships or broad policy interests or smaller research resources use the media, congressional contacts, and public pressure to influence policy development. The scope and purpose of the policy being developed are important because they affect both strategy and organizational requirements for group participation. Narrow fiscal decisions such as those related to subsidies, grants, and so forth, require more specialized information and less intergroup alliance building than broader regulatory or redistributive policies. Single program/grant policies foster continuing direct group-agency-committee ties, while the broader program often loses its original outside group support when the coalition supporting its passage dissolves once the congressional vote is taken. Noneconomic and general issue groups often work for innovative change such as new programs or bureaucratic reorganization, while more specialized groups wait for the less publicized second round of policy development that occurs when programs return to Congress for refining and refunding.

Both Congress and the executive branch, especially the presidential office, participate in policy development. Although the President is often called "chief legislator," a reference to his role in providing annual budget and legislative programs, Congress is not dead, since only Congress can pass the legislation required to initiate governmental action. Presidents have advantages when seeking innovative program developments, for they have at hand the coordination machinery of the Executive Office, plus the moral persuasion powers of the office to use as administrative and public support tools for the development of policy priorities and legislative initiatives.

Although Congress has taken the lead on many pieces of innovative legislation ranging from social security to environmental and consumer protection, both its size and lack of internal policy coordination procedures preclude innovation as a general rule.[2] Congressional policy development emphasizes the more common incremental form of policy development—that which modifies existing laws, reorganizes bureaucratic divisions, increases efficiency, redistributes appropriations. In its usual policy-making role, Congress airs options and negotiates responses.

The legislative program itself is developed within the bureaucracy in a time-consuming process beginning at least a year before the program is presented to Congress.[3] The sequence begins with the collection of outside proposals from task forces, presidential commissions, academics in residence within government, government-sponsored think tanks, private research facilities, bureaucracy subdivisions, and clientele groups. Policy planning staffs within each department and agency collect the ideas and develop their own programs which are reviewed by OMB and then submitted to the President.

Since the receptivity of departments and bureaus to new ideas is often blocked by vested interests in the action centers, presidents have devised various means to supplement agency offerings with other inputs. Presidents Kennedy and Johnson relied on task forces tied directly into the Executive Office as a source of new idea packages. For example, in 1967 Johnson established fifty separate task forces for domestic policy areas. Their ideas were submitted to White House assistants and then sent to the agencies, via interagency task forces, for review. This sequence reversed the usual process in order to secure the input of new ideas, but not without an increase in agency wariness. Most often the task forces did not include the interest groups dominant within that issue's action centers since the approach was keyed to development of alternative ideas. Instead, membership was used as a means to co-opt "relatively powerful but essentially conservative elements of society"[4] by immersing them in actual problems (for example, ghetto life) and then showing them the range of available options. A consensual form of decision making, which emphasized nonpublicized bargaining until a decision acceptable to all was reached, reinforced this co-optation. Indeed, groups often prefer to avoid representation on such panels precisely because the prestige and informational advantages are outweighed by the loss of flexibility in terms of criticizing a program once it is made public.[5]

Generally presidents play a dominant role in setting overall policy priorities and developing redistributive programs. Since redistributive policies require coordination of many bureaucratic elements in the service of an overriding goal, the supporting argument is generally couched in value terms. This permits the President to dominate by virtue of his public leadership position, reinforced by his administrative control within the bureaucracy. Thus priority programs or innovative programs such as Kennedy's Trade Expansion Act, Johnson's commitment to civil rights legislation, Nixon's assault on crime lend themselves to presidential leadership and are processed through presidential level action centers.

When regulatory policies are concerned, presidential involvement varies with the degree of change involved, the scope of the policy, and the President's own electoral commitments. The President may encourage accommodation among interested groups either as a quiet broker within the White House or by publicly using his office to generate mass attention. For example, using the first technique, President Johnson created a federal aid to education bill for both public and parochial schools with enough aid to prevent a "veto" by the

Catholic Church and enough assurances to satisfy the National Education Association.[6] Similarly the main presidential contribution to passage of a strong civil rights bill in 1965 was prevention of horse trading that would have watered it down. "In a private session in his office with Clarence Mitchell of the NAACP and Joseph Rauh of the ADA, Johnson pledged there would be no changes in the bill. . . . Johnson reiterated he wanted the Senate to pass the bill intact."[7] By contrast, in a public display of persuasiveness, President Johnson appeared on television at 11 A.M. on March 26, 1965, to publicize his new Medicare bill and introduce the Democratic congressmen who would be instrumental in its passage. He then gave the public a demonstration of his " 'Johnson treatment' as he 'reasoned' with medicare opponent Senator Byrd and pulled forth his public promise to hold hearings on the bill as soon as the House had acted."[8]

Usually when developing regulatory policy, interested groups use a bargaining process to form issue-oriented coalitions which then work with the entire Congress to pass the agreed upon program. This means that once the legislation has been passed, the ad hoc coalition dissolves again, and implementation and evaluation of the new regulations reverts to single-issue action centers. For example, the Coalition of Concerned Charities, an ad hoc congressional lobbying group composed of eighty charities ranging from the American Cancer Society to the Camp Fire Girls, has been working for seven years to rewrite the tax provisions that prohibit 501(c) (3) tax-exempt organizations from lobbying. Once their goal is secured, these groups will go their separate ways, some even preferring not to take advantage of the new lobbying limits for which they worked through the coalition. The coalition's group relationship with Congress will dissolve into individual charity's relationships with the IRS.

Agency-clientele relationships permit groups that did not participate in the initial policy process to work with mid-level action centers to flesh out new programs and seek beneficial rewordings of new law. Presidents rarely intervene at this level, partially because these subgovernments are almost immune to presidential prerogatives, partially because the implementation requires decision-making detail and expertise related more to program than politics.

Presidential involvement in distributive decisions, those material dispersements of government largesse such as capital construction projects, postal rates, or crop subsidies that affect only narrow segments of the population, is similarly rare. The tendency is for those interested in a specific decision to concentrate on the limited number of key congressmen necessary to win. The bureaucratic and clientele partners in mid-bureaucracy action centers provide backup support and advice.

> The currency of power in distributive policy decisions seems to be one of technical information and expertise . . . it is a process in which "experts" from executive agencies, congressional committees and subcommittees, and concerned interest groups come together to determine who gets what from the government larder.[9]

In general, the more specific, limited, and technical the policy decision, the more independence accrues to mid-bureaucracy action centers.

To summarize, the scope and innovativeness of a program will influence the relative dominance, indeed even the possibility for participation, by congressional and executive branch actors. The President is more involved in redistributive policies, least in distributive; the congressional role is the reverse. Mid-level bureaucratic entities and their clientele groups are most active in relation to regulatory policies. Interest groups work both ends of the street. To secure their own goals, group access lines follow policy power rather than organization chart relationships.

Often interest groups will operate along both alliance levels simultaneously. This was the case when the dairy cooperatives offered $2 million to President Nixon's reelection campaign in order to ensure that they would be an exception to the presidentially announced policy of ending all federal price support programs. Price supports are normally regulated through the USDA/agriculture committees/agriculture groups mid-level action center. While President Nixon persuaded Secretary of Agriculture Clifford Hardin to reverse his earlier price support level decision, the AMPI lobbyists generated support from mid-level action center personnel to ensure Nixon's success.

Over 13,000 letters went from milk producers to USDA; over 50,000 letters were sent to Congress. More than 125 congressmen wrote USDA in favor of an increased price support level. At the same time twenty senators and thirty representatives initiated legislation to remove USDA's power to set that year's milk price supports. Lynn Stalbaum, AMPI's lobbyist, felt that this pressure was crucial in getting USDA acquiescence to the presidential reversal decision. As he explained it:

> Looking back, I think this strategy made a crucial difference, even though the threat to have Congress take over the jobs was really an idle threat, for that year anyway. We forced the Department of Agriculture to take a second look because no department . . . wants to have that kind of power taken away from it. The numbers of members of Congress who were willing to support us was impressive. . . .[10]

Thus mid-level subgovernment action provided the backup muscle to support AMPI lobbying efforts along the presidential action center level.

More often, groups play action center levels or action center participants against each other. For example, EPA was supposed to issue guidelines mandating the use of returnable bottles on federal premises. However, the draft guidelines just happened to be leaked to beverage lobbyists who in turn produced a thirty-eight page lobbying package to stimulate mail to Congress. In response, 200 congressmen wrote EPA, and the guidelines, when issued, were weaker.[11]

Let us consider four examples that illustrate varieties of group/Congress/administrative/presidential interactions in developing redistributive, regulatory, and distributive policies.

Redistributive Policies

Two examples of redistributive policies passed by President Lyndon Johnson reflect the extremes of interest group participation in the development of a coalition to support passage of legislation. In the first case, the war on poverty, the President worked alone with his bureaucratic allies to devise a massive, multifaceted attack on the causes of poverty. By contrast, the second example, aid to elementary and secondary school education, illustrates the President as coordinator of a new coalition alignment orchestrated to fit his redefinition of the aid to education approach.

WAR ON POVERTY. This program has often been described as the archetype of domestic redistributive programs that are creatures of the presidential planning apparatus. Yet in certain aspects it is actually an exception to the processes related to presidential policy planning. First, it was completed within six months of Johnson's signal to create poverty elimination plans, whereas usually such an order would take one to four years to move through the processes. Second, it was developed and passed with only token congressional involvement in creation of the programs. Third, instead of using interest groups as idea resources and co-opted public supporters, the presidential apparatus ignored outside group contributions or gave them only token participation. Instead of providing the motivation and push for the initial legislation, groups spearheaded the criticism and complaints that produced congressional program modifications in subsequent years.

The war on poverty had its origins in a more limited program initiative approved by President Kennedy only days before his assassination. When President Johnson was told of the plans, he enthusiastically adopted the idea, expanding it into a "war on poverty." His demand for immediate action was frustrated by interagency quarreling over whose clientele would lose what when the community action program was implemented.

> The Labor Department, for example, wanted more emphasis on youth employment but thought that too much emphasis might jeopardize the prospects for its own youth-employment opportunities bill, then pending before Congress. The Department of Agriculture was interested in developing local leadership in rural poverty programs, and Commerce thought that the role of local business leaders had been inadequately stressed. HEW feared that local community-action agencies might bypass the department's important clientele groups, . . . Spokesmen for Interior protested that their Bureau of Indian Affairs was also in the poverty business and should be included.[12]

To end the hassles, Johnson appointed Sargent Shriver, President Kennedy's brother-in-law and former director of the Peace Corps, to head a task force in charge of developing the legislative package. Since the obvious need required for program development was established, Shriver now sought salable ideas, ideas to produce immediate results.

Building upon the work already accomplished, he sought out experts in business, academia, foundations, and from the various agencies. Within six weeks Shriver had completed his work and his bill, the Economic Opportunity Act (EOA), went to Congress.

The House Education and Labor Ad hoc Subcommittee on Poverty Programs began instant hearings stacked in favor of the legislation. By August 1964 it had passed both houses with only minor modifications: one program emasculated, two added, and the requested appropriations cut by 20 percent. However, by 1966 Congress was responding to complaints from the localities. Since 1967 the programs in the original Economic Opportunity Act have been modified, reorganized, restructured, refinanced and, at one point almost eliminated, by a Congress engaged in the process of policy initiation the second time around.

The development of the Economic Opportunity Act is a perfect example of presidential innovative initiative and interagency problems in developing broad policy. But the act was unusual in its lack of participation by affected groups.

> The EOA was "legislated" largely within the executive branch and, indeed, without prodding from congressional or other "outside clienteles". . . . The emergence of poverty as a public issue was all the more remarkable because it occurred without the goading of a public "crisis" and because it involved a clientele with relatively little political voice.[13]

Organized groups were ostentatiously courted by Shriver to co-opt them and make them feel important, but their role was largely symbolic. The poor, unorganized as a dues-paying national association, were not even symbolically questioned about the act that made poverty into a major public issue.

"Maximum feasible participation," a key phrase in the legislation, which was interpreted to mean local participation by representatives of the poor, was later seen as a way to forge interest groups among the poor. Yet in the early policy development stage it was only an OMB suggestion to apply an old reform idea tried in youth programs to a new subject matter area. By 1970 the bureaucratic apparatus created by the EOA had been demolished, transferred, or redefined. Its demise reflected in part its lack of a strongly organized supportive clientele that could have developed an action center with sufficient strength to preserve the program once the President moved on to other priorities. Cuts and program shutdowns instituted in 1966 belatedly led to creation of an Office of Economic Opportunity (OEO) clientele constituency composed of Community Action Agency executives and lobbying by constituents whose jobs and opportunities were affected. Indeed, those aspects that remain, such as manpower training programs or legal services for the poor, survived precisely because groups were willing to fight for their retention.

AID TO EDUCATION. On January 12, 1975, President Johnson sent a message entitled "Toward Full Educational Opportunity" to Congress along with his legislation for $1.5 billion in aid to elementary and secondary schools.[14] Eighty-seven days later with only a few minor House committee amendments to its language, the bill passed Congress, with Senator Wayne Morse, as Senate sponsor, agreeing to pass the House bill, comma for comma, in order to eliminate the need for a conference committee. On April 11, 1965, by the ruins of the one-room schoolhouse where he learned to read, Lyndon Johnson signed the bill, calling it, "the most important bill I will ever sign." How was Johnson able to end the twenty-year stalemate that pitted Catholics, blacks, conservative business and farm organizations against educators, PTAs, Protestant and Jewish groups? The answer lay in a change of legislative emphasis that reformulated the argument permitting the participants to regroup along lines that paralleled favorable public interest sentiment for aid to education.

The pre-1965 lineup was polarized over three issues: segregated educational facilities, aid to parochial schools, and local fear of federal domination of local school systems. The 1964 Civil Rights Act eliminated the segregation issue by requiring nondiscriminatory application of all federal programs. The fear of federal domination through conditions ("strings") tied to grant money and the implacable hostility to any parochial school aid was lessening as schools felt the money pinch. During the sixties, the expansion of school populations concided with the beginnings of state and local fiscal problems. Six million children (14 percent) of the 40 million children in elementary and secondary schools were in Catholic parochial schools. These schools were among the first to publicize the constrictions caused by rising enrollments and declining revenues.

The political scene was also subtly new. The 1964 Democratic landslide brought in large congressional majorities; and for the first time, Roman Catholics represented the largest religious sect among them. Secondly, public opinion, nudged by the ecumenical spirit and educated by the "Catholic" issue in the election of President John Kennedy, was inclined toward a combination of aid to both public and private schools. Finally, just as the war on poverty reflected the personal intensity of Johnson's childhood experiences, so too did his emphasis on public education reflect his early career as teacher and lobbyist for the Houston Teachers Association.

During 1964 Johnson asked John Gardner to head a task force to study new ways of aiding education. The task force report suggested playing to the public success of the Economic Opportunity Act by couching aid in terms of poverty and by using the aid to impacted areas formula that would benefit 90 percent of all school districts in America since almost each one had at least one pocket of poverty that could qualify for such funds. The church-state issue was diffused by focusing the aid on children, applying the Supreme Court's "child benefit" theory which held that assistance to children did not violate the establishment of religion prohibition in the First Amendment. Linking the two ideas together in his Education Message, Johnson said: "Poverty has many roots, but the tap root is ignorance." The contents of the bill gave funds to public school districts with low-income families, provided money for public-private school shared time and special services such as educational television and allowed both public and private schools to use the funds to increase library and instructional resources.

The contents of the bill were carefully drafted to create the necessary interest group coalition. For example, the unprecedented money for libraries added new groups such as the American Book Publishers Council, the American Textbook Publishers Institute, and the American Association of School Librarians to the support coalition. In addition Johnson assigned key members of his cabinet and office to woo both sides of the traditional education lobby. In *The Vantage Point,* Johnson's account of his presidency, he says:

> Education Commissioner Francis Keppel met with high-ranking prelates of the church who assured him that they were not eager for a court

> test over any program that would give direct aid to parochial schools. Jack Valenti [presidential assistant] served as our liaison with the Vatican's Apostolic Delegate to the United States. . . . Lew White of the White House staff dealt with the Jewish organizations; Henry Hall Wilson worked with the southern leaders; Douglas Cater and Commissioner Keppel remained in close touch with the powerful education lobbies. Our strategy was to line up all available support in advance. . . .[15]

Neither of the church organizations was delighted with the compromise, but the Protestant National Council of Churches did not wish to appear to be blocking "educational opportunity," and the Catholic Conference, recognizing the token support as a foot in the door, remained supportively neutral.

Johnson met once publicly and twice privately with the major educational group, the National Education Association, to persuade them to compromise on their position against aid to private schools. Realizing that this year the bill would pass, the NEA joined the support coalition for purely political reasons.

> Fear over possible exclusion from the policy-making process helped persuade NEA to go along in 1965. . . . [To have been on the minority side] would have left the NEA without influence during the critical period after passage when the administrative regulations were being drawn up. . . . If for no other reason, the NEA could not afford to be with the losers the year federal aid finally got enacted. . . . The NEA's principal reason for being was the passage of federal aid to education legislation. . . .[16]

The pell-mell congressional pace was designed by Johnson to secure passage "before lobbyists in the special groups could congeal the opposition." It also limited the amount of time in which to reargue the church-state issue that still dominated the hearings. At times during the House floor debate, "there were two members of Mr. O'Brien's [congressional] liaison staff outside the House chamber, plus White House aides Marvin Watson, Douglas Cater, and Bill Moyers, an official of the Democratic National Committee and three representatives of the Department of HEW—in addition to administration-coordinated lobbyists from the NEA and other private groups."[17] When Rules Committee Chairman Howard Smith, an implacable foe of the measure, introduced an amendment to permit citizen test cases of the law's constitutionality, an amendment that would have led the Catholic Conference to oppose the bill, Johnson sent word to defeat it on a party vote. The Smith amendment was defeated by an unrecorded voice vote. In sum, we see that this entire piece of legislation was constructed and passed with an eye to the outside interest group coalition whose support presence would produce the necessary environment for congressional acceptance of the Johnson compromise.

Regulative Policy: Cigarette Advertising

The issue of health and smoking provides a typical example of action center trade-offs wherein each side uses its best arena for development of preferred policy regarding government regulation.[18] The prestigious health charities working with the Public Health Service and the surgeon general focused public attention on smoking's health hazards with a report calling for remedial action by government to protect citizens' health. The report and public response to it led to FTC hearings and a preliminary announcement that henceforth health warnings would be required on all cigarette packages and in all advertising.

The tobacco lobby assessed its strengths and decided first to cooperate in the FTC hearings and then checkmate any agency action in Congress where its southern geographical concentration, coupled with the economic importance of tobacco, campaign contributions from tobacco interests, and the advantage of friends in senior positions gave it clout. An ad hoc alliance of the PHS and the cancer charities called the National Interagency Council on Smoking and Health, which had generated the pressure behind the 1964 report, managed to wage a letter-writing campaign in 1965, but it was outclassed. The alliance's congressional clout was minimal, and its administrative allies either cared more for competing programs (for example, USDA and tobacco price supports) or had gone as far as they dared to go (for example, the FTC ruling).

Before the FTC acted, the tobacco lobby quickly moved to persuade Congress to hold hearings. Then the FTC was asked to delay the effect of its rulings until after Congress had acted. The lobby's strategy was to try to get by with a self-regulation code, but if necessary to agree to a modified package warning and prevent warnings in advertisements by blocking further FTC action. Their lobbyist, former Senator, Earle Clements, advised them

> to play down the health issue, emphasize the importance of cigarettes in the nation's economy, remind the media of their financial stake in cigarette advertising, oppose all regulatory legislation, but settle for a package warning if they had to give in on something.[19]

The Senate Commerce Committee was targeted as the focal point of tobacco's efforts since it was assessed as an influential but ambivalent ally. The hearings were orchestrated by the manufacturers through a lawyer's committee composed of representatives from the top six tobacco companies to show that medical opinion was split over the report (remember the AMA had been silenced for $10 million), that the antismoking senators were extremists, and that drastic measures would have adverse commercial consequences. The result was a law, couched in public health terms, that required a mild warning on cigarette packages, no advertising warnings, and, most importantly, forbid the agencies or individual states from taking any other action until 1969. The compromised label read: "Caution—cigarette smoking may be hazardous to your health."

Congress appropriated only $2 million to establish a National Clearinghouse on Smoking and Health to continue smoking and health education and research programs. Meanwhile the cigarette companies spent over $200 million to advertise smoking, and the USDA continued to give away $1.8 million in tobacco crop support subsidies. The *New York Times* called the law "a shocking piece of special-interest legislation."[20] Or as Senator Frank Moss summarized the action: "In exchange for 11 words on the side of a package, Congress exempted the cigarette industry from the normal regulatory processes of federal, state, and local regulations."

By 1969 when the act came up for renewal, the tobacco lobby was set to perform the same routine, but the public opinion climate had changed. New organizations such as ASH (Action on Smoking and Health) and GASP (Group Against Smokers' Pollution) joined the traditional health charities to fight for the two-thirds of the population who do not smoke. Since 1967 when John Banzhof III successfully prodded the FCC to action with a citizen's complaint letter asking the Commission to apply the "fairness doctrine," designed to ensure equal time for controversial topics, to cigarette advertising, opposition to cigarettes has become acceptable, even chic. A Harris poll found that Americans favored advertising restrictions by a ratio of 5:4.

In Congress the House still responded to the economic clout of the tobacco lobby by passing a status quo bill, but the Senate version included provisions upholding an FCC ban on all radio and television advertising and strengthened the language of the label warning. The compromise bill prohibited radio/television advertisements after 1971, and strengthened the warning to read, "Caution: The Surgeon General has determined that cigarette smoking is dangerous to your health" (still weaker than the FTC version that would have included the phrase "may cause death").

Thus, within a four-year time span, the context within which public policy is made had shifted from purely economic considerations to include health problems as well. Congressmen sensitive to the new proconsumer and health trends changed the balance of power and, in the process, reduced the strength of the old USDA/southern congressmen/tobacco industry action center in favor of a new public health/antismoking/FCC action center.

Distributive Policy: The Highway Lobby

Police development at the distributive level involves departments, committees, and outside interests united in long-standing relationships.[21] However, the 1971–73 effort to force the appropriation of highway trust funds for mass transit purposes illustrates the possibility for internal power rearrangements within an action center when public opinion supports new group players. The Highway Action Coalition found new access points provided by creation of the Department of Transportation (DOT) and the 1973 passage of new Senate rules of procedure. With this leverage, they challenged the traditional highway action center and, three years later, scored their first victory.

The Highway Trust Fund (HTF) was established in 1956 by collecting taxes on gasoline, tires, commercial truck weights, etc., in a separate fund to be used for construction of the 42,500 mile interstate highway system. The total project, to be completed by 1980, will cost $76.3 billion. Six billion dollars annually is allocated to states and localities. Since the federal government pays 90 percent of all costs, it is the most massive public works project in the country. Every congressman is an "inside lobbyist" for this perfect pork barrel. For congressional supporters of the HTF, "extra goodies" can be written into the legislation such as the additional 10,000 miles of priority roads promised to Speaker Carl Albert and two Rules Committee members in order to win their secret support in 1973.

The traditional highway action center is composed of the Bureau of Roads, the Public Works Committees, and the highway lobby, an alliance of rubber, construction, asphalt, automobile, and oil industries, car dealers and renters, bus and trucking companies that use the interstate system, banks and advertising agencies that have them as clients, the AAA and other motorist lobbies, and state and local officials who benefit from the subsidy. They were challenged in the early 1970s by the Governor's Conference, the Conference of Mayors, and the Highway Action Coalition composed of environmentalist groups, Common Cause, the Institute for Rapid Transit, the Teamsters, and the United Steel Workers. For these groups it was an important social issue, a question of national priorities—pollution, urban decay versus a balanced national transportation policy. For the highway clique it was economic self-interest—preservation of their trust and their predominant transportation subsidy position.

By 1971 the tenor of the times was antiroads. Pollution, traffic congestion, urban dislocations caused by interstate highway building, the emergence of vocal citizens groups opposing environmental degradation, and increasing public support for mass transit systems created an opportunity to attack the highway action center. Department of Transportation Secretary John Volpe with the support of President Nixon was for diversion of trust monies for mass transportation since his new department's political base would be strengthened if the original action center lost power.

DOT backed a Muskie/Baker Senate amendment to give states the option of spending their share of the $800 million of urban highway funds on mass transit, buses, or railroads. In the 1971–72 congressional process, the amendment passed the Senate, but was removed from House consideration by a Rules Committee decision that it was not germane to the bill. In conference, the Senate lost its amendment but won the right to seek reamendment in 1973.

By 1973 action center congressional leaders were either more moderate or had been pushed to favor diversion. For example Chicagoan John Kluczynski, chairman of the House Roads Committee was told to support diversion or Mayor Daley would force him into a tough primary fight. Going the other way, Senator Humphrey was backed into voting against the Muskie/Baker amendment, even though he was a cosponsor, by the pressure from his Minneapolis colleague, John Blatnik, chairman of the House Public Works committee.

The lobbies used traditional measures. Both sides harked back to their electoral clout: the highway lobby to its campaign contributions, the environmentalists to their vote power victories. The roadbuilders created a Road Information Program that spent $1 million on advertisements for its side. Both sides used constituent pressure. For example, 150 highway contractors from Georgia lunched with their representatives and at the end of lunch asked each congressman to announce how he planned to vote. The Highway Action Coalition also used selected constituents to approach selected congressmen.

> Georgia's freshman Senator Sam Nunn voted for diversion after calls from Georgia Governor Jimmy Carter (who responded to a plea from Chicago's Richard Daley relayed by the chairman of the Chicago Transit Authority), Atlanta Mayor Sam Massell (calling at Governor Sargent's request), and DOT Secretary Brinegar.[22]

The 1973 Conference Committee scene was a repeat of 1972, but with a difference. When prohighways Senator Jennings Randolph sought to stack the Senate conference team to support his view, John Kramer of the Highway Action Coalition protested to Senator Kennedy. Kennedy and Muskie protested to Senate Majority Leader Mike Mansfield, and the new Senate rule requiring conference teams to mirror the floor vote was enforced. Randolph changed the committee. The conference deadlocked for ten weeks. The final compromise reached after twenty-nine sessions accepted the Muskie/Baker proposal to take effect in the third year, but kept the House interstate transfer system which allows states to cancel one freeway and substitute another for it. Despite the coalition's concessions, it was a defeat for the highway lobby: the trust had been busted, or tapped—$200 million for buses in FY 1975, $800 million for buses and trains in FY 1976.

Then, just as the conference report seemed ready to sail through, the Office of Management and Budget said they would call for a pocket veto since the spending levels in the bill were too high. At this point, Congressman Wright, highway lobby proponent but now angry at this insult to Congress, announced that he would not bring the measure to the floor without an Administration promise of passage. House Minority Leader Gerald Ford assured the White House that this was no bluff. Within an hour, DOT Secretary Claude Brinegar promised that Nixon would sign, and the bill passed on the last day of the summer session.

These four case studies illustrate the importance of individual-interest group relationships in the development of public policy. In each case except EOA, policy content reflects the ideas of the most powerful, most vocal, most organized, and most strategically located actors. Executive branch compartments, the presidential entourage, interest groups, and congressional decision makers work through action centers regardless of the issue at hand, but the issue itself determines the relative importance of the various participants within that action center. Thus the President's personal role in developing the war on poverty and the aid to education act structured the action coalitions (despite the difference in their composition) along the personal, partisan lines of presidential level action centers, while both the smoking and health issue and the use of highway trust funds operated within the context of mid-level action centers.

POLICY IMPLEMENTATION

Implementation may be defined as a course of action that applies public policy to perceived problems. *Administration* in this context refers to the pattern of activities in the action centers that supervise implementation. Although the concept of action centers seems to imply an internal unity of purpose, this is rarely the case. Action center participants are drawn together by a common *need* for decisions on particular subjects and issues, but they are likely to disagree on the centers of those decisions. A common viewpoint among all actors would be nice, but it is both unlikely and not really necessary.

For example, in broad terms the smoking/health action center includes tobacco companies, processors, manufacturers, advertising agencies, television stations, shopkeepers, tax collectors, farmers, vending machine companies, retail stores, cancer research institutes and supporting interest groups, antismoking groups such as ASH, consumer groups, the medical associations, and various government entities including the Public Health Service, USDA, the Treasury (balance of payments), the National Institute of Health, and assorted congressional committees. This diversity of membership enabled the health coalition to circumvent the tight "tobacco as an economic resource" subgovernment and create a new pattern that enhanced its own power—yet still within the broad action center.

When the reality of multiple, separate subgovernment relationships within a broader issue-based action center is linked with the congressional tendency to write vague legislation, it is clear that those who lose in the writing of policy will seek to recoup during its implementation. Speaking more positively to the same point, Louise Dunlop, Environmental Policy Center lobbyist, said that if her side won the bill to regulate strip mining of coal, then lobbying does not end; "the lobbying effort will shift to getting tough administrative regulations written under the law."[22]

As David Truman explained: "Administration of a statute is, properly speaking, an extension of the legislative process."[24] A law really only represents the balance of forces aligned during the drafting and legitimating parts of policy development. Since a bill is always a compromise, its language conceals competing purposes. Administrative rule-making discretion permits an agile administrator to manipulate commas and clauses so as to strengthen certain purposes and render others of only symbolic value. The addition of sex to the antidiscrimination language of the 1964 Civil Rights Act initially meant little because the bureaucracy interpreted its job to be enforcement of racial minority rights rather than elimination of discrimination against women.

Or administrators can impose conditions to be met before an act becomes operative in order to influence the distribution of federal largesse. Thus once the food stamp program was put under the control of the southern-dominated, segregationist USDA, it was logical to foresee an emphasis on the amount to be paid by the poor as a condition of participation—an emphasis that turned the program from a poverty alleviation measure into a surplus commodites distribution program. Both purposes existed in the same act, but the choice of implementing agency determined their relative importance in structuring application of the law.

In 1974 an environmental law specialist catalogued four ways in which administrative fiat counteracted legislative intent:

1. Abuse of past administrative interpretations accomplished by skipping around among precedents until one can be found that might be made to fit the current situation.
2. "Technique by ratification" whereby inconsistent rulings not countered by Congress in a new statute are assumed to be legitimate.
3. Arbitrary departures from statutory language by reinterpreting the law as practiced.
4. Ignoring statutory deadlines that permit outlawed practices to be continued for a longer period of time.[25]

He concluded that the first task of environmental lawyers "is establishing that a governmental decision is governed by law rather than being the matter of administrative discretion that agencies too often make it."

Sometimes administrative rule making not only favors a group, but actually delegates discretionary policy-making authority to it. Such is the case in the Department of Labor's implementation of section 13-c of the Urban Mass Transit Act of 1964 which requires that department to approve any grants made by the Department of Transportation through a city or transit agency for use in mass transit. Labor unions lobbied for insertion of the section in order to ensure that federal grants did not worsen their working conditions or eliminate any of their jobs or wage rights. The Department of Labor has operationalized this labor concern by referring all applications under section 13-c to local transit unions for approval. The local unions have used their veto power as a lever to bargain for increased local benefits which in turn has led city governments to reconsider their use of this grant program. Thus a departmental decision that reflected its consituency interests effectively has stalemated the more general purposes of the act which were to assist in the development of urban mass transit systems.[26] The ICC has delegated its power to establish interstate rates to 148 "rate bureaus" which are really regional associations of truckers. Rate wars are impossible because the truckers, backed by the ICC's authority, can "veto the rates of their competitors."[27]

To increase their chances for administrative input, groups develop the bureaucratic action relationships discussed earlier. Such access is more stratified, permanent, and predictable than access to congressional decision-making processes where people and policy emphases reflect the election returns. The impact of policy content and personality are structured in the executive branch by bureaucratic institutionalization of consultation/support procedures, by ties of professionalism, and by shared decision-making routines. The functional relationship wherein private groups—contractors or supervisors—perform governmental duties that have been delegated to them further enhances the aspect of permanency.

Generally programs are packaged in specific terms because the bureaucracy needs to elicit the maximum amount of congressional and clientele support. Fragmentation of the bureaucratic structure enables some groups to carry this to its logical conclusion: establishment of a separate entity to administer each separate program. The lucky group then enjoys four freedoms: "freedom from financial control by the Congress, freedom from independent audit by the comptroller general, freedom from budget review by the President, and freedom to use federal funds."[28] Thus the same groups that act defensively in the legislative arena to protect vested interests, act offensively in the executive arena in developing bureaucratic entities that maximize their tunnel to the federal mint and minimize access for competitors or overseers.

GROUPS AND REGULATORY AGENCIES

As we saw in Chapter 9, regulatory agencies are favored recipients of interest group group attention for three reasons. As arms of Congress, they are legally separated from presidential control, a separation that also precludes presidential protection when the agency wishes to overrule clientele interests. Additionally, an agency needs group support more than other executive departments because continuing congressional support requires orchestration of constituent praise and evidence of regulatory progress. This final condition leads to a third dependency relationship since agency progress depends on compliance and cooperation from those regulated.

> If the required amount of cooperation is not forthcoming, the organization will fail to accomplish its objectives and hence to satisfy its supporters. Those who are regulated must generally approve of, or at least accede to, these programs. Administrative regulations cannot be enforced against a generally hostile public.[29]

These relationships are illustrated by the workings of the Food and Drug Administration (FDA), an independent regulatory commission staffed by approximately 6,500 employees, with a budget of $200 million. It was created to keep the consumer safe from hazardous substances in food, drugs, and cosmetics. Its procedures incorporate three kinds of mid-level bureaucracy-group relationships:

- industry consultation formalized in advisory committee roles,
- adversary relationships with consumer groups attacking the entrenched industry positions, and
- groups in a contractual relationship which permits them to perform governmental functions.

One FDA responsibility (assigned by the 1962 amendments to the Food, Drug, and Cosmetic Act) stipulated review of all prescription drugs—both new drugs seeking premarketing approval and all drugs approved between 1938 and 1962 in order to make sure that they meet current efficacy tests (that is, that they work).[30] To review the old drugs, FDA hired the National Academy of Sciences and its research affiliate, the National Research Council. Their task was to validate 16,000 individual claims made on behalf of 4,000 drug products. Their fee was $843,000. The study began in 1966 with expectations that it would take a decade to complete. Similarly, work has been contracted out to private institutes for review of ingredients on the FDA's "generally recognized as safe" (GRAS) list of acceptable food additives, a review necessitated by the finding that cyclamates, once on the

GRAS list, were shown to cause cancer in animals. For $250,000 the Franklin Institute was hired to do a literature search of all information on additives accumulated in the last fifty years. The references are being read by the Federation of American Societies for Experimental Biology which will evaluate the safety of each additive.

To review the efficacy of over-the-counter drugs as mandated in the 1962 act, the FDA adopted the advisory commission approach in order to open the process to interested groups and, at the same time, decrease decision-making time by moving from an item-by-item decision base to category decisions. Peter Hutt, General counsel of FDA, divided the drugs into twenty-seven categories and assigned them to seventeen advisory councils consisting of paid experts and unpaid representatives of consumer and drug interests. The panels were charged with developing monographs containing approved lists of ingredients and approved labeling for drugs in each category. Manufacturers can then feel safe if their products are within the new guidlines. If they are not, the manufacturer may petition to change the monograph, or change his own product, or file a new drug application.

The system has been criticized in a congressional committee report as a device to short-circuit examination of drugs by FDA staff. The charge is made that these committees are delay mechanisms permitting dubious products to remain for sale while an advisory council deliberates. Another criticism is that the panels are really designed to co-opt physicians rather than to make medical decisions, since often the FDA withholds crucial information from the committees. For example, a panel approved Alka-Seltzer with aspirin, overruling its previous decision, after FDA lawyers told them their previous decision would not stand up in court. Similarly, a panel approved use of Depo Provera as an injectable contraceptive, presumably because they had not seen laboratory studies linking the drug to cancer in animals.[31]

Both group-agency systems are attacked by consumer groups such as the Health Research Group, Consumers Union of the U.S., and the Consumer Federation of America who feel the rules and membership of the agency inevitably skew its decisions away from the public interest toward private interests. Since almost half of the top executives at FDA come from their regulated industry, they tend to expect an adversary relationship and complaints from public outsiders (that is, consumer interest groups), rather than seeing their own role in government as one of championing that public interest—a perception that could lead to development of the same kind of consumer-agency working relationship that currently exists with industry.

Weak resources of consumer groups make it difficult for them to send staff through the halls of FDA to challenge officials' perceptions and the built-in biases of FDA decision routines. It is almost impossible for small, understaffed, underfinanced groups with broad goals to develop the same expensive, sophisticated, intimate, technical, and informational relationships that industry companies and trade associations formed decades ago. As the president of the Pharmaceutical Manufacturers' Association said:

> We play a constructive role with the FDA. . . . We have the best trained and greatest number of experts in the drug field. We give lots of comments and advice. We have a constructive, non-acrimonious relationship.[32]

The importance of this relationship is not immediately evident to those outside the implementation process. For example, to prove FDA independence, an official said: "We can't get a bill passed that they don't approve. On the other hand, if we present total, all-out opposition, they can't get an okay either."[33] His defense sounds more like symbiosis than autonomy. In terms of rule making, these contractual and advisory committee relationships, reinforced by the industry-related backgrounds of FDA officials, can mean real clout. At congressional hearings in 1974, FDA employees testified that "every time they made a decision to keep a drug off the market, they were called on the carpet, had their decisions overridden, their objections were removed from the files, and in many cases they were transferred out of their fields of expertise."[34]

The twenty-year battle over the use of red dye #2, an all-purpose dye used to make white foods whiter and red foods redder,[35] is a perfect example of industry implementation influence. Here industry stakes are high: red dye is worth $4.5 million to its producers, and is used in over $10 billion worth of food. From the health viewpoint, a series of studies over the last twenty years have shown that the dye has carcinogenic potential. However the findings were somewhat ambiguous, so in industry's interest the FDA delayed a final verdict fourteen times in fifteen years. Finally heavy public pressure from Congress and citizens groups, plus a GAO report criticizing delays as an unnecessary risk to public health, led to a ban, beginning February 13, 1976, on all future use of red dye #2 in food, drugs, and cosmetics.

The FDA illustration is not unique. A 1975 Senate committee study of the Civil Aeronautics Board (CAB) concluded that: "CAB has for the last five years regularly violated its own rules . . . while acting to protect the interests of the airlines at the expense of the traveler."[36] Examples include postponement of new route cases and adoption of a major transportation policy at the request of the airlines without public hearings, although such hearings are mandated by section 4 of the Administrative Services Act. Another study found that the Federal Energy Administration (FEA) regularly favored big oil companies over small ones in collecting penalties for pricing violations: $800,000 was collected in fines from small oil companies, while fines of $267 million were never levied on the majors. The U.S. Geological Survey invited twenty-three oil executives to draft standards for antipollution equipment for offshore drilling. As Jack Anderson commented: "This is a little like putting Dracula in charge of the blood bank."[37]

Groups also secure policy-making influence by fitting their organizational structure to government's so that their mutual dependency is reinforced by the placement of government programs. The Veterans Administration, veterans organizations, and veterans affairs congressional committee exemplify such an action center. The VA budget is the third largest in the bureaucracy; it employs the second largest number of personnel, and is responsible for an enormous grab bag of social, economic, wefare, and educational programs for veterans.

The influence of established veterans associations is so strong in VA policy development that the major programmatic emphasis is on nonservice-connected programs for "old soldiers" despite greater public support for (and expectations of) substantial benefits for those returning from the latest war. Consequently over half the 1972 budget went for pensions for survivors and dependents of all wars since and including the Civil War. The action center gains power and independence from its insulated program, so efforts to put veterans programs into their functional agencies have been sidetracked. In this way the government, through organizational separation and assistance coordinated by recipient rather than function, has led veterans to organize as a separate interest.[38]

GROUPS AND THE PRESIDENTIAL ACTION CENTER

The previous examples of implementation have all been concerned with mid-level action center relationships. Yet relationships also occur along the presidential action center axis as illustrated by International Telephone and Telegraph's (ITT) maneuvers between 1969 and 1971 to prevent antitrust actions aimed at divesting them of three companies, Grinnell Corporation, Canteen Corporation, and Hartford Insurance Company. As Thomas Burns summed it up:

> The moves by ITT, Congress, and the administration were political and industrial diplomacy of the highest order: the company, determined and desperate, seeking to avoid the loss of the Hartford Insurance Company at all costs; the Justice Department, its crusade against ITT cooling, attempting to retain a trustbusting image while backing down by degrees; the administration trying to maintain an air of neutrality while rooting for ITT and pep-talking Geneen.[39]

The antitrust attack on ITT, spearheaded by Assistant Attorney General Richard McLaren of the Antitrust Division of the Department of Justice, began in April 1969 with clearance from John Ehrlichman, counsel to the President, for a suit seeking divestiture of Canteen Corporation from the ITT conglomerate. Later suits were begun seeking divestiture of the other two companies. To counter these moves, Hal Geneen, president of ITT began a two-pronged campaign in which his Washington office, headed by Bill Merriam and Tom Casey, would deal with Justice Department officials, and he would meet with White House and cabinet-level members of the administration. Their approach was to argue that McLaren was basing his case on "bigness" per se as a cause for antitrust action, a position counter to the stated administration decision not to challenge corporations on the basis of their economic concentration or size. Since President Nixon was known to be especially solicitous of business community interests and very concerned that the bureaucracy obey him, the ITT policy line was clearly designed to split those with decision-making responsibilities from those with implementation responsibilities.

Within months of the initial suit, Geneen was making the rounds of top cabinet officials: during the next eighteen months he had appointments and continuing correspondence with Vice President Spiro Agnew, Secretary of Commerce Maurice Stans, McLaren, and presidential assistants Ehrlichman, Flanigan, and Peterson. He also met with the Attorney General, despite the fact that John Mitchell, because of his previous private law practice involvement, had left decisions in this case to Deputy Attorney General Richard Kleindienst. Geneen's purpose was first, to lobby for his version of mergers, and then more specifically, to delay the government appeal process in the Grinnell case. To support the ITT case, Geneen used information gained from others negotiations with McLaren to prove the antiadministration bias of his argument.

The day before the appeal was to be filed, Ehrlichman reported to the President that despite his appeals to the Justice Department to "cool it," they were determined to file. With that the President exploded, accused McLaren of deliberately defying his policy line, and called Deputy Attorney General Kleindienst to order the appeal dropped. In this conversation Nixon said:

> I don't want to know about Geneen. . . . I don't know whether ITT is bad, good, or indifferent. But there is not going to be any more antitrust actions as long as I am in this chair. . . . The IT&T thing - stay the hell out of it. Is that clear? That's an order. The order is to leave the God damned thing alone. . . . Don't file the brief. . . . My order is to drop the God damned thing.[40]

Kleindienst then met with McLaren and directed he apply for a one-month extension.

Having won a grace period, Geneen sent investment banker and ITT director Felix Rohatyn to see Kleindienst and in a series of meetings convince him of the economic peril that would follow ITT's divestiture of Hartford Insurance Company. White House aide Flanigan also assisted in the persuasion process by recommending Richard

Ramsden, an ex-White House fellow, to research the issue. McLaren approached from this tack, accepted the economic rationales, and agreed to make a settlement whereby ITT would give up several important companies, not merge with any large companies for ten years, and keep the insurance company.

It was while these negotiations were being concluded that, ITT became involved in the issue of site selection for the 1972 Republican national convention. No clear connection between this offer and the ITT antitrust settlement has been established, but it is true that Mitchell, Haldeman (Nixon's chief of staff), and several others knew of the $400,000 convention offer during the period of the final antitrust settlement negotiations. Dita Beard assumed a relationship in a confidential letter to her boss Bob Merriam which said:

> I am convinced . . . that our noble commitment [$400,000] has gone a long way toward our negotiations on the mergers eventually coming out as Hal wants them. Certainly the President has told Mitchell to see that things are worked out fairly. It is still only McLaren's mickey-mouse we are suffering.[41]

Since many White House and cabinet members knew of the two deals, it is likely that they affected each other. Geneen did get his settlement, and Nixon his convention site. Senator Kennedy summarized the case when he said:

> The sustained and sophisticated ITT antitrust lobbying effort from 1969–71 is a tribute to the advanced state of the lobbying art. Any cabinet member or White House aide who was not contacted by ITT must now be suffering from a feeling of second-class citizenship.[42]

Once again, action along established patterns of interaction produced results that changed the intent of a law through the process of implementation.

In all of these instances the time lag between presidential signature on a bill and its eventual application to the issue, coupled with complicated bureaucratic rules of procedure, and the importance of defining legal details and semantic nuances make the implementation process a minefield for the unwary or uninitiated and a gold mine for those having passages of safe conduct. The top 500 corporations, big labor and the national trade associations, the prestigious professional societies and research institutes, the elite of civic and civil rights groups —all these have long-established relationships with administrators. Newcomers must either create their own bureaucracy, as in the case of EPA, or challenge the established order through petition, publicity, and aroused public opinion.

POLICY EVALUATION: POLICY CYCLES

Attacks on established subgovernments are one of the most visible forms of group input in the final policy stage: evaluation. Yet as that statement makes clear, to consider evaluation as the end of the line is to see the limitations of conceptualizing the policy process as a linear sequence. Evaluation occurs at all stages of the policy-making process. The highway coalition lobby used Congress to challenge the highway lobby action center; the smoking-health controversy saw challenge in Congress contested by challenge in the PHS, FTC, and FCC. Women, thwarted in their efforts to find a male bureaucracy interested in fighting for their rights, formed a new organization, NOW, and launched a vigorous fight for a change in the basic ground rules of implementation, namely, a constitutional amendment guaranteeing sex-based equality.

All of these actions are taken on the basis of policy evaluation, the analysis of policy as it is applied to the problems it was intended to solve. Questions arise such as: Which goals sought are being realized? Which publics are getting relief from their initial problem? At what costs? How much public support for government is being won or lost? What kinds of new problems are being created? How do the new issues affect the old solution? How has the world changed during the time lag between perception of a problem, development of an issue, creation of a policy, and implementation of its goals?

Just as at any other stage in the process, one's answers to such questions reflect Mile's law: "Where you stand depends on where you sit." Often groups will be pleased initially with the public product, but as it remains in its original mold and the world turns, the same group becomes increasingly critical. Criticism and praise can come from a variety of sources: individuals such as Ralph Nader, Michael Harrington, or Daniel Patrick Moynihan; presidentially appointed evaluation commissions such as the Kerner Commission on Civil Disorders, the President's Commission on Higher Education; or interest groups themselves.

The manner in which groups protest policy implementation reflects their own relationships with the bureaucracy and their own internal resources. For example, dissatisfied Vietnam veterans, piqued by VA emphasis on older veterans' needs, stayed within the confines of their action center: two sides of the subgovernment—the Veterans organizations and the congressional committees—in effect ganged up on the third, the Nixon appointed VA administrator, and had him replaced. Similarly, members representing economic interests on advisory committees use their advance knowledge of coming events to protect their economic advantages by denying OMB clearance for surveys needed to draft new regulations or by interpreting vague language in their own favor.

Noneconomic and public interest groups often issue reports or form coalitions for the purpose of gaining media assistance in influencing patterns of change. For example, the League of Women Voters, National Urban Coalition, Center for Community Change, and Center for National Policy Review made a preliminary report in 1974 designed to influence Congress when it considered extension of the federal revenue sharing act in 1976. The report, based on interviews with thousands of local political and community leaders, criticized the current spending procedure for its lack of openness, lack of meaningful public participation, and nonenforcement of equal opportunity employment legislation.[43] In 1975 twenty-two civil rights and civic organizations sent a public letter to President Ford expressing similar dissatisfaction with the program.

Sixteen representatives of the Leadership Conference on Civil Rights met with President Ford on June 14, 1976, to request that he not introduce legislation to limit court-ordered busing. The President listened, but did not say he would ask the attorney general not to seek a new busing test case, nor would he promise not to introduce legislation.

Other groups use congressional hearings as a forum for airing their views on public policy. Thus, the National Urban Coalition used hearings of the Joint Economic Committee to explain its plans for an alternative federal budget that emphasizes national economic and social ills. Ralph Nader has used hearings to highlight the issues of automobile safety, pollution problems, lack of consumer interest within the bureaucracy, and other reforms. Common Cause waged a four-year media, constituency, and legal campaign to persuade government officials that public financing of elections was a necessary solution to the crisis of confidence in government created after the Watergate scandals.

Many groups sue to force changes. When President Nixon impounded funds for waste treatment plants, several cities and states sued successfully. The National Abortion Rights Action League has threatened to sue to block antiabortion restrictions on Medicaid money. The Food and Research Action Center sued President Ford for impounding $40 million earmarked for meals for the elderly. The El Paso Natural Gas Company spent a decade in and out of court to protect its empire from government regulation.

Outsiders desiring major policy changes are usually forced to use publicity generated by strikes, boycotts, or mass media advertising campaigns. For example, in 1974, the maritime unions, fully supported by the AFL-CIO hierarchy, established a boycott against U.S. grain sales to the Soviet Union. Citing higher food prices, insufficient use of American ships, and no guarantees of limited impact on internal consumer prices as their reasons, the men refused to load the grain on ships. The boycott led to a temporary suspension of grain sales and finally, six weeks later, an agreement with the White House that met labor demands and permitted shipment of current orders. Here, the evaluation of labor, that an international agricultural policy was detrimental to their own interests, led them to use publicity and obstruction in order to have an impact on action centers ordinarily off-limits to them.

The decline of the war on poverty to a negotiated peace illustrates the effects of time and competing evaluations on the content of policy. "The process of achieving any one public's preferences is perforce inexact and incremental,"[44] but the tug of war it engenders explains many policy inconsistencies. Thus, Congress, initially excluded from development of the war, responded to complaints from local officials similarly excluded from its implementation and amended the law to include local political control in administering the programs. Thereby died one bureaucratic goal: to develop independent interest group representation for the ghetto poor "within the system." In subsequent years, as infusion of money failed to produce immediate educational change or statistically significant increases in employment rates, Congress killed EOA by increments: they cut appropriations, reorganized the original bureaucratic structure, and finally ended the war with a few pieces still intact, but scattered throughout the presidential bureaucracy.

SUMMARY

Policy making is a continuous activity, in which interest groups participate at those points and those times that seem most likely to be influenced by whatever resources the group controls. Since the development/implementation/evaluation schedule varies from issue to issue, and since public opinion provides different frameworks as mirrored in the agenda of public priorities, any one group may be active in all three stages at the same time, but on different issues.

The action center locus of decision-making activity is perfectly attuned to policy participation from the viewpoint of groups. The primary group role as information broker, directly in the form of supplied data or indirectly through appointments, keys groups toward the decision-making level where information is a primary influence resource. By supplying data for decisions, groups get a chance to develop the options from which policies are later chosen. Dispersed pockets of authority within the executive branch and the congressional committee system provide an institutional setting for discrete, issue-related, materially oriented groups to create alliances that will produce their goals.

Public interest groups, ad hoc coalitions, and civil rights groups are at a disadvantage in this system unless they can gain support from the two broadest decision forums: votes on the floor of Congress or backing from the presidential office. Without such access, these groups need to go the indirect route of generating policy by making public opinion an important policy consideration.

However those groups with sophisticated resources of leadership and money may seek access to the elected branches of government by using the court system to get a redefinition of important rules of the game or a reinterpretation of legislative clauses. The techniques of court lobbying are discussed in the next chapter.

NOTES

1. Adam Yarmolinsky, "Ideas into Programs," eds. Thomas Cronin and Sanford Greenberg, *The Presidential Advisory System* (New York: Harper & Row, 1969), pp. 94–95.
2. See Richard Pious, "Sources of Domestic Policy Initiatives," in *Congress Against The President,* ed. Harvey Mansfield, Sr., pp. 98–111. (New York: Proceedings of the Academy of Political Science, 1975).
3. See Cronin and Greenberg, *The Presidential Advisory System,* pp. 94–95.
4. Norman Thomas and Harold Wolman, "Policy Formulation in the Institutionalized Presidency: The Johnson Task Forces," in Cronin and Greenberg, *The Presidential Advisory System,* p. 135. Information in this section is drawn from this article, pp. 124–43.
5. See David Truman, *The Governmental Process* (New York: Knopf, 1951), p. 461.
6. David J. Vogler, *The Politics of Congress* (Boston: Allyn and Bacon, 1974), pp. 232–33.
7. Rowland Evans and Robert Novak, *LBJ: The Exercise of Power* (New York: Signet Books 1966), p. 379.
8. Richard Harris, *A Sacred Trust* (New York: Pelican Books, 1969), p. 190.
9. Vogler, *The Politics of Congress,* p. 230–31
10. David Sheridan, "The Lobbyist: Out of the Shadows," in *Watergate: Its Effects on the American Political System,* ed. David Saffell (Cambridge, Mass: Winthrop Publications, 1974), p. 244; and also from U.S., Congress, House of Representatives Judiciary Committee, *Statement of Information,* 93 Cong. 2d sess., May-June, 1974, Bk. 6, p. 22.
11. Jack Anderson, August 27, 1975.
12. John Bibby and Roger Davidson, *On Capitol Hill,* 2d ed. (Hinsdale, Ill.: Dryden Press, 1972), p. 231; see also John Donovan, *The Politics of Poverty* (Western Publications, 1967), p. 9; J. Clarence Davies III and Barbara S. Davies, *Politics of Pollution,* 2d ed. (Indianapolis: Pegasus, 1975); Speech by Chairman Fredrick Engman, Federal Trade Commission, October 7, 1974.
13. Bibby and Davidson, *On Capitol Hill,* p. 226.
14. This data is drawn from Frank Munger, "Changing Politics of Aid to Education," in *Issues and Perspectives in American Government: Read-*

ings, ed. Joseph Palamountain et al. (Glenview, Ill.: Scott, Foresman, 1971), pp. 534–40; Lyndon Johnson, *The Vantage Point* (New York: Popular Library, 1971), pp. 206–12; Eric Goldman, *The Tragedy of Lyndon Johnson* (New York: Dell, 1969), pp. 350–65; Thomas Dye, *Understanding Public Policy* (Englewood Cliffs, N.J.: Prentice-Hall, 1972), chap. 7

15. Johnson, *The Vantage Point,* pp. 209–10.
16. From Eugene Eidenberg and Roy Morey, *An Act of Congress,* p. 77, quoted in Dye, *Understanding Public Policy,* p. 142.
17. Alan Otten, "By Courting Congress Assiduously, Johnson Furthers His Program," in *The Modern Presidency,* ed. Nelson Polsby (New York: Random House, 1973), p. 193.
18. Information for this case study was drawn from Susan Wagner, *Cigarette Country* (New York: Praeger, 1971); Joseph Goulden, *The Superlawyers* (New York: Weybright and Talley, 1972), pp. 130–32; Elizabeth Drew, "The Quiet Victory of the Cigarette Lobby," *Atlantic Monthly,* September 1965, pp. 76–80.
19. Wagner, *Cigarette Country,* p. 149.
20. Ibid., p. 164. The next quotation is on p. 165.
21. This case study is based on information in Congressional Quarterly, *The Washington Lobby,* 2d ed. (Washington, D.C: Congressional Quarterly, Inc., 1974), pp. 128–31; David Martin, "Heading the Highway Lobby Off at the Overpass," *Washington Monthly,* November 1973, pp. 47–54.
22. Martin, "Heading the Highway Lobby Off at the Overpass," p. 50.
23. *New York Times,* May 8, 1975.
24. Truman, *The Governmental Process,* p. 439.
25. *New York Times,* February 11, 1974.
26. *New York Times,* November 16, 1975.
27. Congressman Bill Archer in U.S., Congress, House, *Congressional Record,* 94 Cong., 2nd Sess., February 26, 1976, p. E870.
28. Harold Seidman, *Politics, Position and Power* (New York: Oxford University Press, 1970), p 3.
29. Herbert Simon, Donald Smithburg, and Victor Thompson, "The Struggle for Organizational Survival," in *Bureaucratic Power in National Politics,* 2d ed., ed. F. Rourke (Boston: Little, Brown, 1972), p. 29.
30. Information is drawn from *National Journal,* February 15, 1975, pp. 250–59. See also Seidman, *Politics, Position and Power,* chaps. 7, 8 for discussion of various government-outside interest relationships.
31. These criticisms are listed in *Congressional Quarterly Weekly Report,* January 13, 1976, p. 223.
32. *National Journal,* February 15, 1975, p. 255.

33. Ibid., p. 256.
34. Ibid., p. 256.
35. This information is based on stories in the *New York Times,* February 28, 1975, and February 12, 1976.
36. *New York Times,* November 16, 1975.
37. Jack Anderson, July 23, 1974.
38. See Paul Starr, "The $12 Billion Misunderstanding: Veterans and the VA," *Washington Monthly,* November 1973, pp. 55–61.
39. Thomas Burns, *Tales of ITT* (Boston: Houghton Mifflin, 1974), p. 98. See also Anthony Sampson, *The Sovereign State of ITT* (New York: Fawcett Crest Books, 1973), chaps. 7, 8; U.S., Congress, House of Representatives, Judiciary Committee, *Statement of Information,* 93 Cong., 2d Sess., May-June 1974, Bk. 5, pts. 1, 2.
40. Ibid., bk. 5, pt. 1, pp. 314–16.
41. Ibid., bk. 5, pt. 2, p. 614.
42. Quoted in Sampson, *The Sovereign State of ITT,* p. 237.
43. *New York Times,* December 20, 1975.
44. Charles Jones, *An Introduction to the Study of Public Policy* (Belmont, Ca.: Wadsworth, 1970), p. 124.

Chapter 11

Lobbying through the Courts

According to myth, American courts are apolitical because they supposedly perform a neutral, mechanical, governmental function—settling current legal disputes merely by applying the constitutional and legal precedents established during the last 20 years. But in the real world courts are important to the policy-making process precisely because, by developing rationales based on old laws and adapting them to current issues, they link new problems and old standards. Laws are not neutral; they bend to accommodate to the needs, values, and wishes of those currently in control. So judges do not *find* answers when they place new disputes alongside old constitutional standards: they *make* them.

The basic apolitical myth spawned another myth which holds that interest groups cannot use the courts for policy-making purposes. This myth is reinforced by rules that prohibit personal badgering of justices, picketing of courthouses, or any form of grass roots lobbying of the judiciary. Yet many groups do use the court system to initiate or implement policy goals precisely because the judicial myth can give a legitimacy to new ideas. Furthermore, judicial power to invalidate laws that contradict the Constitution is a policy-making power which some groups that have "lost" in Congress and the bureaucracy try to use to alter policy initiation or implementation that runs contrary to their goals.

A further myth suggests that courts are undemocratic because federal justices are appointed by the President rather than elected by the people. In reality, justices, although not democratically elected, are often democratically motivated because their power rests on the benevolent "justice for all" myth. As in *The Wizard of Oz,* if the curtain of impartial justice and neutral law were dropped, we would see politically astute men moving levers to accommodate change without revolt. Paradoxically, the myth gives justices a flexibility to extend their "constitutional" beneficence to aid rising minorities or assist in the resolution of issues that elected officials feel are too hot to handle. In so doing, they can open the system to those groups that cannot or prefer not to fight their battles through Congress or the executive bureaucracy.

Even accepting the reality of group participation, those who seek evidence of lobbying in the courts often find it difficult to pick up traces of participation. Ours is a system of adversary justice in which individuals with real, personal injuries joust with words, and the notion of third party or outside group involvement seems to upset the balance. "Each party to the contest has his champion—an attorney—and judgment and justice alike are presumably forged in a crucible which is heated by the intensity of the conflicting interests."[1] The current debate over the notion of public interest lawyers, who use the judicial process to seek change for the public at large, is really in part a debate over a two- or three-party adversary system.

Ralph Nader is the personification of the public interest lawyer. He sues as a means of publicizing and reordering the interwoven web of relationships between private economic interests and the state. Nader would have lawyers balance client's interests against the public's interest "and if the two do not coincide, he [the lawyer] should then urge his client to take a broader view of his best interest."[2] By contrast, the more traditional, typical view of the Washington lawyer, as espoused by Lloyd Culter, holds that: "The public interest is best served when all sides of such a controversy have the benefit of skilled advocacy. . . . Where the public interest truly lies can best be determined by the presentation of opposing views in the proper forum."[3]

John Banzhof, a dapper, noncrusading, pragmatic, public interest lawyer seems to combine both viewpoints. He sees legal pressure as a way to produce change, but he wants to "go into areas where I can find a confluence of important problems and a point of legal leverage. . . . And if you're going to spend the rest of your life suing, you might as well sue the bastards."[4] He does. Remember that it was his appeal to the FCC to permit antismoking, prohealth commercials to be aired as a public service antidote to cigarette advertisements that provided just the prod needed for the FCC to overcome the influence that still lingered from the cigarette lobby's 1965 congressional victory over its health adversaries. "The FCC had within it an ovum, and Banzhof supplied the sperm."[5]

In this chapter we will go behind the myths and trace the methods used by interest groups seeking judicial policy responses in the interests of both narrow and broad group goals.

COURT STRUCTURE AND PROCESS

The court system is complicated by its federal nature: parallel state and national court systems coexist, have overlapping jurisdiction in many subject areas, and often both participate in a single decision-making sequence, as when a case begun in state court raises federal issues and, consequently, is appealed to a federal appellate court. We will concern ourselves here with the federal court system: ninety-seven district (trial) courts, eleven circuit courts of appeal, and one Supreme Court. As the third branch in a system of checks and balances, the judiciary plays an important policy-making role. "The guerrilla warfare which usually rages between Congress and the President, as well as the internal civil wars which are endemic in both the legislature and administration give the judiciary considerable room to maneuver. . . ."[6] Like the other institutions, courts are required to make choices among competing alternatives and, in so doing, reward some and deprive others. Yet the courts' role differs from the legislative and executive, reflecting differences in structure and procedure.

Structurally the courts have two strengths and several weaknesses. First, court personnel have a personal flexibility denied elected representatives because federal judges are appointed for life (removable only by impeachment), with guaranteed salaries. Thus, although a part of the dominant ruling elite in cultural, ideological, and economic terms, justices are often able to champion controversial theories or values that elected representatives are unable to push: for example, civil rights for blacks and criminals, as well as equality for school children, travelers, urban and suburban voters.

On the other hand, life tenure, plus the built-in status quo bias of the judicial decision-making process, often leave courts as the final redoubts for defensive interests that have lost ground in elected arenas. According to traditional wisdom, losers go to court:[7] for example, business in the 1920s, unions in the 1930s, blacks in the 1940s. A classic example was the Hughes' Court's negation of New Deal legislation, twelve statutes in six months, in a losing effort to protect laissez-faire capitalism.

> . . . Groups whose strength has diminished in other segments of the governing institution . . . use the rules, the high costs, and the technical procedures of the judiciary to perpetuate their power.[8]

Personal independence thus gives justices the flexibility to salvage losers or support rising newcomers without fear of voter retribution.

Second, the court's strength lies in the public's identification of its activities with the symbolism inherent in the Constitution. Just as myth hails law as neutral and the Constitution as immutable, so too it describes judicial decision making as impartial, impersonal, and just.[9] Courts use this legitimacy to advance or retard the policy consensus of the elected branches. Such symbolic support for American values of equality, opportunity, freedom, and fair play may not change current outputs, but it can affect policy by injecting new considerations into the public arena.

> Providing effective access to participants who wish to take part in decision-making, placing issues on the agenda of public opinion and of other political institutions, providing an imprimatur of legitimacy to one side or another that may affect its ability to attract adherents, mobilize resources, and build institutions—these are all important parts of the policy-making process.[10]

Thus litigants can capitalize on these aspects of independence "to force intelligent planning in the public interest" and to show elected decision makers "that there is another avenue of redress for the citizen."[11]

Countering these strengths is the dependence of the courts on both legislature and executive for personnel, budget, and even the scope of their appellate jurisdiction, which is granted by Congress, not the Constitution. Furthermore, courts have no armies to force compliance with their rulings. They must await executive help. Eisenhower sent the National Guard to Alabama to enforce the Court's school integration ruling, but when Presidents refuse to cooperate as Nixon and Ford did on the busing issue, Court pronouncements are unlikely to become applied policy. Aware of these weaknesses, justices use doctrines such as "ripeness," "political questions," and "judicial self-restraint" to save face and avoid making decisions that are likely to be resisted by those charged with implementing them. Thus presidents are never checked for abuse of war powers while a war is in progress. Nevertheless imaginative use of language to justify decisions often permits a court to pursue an independent course while protecting its flanks.

Courts have several ways of packaging policy, ways that vary in visibility and assertiveness: they can act negatively by vetoing policy outright; they can act positively, extending old acceptable powers into new areas; or they can accept, without comment, changes in typical behavior patterns. The first option has the most potential for challenge from competing policy centers, the last format provides an innocuous way to legitimize behavior patterns without providing material for further argument.

Judicial procedures also inhibit the court's policy-making role. Courts cannot seek out an injustice and decide to fix it. Issues must be contained in the cases that enter the court system. In this sense, courts are passive instruments, activated by litigation. Even when courts do consider cases, the impact may not be as broad as desired, since legally, decisions apply only to the actual parties to the suit or the specific class of persons they represent.

Yet despite the formalities of the process, some flexibility is introduced by *judicial discretion* in accepting cases and by the nature of legal reasoning itself. To take the latter first, legal reasoning is not simply the logical application of clear precedents to current situations. It is circular, expedient, practical: changing old rules to fit new situations.

> . . . The kind of reasoning involved in the legal process is one in which the classification changes as the classification is made. The rules change

> as the rules are applied. . . . The categories used in the legal process must be left ambiguous in order to permit the infusion of new ideas, . . . The process is one in which the ideas of the community and of the social sciences, whether correct or not, as they win acceptance in the community, control legal decisions.[12]

As Justice Oliver W. Holmes said, "The life of the law has not been logic: it has been experience, the felt necessities of the time, the prevalent moral and political theories . . . even the prejudices which judges share with their fellow-men. . . ."

Judicial discretion in accepting cases illustrates the pragmatic flexibility inherent in judicial reasoning. Courts possess gatekeeping powers such as the doctrines of standing, justiciability, jurisdiction, political questions, ripeness, mootness, and so forth, which essentially determine who wins access to the court system. Use of these powers enables courts "to determine which demands they will address and how fully they will consider those that they do address."[13]

Consider the major criterion from the interest group perspective: *standing to sue,* that is, the initial decision to grant access to a court. Forty years ago, Justice Brandeis in *Ashwander* v. *TVA* said the Court could consider only "real, earnest, and vital controversy between private individuals. . . . It is no part of the judicial function . . . to decide cases in which merely the public interest is at stake." Today as government involves itself in more functions of daily concern to citizens, as concern for common properties of air, water, diet, and so on increases, as trust in government decreases, more groups turn to the courts. Prior to 1975, the Supreme Court responded by expanding its standing doctrine to include more and more varieties of "public interests."

> . . . The standing criteria partake as much of diplomacy as of law. These rules are not dogmas. . . . They are . . . means to assist federal judges in timing their decisions on substantive issues to obtain a maximum effect on public policy with a minimum of conflict with other governmental officials.[14]

To keep the court process adversary instead of advisory, standing criteria mandate that the cases involve real injuries to the parties involved in order "to assure that concrete adverseness which sharpens the presentation of issues upon which the Court so largely depends for illumination of difficult constitutional questions."[15] Within the last decade the definition of "personal stake" has been expanded from economic issues to include a variety of nonpecuniary issues—social, aesthetic, recreational, and conservational.[16] The Court also expanded the notion of "individual injury" to include members of the public on public issues, in both citizen and taxpayer suits. The Court reasoned that: "To deny standing to persons who are in fact injured simply because many others are also injured would mean that the most injurious and widespread government actions could be questioned by nobody."[17]

The impact for interest groups of this judicial loosening is dramatically illustrated by the rise of environmental law as a new and successful field. Prior to 1967, environmental litigation was extremely rare because the courts adhered to the "public nuisance rule" whereby citizens in situations where all suffer equally must be represented in court by a public official.[18] Needless to say, given the buddy system of policy development, this rarely happened. Then in 1970 environmentalists were handed a tool that might be used to gain "standing": Congress passed the National Environmental Protection Act (NEPA). Its key section requires government agencies to prepare environmental impact statements before initiating actions with environmental consequences.

Court review is not specified in the law, but courts opted for the oversight role implied in NEPA's provisions because it came at a time when the notion of stricter review of administrative processes was already percolating through the courts.[19] NEPA provided "a surrogate review mechanism" for those anxious to review agency action more stringently. Proenvironmental rulings were welcomed in the early 1970s climate of opinion, so the courts were praised for their aggressive role.

Between 1970 and 1973, 149 separate litigations, often involving more than one opinion, were initiated under NEPA. The new access route generated a host of environmental public law firms such as the Sierra Club Legal Defense Fund, the Environmental Defense Fund, the National Resources Defense Council, and the Center for Law in the Public Interest. Their litigating range is very broad. The Environmental Defense Fund, for example, works on seventy or more cases simultaneously—related to issues such as energy, land use, sea otters, noise, whale preservation, pesticides, environmental health, water resources, and highways.

In sum, standing benefits both sides. Some new interests may have a day in court. However, a Court can use its gatekeeping functions for self protection or as a form of limited initiative in selecting areas where the policy situation is current, fluid, and amenable to judicial action. For example, since 1975 the justices have been less inclined to continue the Court's precedent-making initiatives of the 1960s.

INTEREST GROUPS IN COURT

Despite the fiction that court decisions involve individuals, the Court ruled in 1958 that groups have "standing to assert here constitutional rights pertaining to the members, who are not of course parties to the legislation."[20] Then in 1963 the Court made it quite clear that litigation could be an essential method for influencing public opinion.

> ... In the context of NAACP objectives, litigation ... is a means for achieving the lawful objectives of equality of treatment. ... It is thus a form of political expression. Groups which find themselves unable to achieve their objectives through the ballot turn to the courts. Just as it was true of opponents of New Deal legislation during the 1930s, for example, no less is it true of the Negro minority today. And under conditions of modern government, litigation may well be the sole practicable avenue open to a minority to petition for redress of grievances.[21]

These groups use the technique of the *class action,* wherein the plaintiffs sue for themselves and all persons "similarly situated." The device saves money in that a case will not become "moot" (no longer a live controversy) during the years it takes to progress from district to Supreme Court, and it saves time because the one decision applies —yea or nay—to all people in the same situation. Equality, apportionment, criminal's legal rights, women's occupational rights—all have been litigated through class action suits.

Public Law Problems

Courts are welcome policy-making forums for groups with a variety of needs. One large category includes "losers" in the administrative or legislative battles who seek judicial redress. For example, Ralph Nader's Public Citizen Litigation Group has sued a variety of targets that stand between it and its goals: the USDA for its new beef grading rules, lawyers who follow minimum fee schedules (as a form of price fixing), the IRS for its political surveillance records, and President Nixon for illegally impounding $5 billion in water quality improvement funds. In each instance, Public Citizen won.

Congress has explicitly provided for outsider's access to the court process in instances where public law problems (that is, problems caused by governmental action or inaction) arise. The Administrative Procedures Act makes provisions for court redress (1) when irreparable injury might result, (2) where the agency is acting outside the scope of its authority, (3) where the futility of pursuing administrative remedies is obvious, (4) where the agency's authorizing statute is attacked as unconstitutional, or (5) where the agency is being deliberately dilatory.[22] Use of these provisions abound in the environmental area: for instance, environmentalists sued HEW to stop the use of DDT, the Department of Interior to stop building of the Alaskan pipeline, and the Federal Power Commission to stop construction of the Storm King electrical power plant.

In some other cases:

- The Sierra Club sued the EPA in order to prevent a weakening of the 1970 Clean Air Act. At Court insistence, EPA was forced to apply a nondegradation policy to air pollution.
- The Association of Physicians and Surgeons sued the secretary of HEW to block implementation of a national review system to monitor hospital treatment of medicare/medicaid patients which was required by the 1972 Social Security Amendments. The court's ruling, affirmed by the Supreme Court, held the doctor's rights to make unfettered medical care decisions were correctly balanced in this case against the public interest in setting standards on care for the needy. The review system has now been implemented.
- The American Public Health Association and Senator Frank Moss sued when the Consumer Safety Product Commission refused to ban high-

tar cigarettes in interstate commerce because they said they lacked jurisdiction. The Court held that the CPSC has such authority under the Hazardous Substances Act which it administers.

- Thirteen states (Connecticut, Massachusetts, Rhode Island, New York, Virginia, Florida, South Carolina, Mississippi, Wisconsin, Michigan, Minnesota, Idaho, and Illinois) sued HEW for withholding social service welfare matching funds on the basis of revised procedures designed by HEW to contain the expanding costs of the program. The Court said the States were entitled to their funds which had been deferred on the basis of that invalid memorandum.

This technique has been so successful that Supreme Court Justice Lewis Powell sent a 1972 memorandum to the United States Chamber of Commerce urging it to emulate such tactics in order to get court support for the free enterprise system. He characterized the judicial arena as "a vast area of opportunity for the Chamber if it is willing to undertake the role of spokesman for American business. . . ."[23]

Outsiders Getting In

Another category of losers are those who need court support, not to rectify a specific policy defeat, but rather to create legitimacy for an entire set of concepts that may or may not already be written into law. Joseph Rauh uses the courts both to protect the rights of unions to organize and to protect the rights of union members to dissent. He won a suit against the National Right to Work Legal Defense and Education Foundation, which had financed over sixty-five union shop suits by members against their own unions, in order to force disclosure of employer-contributors to the foundation. He has also won court fights protecting the rights of insurgents to challenge current union leadership. The most famous of these was the 1972 reform fight that ousted UMW President W. A. "Tony" Boyle.[24]

The classic example of "outs" using the court system to get "in" is the NAACP's sixty-year history of litigating for equality. The NAACP was founded in 1909 with the goal of making racial prejudice "unfashionable." Initially the organization utilized the whole spectrum of lobbying techniques but soon found that petitioning Congress was like hitting a blank wall. "The institution was insulated against

Negro claims. The size and character of the southern delegation, the committee system, seniority, and cloture in the Senate doomed Negro efforts."[25] So, beginning in 1915, the NAACP turned to the courts to implement broad principles of equality through a series of issue-related court decisions and accompanying opinions designed to increase the acceptability of such ideas in legal circles and among the public at large. By 1939 the caseload was sufficiently large and important for the parent organization to create a separate litigating institution, the NAACP Legal Defense and Educational Fund as an incorporated tax-deductible entity.

Since then the NAACP has monopolized the racial discrimination field: over two-thirds of all such cases are sponsored by the fund, over fifty Supreme Court victories attest to the excellence of its efforts. Its monopoly in numbers and quality has given the NAACP an excellent reputation *within the court hierarchy.* This point is important in understanding the preconditions for group success in the court system where only a handful of men make key decisions; their esteem is won by diligence and intelligence rather than votes. Their world is the small world of lawyer elites, who know each other and respect each other for the value of their work. Groups unable to command the resources for congressional access such as money, membership status, and/or socially acceptable programs, but which have leadership resources and group cohesion may find that the court system provides a perfect setting for maximizing the effect of the resources they do have while developing those attributes that earn legislative attention.

The NAACP prefers to initiate cases in order to ensure that proper questions are raised and considered, since it is the district court record and opinion that forms the basis for appellate decisions. The NAACP uses pressure but with "courtesy, dignity, and authority. Its briefs have been models of legal craftsmanship."[26] The technique used by the NAACP is exemplified in one of its first attempts at implementing a court strategy—the attack on the use of racial covenants, a practice sanctioned in previous court decisions that permitted neighborhoods to retain their ethnic homogeneity by forbidding sales to "outsider" classes such as blacks. In the mid-1940s a half-dozen cases contesting racial covenants were initiated in courts in various sections of the country. The lawyers for these cases met regularly during the succeeding years in order to coordinate arguments, divide responsibilities for legal research, minimize duplication of effort, and build strong records for each case since no one knew which case(s) might be accepted by the Supreme Court.

To compensate for a lack of favorable legal precedents, the NAACP utilized the "Brandeis" brief, which emphasizes sociological, psychological, and economic data relevant to a legal decision. Articles "planted" in leading law journals stressed the sociological rather than biological sources of black problems and argued a new interpretation of "state action" which introduced the notion that inaction was as much a policy as action. In 1947 when the Supreme Court finally agreed to hear four restrictive covenant cases on appeal, the constitutional issues were argued; the NAACP won.

> Analysis of victory in the restrictive covenant cases forces the conclusion that this result was an outgrowth of the complex group activity which preceded it. Groups with antagonistic interests appeared before the Supreme Court, just as they do before Congress or other institutions that mold public policy. Because of organization, the lawyers for the Negroes were better prepared to do battle through the courts. Without this continuity, money, and talent they would not have freed themselves from the limiting effects of racial residential covenants, notwithstanding the presence of favorable social theories, political circumstances, and Supreme Court justices."

The same technique has proven successful in eliminating the concept of separate but equal education, in opening the housing market, and in extending the franchise to blacks.

Policy Tacticians

There is a final category of groups interested in court processes: those who seek judicial assistance in publicizing facets of an ongoing policy debate in order to focus congressional or bureaucratic attention on the issue. Such was the case of the Common Cause litigation strategy during its four-year effort to pass a campaign finance law that included provisions for public financing of campaigns, broad reporting provisions, a strong enforcement agency, and strict limitations on campaign contributions and expenditures.[28] Since most legislation is written to rectify the worst or the most obvious of past abuses, Common Cause used litigation to press its view of what these abuses were. Cases were initiated that pinpointed areas of excessive dependence on private campaign donations or lax enforcement of existing laws and thereby forced Congress to deal with the issues that were raised.

In addition, court procedures helped Common Cause to acquire the necessary information for influencing both legislators and the public at large. The judicial process provides for the technique of "discovery" whereby those given standing to sue can subpoena witnesses and material in order to accumulate the evidence necessary for defense of their position. Using this tool, Common Cause litigation forced open the cracks in the story told by Nixon's Finance Committee to Reelect the President. Pressures from the court process led to piecemeal release of data that indicated President Nixon circumvented a reform campaign finance law which he had reluctantly signed by collecting $22.9 million (40 percent of the total money he collected) in unreported donations before the new law went into effect. This data, well-publicized, forced Congress and public alike to the conclusion that public financing was necessary to take the elements of coercion and bribery out of presidential campaign politics.

To summarize, groups include the court as a policy-making forum for various reasons. Some use the courts to modify specific decisions made by the bureaucracy or to redefine statutes in a more favorable light. Others use the courts to generate controversies that will put issues on the formal agenda of government or influence the content of legislation under consideration. In both these situations, the interest groups are already policy players using an alternative forum for their ideas. Public relations and public opinion aspects of court decisions provide leverage for such groups.

However, for a third category of groups, those that have not yet achieved the status of policy participant, the courts are not an alternative source of access but the *only* source. For these groups court protection and assistance is necessary in order to legitimize controversial policies, place new ideas on the public policy agenda, or publicize rising groups and their needs. While others choose the courts as the arena for a particular policy round, these groups use the courts as entry into the system itself. Consequently they usually seek broad, value-related changes that will force other actors to pay attention to the specifics of their goals. The difference here is between using the courts as part of one's basic long-range strategy or using the courts for tactical purposes. When asked, justices are thus in a position to support rising groups, waning groups, and groups in transition from "out" to "in" or vice versa.

LOBBYING THE COURT

Notions of judicial neutrality and nonpartisanship—the same qualities that make the Courts attractive as a policy-making alternative—also prevent the use of traditional lobbying techniques. It is illegal to picket justices or bombard them with mail or bribe them or in any way seek to influence the person of a judge. Therefore when lobbying the court, groups have three main techniques available to them: influencing the appointment of judges, influencing the content of cases and decisions, or affecting the implementation of court decisions. Strategy in any given instance is related to the current policy climate and organizational strengths and goals just as it is for any other form of lobbying.

Appointments

It has been estimated that new justices reach the Supreme Court approximately every twenty-two months, thus ensuring that Court opinions will be only slightly "out of line with the policy views dominant among the lawmaking majorities of the U.S."[29] Indeed FDR's extreme plan to "pack the court" with New Dealers resulted from frustration: by a fluke he was in office for five years before the first Supreme Court vacancy occurred. Most presidents wish to place like-minded men on the Court as a way of guaranteeing support for their policies once their own term has ended. When President Nixon appointed law-and-order advocates to the Court, he was simultaneously selecting men who shared his policy beliefs, fulfilling a campaign pledge, and responding to public outcries that the Warren Court had "dangerously coddled" criminals.

Rejection of a presidential choice of appointee is the exception, not the rule. Fewer than one-quarter of all federal court nominations are rejected. Usually interest groups are consulted in advance to prevent the embarrassment of a failure to confirm a presidential nominee. The most obvious example of such consultation has been the American Bar Association's (ABA) continuing attempt to routinize prior screening by their Committee on the Federal Judiciary before nominations are sent to the Senate.[30] The committee's success record has been mixed:

- Eisenhower used it for all federal district and circuit court appointments,
- Kennedy informed it after his selections and prior to confirmation,
- Nixon began to use it after his nominations of Clement Haynesworth and G. Harrold Carswell were rejected by the Senate.

Reluctance to use the ABA arises when presidents disagree with ABA philosophy, since its ratings tend to be based as much on a candidate's attitudes as his professional qualifications.

The definition of other "powerful" groups to be consulted prior to nomination changes with the times.

> In the years following the Civil War, during which the influence of large corporations on governmental policy making was unchallenged, the influence of railroads on Supreme Court appointments was noticeable. Today such influence is lacking. Judging from . . . recent defeats of presidential nominees, however, it would appear that labor and civil rights groups have wielded considerable influence over decisions concerning judicial personnel.[31]

In 1916 the appointment of Louis Brandeis was opposed by the ABA and business groups who were using the courts as a bulwark against regulatory legislation, and feared his progressive position would be detrimental. In 1971 a similar coalition of conservative forces challenged Justice Fortas's move from associate to chief justice, partly to snub President Johnson and partly in retaliation for Fortas's liberal votes on criminal rights, civil liberties, separation of church and state, and other personal freedoms issues. Brandeis won despite the storm; Fortas withdrew.

In 1969 and 1970 the labor-civil rights coalition forced defeat of two successive Nixon nominees—Clement Haynesworth and G. Harrold Carswell—on charges of questionable ethics, poor civil rights records, and incompetence. The Carswell fight presented several problems for the opposing groups. First, it meant the second Senate rejection of a presidential nominee for the same Supreme Court seat, when even one rejection goes against custom. Second, time was a crucial factor for two reasons: (1) hearings began within a week of the nomination; (2) other legislation of importance to these groups, such as revision of the 1965 Voting Rights Act, was on the Senate floor. To be successful, the groups had to quickly generate enough counterpressure to nullify the natural influence of the President and thereby create a milieu in which the appointment might be decided on its merits.

The Leadership Conference on Civil Rights, which led the opposition lobbying effort, had to decide who would be its inside lobbyists; how the press could be involved, especially in the investigative work; how the issue could be made bipartisan; how to publicize the issue favorably to the mass public; and how to circulate information so that senators would be informed in time. Within days of the nomination announcement, lobbyists for the Leadership Conference, the ADA, NAACP, AFL-CIO, and UAW met with staff members for Senators Bayh, Kennedy, Hart, and Tydings to plan strategy.

Despite the disadvantages of timing and overcommitment to other goals, the groups succeeded in finding enough documentation of Carswell's civil rights bias and poor judicial performance to complement the counterproductive White House lobbying and Carswell's own self-defeating lying during the Judiciary Committee's nomination hearing. For example, the national ABA found Carswell qualified, but the coalition nullified this fact with a letter from the equally prestigious New York City Bar Association urging Carswell's defeat, plus letters from establishment lawyers and well-known law professors opposing the appointment. Carswell's nomination was defeated 45 to 51. The conference's victory demonstrates that the Court's policy-making role is important enough to some groups to warrant major efforts to influence the nomination/confirmation process.

Court Decision Content

An attack on a presidential nominee may occur once in a decade, but the sophisticated, reasoned, tactful, scholarly, low-keyed use of the written word to influence court decisions occurs daily. Petitions, demonstrations, threats, bribes are illegal and counterproductive. But,

> a well-reasoned and ably written brief, be it by one of the litigants or a brief *amicus curiae;* a persuasive oral argument on behalf of an issue at bar; a timely, thoughtful, and convincing book, monograph, speech, or law review article on the general or specific issue; a strategically timed use of a bona fide test case—that type of influence, as well as the intriguing concept of the "climate of public opinion," falls into a different category.[32]

The importance of group manipulation of language reflects Court rules of procedure which emphasize adherence to precedents whenever possible, consideration only of issues raised in earlier decisions, and then evaluation of constitutional questions only when no narrower answer will suffice. Interest group "lobbying on paper" provides a way to plant seeds of change, a means of introducing new ideas to old judges and making new interpretations seem logical adaptations of old doctrine.

Test cases are cases that, by definition, can be decided either way since their purpose is to challenge existing public policy, usually by having a litigant sue in the name of a class of affected people. The probable outcome is a toss-up. A decision for the group sets the stage for changes in public opinion and challenges to policy from other governmental actors. A loss for the group means preservation of the current status quo.

In test cases the actual person who provides the real case or controversy is less important than the constitutional principles argued in the case. Thus the point of *Brown* v. *Board of Education* was important because it would affect the right of all children to attend integrated school systems. *Common Cause* v. *the Democratic National Committee (DNC)* granted Common Cause and all its members as political activists and voters constitutional rights to an undiluted vote. Establishment of constitutional protection for rights makes such cases pivotal in the development of policy-making precedents because the decision may open entire fields of new policy development.

Since the point is to provide a fulcrum for change, timing is crucial. Leadership and organizational skill are required to "pick the right case at the right time and bring it before the right judge. Such decisions are as crucial to the outcome of litigation as the choice of time, location, and weapons is to the results of a military campaign."[33] Skillful handling of test cases by organizations permits their litigants to compete equally in court with government representatives since the organizations provide an expertise, continuity, and financial resources that few individuals could provide. Consider the Jehovah's Witnesses, a religious sect that has never been popular in Congress, but won forty-five of the fifty bona fide test cases that they carried to the Supreme Court between 1925 and 1950.

Just as groups lobbying Congress seek media support to build a climate of public opinion for their policies, so legally oriented interest groups seek to build a favorable opinion climate within the narrower confines of the legal profession. It has been said that justices make law with one eye out the window and the other on election returns. Or as Justice Frankfurter more elegantly phrased it: "Can we not take judicial notice of writing by people who completely deal with these [current] problems? . . . How to inform the judicial mind, as you know, is one of the most complicated problems."

Congressman Wright Patman criticized the planting of relevant articles as "lobbying through law reviews," which he called unfair because it "adds new information unknown to others."[34] Yet this is a common technique that has been used by the NAACP in the restrictive covenant cases, by groups in favor of state control of offshore oil, by business interests opposed to antitrust litigation, by reapportionment experts anxious to write "one man, one vote" into the Constitution, and many others.

Midway between the test case sponsored by an interest group and a piece of favorable scholarly analysis in a law journal lies the *amicus curiae* (friend of the court) *brief.* Instead of developing their own cases as litigation vehicles, specialized, legally oriented groups often broaden their scope and involvement by becoming active at the appellate level through the device of the *amicus* brief. These briefs supply new points of law, provide needed expertise, or add important moral arguments that are relevant but might detract from the main arguments in the official briefs offered by the litigants. Politically speaking, a broad coalition of organizations, representing diverse constituencies, but united in terms of a case, can provide political support for the formal party to the case by acting as an alliance of *amici.*

Until 1949 anyone could file an *amicus* brief since permission to do so was freely given by the Court. Abuse of the privilege led to its curtailment. Currently such briefs are filed in three to four dozen cases yearly, primarily by the ACLU, NAACP, AFL-CIO, American Jewish Congress, and National Lawyers Guild. For example, in the racial covenant cases, nineteen groups ranging from the AF of L to the Congregational Church filed on behalf of the NAACP; five pro-real estate groups filed for the defendants. In *Gideon* v. *Wainwright,* twenty-four *amicus* briefs were filed supporting Gideon's right to free counsel; two supported the State of Florida. In *DeFunis* v. *Odegaard,* eight *amici* supported DeFunis's argument of reverse discrimination; nineteen supported the University of Washington's stand.

A major drawback to using *amicus* briefs instead of initiating cases is the inability to control the development of case content. This drawback led the American Civil Liberties Union (ACLU), a national nonpartisan organization that promotes First Amendment individual rights and liberties, to shift from a predominantly *amicus* role to a direct litigation emphasis. The former technique permitted involvement in a greater number of suits, but taking direct cases has increased the ACLU's organizational importance within the judicial policy system. "Direct representation is now the way of Union life, *amicus* participation the exception."[35]

When ACLU entered the field of women's rights by establishing the Women's Rights Project as a separate unit to deal with sex discrimination, it combined the three informational lobbying techniques in order to create a climate for judicial rethinking of the unconscious sex bias evident in the history of decisions related to such discrimination. Between 1971 and 1975, WRP handled thirty-seven cases; in 1975 sixteen cases were filed jointly with others, eight were handled through *amicus* briefs. In each instance cases were selected to create the NAACP-type of sequential movement and incremental change that eventually sets new public policy.

For example, in creating a line of precedents that would eliminate gender labels, the Women's Rights Project extended to other preferential treatment areas an earlier victory in *Reed* v. *Reed,* which held unconstitutional an Idaho law giving males preference in appointments to administer estates. In their next major test case, *Frontiero* v. *Richardson,* the Court held that setting different standards for determining eligibility of male and female dependents to secure military dependents' benefits was a violation of the due process clause of the Fifth Amendment. The Women's Project built on this victory in *Weinberger* v. *Wiesenfeld,* which held that paying Social Security survivors' benefits only to mothers was unconstitutional. "The basic argument in all these briefs came from the *Reed* brief, the "grandmother" brief."[36]

It has been argued that the use of *amicus* briefs and test cases as a form of interest group influence on Court decisions has been vastly overrated. The majority of Court cases involve narrow, ad hoc, private controversies between "individual commercial, proprietary, or private interests" with no backstage organizational maneuvers "intervening between the attorney and his business client."[37] Indeed this is accurate. However, as the examples in this chapter suggest, *amicus* briefs and test cases are not scattered randomly across the policy spectrum. They are used predominately in the area of civil rights and liberties where "special interest groups are now succeeding in organizing the flow of much of . . . [this] litigation that reaches the Supreme Court, and in using it to promote their causes."[38]

Twenty-one of the fifty-two cases involving personal rights accepted by the Supreme Court in its 1967–68 term were brought by the NAACP, ACLU, and American Jewish Congress (AJC). Of the 2,600 Court cases involving civil rights litigation between 1955 and 1962, 1,400 were handled by private lawyers, the bulk of them being members of fifty law firms (which includes the litigation divisions of the ACLU, NAACP, and other similar groups.)[39] The policy impact of these groups led to formation of a counter group, Americans for Effective Law Enforcement, to provide expert *amicus* support in favor of capital punishment, limited rights for welfare clients, neighborhood schools, and so forth.

Basically the issue over the importance of *amicus* briefs as an interest group technique involves apples and oranges. Indeed, those groups using this technique are few in terms of all Court supplicants and indeed the percentage of cases in which they serve an interest group function of defining issues for a larger policy context is few in terms of overall Court output, but neither of these two truths negates the fact that the social welfare, civic, and civil rights groups that provide the bulk of *amicus* services do so in order to create a foundation for policy by legislation or administrative implementation. Thus to judge the technique by case quantity or in purely internal court terms is inherently unfair, since its purpose is to extend the political possibilities of the courts beyond the court process.

Effecting Implementation of Court Decisions

Losers who go to court may lose again, or winners may need to ensure that the victory is translated from words to deeds. In either case, group participation follows the action back down the court system hierarchy to the initial district court that is usually charged with implementation of appellate decisions. Here judges who live in the area are vulnerable to the powerful community forces that may have won early rounds in the litigation battle. These forces can frustrate implementation for years as evidenced by the busing controversy of the 1970s which has its roots in the school integration decision of 1955. The practice of redlining neighborhoods, which restricts mortgage availability and creates racial housing patterns, is today's version of the restrictive covenants outlawed thirty years ago. Such community obstinacy suggests the distance that often must be traveled between winning symbolic court language and its actual implementation in the real world. The Court can create new symbols; it cannot make them come alive.

Yet research suggests that in terms of specific holdings, that is, the actual dispute settled in court, decisions are usually implemented. However, as issues are broadened in the public mind and extended by inference to other events not included in the original opinion, current politics may intervene. If lower courts or legislatures or executives choose to misinterpret or not apply decisions that the interest groups involved feel are relevant, then those groups must return to court or lobby again at the implementation level.

Basically there are five ways to nullify a Supreme Court decision. In some instances the Court can be persuaded to overrule itself as it did on the issue of reapportionment. Secondly, groups can lobby

Congress for legislation reversing a Court decision. The Cement Institute did this in 1949 when it succeeded in having legislation passed to reinstitute the base point pricing system invalidated a year earlier by the Court. Those interested in state control of offshore oil rights succeeded in passing the Submerged Lands Act of 1954 which invalidated the Court's decision in favor of national control.

Two variations of defiance involve lower courts' rejections of Supreme Court decisions. One form involves raising new legal issues after the case is remanded to the district level. Between 1941 and 1951, 175 cases were remanded; forty-six involved further litigation; in approximately one-half of these instances, the party that won in the Supreme Court lost in the state courts. Courts can also ignore decisions or governors can oppose them by force. Remember the picture of Alabama Governor George Wallace standing in the school house doorway to personally block integration?

The most drastic form of nullification is passage of a constitutional amendment. Amendments Eleven, Thirteen, Fourteen, and Sixteen represent victories in this effort, but it is a difficult task to accomplish as evidenced by attempts to "amend" Court decisions forbidding prayers in public schools, requiring apportionment on the basis of one man, one vote, or prohibiting abortion. Proponents of the Equal Rights Amendment, which needs ratification by four more states before 1979, justify the amendment in terms of previous Court decisions that have eliminated sexual equality from the purview of the Fourteenth Amendment.

Since the policy process is a continuing one, groups that challenge legislative or executive decisions in the courts can expect to play another round. "The leverage provided by litigation depends on its strategic combination with inputs at other levels."[40] When litigation is part of an integrated lobbying strategy, as illustrated by Common Cause's development of the public financing of elections issue, it has more permanence and clout than when it represents an ad hoc side trip to court or presents unexpected or new agendas for change.

However it is unrealistic to expect Court success to provide both substantive and symbolic rules changes. The former is outside its powers, although the more divided the other policy makers are, the more likely it is that a decision will have tactical impact.

> Litigation then is unlikely to shape decisively the distribution of power in society. It may serve to secure or solidify symbolic commitments. It is vital tactically in securing temporary advantage or protection, providing leverage for organization and articulation of interests, and conferring [or withholding] the mantle of legitimacy.[41]

SUMMARY

Justice Frankfurter saw the Court as "a good mirror, an excellent mirror . . . of the struggles of dominant forces outside the Court." In this struggle, judges may give a leg up to rising groups or groups whose policies have received academic acceptance but are still new to the public at large. However, its institutional weaknesses, such as lack of enforcement powers and formalized decision-making processes, limit the amount of significant change that can be anticipated from any Court action.

Courts may alter the distribution of prizes on specific policy issues as indicated by the current plethora of environmental/industrial growth cases. In terms of group development per se, courts can confer a legitimacy that leads to membership growth and resource development. "For example, the civil rights decisions culminating in *Brown* contributed to the growth of civil rights organizations like SCLC, CORE, and SNCC that became active in the streets as well as in the Congress."[42]

Courts may legitimize an idea as they did in promoting strong national government and the later development of government-supervised free enterprise. Court decisions may force other governmental actors to deal with issues such as equality, hunger, poverty, and individual rights.

Expectations regarding proper judicial behavior, restrictions on decision-making procedures, and the structural peculiarities of the court system alter the traditional forms of lobbying. The written word substitutes for direct or grass roots lobbying; time, money, and leadership skills become more important than campaign contributions or vote power. But essentially, the group goal is the same as in all other governmental decision-making forums: to influence the content of policy decisions by affecting the persons in decision-making positions and/or finding ways to get the group's information to the right place in the most acceptable form at the most propitious time.

NOTES

1. Glendon Shubert, *Constitutional Politics: The Political Behavior of Supreme Court Justices and The Constitutional Policies That They Make* (New York: Holt, Rinehart & Winston, 1960), p. 69.
2. David Riley, "The Challenge of the New Lawyers: Public Interest and Private Clients," 38 *George Washington Law Review:* 587.
3. Quoted in Joseph Goulden, *The Superlawyers* (New York: Weybright and Talley, 1972), p. 325.
4. Joseph Page, "The Law Professor Behind ASH, SOUP, PUMP, and CRASH," in *Styles of Political Action in America,* ed. Robert Wolff (New York: Random House, 1972), p. 126.
5. Ibid., p. 121.
6. J. Roche, "Judicial Self-Restraint," in Shubert, *Constitutional Politics,* p. 214.
7. David Truman, *The Governmental Process* (New York: Knopf, 1951), pp. 494–95.
8. Ibid., p. 487.
9. See Walter Murphy and C. Herman Pritchett, eds. *Courts, Judges and Politics* (New York: Random House, 1961), p. 188.
10. Jonathan Casper, "The Supreme Court and National Policy Making," *American Political Science Review* 70 (1976): 63.
11. Both quotations from J. Sax, "Environment in the Courtroom," *Saturday Review,* October 3, 1970, p. 57.
12. Edward Levi in Murphy and Pritchett, *Courts, Judges and Politics,* p. 375.
13. Lawrence Baum, "The Judicial Gatekeeping Function: A General Analysis and A Study of the California Supreme Court" (American Political Science Association paper, 1975), p. 3.
14. Murphy and Pritchett, *Courts, Judges and Politics,* p. 246.
15. *Baker* v. *Carr* 369 U.S. 186,204 (1962).
16. See *Association of Data Processing Service Organizations* v. *Camp,* 397 U.S. 150 (1970); *U.S.* v. *SCRAP,* 412 U.S. 669 (1973).
17. Ibid., p. 688.
18. Sax, "Environment in the Courtroom," p. 55.
19. See Frederick Anderson, *NEPA in the Courts: A Legal Analysis of the National Environmental Protection Act* (Baltimore: Johns Hopkins University Press, 1973), pp. 15–23.

20. *NAACP* v. *Alabama,* 357 U.S. 449 (1958).
21. *NAACP* v. *Button* 371 U.S. 415, 425 (1963).
22. See Murphy and Pritchett, *Courts, Judges and Politics,* p. 240.
23. Jack Anderson, September 28, 1972.
24. *Business Week,* February 10, 1975, p. 94.
25. The factual data in this section are from Clement Vose, *Caucasians Only* (Berkeley: University of California Press, 1967), pp. 36–37.
26. Ibid., p. 49.
27. Ibid., p. 252.
28. See Carol Greenwald, "The Use of Litigation by Common Cause," (American Political Science Association paper, 1975).
29. Robert Dahl, "Decision-Making in a Democracy: The Supreme Court as a National Policy-Maker," *Journal of Public Law* (Fall 1957).
30. There are several studies of group influence on appointments, including Joel Grossman, *Lawyers and Judges: The ABA and The Politics of Judicial Selection* (New York: John Wiley and Sons, 1965); Henry Abraham, *Justices and Presidents* (New York: Penguin Books, 1974); Richard Harris, *Decision* (New York: E. P. Dutton, 1971).
31. Harmon Zeigler and Wayne Peak, *Interest Groups in American Society,* 2d ed. (Englewood Cliffs, N.J.: Prentice-Hall, 1972), pp. 194–95.
32. Henry Abrahams, *The Judicial Process,* 3d ed. (New York: Oxford University Press, 1975), pp. 230–31.
33. Murphy and Pritchett, *Courts, Judges and Politics,* p. 280.
34. Quoted in ibid., p. 309.
35. Dorsen, *Civil Liberties,* March–April 1968, p. 6.
36. See Ruth Cowan, "Litigation as a Strategy in Women's Rights Politics: An Examination of the ACLU's Women's Rights Project" (APSA paper, 1975), p. 20.
37. See Nathan Hakman, "Lobbying the Supreme Court," in *The Federal Judiciary System,* eds. T. Jahinge and S. Goldman (New York: Holt, Rinehart & Winston, 1968), pp. 52–53.
38. *New York Times,* January 21, 1968.
39. Ann Ginger, "Litigation as a Form of Political Action," in *Legal Aspects of the Civil Rights Movement,* eds. Donald King and Charles Quick (Detroit: Wayne University Press, 1967), pp. 198–203.
40. Marc Galanter, "Why the 'Haves' Come Out Ahead: Speculations on the Limits of Legal Change," 9 *Law and Society Review* (Fall 1974), pp. 95, 151.
41. Ibid., pp. 149–50.
42. Casper, "The Supreme Court and National Policy Making," p. 63.

IV

Who Makes Policy ?

Chapter 12

Policy Patterns: Elitist, Pluralist, or Other?

In order to become a member of the public policy-making system, political interest groups need access to governmental institutions where decisions are made. Without access, there can be no influence; without influence or the possibility of becoming influential, why play? Questions such as who has access, for what purposes, under what conditions, with what consequences, intrigue political observers. They are implicit in our definition of politics as the study of influence and the influential, as well as our definition of public policy making as the authoritative allocation of resources and values in society. The very title of this book, *Group Power,* assumes one answer, namely, that groups do have meaningful access within the political system, but it does not tell us who gets what, when, and how.

Such questions have been the subject of continuing debate among social scientists. Some feel that government is run by a *power elite* who make all significant decisions without any imput from the rest of the citizens. This view sees the policy system as closed, with no competition among groups. The opposing viewpoint, known as *pluralism,* sketches a policy system composed of ad hoc, issue-oriented coalitions open to all interested participants in an environment of free competition among groups. Between these extremes lie an assortment of theories that see group activity as either hampered or encouraged by the kinds of relationships formed between outside groups and governmental decision makers.

In this chapter we will examine several of these policy-making theories in order to assess the conditions that affect competition and openness within the system and to consider the various sorts of relationships that develop between public and private decision makers. We will use examples from the world of the military-industrial complex as a common thread to facilitate comparisons among the various theories.

The military-industrial complex is an informal coalition of public and private groups with vested interests, psychological and material, in the development of weapons and other forms of military support. President Dwight D. Eisenhower coined the term, "military-industrial complex" in his farewell address to the nation when he warned that:

> This conjunction of an immense military establishment and a large arms industry is new in American experience. The total influence—economic, political, even spiritual—is felt in every city, every statehouse, every office of the federal government. . . . We must guard against the acquisition of unwarranted influence, whether sought or unsought, by the military-industrial complex. . . . Only an alert and knowledgeable citizenry can compel the proper meshing of the huge industrial and military machinery of defense with our peaceful methods and goals so that security and liberty may prosper together.

Everyone acknowledges its existence and influence, yet it is difficult to describe. It has no single address or phone number; only a parent —the Department of Defense. The DOD is the "primary employer, contractor, purchaser, owner, and spender in the nation."[1] During the 1960s the Department of Defense owned over $200 billion in domestic assets, plus 429 major bases and 2,972 minor bases overseas. In 1966 national defense expenditures were 40 percent of the budget, 7.7 percent of the GNP (gross national product); a decade later in FY 1976 these outlays accounted for 27 percent of the federal budget, 5.9 percent of the GNP. Yet in dollar amounts the numbers have been increasing, from $56 billion in FY 1966 to $94 billion in FY 1976, which is $17 billion more than the cost for military expenditures at the height of the Vietnam War.

Domestically this money can help to prime the economy: $1 billion by DOD can create 75,812 jobs.* The Pentagon annually signs con-

*A $1 billion expenditure by state and local governments on health can produce 80,041 jobs; on education, 104,019 jobs.

tracts with approximately 22,000 prime contractors and 100,000 subcontractors. The 1968 payroll for *only* the employment of civilians *directly* involved in defense work was over $8.5 billion.

The military-industrial complex is big business—thousands of companies, millions of people, billions of dollars. It includes the Department of Defense, the National Aeronautics and Space Administration, the Atomic Energy Commission, the President as commander in chief, over a dozen congressional committees, and the governments of states such as New York, Massachusetts, California, and Florida, where concentrations of defense-related industries are important to the state's economy. The private sector drawn to the complex includes all contractors from AT&T on down to the manufacturer of government-specified screws, trade associations representing all related businesses, the various armed services, veterans and their organizations, and ideological groups or one-issue coalitions promoting war, peace, or specific means to either end.

The complex is huge, but is it unified or fragmented? Is it open to outside influences or closed to all but top generals and presidents of the top twenty-five defense contractors? Where are the access points within the complex? Who uses them? What access points does the complex use? Indeed, can we speak of the military-industrial complex as if it were a single entity or is it really a conglomerate of related groups going in separate directions with separate interests and acess points? These questions can be asked about participation in any public policy-making arena. The theories applied here to decisions within the military-industrial complex can be applied to other policy areas as well. The answers outline the rules of participation, competition, and access that set the boundaries of meaningful group activity.

A POWER ELITE

"Government is always government by the few, whether in the name of the few, the one, or the many."[2] Once a small group of people expands past three, the division of labor that creates leadership positions begins. Leaders, the few people who have decision-making power, may be termed *elites.* The overwhelming majority of economic and political high-ranking decision makers "are recruited from the well-educated, prestigiously employed, older, affluent, urban, white, Anglo-Saxon, upper and upper-middle class, male population of the nation."[3] Similarity of backgrounds among members of the elite supports a consensus on American values and rules of the game, and breeds an inclination to maintain the favorable status quo.

Consequently changes occur only incrementally, giving the elites time to slowly redefine their own values. Conflict within the elite is limited to specific issues rather than ideological disputes. Although new members may join elite ranks, they rarely disturb the incremental pace of change because, during a gradual process of assimilation into this status, they learn to accept the current elite consensus on "the sanctity of private property, limited government, and individual liberty."[4]

Drawing on these general concepts, C. Wright Mills elaborated a theory of the *power elite*[5] which he characterized as government by the few in the name of themselves. His policy-making model envisioned a pyramid in which biased rules of the game were designed to create a small clique of key military, economic, and political leaders at the top who controlled all major decisions. Divisions on the pyramid separated the top decision makers from the middle layer of minor decision makers and the bottom layer, the masses of average citizens.

In his theory, power is a class attribute; instead of flowing vertically from the citizens to their rulers or vice versa, it flows horizontally through the major institutional decision-making points—the military command, the presidential office and top cabinet advisers, and leaders of the 500 major corporations. Mills writes:

> If we took the 100 most powerful men in America, the 100 wealthiest, and the 100 most celebrated away from the institutional positions they now occupy, away from their resources of men and women and money, away from the media of mass communication that are now focused upon them—then they would be powerless and poor and uncelebrated. For power is not of a man. Wealth does not center in the person of the wealthy. Celebrity is not inherent in any personality. To be celebrated, to be wealthy, to have power, requires access to major institutions, for institutional positions men occupy determine in large part their chances to have and to hold these valued experiences.[6]

Yet the closed nature of this institutional power circuit is reinforced by the tendency for incumbents in these positions to share similar upper-class, high socioeconomic backgrounds, interests, and values. Their overlapping memberships on prestigious philanthropic, art, and educational boards of directors, plus common employment at the pinnacle of legal or corporate power, solidifies the institutional power monopoly with ties of friendship, shared references, and experiences.

For example, Robert McNamara, now president of the World Bank was secretary of defense from 1961 to 1967, and before that president of Ford Motor Company. Another automobile company president, George Romney of American Motors, was secretary of Housing and Urban Development, and before that governor of Michigan. Cyrus Vance, President Carter's choice for Secretary of State, was chief negotiator at the Paris Peace Conference on Vietnam, had previously been secretary of the army and undersecretary of defense. In private life he has been a member of a prestigious Wall Street law firm and on the boards of Pan American World Airways, Aetna Life Insurance Company, IBM Corporation, Council of Foreign Relations, American Red Cross, the University of Chicago, and the Rockefeller Foundation.

The links between military and corporate decision makers are cemented by time and similar career histories. In 1969, 2,124 former high-ranking officers were employed by the 100 largest military contractors. Between 1969 and 1972, industry recruited 1,101 Pentagon officials; the Pentagon hired 232 corporation executives for policy-making bureaucratic positions. Secretary of Defense James Schlesinger, for example, was previously chairman of the CIA, before that chairman of the Atomic Energy Commission, and before that an economics professor at the Rand Corporation, a research affiliate of the Pentagon. These social and associational relationships create Mills's "conjunction of institutional and psychological forces,"[7] which are at the core of the power elite. For Mills the military-industrial complex is a prime example of the power elite. The relationship between military decision makers and corporate managers is one of cooperation in which "each component of the complex, by protecting its own interests, maximizes the collective power of the complex."[8] This symbiotic relationship is a perfect example of a small, closed, interwoven power elite making literally life-and-death decisions without reference to the wishes of the masses who will be affected by their actions.

The basis of their power lies in the post-World War II preoccupation with national security in an age of nuclear insecurity. If, as assumed, World War II was the result of military weakness, then security lies in military strength. But what is military strength in an era when nations stockpile nuclear warheads they can never use? Should the United States seek a supremacy of military weapons, or only military sufficiency, or perhaps total disarmament? The assumption that superior hardware will provide national security leads to a cycle of expansion in which money is poured into research and development of new generations of weapons, aircraft, naval carriers, while diplomats work simultaneously to limit the military frontiers through treaties and alliances.

This debate, coupled with American leadership of the Western world, has made the military a predominant partner in governmental decision making. The United States economy is "at once a permanent-war economy and a private-corporation economy. American capitalism is now in considerable part a military capitalism, and the most important relation of the big corporation to the state rests on the coincidence of interests between military and corporate needs, as defined by warlords and corporate rich."[9]

Sophisticated research and technology have bred a new form of industry, one geared exclusively to weapons development. In monetary terms, since World War II the United States has spent $1.2 trillion on defense; over one-half of which, $700 billion, was spent between 1963 and 1973. In 1971 one-half of all defense dollars went to aircraft and missile manufacturers. In the 1960s ten of the top fifteen defense contractors received more than one-half of their total sales from defense contracts.

Currently the largest contractor is Lockheed Aircraft Corporation with $1.7 billion in government contracts (88 percent of its total business). Of the top ten contractors in fiscal 1973, only American Telephone and Telegraph and General Electric Corporation were among the 100 largest industrial corporations in America. The others were medium-sized giants, but their economic impact can be very important.

For example, during the 1967 debate on creation of an antiballistic missile system, it was pointed out that this one project involved over 15,000 companies including General Electric, Sperry-Rand, General

Dynamics, McDonnell Douglas, and Thiokol Chemical Company. Twenty-eight of the major contractors employed 1 million people in 172 congressional districts located in forty-two states.[10] Current discussion of the need for a B-1 nuclear weapons carrier, translated into jobs and dollars means 70,000 jobs in its current development phase, plus 192,000 jobs at the peak of production. The $2 billion spent by 1975 meant jobs for 5,000 businesses in forty-eight states.[11]

Few companies are equipped to design esoteric modern weaponry or act as resource pools, holding in readiness scientific experts available to research future projects. Consequently the Pentagon is as interested in sustaining them, as these companies—short on competitive marketing and distribution skills—are in being sustained. "Much of the plant of the specialized defense contractors is owned by the government. Most of their working capital is supplied by the government through progress payments—payments made in advance of completion of the contract. The government specifies what the firm can and cannot charge to the government."[12]

Allied with the Department of Defense, or NASA or AEC, these firms are protected from the normal capitalist marketplace by a self-contained system in which sweetheart contracts, negotiated between friends, have built-in profit margins, long-term schedules, and other amenities to soften risks for the contractors who must face the "unk unks," the unknown unknowns," that arise whenever someone contracts to produce something not yet invented. After acquiring a contract, which may take years and may run for years, the contractor becomes more closely affiliated with the military position since he becomes a quasi-government agent distributing subcontracts on the basis of any criteria his company desires. The result has been a system of cost overruns, late delivery, and poor performance that have bedeviled every major contract in the 1960s and early 1970s. The creation of such multibillion dollar fiascos is the result predicted by Mills in his description of this power elite.

PLURALISM

Pluralism is often called "the thinking man's democracy." It tries to reconcile the existence of a large, modern, heterogeneous technocratic society with democratic notions of individual self-development through participation in civic decisions that affect the quality of one's life. For every person to participate directly in all such decisions, from the amount of sulfur dioxide allowed in the air we breathe to the number of strontium 90 particles in a quart of milk to the details of the international seabed treaty, is clearly a human impossibility. Yet democratic values—human dignity, legal equality, liberty, and First Amendment freedoms to speak, write, assemble, and pray—are an essential part of the American commitment. The pluralists have tried to accommodate the notion that participation in public decisions furthers such public values with recognition of the fact that millions of Americans cannot be intimately involved in billions of specialized, technical, public policy decisions.

The dictionary definition of *pluralism* is the "assumption that democracy can exist in a [heterogeneous] society where a variety of elites compete actively in the decision process for the allocation of values, that voters can choose from among them, and that new elites can gain access to power through the same political processes."[13] Competition, open access, meaningful electoral ties to the citizenry, and the continuous evolution of new elites composed of new political actors become the modern equivalent of independent individual action on every public policy. If policy making is compared to a game, then interest groups are teams that substitute for individual players. Rules of the game such as majority votes, minority rights, and multitudes of decision-making umpires force the players to compromise, negotiate, and accommodate in order to win their policy goal.

Pluralists see a meaningful role for the common man: public opinion sets the outer limits of permissible public policy, and electoral actions make more specific demands. Thus, the military-industrial complex may create a Vietnam War, but pluralist pawns will checkmate President Johnson so that he declines to run for a second term. It is also assumed that those who want to participate indirectly in politics may be active in organizations which then act as their surrogates in the public policy process. Implicit in this assumption is the notion, discussed in Chapter 2, that group cohesion rests on a sense of democratic accountability between leaders and members so that the goals the elite pursue are accurate reflections of the members' wishes.

Pluralist theory assumes that within the public arena there will be countervailing centers of power within governmental institutions and among outsiders. Competition is implicit in the notion that groups, as surrogates for individuals, will produce products representing the diversity of opinions that might have been possible in the individual decision days of democratic Athens. To support this contention, the pluralists call attention to the constitutional distribution of official power and the ways decisions are actually made to resolve real issues.

To take the constitutional system first, checks and balances among governmental institutions, plus federalism, multiplies separate decision-making centers or access points for interested groups.

> Actual authority tends to be dispersed and exercised not solely by governmental officials but also by private individuals and groups within society. Moreover the power structure tends to be segmented: authority over one question rests here and over another there. . . . On one matter, the President's decision may govern; on another, the wishes of the heads of a half-dozen industrial corporations will prevail; on a third, organized labor or agriculture will win the day; and on still another, a congressionally negotiated compromise completely satisfactory to none of the contenders may settle the matter.[14]

Since elite theorists view power as stratified along institutional levels of society, they acknowledge these features of the constitutional system while simultaneously denying that they affect the content of major decisions. But what is a *major* decision? Elitists use circular reasoning to solve the matter; they either say that major decisions are elite decisions and vice versa, or define elites as decision makers. Pluralists break down "major" policies into their component parts. For example, new weaponry systems, the employment effects of defense industries, balance of payments problems, oil deposits, and entangling alliances are issues that may separately be of large or minimal importance; together they are part of the policy situation called cold war.

Such separate issues provide the pluralist focus for power; the pluralists then define power in terms of active participation within these decisional frameworks. Thus there is no sovereign, monolithic, elite power bloc. Power is tied to issues, with different patterns emerging as a reflection of the congeries of interests attracted by a specific problem. Groups feed on the parts of the policy process as bees feed from flower to flower. Robert Dahl, a modern exponent of pluralism, explains this limited, sequential, separate view of public policy as incorporating an incrementalist perspective, which he defines as the belief that "problems are separable, can be dealt with satisfactorily by piecemeal adjustment, and can be solved by limiting the scope of conflict, cooperation with others in searching for solutions and accepting compromises."[15]

While elite leadership is based on occupational position, pluralist leadership emerges from situational factors that propel people to the fore because of their knowledge or personal attributes of charisma and organizational skills. Again, leadership is issue-oriented, issue-created. Cesar Chavez leads farm workers, I. W. Abel leads steel workers, David Rockefeller speaks for the Chase Manhattan Bank, but the wealth of Rockefeller does not automatically make him the most powerful of the three—unless the issue is money. All are key spokesmen for their interests in their own area of competency. In this sense the pluralist concept of power is "situational and mercurial; it resists attempts to locate it. . . ."[16] Power is a relationship consisting of a person, his/her occupational niche, and the context of the issue being resolved.

The power elite theory does not deal with notions such as the uses of power. It implies power from a job description and then assumes its use. Pluralists focus on issue action and discount *potential* influence; the only relevant actors are those who play in the game. Public policy, then, reflects majority desires in the sense that it is an accommodation of the prevailing activist interests concerned with that specific policy. Once the issue is negotiated through the byways of fragmented power in Congress, the bureaucracy, and perhaps the court system, the product is presumed to answer common needs in the sense that specific tangents have been rounded off in this bargaining process.

A CASE IN POINT: THE SUPERSONIC TRANSPORT PLANE (SST)

The SST is a technological dream aircraft designed to fly 300 commercial passengers at 1,800 miles per hour. It was promoted by the Air Force as an indirect way to maintain its reservoir of skilled aerospace scientists and technicians despite failure to secure clearance for a new generation of manned fighter bombers. Theoretically the SST was a privately developed commercial venture designed to transport persons at commercial profits, but actually costs were apportioned on a 90:10 ratio with government subsidizing research to the tune of $864 million between 1961 and 1971. However, since it was to be a private transportation carrier, SST personnel were part of the Federal Aviation Administration (FAA), later merged into the Department of Transportation (DOT), instead of under Pentagon supervision.

Yet in reality control of the project was in the hands of the military-industrial complex as illustrated by the interlocking backgrounds of the key government decision makers. Secretary of Defense McNamara sponsored the project and gave it an initial top industrial priority rating equal in importance to top military work.[17] Air Force influence continued through President Johnson's appointments of Air Force General William McKee as head of FAA and Air Force General Jewell Maxwell as director of the Office of Supersonic Transport Development. With the Nixon takeover, General Maxwell's position was filled by William Magruder, formerly an employee of Lockheed Aircraft Company. The winners of the SST design competition were Boeing Company and General Electric, both consistently among the top ten defense contractors.

Looking at these actors, the SST seems just another example of a Pentagon power elite decision to create a commercial venture in order to sustain desirable activity levels within their aerospace industries. However, from a less encompassing perspective, the history of SST funding lends itself to the pluralist interpretation of public policy making. Two additional sets of participants—congressmen and outside interest groups—appear. These actors are ignored by the power elite analysis, yet in the case of the SST their activities killed the project in the name of a reordering of national priorities (surely a topic important enough to belong to the power elite alone). To the leader of the anti-SST congressional forces, Congressman Sidney Yates: "The SST has become the symbol of resistance to unbridled technology and science." Using the pluralist mode of analysis, the decisions of 1970 and 1971 that terminated the SST project indicate a complex interaction of events, attitudes, and groups that reduce the power elite monolith to a jumble of competing entities.

Indications that the SST was in trouble appeared in a 1969 report prepared at President Nixon's request which recommended withdrawal from development of SST prototypes. The President suppressed this report and a similar one from an outside panel of scientists, and recommended continued research and development appropriations of $290 million in 1970 and $134 million in 1971. In earlier years such small amounts of money passed routinely since Congress declined to second-guess the executive on aerospace issues; for example, in 1964 the first request to cut off SST funds was summarily rejected, 109–26.

But by 1970 the decisional context had changed. The SST was caught in the vortex of shifting public attitudes as national priorities were being debated. Termination of the $5 billion SST program became a national symbol for those seeking to end the automatic subsidy of American technology for its own sake, rather than to achieve the good life for Americans. In addition, two new rules made it easier for nongovernmental participants to follow official actions (as a first step in influencing them). First, in 1969, the environmental movement achieved passage of the National Environmental Protection Act which created procedures requiring initial determination of the impact of new technology on all aspects of the environment. Second, the 1970 Legislative Reform Act changed the teller vote procedure in the House of Representatives to require that, on request, individual's votes be publicly recorded. Since only a handful of representatives are required to initiate the procedure, it provides a way for opponents of a measure to get an accurate head count; it also generates sufficient publicity and media coverage to motivate congressmen to attend floor debates and vote.

The 1970 SST fight centered in the Senate where Senator William Proxmire and a Coalition Against the SST argued environment versus technological overkill. The coalition was formed in 1970 by fifteen national organizations and fourteen state and local groups that used environmental data such as the atmospheric dangers to the ozone layer and noise pollution from sonic booms to document the possibility of SST-induced environmental disaster. By a vote of 52 to 41, the Senate voted to terminate the $290 million appropriated by the House for the SST. In conference committee the House figure was restored, only to have Senator Proxmire successfully threaten to filibuster the bill. As the 91st Congress entered its last week of existence, a compromise was reached providing $210 million through March 30, 1971.

The focus of the debate in 1970 was environmental effects, so the government concentrated on eliminating them before March 1971, by modifying the plane's engine, agreeing not to reach sonic boom speeds over land, and producing scientists to dispute the coalition's atmospheric consequences arguments. In 1970 the White House, industry, and labor had not worked actively to support the program; in 1971 they responded. With governmental blessing, the key contractors and labor unions formed the American Industry and Labor Committee for the SST which raised $350,000 for a massive public relations campaign. Full-page advertisements ran in all major newspapers headlined: "Announcing International SST Service . . . the best that rubles could buy"—implying that our failure would be the Soviet's economic gain. Bumper stickers poked at Senator Proxmire, from Wisconsin, the dairy state, with the message: "Proxmire Eats Margarine."

The administration led the fight all the way, by restructuring the debate to focus on issues of jobs and national prestige instead of environmental damage. Secretary of the Treasury John Connally told a House committee: "We dare not be so timid as not to produce an SST on an experimental basis." DOT secretary, John Volpe said: "The appeal I make to you . . . represents my deepest conviction. It is devoid of politics. . . . We have gone too far, invested too much, and are too near our goal to let all this go down the drain with no tangible results."

Congressman Gerald Ford, leader of the pro-SST forces in the House, shouted in debate that "If you vote for the SST you are ensuring 13,000 jobs today plus 50,000 jobs in the second year, and 150,000 jobs every year over the next ten years." To which SST opponents responded: "If the SST is such a profitable undertaking, why does the United States government, that is, the taxpayer, have to put up 80 to 90 percent of the development costs?"

The environmentalists concentrated on the new congressmen and swing voters; the pro-SST lobby focused on those previously against the measure. President Nixon spoke personally with these individuals. In the most famous episode he sent a hand delivered letter to SST opponent, Republican Senator Margaret Chase Smith of Maine indicating that he would rescind his order to close the Portsmouth, New Hampshire, naval base which employed many of her constituents. Interpreting this as a crude bid for her vote, Senator Smith read the letter aloud to her colleagues, reprimanded the President for his timing, and voted against the SST appropriation.

In March 1971 both the House and Senate voted by slim margins to delete SST funds, but the issue surfaced again in the guise of an amendment to the fiscal 1971 supplemental appropriations bill considered by the House in May. The $85 million there, intended to compensate Boeing and General Electric for the SST cancellation, was turned into a plan to continue the project. Arm twisting and logrolling produced a four-vote margin of victory for Republicans who supported the administration's pro-SST position. Then, two days later, William M. Allen, Boeing's chairman of the board said it would cost $500 million to $1 billion to successfully complete the project. The White House conceded these estimates as compared to $178 million to terminate the project and the fight was over. The Senate voted to cut off the funds, and was upheld in conference. The SST project was dead.

From the pluralist perspective, competitive groups developed to reflect the countervailing attitudes in the country, and the final decision was negotiated over a two-year period with input from all interested groups. Thus in this decisional context, power was dispersed, participation was encouraged, and a public solution produced, a solution that clearly ran counter to the wishes of the "power elite."

The power elite and pluralist theories of public policy participation are diametrically opposed on degrees of openness, circulation, and competition of elites. Power elite theory stresses a horizontally layered structure with all meaningful political power concentrated in the top layer. This layer, consisting of the major military, corporate, and political executives, creates policies within the framework of its own needs and world view, without reference to the citizenry affected by its actions. The elite is closed to competition either from outside individuals or meaningful policy alternatives because participation is determined by institutional position rather than the individual or issue.

Pluralist critics argue that this model is too rigid, the locus of power impossible to verify factually, and that, in reality, elites do not govern without the acquiescence of the citizen majority. Rather elites govern by default, entering the power vacuum created by general citizen disinterest in the details of public policy. Nevertheless, when citizen opposition to an issue is mobilized, the power elite is not homogeneous enough, closed enough, or powerful enough to resist the influence generated by widespread prolonged citizen disapproval. The SST, Vietnam War, and Watergate crisis vary in scale, but all bear witness to elite capitulation to an opposition's demands.

The pluralist countertheory focuses on processes and procedures rather than institutional or class positions. Policy makers are defined as those active on behalf of any specific policy. Public decisions are arrived at by bargaining, negotiation, and compromise among scattered actors and assorted institutions. Procedural duplications (for example, eight major congressional votes on SST funding in 1971 alone), plus multiple decision-making centers (for example, White House, Pentagon, Congress), in theory create countervailing groups and diffuse power which, in turn, guarantees openness, circulation among elite decision makers, and meaningful competition. This emphasis on fragmentation, duplication, and competition creates a practical procedural equivalent for the impractical classic democratic requirement of direct individual participation in public decisions affecting the quality of life.

PLURALISM THROUGH CRITICS' EYES

Pluralistic theory has been challenged from the point of view of its value assumptions and in terms of actual policy making. The root of the *democratic values problem* lies in the attempt to create a group equivalent of rational direct individual participation. Since the group is conceived of as a substitute for such activity, it must incorporate the decision-making and leadership opportunities that will facilitate development of each member's human potential, and enable the group to be an authentic substitute when it acts as spokesman for its members' interests.

Yet Freud and public opinion polls tell us that most individuals do not naturally want to lead or take a detailed interest in politics. Organization itself provides a recognized division of labor based on the assumption that a few are leaders, the majority are led. Consequently private groups are not models of internal democracy as required by the normative bias of pluralism. The issue is summarized by Henry Kariel, a leading critic of theoretical pluralism, as follows:

> organized labor (or, for that matter, organized business) is decidedly not some sort of private, close-knit group of individuals who are in general agreement on life's ultimate objectives. . . . American constitutionalism and an advanced technology, intimately linked, have encouraged a trend toward policy formation within a plurality of entrenched oligarchies. . . . The rights of members to dissent, and to make their dissent effective, are not being habitually exercised in the giant-size group, even where such rights are nominally granted. And this is the case despite the wide range of interests which organizations contain. . . . To stabilize the social organism, incumbent leadership relies either on loyalty freely pledged or on the coercive tactics which monopolistic positions make possible. It avails itself of plebiscites, mood engineering, need manipulation, or more forthright economic sanctions."[18]

Consequently it is inaccurate to equate group participation in public decision making with individual activity.

In terms of policy making, the pluralist notions of *competitiveness and openness have also been questioned.* Pluralism and its corollary theory of the automatic generation of groups to represent interests are undermined by reality. Some interests float for years among the general population without finding an organizational form. This is especially true for categoric groups based on age, sex, and race, since they often lack an issue specific enough to encourage organization. When interests do organize, they tend to defend their potential pool of members by barring rival organizations as illustrated by labor's attitude against dual-unionism which would give workers a choice of competing representatives in any one occupation. Trade associations similarly stake out their turf, thereby encouraging the development of multitudes of narrowly based complementary associations. Even among broad-based organizations, the tendency is to divide the membership field so that it represents different geographic bases or emphasizes different occupations. Thus there is little true rivalry within areas of group interest.

In a more systemic sense, William Gamson argues that pluralism creates a system of "stable unrepresentation"[19] that keeps incipient competitors from entering the political game. Even for those already playing policy politics, some game moves create collusion among strange bedfellows instead of competition between strangers. The pluralists assume that a multitude of pressure points will create cross-pressures leading to conflict, but a multitude of points can also lead to accommodation if parallel interest groups use parallel access points to gain parallel goals.

This is evident within the military-industrial complex where "each component of the complex, by protecting its own interests, maximizes the collective power of the complex."[20] The parallel form of the system is reinforced by the inclination of each branch of the military to develop its own sources of supply. For example, the Navy did not want to buy the F-111 fighter airplane designed for use by both the Navy and Air Force because "the admirals [could not] stand the thought of buying what they consider an Air Force plane produced by an 'outside' contractor."[21] This helps to ensure that 50 to 60 percent of all military contracts are arranged with a single source that bids, wins, and delivers the product. Thus competition becomes cooperation because, if each service has separate contractors, there is no competition. The policy process leads to formation of complementary organizations and procedures of accommodation.

Meaningful competition is further weakened *by inequalities in the balance of power among policy-making participants.* Pluralism implies an equality among groups when it presupposes the creation of countervailing groups, or assumes that all groups will have effective access points within the decision-making system. However, in reality there are vast areas of dispersed power, citadels of concentrated power, and pockets of powerlessness. The primary distortions come from concentrations of power which may assume a variety of forms.

Some corporations cannot be ignored because they have too important an impact on the economy. "Neither the administration nor Congress dares allow a major employer to go down the drain. . . . [The government] is compelled, therefore, to shape national policy in terms of protecting the great corporations instead of letting the economy make deflationary adjustments."[22] Groups whose members provide a professional service, be it doctors on slowdowns to direct attention to malpractice insurance rates or sanitation men on wildcat strikes to preserve the sanctity of their contracts, have a potential power based on official recognition of the need for their services. Groups with the intellectual resources required to design nuclear reactors, purify water, or measure particles in the air, all have power concentrated near the decision-making center of their issues because their knowledge is required to make the decisions.

Most decision-making action centers have inner and outer circles of participants. Inner circle members are those with ties to the official participants, lobbyists, or groups that have the relevant information, membership prestige, wealth, expertise, or whatever resources are valued in terms of that particular issue. The outer circle are the newcomers—either newly formed groups or "Johnny-come-latelies" who are currently interested in the issue. Even changes in the rules of the game may not alter the significance of this two-tier arrangement as illustrated by the Freedom of Information Act which was supposed to open up government for the average citizen by permitting access to most government records. However, instead of access for outsiders, a study of its use vis-à-vis regulatory agencies suggests that the insiders, those being regulated who already have close ties to the agencies, are using the act to pry advance information from the bureaucracy and thereby cement their favored positions.[23] This kind of inequality of access and positioning supports the notion that "a deliberate pluralistic diffusion of power . . . will enforce the concentration of power in private hands. . . . [In effect] an existing balance of power [is] officially cemented."[24]

Pluralists like E. E. Schattschneider may agree with the critics that "pressure politics . . . is skewed, loaded, and unbalanced in favor of a fraction of a minority,"[25] but they disagree with the conclusion that weak government joins private power for its own support. They view government as the neutralizer of this private power. "It is the function of public authority to modify private power relations by enlarging the scope of conflict."[26] In Schattschneider's view, losers take their case to the government in order to enlarge the number of participants and alter the consequences. "The function of democracy has been to provide the public with a second power system, an alternative . . . which can be used to counterbalance the economic power."[27] The SST provides such an example, since the research continued quietly for ten years as an in-house bureaucratic decision. Controversy arose when Congress, awakened to the problem by the environmentalist coalition of losers, challenged the Pentagon and reversed the power equation.

The flaw in this kind of competitive challenge interpretation stems from the provisions that Schattschneider, explicitly, and other pluralists implicitly, require as preconditions for such freewheeling, balanced policy making. His major condition is open, meaningful participation in the choice of alternatives to be considered and the conflicts to be emphasized, since these selections determine "the allocation of political space"[28]—the players and the rejects. Schattschneider's conditions do not seem feasible or probable to his critics.

Sociologists such as David Riesman do not see sufficient independence of thought and quality of leadership to produce a pluralist state. For Riesman, the last American ruling class was made up of the businessmen behind President McKinley in the 1890s, who went into politics to produce conditions conducive to business expansion. Guided by their own internal sense of morality and well-defined goals, they led and the workers followed.

Today a consensus of purpose is nonexistent and power is dispersed. Individuals do not impose ideas on groups; rather *groups provide ideas for "other-directed" individuals.* Leaders are brokers who manipulate coalitions of groups in order to create successful policies. The modern substitute for the 1890s business oligarchy is "a series of groups, each of which has struggled for and finally attained a power to stop things conceivably inimical to its interests, and within far narrower limits, to start things. . . . Among the veto groups, competition is monopolistic; rules of fairness and fellowship dictate how far one can go. . . ."[29]

While Riesman traces the problem to modern dependence on others for our ideas, our conscience, and our needs, other observers trace pluralist inequalities to insiders' manipulation of procedures so that certain values, questions, and alternatives can never reach the stage of public discussion. One form of this bias that precludes open, equal competition is the *"nondecision."* Nondecisions are "a means by which demands for change in the existing allocation of benefits and privileges in the community can be suffocated before they are even voiced."[30] This can be accomplished in a variety of ways.

Force is the most obvious and direct means of preventing private conflicts from going public. Power can also be used more subtly to intimidate or co-opt challengers to the system; for example, A. E. Fitzgerald, the employee who blew the whistle on the C-5A cost overruns, was dismissed from his job.

Co-optation is another way to stifle conflict. It covers a variety of behavior patterns, ranging from a state of mind that makes doubters into adherents to a working relationship that occurs when groups assume governmental responsibilities. For example, prime contractors in the military are psychologically tied to the military system by the revolving employee relationships within the complex, and physically tied by the borrowed power given them in their role as "official" allocators of subcontracting resources. Kariel explains that while cooperation may begin as a way to provide equal representation of interests, it results in unrepresentative policies because it permits "the well-situated firm [that is, the contractor] to improve its situation by using the government as its outpost."[31]

At a more symbolic level, nondecisions are implemented by invoking existing rules, values, and precedents to strengthen the bias of the system against challenge. Listen to the military cry of "Communist menace," "Military superiority," "National security!" A new generation of weaponry and carriers—planes, ships, tanks—was planned by the Nixon administration to provide for the economic needs of the military-industrial complex in the post-Vietnam peace. The consequence of this policy, as former Secretary of Defense Clark Clifford pointed out, is that we are still creating a confrontation military force in an era of negotiation. "Thus we face a paradox of an increasing budget for military purposes in a world in which all the political signs point to contingencies calling for United States military action being less rather than more."

The nondecision answer is that the values of military security are embedded within the society itself. The question as to whether a military-industrial complex prevents peace would produce the following response: "The answer is inextricably embedded in the mainstream of American institutions and mores. Our concept is not that American society contains a ruling military-industrial complex. Our concept is more nearly that American society *is* a military-industrial complex. . . . The requirements of a social system geared to peace . . .

share a pattern of resource distribution which is different from the one the world now has."[32]

A CASE IN POINT: THE LOCKHEED BAILOUT

The various patterns of imbalance noted by critics of pluralism can be illustrated by a series of examples of government bailouts "when companies get too big to fail."[33] Between 1959 and 1973 the Pentagon, under authority from P. L. 85–804 passed as part of the Korean War emergency legislation package, increased contract prices in order to assist 3,652 companies whose bankruptcy would not be in the national interest. Such assists totaled over $86 million.[34]

Dwarfing these continuing assists was the major price increase of $1 billion on the total contract purchase price of Lockheed Aircraft Company's C-5A giant transport airplanes. Originally the C-5A contract was awarded under a new cost-saving procedure called "total package procurement" which was designed to eliminate the expense of cost overruns by setting a fixed price for the total research/development/manufacturing process. The Lockheed contract fixed the price at $2.6 billion for 120 planes, but the fine print included loopholes designed so that "neither of us [the Pentagon or Lockheed] would lose our shirt."[35] However, Lockheed had submitted an unrealistically low bid in order to win the contract, so it should have been no surprise when A. E. Fitzgerald told the congressional Joint Economic Committee that the C-5A program was $2 billion in the red. Pressure generated by Congress and the press led to renegotiation of the contract. The Air Force order was also reduced from 120 to 81 planes as an economy measure. Seventeen months of negotiation led to Lockheed's acquiescence in a penalty of $200 million as a fixed loss on the contract.

During this time horror stories repeatedly appeared detailing C-5A deficiencies. For example, after Congress passed the 1972 fiscal year defense appropriations bill, it was announced that eight days before a jet engine had dropped off one of the C-5A's while the pilot was making routine checks prior to takeoff. Earlier, on March 19, 1971, Deputy Secretary of Defense David Packard told a secret session of the Senate Armed Services Committee that: "The only problem with the landing gear is that it won't always go down when you are trying to put it down, which usually causes some difficulty." This testimony was not declassified until the following year when the General Accounting Office documented the sorry history of C-5A problems. The GAO estimated that "the ill-fated C-5A suffers a major technical breakdown once an hour during every hour of flight time . . . the landing gear alone will fail once every four hours."[36]

During this period, Lockheed was making profits in its missile and rocketry division, and progress in its manufacture of a commercial airbus, the 400-passenger TriStar, L1011. Then three days after Lockheed's acceptance of the $200 million penalty on the C-5A contract overruns, Rolls Royce, the British firm that was subcontractor for the TriStar engines, declared bankruptcy. The British government wanted proof of Lockheed's financial stability if they were to guarantee delivery of the engines. If Lockheed were to drop the British engines and buy the General Electric ones, which were used in the rival DC-10s produced by McDonnell Douglas, the TriStar would be more expensive and require adjustments to incorporate the new engine.

Lockheed had a $1.4 billion investment in TriStar's development: $400 million lent by a twenty-six member consortium of banks, $375 million from Lockheed itself, $350 million from suppliers, and $240 million in deposits from its two biggest customers, TWA and Eastern airlines. Lockheed had 103 firm orders and 75 options for the jumbo jets. They estimated that they had to sell 265 planes to break even, a figure increased to 300 planes in 1975 estimates.[37] Meanwhile, the competition, McDonnell Douglas had orders for 127 planes, 96 options, and had already delivered its first two DC-10s. Thus, in a "soft" market, when many planes were flying with surplus capacity, the competition had cornered more of the probable market and already begun delivery. Lockheed was behind; an engine switch would increase the time gap.

Aware of these marketing uncertainties and the C-5A penalty, the bank consortium was not eager to put up an additional $250 million guarantee without government backing. Lockheed declared that without the loan to tide them over they would be forced into bankruptcy. On May 13, 1971, the administration sent Congress legislation to guarantee the $250 million Lockheed loan. Since this was an example of a prime military defense contractor in trouble on a commercial venture, the arguments could have been couched either in terms of the national security bailout rationale used for the C-5A crisis or the economic catastrophe scenario used to preserve other giant corporations such as Penn Central or American Motors. The administration chose the latter rationale, emphasizing that 17,000 people worked on TriStar at Lockheed plants, 14,000 were employed by TriStar subcontractors, and if Lockheed went bankrupt it would mean 60,000 jobs in twenty-five states.

Treasury Secretary John Connally said Lockheed's bankruptcy would have an adverse effect on the economy, diminish competition within the aerospace industry, depress our balance of payments since we would lose overseas sales of the L1011, and increase unemployment in a period of recession. Speaking in San Clemente, California, President Nixon told a news conference: "Lockheed is one of the nation's great companies. It provides an enormous employment lift to this part of the country and I am going to be heavily influenced by the need to see to it that . . . after taking the disappointment of not getting the SST, . . . that California does not have the additional jolt of losing Lockheed."

Since the issue was considered in the context of domestic economic consequences, it meant that bailout hearings were held in financial rather than military congressional committees, government lobbying efforts were spearheaded by the Treasury Department on behalf of the bank consortium, and private lobbying efforts were directed by the affected unions. The unions staged mock unemployment lines, flooded Congress with half a million pieces of mail, and placed full-page ads in Washington newspapers stating that: "Our jobs, families, and our careers are at stake." Lockheed officials spoke to every congressman at least once during the two-month campaign. "They were soft sell and professional—very impressive."[38]

A *New York Times* editorial of May 23, 1971, asked the key questions: If the TriStar airbus has excellent marketing prospects

> why do the commercial banks that have been working closely with Lockheed not lend it the additional money? Why should government bear the risk? Or, if Lockheed is not soundly managed and the prospects for the L1011 are dubious, why should its management be rescued?

> Where is the evidence that the national economy stands in peril if this rescue operation is not rushed through? Are there not more serious risks to the effectiveness of the American economy if a precedent is established for rescuing huge and inefficient corporations and substituting government decision making for private commercial lending decisions?

Business opinion was divided. Aerojet-General Corporation president Jack Vollbrech said government support would prove that "if you fail big enough, you don't fail."[39] Ian MacGregor, chairman of American Metal Climax, said, "A Lockheed bankruptcy would be like hard frost hitting spring flowers."[40] Senator William Proxmire countered administration arguments by pointing out that in fact the administration's figure of 60,000 jobs could be reduced to 6,583 jobs specifically related to TriStar production, and if the TriStar were eliminated, these workers could probably move over to the competition amd make DC-10s. He called the administration's plan a reward for bad management that provided "an example of socialism for big business and free enterprise for Mom and Pop stores."[41]

The House Banking and Currency Committee led off the congressional process with July hearings. In executive session, the members ignored a staff study opposing the guarantee and reported out a broader bill authorizing the government to guarantee loans of up to $250 million to individual businesses up to a total of $2 billion outstanding at any one time. An agreement was then reached to return the bill to its original limited form through floor amendments in order to secure the backing of the Banking Committee chairman, Wright Patman. The bill passed the House on July 30 by three votes. Meanwhile the Senate Banking, Housing, and Urban Affairs Committee held hearings. Senator Proxmire called them biased, since "in the end the administration was unable to provide a single independent public-interest witness to support it. Everyone who testified for the loan had a financial stake in the guarantee."[42]

The Senate antiloan forces filibustered for two weeks in an effort to delay passage until after the planned August 6 recess. Finally after the House passed the limited version of the bill, the Senate agreed to a final 160 minutes of debate on August 2, 1971. President Nixon made a half-dozen last-minute phone calls, and the final vote was 49 to 48 as the Senate passed the House bill without any amendment. The vote pattern in both the House and Senate crossed ideological and party lines and settled on constituency influence. Districts encompassing Lockheed subdivisions or one of its major contractors voted for the bailout; McDonnell Douglas and General Electric districts voted against the bill.

The Lockheed bailout battle illustrates the varieties of power imbalances discussed previously: the *intensity* imbalance of those with jobs at stake versus a moderate effort to attain the probable outcome of increased business; the *corporate position* imbalance symbolized by Lockheed's rankings as the largest defense contractor and one of the top 100 American corporations; the *priorities* argument of tangible versus intangible goals, and domestic versus national security arguments; the *information* imbalance as Treasury Department releases countered Senator Proxmire's independent studies; and the *power* imbalance created by the decision-making context—a mild recession, a beleaguered defense contractor harassed by C-5A difficulties, a national debate on American priorities, and competing congressional factions fighting to place the issue within their own spheres of power. All participants were not equally represented, all facets of the problem not equally weighted, all expertise not equally available. Thus, the system in action seemed a revival of George Orwell's commandment in *Animal Farm:* "All animals are equal, but some are more equal than others." To the extent that this is true, the conditions for effective pluralism as a substitute for democratic participation are not met.

SUMMARY

This chapter has examined three perspectives for viewing outside competition within the public policy-making sphere. Both pluralism and elitism suffer from the defect of perfectionism: no elite in a constitutionally representative nation is wholly impervious to the general political climate; no clique of decision makers is large enough to encompass all interested groups. If by the process of elimination that leaves an answer from the middle position, then questions center on the impact of outside groups. When are groups influential? On what kinds of issues, under what circumstances? What is the contribution of groups to the American public policy-making process? We will address these questions in the next chapter.

NOTES

1. James Clotfelter, *The Military in American Politics* (New York: Harper & Row, 1973), p. 51.
2. Harold Lasswell, quoted in Thomas Dye and Harmon Zeigler, *The Irony of Democracy,* 3d ed. (North Scituate, Mass.: Duxbury Press, 1975), p. 3.
3. Ibid., p. 130.
4. Ibid., p. 5.
5. C. Wright Mills, *The Power Elite* (New York: Oxford University Press, 1956).
6. Ibid., pp. 10–11.
7. Ibid., pp. 292, 288.
8. Clotfelter, *The Military in American Politics,* p. 70.
9. Mills, *The Power Elite,* p. 276.
10. Congressional Quarterly, *Legislators and Lobbyists,* 2d ed. (Washington, D.C.: Congressional Quarterly, Inc., 1968), p. 51.
11. Peter Ognibene, "The Air Force's Secret War on Unemployment," *Washington Monthly* (July-August 1975): 59.
12. John Galbraith, *How to Control the Military* (New York: Signet Books, 1969), pp. 32–37.
13. Jack Plano and Melton Greenberg, eds., *The American Political Dictionary,* 3d ed. (Hinsdale Ill.: Dryden Press, 1972), p. 14.
14. V. O. Key, *Politics, Parties and Pressure Groups,* (New York: Thomas Y. Crowell, 1964), p. 7.
15. Robert Dahl, *Democracy in the United States: Promise and Performance,* 2d ed. (Chicago: Rand McNally, 1972), p. 53.
16. David Riesman, *The Lonely Crowd* (New Haven: Yale University Press, 1961), p. 223.
17. Seymour Melman, *Pentagon Capitalism* (New York: McGraw-Hill, 1970), p. 82.
18. Henry Kariel, *The Decline of American Pluralism* (Stanford Ca.: Stanford University Press, 1961), pp. 66–68.
19. William Gamson, "Stable Unrepresentation in American Society," *The American Behavioral Scientist* (November-December 1968): 18–19.
20. Clotfelter, *The Military in American Politics,* p. 72.

21. Congressional Quarterly, *Legislators and Lobbyists,* p. 60.
22. *Business Week,* January 27, 1975, p. 16.
23. Ognibene, "The Air Force's Secret War," p. 59.
24. Kariel, *The Decline of American Pluralism,* pp. 74–75.
25. E. E. Schattschneider, *The Semi-Sovereign People,* (Hinsdale, Ill.: Dryden Press, 1975), p. 35.
26. Ibid., p. 40.
27. Ibid., p. 121.
28. Ibid., p. 68.
29. Riesman, *The Lonely Crowd,* p. 213.
30. Peter Bachrach and Morton Baratz, *Power and Poverty: Theory and Practice* (New York: Oxford University Press, 1970), chap. 3.
31. Kariel, *The Decline of American Pluralism,* p. 100.
32. Marc Pilisuk and Thomas Hayden, "Is There a Military-Industrial Complex Which Prevents Peace?: Consensus and Countervailing Power in Pluralistic Systems," in *The Bias of Pluralism,* ed. William Connolly (New York: Atherton Press, 1969).
33. *Business Week,* January 27, 1974, p. 16.
34. *New York Times,* April 30, 1973.
35. Congressional Quarterly, *Power of the Pentagon* (Washington, D.C.: Congressional Quarterly, Inc., 1972), p. 88.
36. Les Aspin, *New York Times,* August 29, 1972.
37. *Christian Science Monitor,* April 17, 1975. By this point Lockheed had 133 firm orders, 69 options, 68 delivered planes.
38. *New York Times,* August 8, 1971.
39. *Christian Science Monitor,* May 17, 1971.
40. *Business Week,* May 15, 1971, p. 41.
41. William Proxmire, *Uncle Sam: The Last of the Big Time Spenders* (New York: Simon and Schuster, 1972), p. 236.
42. Ibid., p. 236.

Chapter 13

Group Influence and Impact

Perhaps it seems absurd, following twelve chapters devoted to the development of interest groups and their pursuit of political goals, to ask whether groups have any influence and whether group activity as a whole has an impact on the American political system. But these questions *are* asked by public policy observers who usually impute too much or too little influence to organized groups. Haven't you heard that "big business runs the country," or "oil companies control Texas Congressmen," or "labor has the Democrats in its pocket." Indeed, ex-lobbyist Robert Winter-Berger calls lobbyists "the single most potent political pressure group in the history of the world. . . . Without the lobbyists, corruption in government would be minimal, simply because the efforts to corrupt would be so disorganized, so diffuse."[1] According to a Harris poll taken in 1975, 72% of Americans feel "Congress is still too much under the influence of special interest lobbies." In 1973, 74% agreed that "special interests get more from the government than the people do;" and that "tax laws are written to help the rich, not the average man."[2]

However, political scientist Lester Milbrath after analyzing the results of interviews with 101 Washington lobbyists concluded that "The weight of the evidence . . . suggests that there is relatively little influence or power in lobbying per se. . . . Favors and bribes are not highly valued."[3] Bauer, Pool and Dexter's study of business influence on trade policy similarly concluded that despite the stereotype of omnipotent pressure groups bowling over recalcitrant officials, their research showed competing interests, all hampered by lack of time, money, manpower and information, who usually were most successful when they reinforced and stimulated activity by others.[4]

An assessment of the power of *any one specific interest group* would fluctuate widely between power and powerlessness because the influence any group commands is strictly bound by the limitations inherent in the group itself: its goals, its access points, its allies and enemies. To predict influence by adding up group assets without considering the context of the action is misleading and naive. Thus one cannot add up separate wins and losses and compute a group power average. However, it is possible to assess the cumulative impact of group activities on the total policy making process. The formation of groups and the way the political rules help or hinder group players does establish a broader pattern of generalized influence on policy output that is a sum total of the group lobbying process rather than a total of group successes.

Using the data we have already examined on the nature of groups, their structural relationships with official policy action centers and their contribution to policy content we can draw some conclusions as to group influence in the overall policy process. In this chapter we will examine this influence from two perspectives: (1) the perspective of the group and (2) the overall functioning of the American political system.

INFLUENCE

Lobbying, lobbyist, interest group, power, influence, rules of the game: all are terms with strong normative overtones that lead to a variety of definitions. Thus definition is a first barrier to any assessment of group activities as influential. The dairy cooperatives' campaign to raise milk price supports illustrates how one incident perceived from assorted perspectives can lead to contrasting evaluations of influence and effectiveness. For example:

- People who worry over the undue influence of special interests could see the dairy cooperatives' success as an excellent illustration of such influence.
- Those who think that a policy product should reflect a wide variety of inputs could, by adding up presidential, USDA, congressional,

constituent and voter pressures, evaluate the price support decision as proof of an open system where relatively small economic interests are able to gain access and influence.

- Purists who equate influence with corruption would consider AMPI's success a reflection of the jingle of dairymen's coins in Nixon's re-election pockets.
- For others, the broker role of groups between citizen/voters and decision makers is illustrated by the sources of AMPI's clout, that is, access through the electoral nomination process, the ability to parley political action funds into a needed decision, and the use of their geographically concentrated voting base as an implicit threat.
- For those to whom influence is derived less from techniques and more from consequences, a comparison of milk price support levels with those of other protected commodities makes the decision seem cheap, localized and unimportant, therefore, an example of limited influence. However, if the milk price support level is computed in relation to expected milk price increases for consumers, then the AMPI victory affects urban America, and becomes an example of power.

So we have come full circle: from negative to positive to negative attitudes towards the episode, and from powerful to participatory to powerful definitions of influence. Let's look at some current definitions of influence in order to scan the range of opinion about this term, before settling on a definition for use in this chapter.

Robert Dahl defines influence as a "relation among actors in which one actor induces other actors to act in some way they would not otherwise act."[5] He then defines power as influence with severer sanctions for compliance. Power and influence so considered are useful terms when we analyze broad notions of politics as a process of conflict resolution or look at government's function of allocating resources and values among competing forces in society. But influence so defined is less useful in relation to lobbying activities, since most lobbying consists of reinforcing the views of friends rather than converting neutrals or forcing enemies to recant.

Power in this sense is an even more unrealistic term to use concerning the activities of political interest groups. Lobbying is primarily an information-sharing enterprise and, as such, its impact depends on timing, content, and sources that may affect decision makers' perceptions of an issue. Only rarely can groups punish officials for their behavior. When a lobby coalition does successfully block the nominations of a Carswell and a Haynesworth for Supreme Court justice, when Senator Tydings says he was shot down by the NRA, or FOE proclaims the effectiveness of its "Dirty Dozen" list, the causal relationship is rarely a direct one between group resources, lobbying techniques and policy result; rather, the group activates certain public sentiments which it then focuses on specific targets. This is the distinction behind Milbrath's denial of lobbying influence. He separates lobbying as a specialized activity of groups from the "considerable influence" of groups based on "the fact that members of groups are citizens and the political system is designed to respond to votes."[6]

One way around the problem of proving causation that is built into power and influence as Dahl defines them is to find some other measure of influence. For example, one could draw on the relationship between access to the policy process and policy success. Thus David Truman said, "The product of effective access . . . is a governmental decision."[7] This oversimplification has been translated by other group analysts into the notion of measuring influence by establishing the ratio of goals won to goals lost.[8] This formulation too is useful in evaluating competitive situations, but irrelevant for discerning lobbying influence most of the time, since it fails to account for most of what we really want to know: the relative importance of particular goals to the group, the degree of acceptance by policy makers, the allocation of costs and benefits, and so forth. Yet if we categorize goals rather than quantifying them, what we discover about group influence tends more and more to be limited to specific situations.

Another version of the access/influence equation has led to study of the horizontal relationships between groups and Congress or groups and an executive agency with influence deduced from the closeness of the relationship or the content of policy outputs resulting from it. Again a causal relationship is superimposed on what may be merely the product of the normal human tendency to play insiders' games.

> Is [influence] merely a close calculation of the costs of accepting or denying the demands of a particular group? Or is it something like role

> theory at work . . .? Is there a role for the spokesman of organized farmers, or organized labor, or organized business, which, with its complementary congressional and administrative roles, better explains what is asked and what is David Truman's idea of access?[9]

The problem of defining influence in terms of group activity is further complicated by the normative bias inherent in most interpretations; that is, pluralists tend to think of group activities as the equivalent of democratic political participation, so their assessment of group influence is positive. Elitists, by definition, consign groups to lesser levels of politics where their impact is limited and their influence unimportant in terms of overall policy consequences. Middle-range cynical pluralists define the influence of groups in terms of public policy content since these scholars accept the pluralists' pragmatic concept of group functions in modern representative societies, but they do not necessarily agree that such activity serves positive democratic functions for society.

Rather than reconcile these definitions or become embroiled in the controversies of group theory, let us be practical and define influence in broad action terms. Thus influence is defined as *group activities designed to alter the probable activity patterns of others.* The definition is not restricted to conflict situations, nor is it restricted to direct communications with official decision makers. Yet, as in our earlier definition of lobbying, it is narrowed by the notion of intent which presumes a thought-out plan. While the final goal may be to affect a government decision, the target of influence may be the media, the public, group membership, and/or public officials. Using this pragmatic definition strategy can be analyzed from the perspective of influence by asking specific questions about the number and position of other actors that the group can influence, the kinds of issues on which the group can have an impact, the political resources used to obtain influence, the degree of change in position that a group can promote, and the costs to both the group and other actors of accepting group influence.[10]

Questions such as these are necessary for realistic identification of influence, because influence is a relationship. As in any relationship, it changes as people, places, and policies change. Therefore, to speak of influence in the abstract, in the generalities of Winter-Berger or Milbrath, is to dilute the analytic value of the term. Lobbyists cannot be all powerful; lobbying cannot be always insignificant. The point is that influence must be embedded in a context: a lobbyist lobbying for a specific program at a specific time in a specific environment with its allies, competition and necessary decision makers similarly specified.

Using this definition of influence, let us apply it to the range of group activities discussed previously in order to reassess them in terms of their effectiveness in creating influence for the group. What resources and conditions maximize the possibility of influence for a group? What kinds of relationships are effective bases for furthering various kinds of group goals? On what types of issues are group activities likely to be most influential? The answers will be found by analyzing influence derived from three types of relationships:

- The relationship *within* a political interest group between the group's potential array of lobbying resources and the kinds of lobbying techniques that it can actually use effectively.
- *Vertical* relationships of groups to policy-making action centers, that is, how close a group is to direct participation as a member of the policy-making team.
- *Issue-oriented* relationships between group lobbying activities and policy decisions concerning timing, content, implementation, and enforcement.

INFLUENCE FOR ANY SPECIFIC GROUP

Group Resources as Lobbying Resources

The lobbyist stands midpoint in a balancing act that requires expending group resources for lobbying purposes while at the same time creating more resources in order to continue the internal development of the group. The weaker the internal ties of the group, the more inhibited the lobbyist becomes in terms of policy requests, institutional access points, and possible techniques which can be implemented effectively. Group attributes or resources that affect lobbying can be categorized according to membership attributes, geographical distribution, organizational/leadership resources, economic resources, and the place of the group and its goals in the economic and social environment.

Membership attributes involve the size of the organization in terms of its percentage of possible members and in terms of its voting potential; the prestige of the occupation represented; the amount of internal cohesion; and the political reservoir of talents among members as derived from their educational backgrounds, available time for political activities, interest in such activities, and so on. For example, the Business Roundtable has membership assets related to size as a percentage of eligible members, prestige, and individual skills Common Cause rates low in terms of percentage of possible members (since anyone could join), high in terms of the voting potential of its members, internal cohesion, reservoir of individual member talents and inclination to participate. The AFL-CIO rates low in terms of percentage of possible members, high in terms of number of members who vote, low in internal cohesion, high in membership reserves for use in political activities.

Geographical distribution translates into lobbying power when federated organizations such as the AMA, the AFL-CIO, the Chamber of Commerce, and AMPI, can ask their local units to use constituent pressures such as letter writing and votes to influence elected officials. When corporations are decentralized so that separate subdivisions are economically important to numerous congressional districts, then the advantage translates into votes (such as on the SST funding) or into corporate equivalents of grass roots mobilization (similar to ITT's assignment of each area manager to the relevant congressmen). Special interests such as sportsmen, environmentalists, gun owners, and geographically dispersed national organizations such as church groups, the League of Women Voters, NOW, or the John Birch Society, which lobby for many issues centered around a core concern, can use their geographical dispersal to generate ground swells of citizen response to Congress, the President, and for electoral purposes.

The degree to which geographical organization is a help or a handicap is directly tied in with the *organizational linkages* and *leadership skills* of the organization. When state organizations refuse to follow their national board's direction as they did in terms of AMA attitudes toward national health insurance and peer review, the national leadership's lobbying effectiveness is weakened. Trade association lobbyist-directors must devote as much time to in-house politicking as to outside contacts. Often lobbyists will seek congressional hearings on a hopeless topic in order to prove their effectiveness to home base, in effect, using up a political IOU for internal organizational purposes. Groups led by charismatic leaders such as Cesaer Chavez, John Gardner, Martin Luther King, or Ralph Nader have the advantage of leader-forged unity, but the disadvantage of developing organizational independence from that one man. When King died, his organization, the Southern Christian Leadership Conference (SCLC), descended rapidly from leader of the fight for national civil rights to its original place as a middle-level regional civil rights group.

Economic resources are important in two forms. One is money—money to assist in electoral campaigns, to offer soft services to candidates, to finance research, pay lobbyists, entertain decision makers. Disclosure of widespread corporate bribery of American and foreign officials in 1975–76 can be explained in the context of internal group needs as a pragmatic response to a situation that violated American laws and norms of corporate behavior but reflected the reality of government influence over business. Basically the money from the corporate perspective was "protection money" paid to guard against the harm inherent in government "power that ranges from awarding contracts and subsidies to withholding approval of new products and facilities."[11]

Second, economic resources translate into political clout when an ITT is so important to the national economy that it receives attention in proportion to that fact rather than the democratically acceptable alternatives of vote power and citizen demand. The military-industrial complex exemplifies a variation of this relationship in which the specialized skills and enormous monetary investments of a Lockheed lead to its bailout. Economic resources in the form of specialized, technical skills from private industry which are not equally available in government create lobbying relationships such as the Pentagon's sweetheart contracts, regulatory agency reliance on its clientele for its basic information, as exemplified by the use of API oil industry data as the basis for development of a federal energy program.

Nevertheless the economic importance of the oil companies or their status as multinational corporations did not prevent the "7 Sisters" from losing their oil depletion allowance tax loophole despite their economic clout and expensive public relations advertising campaigns. Ten years earlier the AMA lost its decade-long, very expensive battle to prevent enactment of Medicare. Common Cause, in its first year of operation, sued the national committees of the Republican and Democratic political parties and won.

In each case the economic resources of those losing interests were countered by a more important, if more ambiguous, group resource: *standing in the general social environment* which surrounds the political system. Truman called this "the most basic factor affecting access."[12] Social standing, in turn, is composed of two separate sets of assets—one tangible, one intangible. The National Red Cross, the American Legion, General Motors, the American Bar Association all have the first—a solid combination of economic/social or cultural status attributes plus money, educated group participants, and a well developed arsenal of lobbying tools. In a sense these assets can be acquired by a group on its own; certainly they can be bolstered and burnished through a group's self help campaign.

However, intangible assets depend upon the relationship between the group as a complex of resources and the current climate of opinion which sets the boundaries for acceptable policy. This aspect of social standing reflects the legitimacy which officials accord the group to act as spokesman for its issues. Perhaps those endowed with tangible social standing assets can acquire this intangible prerequisite for influence with ease. But legitimacy may also be bestowed on scruffy groups such as protest organizations which also are perceived as legitimate spokesmen for legitimate demands. Thus, two "public goods" such as economic development and ecology can divide groups with identical resource assets into separate sides based on their situational, issue-based legitimacy.

> The power of the pressure organization seems to be that it is recognized as the voice of its supporters. Thus, what it says is endowed with a kind of canonical authority as the expression of their point of view. Its power lies in that slight aura of legitimacy, not in having any capability for persuasion or coercion.[13]

Thus ironically the most basic resource is one that can be preserved or developed by selecting one's members, utilizing the media, and establishing a spokesman role for the group in ways that enhance the group's standing among the general public; but in the end precisely because this resource is based on officials' perceptions of the larger public, it is the one resource that is the most vulnerable to the vicissitudes of public opinion and the impact of catalytic events in the general decision-making environment. Groups cannot always control their social acceptance: witness the oil companies, once grand baronies dispensing free glasses and towels with a full tank of gas, and then reduced by the gas crisis and embargo in the mid-1970s to engaging in an extensive grass roots public relations campaign in order to refurbish their shiny image.

The contextual limitations of specific group influence are especially evident when groups challenge existing rules of the game in order to advance their own status. Public interest organizations used the general public revulsion to Watergate to press for specific procedural changes: open congressional committee meetings, elimination of automatic seniority for congressional committee chairmen, and public financing of presidential general election campaigns. Each reform provided access for the public and for groups previously not admitted to the insiders' club.

Nader, pre-Watergate, tagged three "Washington lawyer" law firms (Covington and Burling; Arnold and Porter; and Hogan and Hartson) as source of "immense power" based on "their tailored capacity to apply know-how, know-who, and other influences." Post-Watergate, on June 13, 1976, the *Washington Star* (the evening Washington, D.C. newspaper) called Nader "the most powerful nonelected politician in America." In each case the assignment of influence must be considered in the context from which it evolved.

In sum, there is no automatic equation by which group resources translate into political resources. By a pyramiding process, a group can generate lobbying resources superior to any of its separate assets. Or conversely, internal weakness can hamper groups that seem endowed with ample economic and social clout. The greater a group's resources, the more lobbying latitude it has, but the policy-making environment acts as an important determinant when groups try to translate assets into effective access.

INFLUENCE FROM POLICY RELATIONSHIPS

Group policy goals and group relations with policy makers must be considered in terms of the policy process itself: A phenomenon marked by internalized duplication, competition within and among decision-making action centers, rules of the game that build in delay, personnel cliques, and information barrages from constituents, election returns, media, and competing organizations. Furthermore, public policies are incremental in thrust, designed in pieces and fragmented among institutional points. Policy content ranges from a nonsense level that sets the number of ridges per submarine screw to symbolic programs such as a war on poverty. Amidst all this it becomes impossible to establish fixed conditions for the development of group influence or fixed criteria for its measurement.

Published sources on group lobbying activities offer little reliable data for those in search of influential groups. Sophisticated observers estimate 5,000 to 10,000 practicing lobbyists in Washington who are interested in domestic issues, only 1000 registered officially in 1974.[14] Registration records also show that 11,432 foreign government lobbyists registered with the Department of Justice in 1974, and 600 executive branch "legislative liaisons" (read "lobbyists") including twelve from the Executive Office were listed among federal employees. The Washington telephone directory shows 1,600 trade associations, professional groups, and unions headquartered in this company town, plus a couple of hundred civic, social, humanitarian, and religious organizations, and dozens of foundations. Adding up the registration list and telephone directory listings will not produce the sum total of those who lobby or those who lobby successfully. Indeed the official lists explain more about the loopholes in current lobbyist registration laws than about the realities of lobbying.

Similarly an examination of the expenditure records required by the Federal Regulation of Lobbying Act reveals total reported expenditures of $9.7 million for 1973. The biggest spender was listed as Common Cause with $934,834. The 159 businesses that filed reports listed only $3,287,561.89 in expenditures. The Chamber of Commerce, NAM, Lockheed, ITT, and thousands of other visible lobbyists did not feel that they came within the law's definition of lobbying or lobbyist. As John Gardner said, "Anyone innocent enough to believe the official lobbying reports would form a bizarre and misleading impression of modern lobbying practices."[15]

Both registration and expenditure filings drastically understate the amount of political interest group lobbying. Nevertheless it is an exaggeration to call interest groups the "animating forces in the political process,"[16] or describe public policy as the "result of the interplay of group interests."[17] Political interest groups are only one category of important actors, working in conjunction with other informational resources to structure the policy debate towards their goals. The probability of successful efforts to influence policy will depend on group access to decision makers and on the nature of the policy decision itself.

Vertical Relationships

The concept of vertical relationships[18] relates to distance from the governmental apparatus. At the innermost level are the co-opted groups that supply government personnel through the revolving door, sit on advisory committees, or act as government agents by supervising federal grants, supplying federal research data, or subcontracting parts of a military project. The next level consists of clientele groups that provide the necessary political support for an executive branch department, regulatory agencies, or a congressional committee. This is the level of subgovernments where close triangular relationships based on mutual needs and personal friendships make the group an unofficial but equal third member of the policy-making scene. Examples include farm interests or commodities and the relevant subcommittees and departments; and the military-industrial complex at the level of each separate service and separate weapons systems.

The third level represents automatic veto status for groups that participate only on specialized topics. The FDA supervisory panels or advisory committees that clear proposed regulations are examples of such groups. These three levels are most closely associated with executive branch relationships where groups, granted territory in legislation, turn to the implementation side to ensure that the law is administered along lines anticipated by the group. Indeed, where a group cannot develop this relationship, its legislative gains may evaporate, as suggested by the blacks' experience with implementation of the 1960s civil rights legislation or educators' experience in trying to expand their role without a department of their own.

The fourth level, where group-policy apparatus relationships are based on specific direct and indirect lobbying techniques, is the level of assumed conflict. However, inter-group conflict often fails to materialize either because no counter interest could be organized or could find credentials for access at this level sufficiently quickly, or because natural enemies decided to work together as when the AMA and tobacco lobby agreed to protect cigarette manufacturers rather than cigarette smokers. Evidence of actions on this level appear in hearings testimony, constituent letter campaigns, personal lobbying of legislators, officials, and staff. Generally the group's participation is structured by the policy at hand rather than any routinized form of interaction with official decision orders.

The fifth level consists of groups that participate at the agenda-building stage where public-directed protests and media events are staged to develop the socioeconomic preconditions for generating a political issue. The sixth, outermost level, is peopled by groups such as the Black Panthers and the Communist Party which reject the existing power structure, preferring instead a role of agitation and resistance. Groups at the fifth and sixth levels are outsiders, but those at level 5 see an advantage in gaining access to higher levels of participation.

Usually groups at the uppermost levels are most likely to be influential in terms of their policy objectives. However, the cases of the SST, the highway lobby, and the tobacco lobby suggest that coalitions of new groups can push new concerns such as public health, environmental controls, and urban deterioration onto the policy scene in order to challenge the status quo. Continued impact after the initial victory then lies in establishing group interest on one of the higher, more permanent levels of cooperation.

Policy Content

Traditional wisdom says that a group is most successful when the issue is most narrowly and specifically related to the group's identified interests. Since they represent direct allocations of money for specific purposes, subsidies provide the data to support this hypothesis. Such winners include the dairymen, tobacco growers until 1969, major oil companies, and ITT as an exception to general antitrust merger prohibitions. Mention is rarely made of losers—the smokers, consumers, and small oil companies—who competed for a different distribution of money and lost. The point is success has several sides: unless there is total unanimity of opinion or total lack of opposition, every winner means a loser.

The narrow spectrum of influence myth also undervalues both the significant role played by catalytic groups in raising issues for public decision and the importance of outside coalitions as a precondition for broad, regulatory action on touchy issues. Groups with broad goals, those pursuing policies requiring widespread costs and/or benefits, join umbrella coalitions for the purpose of merging resources. That the lobbying vehicle is a coalition instead of a single group is immaterial in assigning influence, since such alliances are but one of many available lobbying tactics. Thus Congress refused to settle the prickly issue of aid to elementary and secondary education until the outside interests had agreed to a compromise. Civil rights legislation was based on a solid performance at all levels of action by several hundred allied organizations.

Redistributive policies such as tax reform, welfare revision, or the war on poverty are generally considered in their entirety only by peak associations such as the Chamber of Commerce. Most interests ignore the total program preferring to alter the policy at the level of specifics. The Economic Opportunity Act was literally dismembered piece by piece every year at reappropriation time. Although group influence is most noticeable in small clauses inserted in legislation or administrative rulings to benefit one company or group, the narrowness of the item should not obscure its importance for the general policy of which it is part. Everyone wants tax reform, but no one wants to lose his own loophole. Seventy-three identifiable clauses of one company benefits in the 1976 tax reform package change the meaning of "reform." Cumulatively such small victories can have enormous policy consequences.

Since redistributive issues are implemented in pieces, group influence, in bureaucratic action centers can counter symbolic ideas with pragmatic reasons to wait or reinterpret. Blacks and women seeking implementation of equal opportunity legislation have been thwarted by such alliances time after time. Often groups disadvantaged by such insider strangleholds over details go to court to seek judicial reinterpretations of the rules that will give them a seat at the same table.

The oil lobbies, in explaining their relative impotence within the 1975 Ways and Means Committee, attributed their decline in influence to the rise of new public interest groups, changes in House procedures that weakened the power of their traditional access points, the national public sentiment against big oil, and the lack of unity among members of the oil bloc. When Frank Ikard, president of API, calls Common Cause and Nader the "two most powerful groups in the U.S.," he is identifying his "enemies," not defining their influence level.[19]

Indeed, the psychological need for groups to attribute failure to the "power" of the other side has inflated the actual performance ratings of many groups. Milbrath found that lobbyists asked to pick successful groups usually identified a member of their opposition. The Chamber of Commerce/NAM merger was justified as one means for business, the "weaker" side, to counter the "excessive influence" of labor. However, labor, unable to successfully negotiate its common site picketing bill past a presidential veto, probably felt business had more influence since, in this instance, business "won."

The role of groups in moving new ideas onto the formal policy agenda is another aspect of group policy influence that is often neglected since it is subsumed under the rubric of public opinion. This two-pronged phenomenon usually involves a political interest in the dual role of generating public interest in a "new" issue—campaign finance reform, clean air, aid to parochial schools—and then communicating that newly aroused demand to decision makers. This initial group advocacy role is especially influential because any subsequent specific allocation of government benefits will be made within that general policy environment already influenced by group activities.

In a Harris public opinion survey commissioned by the Senate Government Operations Committee, this aspect of interest group activity was positively perceived. "Both the public and state and local leaders agree that 'groups of citizens and organizations are having more effect in getting government to get things done compare with five years ago.' "[20] When asked to name examples of such groups, citizens volunteered civil rights groups, business groups, Nader's group, church, educational, environmentalist, fraternal, and veteran's organizations.

These examples correspond to a similar listing in which people were asked to name the most influential Americans and rate the most powerful institutions. On the big twenty list, the only nonpoliticians were evangelist Billy Graham, publisher Katherine Graham, and three interest group leaders: George Meany (#4), Ralph Nader (#12), and John Gardner (#19). Interests ranked among the most powerful institutions included labor unions (#5), industry (#10), lobbies and pressure groups (#11), educational institutions (#18), minority organizations (#19), military (#21), and organized religion (#23).[21]

In the Harris poll respondents were asked to evaluate five specific citizen efforts during the 1963–73 decade: civil rights protest marches, antiwar demonstrations, antibusing protests, ecological group efforts to stop pollution, and local crime control campaigns. The public rated the civil rights and environmentalist efforts as highly positive and effective in terms of policy results; while 49 percent assessed the antiwar movement as having no policy impact, and 59 percent felt that antibusing demonstrations have not been effective. Thus the two efforts that resulted in the most new legislation were judged by the public to be the most successful.

Summarizing the relationship between individual group needs and the group's effectiveness in influencing government to respond positively to its position, the evidence in this book suggests that influence is indeed relative. Any group's chances for successful input are affected not only by its own resources and policy-process relationships but also by factors beyond group control such as currently operating rules of the game and currently popular policy priorities. When group goals and public priorities coincide, groups are most able to be influential. Groups that win can, over time, turn a series of small, narrow victories into a consistent governmental policy focus.

GROUP IMPACT ON THE AMERICAN POLITICAL SYSTEM

Identifying the influence of any one group at any one point in time stops a dynamic process and by freezing the action distorts it. Even when group action is correctly observed, the measurement of group influence is inevitably inaccurate because it only isolates part of pyramiding series of complex relationships. However, it *is* possible to step back from the particulars and generalize from the character of group involvement to the impact of such involvement on the political system as a whole. This is done not by aggregating separate instances of group influence, but rather by assessing the consequences of group organization and group policy participation as it affects the broker-communication function that groups perform in a representative society.

When groups explain the outlines of public sentiment (often developed under group auspices) to official decision makers and convey the government's response back to their members, groups act as communications couriers. However, the notion of groups as brokers does not imply that groups have equality of access or success. More established, prestigious and economically/socially acceptable groups and group goals are likely to have favored lines of communication with key decision-makers. Newer groups and the issues they sponsor may be relegated to indirect access points or subjected to indefinite delays.

Separation of powers, checks and balances, and federalism are all rules of the game that encourage multiplicity of access points but that simultaneously create opportunities for insiders to protect their established access lines at the expense of newcomers. The rules of the game also ensure delay—delay in bridging the gap between private problem and public issue, delay in organizing new interests to play in the policy game, delay in adopting an official approach to the new problem, delay in acquiring the skills and contacts required to play the game well. The universe of political interest groups reflects these inequities in our rules of the game. Groups per se may manipulate and modify the rules, but they are a product of, rather than producer of, the basic policy system.

Registration data and reported expenditure figures do not explain the impact of groups on the system. Assessing the impact of a group in terms of its own goals can give us some idea of comparative effectiveness among groups, but it tells us nothing of the cumulative impact of such activity for the functioning of the system. The cumulative effect of group activity that creates its impact on the American system as a whole is derived from the operationalization of group functions. Elitists say most groups, like most political actors, have little impact on real decisions, so we can ignore them. Pluralists view groups as modern reincarnations of the virtues of direct democracy—a view as naive and oversimplified as its elitist opposite. Taking the middle position of flawed pluralism, or biased participation, let us project the impact of key group functions in order to draw a cumulative portrait.

Let us agree that groups serve the democratic function of linking individuals to society whether or not their internal organizational structure resembles the popular participation machinery of the democratic state. Three-quarters of all American adults say they have belonged to some group at some point in their lives. One-third of all American adults say they have been group office holders. This one-third tends to be the politically active one-third of the population which in turn tends to be above the mean in age, income, and education. Again, the interest group system, rather than inventing a bias, reflects the bias already evident in other aspects of the social system.

Bias appears not only in group membership but also in group representation of particular viewpoints. There is never a guarantee that all points of view on an issue will develop or mobilize and organize with equal effectiveness or simultaneously. Organization is itself a mobilization of bias, since it presumes an ordering of resources to produce a goal. When an organization goes to government, it may accurately reflect public sentiments that have turned a problem into an issue. By the end of the policy-making sequence, time or events may have rendered the initial group perceptions inaccurate or out of date. Yet further inequality is produced by unequal resources and access, and distortion caused by the inherent complexity of the policy process may appear at this point. In the 1974 strip-mining battle, of twenty registered lobbyists, eleven worked for the American Mining Congress, two for nonprofit environmental projects. The numbers indicate the inequality.

The unrepresentative portion of American society active in groups, the lopsided evolution of groups on all sides of a question, and their unequal resources accumulate bias toward the status quo. This tendency is reinforced by the policy system itself. Groups seeking to broker current demands are caught in a policy process that mandates delayed, sequential, incremental solutions. The system best accommodates seasoned change—change that has worked its way in and through the pockets of official power, that is, the action centers.

In a modern industrial nation where each elected representative is responsible to a half-million or more people there is clearly a need for supplemental representation of economic, ideological, psychological, and social needs, demands, and desires of citizens. Political interest groups, serving this function, are an imperfect conduit. Organized political interest groups represent the active citizenry, thereby exaggerating the role and resources of participation, ignoring numerical majorities of the disinterested, ill-equipped, or politically apathetic. The policy system, by making individually effective groups partners in an action center, further skews the system away from diffuse majority needs towards policies that embody the specific economic, social, or civic demands of groups. Regardless of the purity of an idea or the breadth of policy intent, the political system in which it is developed mandates line-by-line implementation, which, in turn, permits group intervention at the level of decision-making detail. Since the final policy is, for practical purposes, the sum of such details, the importance of group intervention at this level lies in its cumulative impact on policy output for the whole system.

In this sense groups carry specialization to its logical conclusion: narrow shifts in minor positions produce major changes. In this way, all groups create and exploit inequities in the public policy-making system. But let us not rush to blame the messenger for the message. Interest groups per se are not the source of bias but mirror only certain participants' needs and act on only certain aspects of policies. Thus the politics of interest group activity simply magnifies flaws already built into the rules of the American public policy game.

NOTES

1. Robert Winter-Berger, *The Washington Pay-Off* (Secaucus, N.J.: Lyle Stuart, 1972), pp. 27, 14.
2. U.S. Senate, Committee on Government Operations, "Confidence and Concern: Citizens View American Government," Part I (December 3, 1973), pp. 29–35.
3. Lester Milbrath, *The Washington Lobbyists* (Chicago: Rand McNally 1963), pp. 353–54.
4. Raymond Bauer, Ithiel de Sola Pool, and Lewis Dexter, *American Business and Public Policy* (New York: Atherton Press, 1963), p. 398.

5. Robert Dahl, *Modern Political Analysis* (Englewood Cliffs, N.J.: Prentice-Hall, 1964), p. 40.
6. Milbrath, *The Washington Lobbyists,* p. 342.
7. David Truman, *The Governmental Process* (New York: Knopf, 1951), p. 507.
8. See Martha Derthick, The *National Guard in Politics* (Cambridge: Harvard University Press, 1965), chap. 1.
9. Phillip Monypenny, "Introduction," in *Pressure Groups in American Politics,* ed. H. R. Manhood (New York: Scribner's, 1967), p. 8.
10. See Dahl, *Modern Political Analysis,* chap. 5.
11. *New York Times,* May 4, 1975.
12. Truman, *The Governmental Process,* p. 265.
13. Bauer, Pool, and Dexter, *American Business and Public Policy,* p. 374.
14. These statistics are from the *Christian Science Monitor,* October 8, 1975.
15. This data and quotation are from *Congressional Quarterly Weekly Report,* July 24, 1974, pp. 1947–49.
16. V. O. Key, *Parties, Politics and Pressure Groups,* 5th ed. (New York: Thomas Y. Crowell, 1964), p. 17.
17. Harmon Zeigler, *Interest Groups in American Society* (Englewood Cliffs, N.J.: Prentice-Hall, 1964), p. 30.
18. This typology is adapted from a suggestion made by Samuel Eldersveld in his article "American Interest Groups: A Survey of Research and Some Implications for Theory and Method," in *Interest Groups on Four Continents,* ed. Henry Ehrmann (Pittsburgh: University of Pittsburgh Press, 1958), p. 187.
19. See "The Oil Battle," in *Current American Government* (Washington, D.C.: Congressional Quarterly, Inc., 1975), pp. 66–72.
20. U.S. Senate, Committee on Government Operations, "Confidence and Concern," pp. 71. Later data from pp. 93–96.
21. "Who Runs America," in *Annual Editions 1975/76* (Guilford, Conn: Dushkin, 1975), pp. 26–28.

Selected Bibliography

General

BENTLEY, ARTHUR F., *The Process of Government* (Cambridge, Mass.: Harvard University Press, 1967). The classic study of interests as the animating forces of American politics.

CHERINGTON, PAUL W., and RALPH L. GILLEN, *The Business Representative in Washington* (Washington, D.C.: The Brookings Institution, 1962). A summary of perceptions of lobbying roles as discussed by twenty-four trade-association and business-corporation "Washington representatives" during a series of roundtable discussions sponsored by the Brookings Institution.

COBB, ROGER W., and CHARLES D. ELDER, *Participation in American Politics: The Dynamics of Agenda-Building* (Boston: Allyn and Bacon, 1972). Presents a conceptual framework of agenda-building as a way of explaining linkage between societal problems and governmental actions.

DEAKIN, JAMES, *The Lobbyists* (Washington, D C.: Public Affairs Press, 1966). An anecdotal but perceptive study of Washington lobbyists and lobbying.

EDELMAN, MURRAY, *The Symbolic Uses of Politics* (Urbana: University of Illinois Press, 1964). An analysis of politics in terms of the underlying symbolic meanings that color the perceptions and actions of players and observers.

GAMSON, WILLIAM A., *Power and Discontent,* (Homewood, Ill.: Dorsey, 1968). A provocative, theoretical analysis of power relationships between decision-makers and non-governmental actors.

———, *The Strategy of Social Protest* (Homewood, Ill.: Dorsey, 1975). A study of a representative sample of fifty-three voluntary groups that between 1850–1945 challenged part of the status quo. Emphasis is on their strategies and organizational characteristics that effected their success.

GOULDEN, JOSEPH C., *The Superlawyers: The Small and Powerful World of the Great Washington Law Firms* (New York: Weybright and Talley, 1971). A journalist's tour of the top Washington lawyers and law firms and their role as mediators between corporate power and political decision-makers.

GREEN, MARK J., *The Other Government: The Unseen Power of Washington Lawyers* (New York: Grossman, 1975). Analysis of the linkage between lawyers, law, and political power, with special emphasis on the policy areas of monopolies, drugs, food, cigarettes, auto safety, transportation, and the media.

KARIEL, HENRY S., *The Decline of American Pluralism* (Stanford, Ca.: Stanford University Press, 1961). Analysis of current interest-group-governmental relationships as in conflict with basic principles of constitutional democracy.

LOWI, THEODORE J., *The End of Liberalism: Ideology, Policy, and the Crisis of Public Authority* (New York: Norton, 1969). A work that is critical of American public policies because they are based on the outmoded policy of interest-group liberalism, which benefits government-related interest rather than generating new approaches to current problems.

LANE, EDGAR, *Lobbying and the Law* (Berkeley: University of California Press, 1964). A realistic, objective discussion of the origins, purpose, requirements and operational meaning of state lobbying disclosure laws. Although dated, the book still stands as a good introduction to the symbolic and real problems addressed by such laws.

McCONNELL, *Private Power and American Democracy* (New York: Knopf, 1966). One of the classic works debunking notions of pluralism as the modern equivalent of democracy. Emphasizes internal organizational relationships and the accrual of power to unresponsive, unresponsible private interests.

MILBRATH, LESTER W., *The Washington Lobbyists* (Chicago: Rand McNally & Company, 1963). Study of lobbyists as a political skill group: the socioeconomic and personal characteristics of Washington lobbyists, their attitudes toward their jobs, and their evaluation of various lobbying techniques.

OLSON, MANCUR, JR., *The Logic of Collective Action: Public Goods and the Theory of Groups* (New York: Schocken Books, 1971). Disputes the basic premise of group theory by developing the argument that groups do not organize rationally to further common traits but rather that rational self-interested individuals organize for more specific reasons; and lobbying when it occurs is usually a by-product of group activity rather than the *raison d'être* for group existence.

SCHATTSCHNEIDER, E. E., *The Semi-Sovereign People: A Realist's View of Democracy in America* (Hinsdale, Ill.: Dryden Press, 1975). Reissue of a classic work that develops the theory of politics as the socialization of conflict and development of alternatives. It critiques group theory but provides fruitful theory for analysis of interest-group activities.

TRUMAN, DAVID B., *The Governmental Process: Political Interests and Public Opinion* (New York: Knopf, 1971). The classic 1950s refurbishing of Bentley's theory, this work applies group theory to the role of groups in American national policy-making. The second edition contains a long excellent survey of Truman's views on two decades of studies sparked by his book.

WILSON, JAMES Q., *Political Organizations* (New York: Basic Books, 1973). This volume offers a theory of the internal processes of voluntary formal organizations as the source of constraints and requirements that affect the behavior of individuals whose policy making base is an organization.

VERBA, SIDNEY, *Small Groups and Political Behavior: A Study of Leadership* (Princeton, N.J.: Princeton University Press, 1961). A basic sociological survey of the literature on small-group behavior. Demonstrates the importance of primary-group relationships in the development of political systems and dissects the concept of leadership from methodological and practical perspectives.

WOOTTON, GRAHAM, *Interest Groups* (Englewood Cliffs, N.J.: Prentice-Hall, 1970). A thought-provoking essay that traces the conceptual and value choices involved in the process of creating definitions. Develops a definition and new classification of interest groups, followed by a discussion of interest-group activities and influence.

Groups in the Political Process

ALEXANDER, HERBERT E., *Financing the 1972 Election* (Lexington, Mass.: Heath, 1976). Fourth in a series of detailed factual analyses on the financing of presidential election campaigns. A well-written and invaluable data source.

ANDERSON, FREDERICK R., *NEPA in the Courts: A Legal Analysis of the National Environmental Policy Act* (Baltimore, Md.: Johns Hopkins University Press, 1973). Analysis of the role of the court system in "making law," specifically in giving meaning to the NEPA's provisions by means of court interpretations of its key provisions.

BARKER, LUCIUS J., and JESSE J. MCCORRY, JR., *Black Americans and the Political System* (Cambridge, Mass.: Winthrop, 1976). Most valuable for its competent treatment of blacks and the legal process.

CONGRESSIONAL QUARTERLY, *The Washington Lobby* (Washington, D.C.: Congressional Quarterly, Inc. 1974). A factual study of Washington lobbies, emphasizing lobbying laws, electoral politics, and congressional activities.

FREEMAN, J. LEIPER, *The Political Process: Executive Bureau–Legislative Committee Relations* (New York: Random House, 1955). A brief but excellent analysis of executive bureau–legislative committee relationships and their impact on policy-making.

HALL, DONALD R., *Cooperative Lobbying—The Power of Pressure* (Tucson: University of Arizona Press, 1969). Analysis of the forms of intergroup cooperation and alliances, with emphasis on the Chamber of Commerce's relationships with other groups.

HERRING, PENDLETON, *Group Representation before Congress* (New York: Russell & Russell, 1967). A classic study, first published in 1929, of the national associations that lobbied and the techniques used to influence Congress.

MAKIELSKI, S.J., JR., *Beleaguered Minorities: Cultural Politics in America* (San Francisco, W.H. Freeman, 1973). A "radical" critique of the pluralist model as a response to the needs and problems of blacks, American Indians, Mexican Indians, students, and women.

O. M. COLLECTIVE, *The Organizer's Manual* (New York: Bantam Books, 1971). A detailed, well-done, how-to book—a guide to practical action for those who would organize to change the current social system. Contains an excellent bibliography and list of existing organizations in various fields.

RIPLEY, RANDALL B., and GRACE A. FRANKLIN, *Congress, the Bureaucracy, and Public Policy* (Homewood, Ill.: Dorsey, 1976). Well-done basic treatment of congressional–bureaucratic policy-making relationships using the distributive/regulatory/redistributive policy categories for discussion and analysis.

RUBENSTEIN, RICHARD E., *Rebels in Eden: Mass Political Violence in the United States* (Boston: Little, Brown, 1970). Analysis of the use of violence by a wide spectrum of groups as a necessary means for these interests to gain recognition by those already within the policy-making system.

SCHLESINGER, STEPHEN C., *The New Reformers: Forces for Change in American Politics* (Boston: Houghton Mifflin, 1975). A study of catalytic groups (women, blacks, labor unions, middle-class liberals, congressional reformers, and selected minorities) most useful for its insights into the tactics groups should have recourse to in order to reach their objectives.

SCHEINGOLD, STUART A., *The Politics of Rights: Lawyers, Public Policy, and Political Change* (New Haven, Conn.: Yale University Press, 1974). A stimulating addition to the impact-compliance literature, concentrating on the relationship between legal values and political outcomes.

VOSE, CLEMENT E., *Caucasians Only: The Supreme Court, the NAACP, and the Restrictive Covenant Cases* (Berkeley: University of California Press, 1959). A classic study of the role of the NAACP in developing a litigation strategy to secure civil-rights policy gains through court decisions; uses restrictive covenant cases as the case-study example.

ZEIGLER, L. HARMON, and G. WAYNE PEAK, *Interest Groups in American Society,* 2d ed. (Englewood Cliffs, N.J.: Prentice-Hall, 1972). An overview of the role of interest groups in the American political system with emphasis on the sociocultural forces affecting a group's roles, formal relationships with government, and the significance of such interest-group activity.

Case Studies

ALFORD, ROBERT R., *Health Care Politics: Ideological and Interest Group Barriers to Reform* (Chicago: University of Chicago Press, 1975). Develops a theory of interest groups in relation to health care policies.

BAUER, RAYMOND A., ITHIEL DE SOLA POOL, and LEWIS ANTHONY DEXTER, *American Business and Public Policy: The Politics of Foreign Trade* (New York: Atherton Press, 1967). Uses the politics of trade from 1953 to 1962 as the vehicle for a classic study of lobbies, especially business, in their relationships with government decision-making.

BROOKS, THOMAS R., *Toil and Trouble: A History of American Labor,* 2d ed. (New York: Dell, 1971). A history of the labor movement from its status as an outside crusade to its current role as a political insider.

EIDENBERG, EUGENE, AND ROY D. MOREY, *An Act of Congress: The Legislative Process and the Making of Education Policy* (New York: Norton, 1969). A readable and informative study of the forces in and out of Congress that shaped the 1965 Elementary and Secondary Education Act.

EPSTEIN, EDWIN M., *The Corporation in American Politics* (Englewood Cliffs, N. J.: Prentice-Hall, 1969). A sympathetic treatment of the power, legitimacy, and impact of the corporate role in American politics.

FARKAS, SUZANNE, *Urban Lobbying: Mayors in the Federal Arena* (New York: New York University Press, 1971). Focuses on the United States Conference of Mayors and its success at lobbying in the field of housing and urban redevelopment.

FELICETTI, DANIEL A., *Mental Health and Retardation Politics: The Mind Lobbies in Congress* (New York: Praeger, 1975). A useful study of the efforts of mental health and retardation groups to win favorable congressional health legislation over the last 20 years.

FREEMAN, JO, *The Politics of Women's Liberation* (New York: McKay, 1975). An analysis of the women's movement as a social movement and then in terms of its impact on public policy.

FRIEDMAN, KENNETH M., *Public Policy and the Smoking-Health Controversy: A Comparative Study* (Lexington, Mass.: Heath, 1975). A valuable source of data about smoking-health politics in the United States, Great Britain, and Canada.

GROSSMAN, JOEL B., *Lawyers and Judges: The ABA and the Politics of Judicial Selection* (New York: Wiley, 1965). A case study of the political role of the American Bar Association in the recruitment of federal judges.

HARRIS, RICHARD, *A Sacred Trust* (Baltimore: Penguin Books, 1969). A well-written, detailed study of the AMA's 30-year battle against Medicare.

———, *Decision* (New York: Dutton, 1971). The story of civil-rights coalition activity to defeat President Nixon's nomination of G. Harrold Carswell for Justice of the Supreme Court.

GUSFIELD, JOSEPH R., *Symbolic Crusade: Status Politics and the American Temperance Movement* (Urbana: University of Illinois Press, 1963). A study of the Temperance movement as an example of the psychological, cultural, and social roots of a moral reform movement.

KING, LAURISTON, *The Washington Lobbyists for Higher Education* (Lexington, Mass.: Heath, 1975). A highly readable neo-pluralist interpretation of the legislative activities of higher education interest groups.

KAUFMAN, RICHARD E. *The War Profiteers* (Indianapolis: Bobbs-Merrill, 1970). A well-written and documented analysis of military-industrial complex interrelationships from the perspective of economic profit.

LIPSET, SEYMOUR MARTIN, AND EARL RAAB, *The Politics of Unreason: Right-Wing Extremism in America, 1790–1970* (New York: Harper & Row, 1970). A comprehensive examination of the psychological, cultural, and social needs to preserve certain values or interests through right-wing appeals to believe in un-American conspiracies. The study is based on data from a five-year University of California study of anti-Semitism in the United States. Winner of the Gunnar Myrdal Prize.

MARMOR, THEODORE R. *The Politics of Medicare* (Chicago: Aldine, 1970). This volume uses the case study of the struggle to pass Medicare in order to analyze agenda-building questions, interest-group conflict, and the nature of the final policy compromise. The last chapter relates the case to general public policy-making approaches.

MEIER, AUGUST, AND ELLIOTT RUDWICK, *CORE: A Study in the Civil Rights Movement, 1942–1968* (New York: Oxford University Press, 1973). An encyclopedic chronicle of the internal conflicts and policies of an important civil rights organization.

PRIMACK, JOEL, AND FRANK VON HIPPEL, *Advice and Dissent: Scientists in the Political Arena* (New York: Basic Books, 1974). Four case histories (the SST, the ABM, insecticides, and cyclamates) analyzing the efforts of scientists to block or reverse federal policies.

REDMAN, ERIC, *The Dance of Legislation* (New York: Simon and Schuster, 1975). An entertaining but thoroughly researched case study of the detailed interactions involved in drafting and passing the National Health Service bill.

Index

Carol S. Greenwald is an Assistant Professor of Political Science at Brooklyn College of the City University of New York. A graduate of Smith College, she received her doctorate from CUNY. Professor Greenwald has written articles and papers on various aspects of lobbying and has served on the New York State boards of directors of the League of Women Voters and Common Cause. As a member of the New York Common Cause Executive Committee, she coordinated legislative issues and strategy for three years.